Selected Writings of Herbert Read

HERBERT READ

Selected Writings

Poetry and Criticism

With a Foreword

by

ALLEN TATE

HORIZON PRESS

New York

First American edition 1964
Published by Horizon Press, New York
Printed in Great Britain
by Robert MacLehose & Co. Ltd Glasgow
All rights reserved

Library of Congress Catalog Card Number 63–21569

Contents

FOREWORD BY ALLEN TATE   *page* 7

I. POEMS   17

II. MOON'S FARM   53

III. LITERARY CRITICISM   79
- 1. The Personality of the Poet (1932)   81
- 2. Psycho-Analysis and Literary Criticism (1924)   98
- 3. Swift (1926)   117
- 4. In Defence of Shelley (1936)   138
- 5. American Bards and British Reviewers (1962)   198

IV. ART CRITICISM   217
- 1. The Modern Epoch in Art (1949)   219
- 2. Surrealism and the Romantic Principle (1936)   246
- 3. The Nature of Abstract Art (1960)   283
- 4. Henry Moore (1961)   298

V. SOCIAL CRITICISM   307
- 1. The Philosophy of Anarchism (1940)   309
- 2. The Politics of the Unpolitical (1943)   327
- 3. Towards a Duplex Civilization (1946)   336

VI. EDUCATION   359
- 1. Education Through Art (1963)   361
- 2. Art and Life (1959)   376
- 3. The Flower of Peace (1958)   388

SELECT BIBLIOGRAPHY   402

Foreword by Allen Tate

It would be improper and I should not be competent to write an *introduction* to a selection from the sixty-odd books of Herbert Read. I am calling these brief reflections a Foreword which might well be subtitled a Tribute, or Homage to An Old Friend. For I first met Herbert Read in the autumn of 1928 at one of the 'Criterion luncheons' in London (the same day I first saw T. S. Eliot), to which I had been taken by F. V. Morley, a friend of both these men who were to become my lifelong friends. Read and I were more nearly of an age, and became friends as soon as his Yorkshire shyness allowed; this took a little time; but the twelve years between Mr. Eliot and myself were like the Grand Canyon that only after some years seemed to silt up until it was no wider than the Potomac above Washington; that is to say, about the width of the Mason and Dixon Line. I am sure that Mr. Eliot would not mind my saying, on the occasion of our friend's seventieth birthday, that thirty-five years ago I felt closer to rural Yorkshire and to Herbert's grandmother Jane Tate than to Cousin Nancy Ellicott and the *Boston Evening Transcript*. I confess that in those days regional symbols did not occur to me: they will do now for something I may have felt then. What I definitely felt, and felt very strongly, was the originality and power of two books by Herbert Read: *Reason and Romanticism* (1926) and *Collected Poems 1913–1925*. These books had a crucial effect upon me, and because this Foreword is an occasional essay, I hope I may be allowed to pursue reminiscence a little further.

In the two or three years preceding 1928 I had read Herbert Read's reviews in *The Criterion*; early in 1927 I read in that journal Mr. Eliot's review of *Reason and Romanticism* and Ramon Fernandez' *Messages*. The review was a detailed comparison of Read and Fernandez, somewhat to the advantage of the latter, whose critical theory Mr. Eliot found the more 'coherent'. At that time I was reviewing French books for a New York trade-journal, and

7

I had read *Messages*. I soon found a copy of *Reason and Romanticism* and read it — to the advantage of Read. Here was a young man (he was scarcely more than thirty) who was struggling with a problem which one now knows would engage him the rest of his life: the synthesis of romantic intuition and intellectual order. (When the word problem came into literary criticism I do not know — possibly from mathematics or economics.) My own 'problem' at that time — it probably still is — was Read's: intuition and/or order. It is a problem the solution of which, unlike mathematical solutions, cannot go beyond the intelligence of one's awareness of it.

Read's awareness has steadily increased over more than forty years. Starting with the Coleridgean theory of 'organicism', he has assimilated to the original doctrine a large number of insights from later philosophers, particularly Kierkegaard, Lipps, Worringer, and Bergson; and after these, T. E. Hulme and Jean-Paul Sartre. These writers have contributed to Read's defense of the romantic 'cult of sincerity', but at the level of metaphysics. I am not prepared to judge how well this metaphysical eclecticism has been achieved; yet it must be acknowledged that no other Anglo-American critic of our time has pursued with greater devotion, learning, and profundity a single theory of the arts. A capital point about Read's criticism that has been ignored or overlooked is the consistency of his performance; one may here and there question his placing of certain writers — Hulme, for example — in the tradition of Coleridge; but there can be no doubt that he has extended the poetics of the master far beyond any horizon that the master could see. This has been due to an historical advantage; for Read knows what Coleridge knew plus what Coleridge could not have known: (1) Coleridge himself and (2) the development by Freud and Jung of certain ideas of Coleridge that foreshadowed a collective unconscious as the source of organic form. After Coleridge rejected Hartley's associationism, he had no other 'psychology' as an empirical reference for his intuitive deductions. It would be Read's claim that Jung's hypothesis of the archetype has given Coleridge his empirical reference for the theory of the Primary Imagination. There is much to be said for this theory; it is an anomaly of contemporary scholarship that the academic 'Coleridgeans' seem to believe it would be unsound 'scholarship' to take seriously Read's synthesis of Coleridge and Jung; for the strict academic must not allow himself to know more than Coleridge knew, or more than his colleagues have said about what Coleridge knew. The great studies of Coleridge in our time are to be found in *The True Voice of Feeling* (1953): 'The Notion of Organic Form' and 'Coleridge as Critic'; and along with these one must read the sequence of eight essays under the general title 'The Nature of Poetry' which appear most handily in *Collected Essays in Literary Criticism* (1938; revised edition 1951). The first two essays, 'Organic and Abstract Form' and 'The Personality of the Poet' (the latter will be found in the present volume) are Read's earliest attempts to ground the distinction between Imagination and Fancy in modern depth psychology. Organic form and abstract form are respectively Imagination and Fancy.*

Having read these essays and others which apply the central insight to an enormous variety of individual writers — for Read's knowledge of English literature is encyclopedic — what may his critic say about the success of his Coleridgean stance in a world that Coleridge could not know? The first test, I believe, is the pragmatic one: he is not the scholar of a 'field', the man who spends his life writing two books and writing a few 'learned articles'; he is a man of letters in the grand style; and whatever one may think at last of his philosophical and psychological enquiries, one must acknowledge the overwhelming evidence of his *literary commitment.* He is a literary critic before he is a psychologist or philosopher. What other critic of our time could write so well of Swift and Shelley, Hopkins and Whitman, Sterne and Henry James? (The essay on James I do not hesitate to say is the best short analysis of James' 'discoveries' by a living critic. Who has read it?) I have cited only a handful of the hundreds of essays that would meet the pragmatic test; I have not referred to *The Tenth Muse* (1957) or to *The Forms of Things Unknown* (1960). Before I leave the subject of Read's criticism I must glance briefly at three essays, one in the latter volume, 'Psycho-analysis and the Problem of Aesthetic Value', the second, 'Poetic Diction', in *Collected Essays in Literary Criticism.*

Since the former essay was written (1950) Read has moved away from Freud towards Jung, whose theory of the collective unconscious seems to suggest a dynamic relation of conscious control

* The other great work on Coleridge, Dr. I. A. Richards' *Coleridge on Imagination*, is epistemological in its method, not psychological, in spite of Dr. Richards' early training in psychology.

to patterns of sensibility recurrent throughout the history of the arts. Jung's collective unconscious thus becomes positive and 'creative', whereas Freud's personal unconscious remains either a dry well into which we drop our frustrations, or at worst a chamber of horrors, Blue Beard's closet, to unlock which spells our doom; or perhaps the doom having been faced symbolically, we come out of the closet with integrated personalities, or, as poets, with integrated poems. Whichever way we throw the emphasis, whether on Freud or on Jung, there is inevitably a springe to catch the critical woodcock, and Sir Herbert is perfectly aware of it, as Jung was aware of it before him: did not Jung warn his disciples that analytical psychology was not criticism and could not provide criteria of 'aesthetic value'? Read tells us that psycho-analysis has 'come to the aid of the philosophy of art in two ways, which are really two stages of application.' The first was to show that 'the power of art *in a civilization* (my italics) was due to its expression of the deeper levels of personality'; that is to say, the primitive, or 'archaic image' (Jung's term), is assimilated to the civilized conscious ego of the poet and by him projected into a language which through our own empathy allows us to share the integration of the archaic and the conscious. But the most important aid is the second: . . . 'psycho-analysis has proved that the significance of the symbol may be, and indeed generally is, hidden; and that the symbol as such need not be representational . . .'. The symbol need not be mimetic; and ultimately it is not paraphrasable.

That would be my gloss on the central aesthetic doctrine of Sir Herbert; but so phrased, it is fairly commonplace. What is not commonplace is the critical mediation that he achieves between a psychologically grounded insight and what I have called the pragmatic test, the application of the insight to the critical evaluation of poetry. The poetry, with Read, always comes first. Would he be as good a critic as he is (he is a very fine one) if he had not striven towards a systematic aesthetic? I do not know how to answer this question. He would at any rate have had a different critical vocabulary.

The essay 'Poetic Diction', which first appeared in *Reason and Romanticism*, was written before Read's studies in depth psychology were fully developed; but there is no indication in the later writings that he has changed his views. Like his first master Coleridge he has constructed a theory in later life which buttresses critical standards that were earlier expressed in the more con-

ventional terms of literary criticism. In 'Poetic Diction' he revives
Arnold's rejection of Dryden and Pope, and though he avoids
Arnold's phrase, 'classics of our prose', he dismisses them with
Dryden's own phrase 'wit-writing'. In the context of Sir Herbert's
later aesthetic speculations 'wit-writing' is the result of reliance
upon the conscious ego which suppresses the unconscious and
organic. Wit-writing is Coleridge's Fancy, a shuffling of 'fixities
and definites.' He cites the concluding lines of *The Dunciad* as
wit-writing, in contrast with some famous lines from *Macbeth*. I
do not see how Shakespeare's lines imply a standard of organic
form which allows us to reject the lines of Pope: I would retain
both, with some awareness of their differences. What I would
conclude from my over-simplified account of Read's theory, as it
is grounded in psychology, is that he remains one of the best
critics in English, not only now but of any age; but one must
point out, without quite knowing what to say about it, that as the
philosophical aesthetics has become more and more elaborate,
there is an increasing divergence between the philosopher and the
poet. May one say that the philosopher is devouring the poet at
the banquet of Thyestes?

Not only the philosopher, but the *political* philosopher: here
the critical doctrine of organicism implies the organic society. I
have strong affinities with Sir Herbert's vision of the anarchic
society (literally, the society without rulers); it is an old American
doctrine going back in the United States to the time Wordsworth
was propagating it in England; its champion with us was Thomas
Jefferson; it was revived some thirty years ago by a group of
Southern writers and renamed Agrarianism. Back of the different
versions of the organic society lurks the myth of unity of being:
the integration of the collective unconscious with the conscious
ego. This integration seems to have been broken up, for Mr. Eliot,
by a 'dissociation of sensibility' in the seventeenth century. (I have
been accused of placing the break-up in the United States at the
year 1865.) The point at issue is not whether unity of being in an
organic society ever existed, or whether it could exist; we must
affirm its necessity, if only to explain the disunity of being which
is the primary fact of the human condition. For the poet, and for
the literary critic, the idea of organicism, regardless of a particular
philosophical perspective, is the postulate, almost the axiom,
from which they must proceed.

I must pass over Sir Herbert's art criticism: I am not competent to discuss it. One surmises that his defense of abstract art is based upon a deduction from the Jungian theory of the archetype: the archetypal symbol need not be naturalistic, representational, or mimetic. As to the literary criticism, I cannot believe that the five essays selected by Sir Herbert for this volume would give a new reader a just notion of his depth and range. But the third essay I want to point out, 'American Bards and British Reviewers', in print I believe for the first time, is one of his most valuable essays. Here he brings together all his superior critical gifts — historical sense, knowledge of American as well as English poetry, subtle perception of stylistic similarities and differences, and profound insight into the alienation, and the reasons for it, of the modern poet everywhere. It should be required reading for the American chauvinists who think that 'American' has ceased to be 'English', and for their British counterparts who do not want English to be American. I would call attention to three points that ought to dispel forever these linguistic superstitions. First, the juxtaposition, in sequence, of passages from Robert Lowell and John Masefield: I thought at first sight that Lowell had written Masefield, and *vice versa*. More than fifty years and the Atlantic Ocean separate the two passages. Read cites the late W. C. Williams' dogma that, since American speech is not iambic, American poetry must not be iambic. Read disposes of this naïve jingoism with the remark that neither is British speech iambic. (It seems that Dr. Williams needed bad theories to write good poetry.)

Having done scant justice to Read's practical criticism, and none at all to his social and his art criticism, I should like to say a word about the essays on education. The philosophy of education will tell us something about Read's poetry, which though greatly distinguished is more limited in range and slighter in body than one might reasonably expect of a man who for nearly fifty years has made the prose ancillary to the verse. His argument goes somewhat as follows: The age of science and the industrial society which through technology has dehumanized man, have made for an increasing alienation of man from the soil. This is the Wordsworthian doctrine; but Read extends it to include his own insight into the Coleridgean Primary Imagination. He goes beyond Wordsworth and Coleridge. For Read, *perception* of physical nature through the archetypes, which are both subjective and objective, the forms being both in nature and in the mind, must be the basis of all education from infancy on. This doctrine has in modern criticism corrected a balance, for the intellectualism represented by men like Eliot, Ransom, and Winters has seen order exclusively as intellectual order; whereas Read sees order in an organic relation of man (perception) and nature (forms), man being both apart from and in nature. This, as I have already intimated, is a difficult doctrine to grasp, but as Read has expounded it in book after book, it is the most searching presentation of the philosophy of romanticism that I know anywhere. What this philosophy seems to leave out, and what I should like to see put in, is what Read would call the 'determinate' element; that is to say, the organic relation of man and nature maintained by an order which goes beyond individual perception — in short, religious order. The autonomous local community, in a society without rulers, would appear to be held together by the right relation of individual perception to tools, materials, and of course nature itself; and Read allows for myth as a binding element. But which myth?

Sir Herbert *uses* myths: some of the finest poems, such as 'The White Isles of Leuce' and the longer 'Daphne', are more than classical allusion. Helen and Daphne are symbols which set the limits of perception. The poem 'Daphne' is perhaps technically the most original work that Read has ever done. I do not say the *best* poem. There are five or six that one might call best: 'The End of a War', 'The Analysis of Love', 'To a Conscript of 1940', 'Any Crucifixion', 'Time and Being', 'The Falcon and the Dove'. I think this is the place to say that I refuse to understand why Sir Herbert included the long philosophical eclogue, 'Moon's Farm', and omitted 'A World Within a War' which is not only a great war poem but a great poem on a great subject: the impact upon the contemplative mind of universal violence, whether the violence be natural or man-made.

For many years I have been puzzled by Read's reputation as a poet. He is slightly younger than Eliot, Pound, and Aiken, but he is one of four poets of that generation who made their first reputations in England: he is talked about but he seems not to influence anybody and there are few references to him when his peers are mentioned. I shall not undertake comparisons; yet he belongs in this company. The three others have written long poems with elaborate formal structures, and these poems try deliberately to embody the spirit of the times. One need think only of *Four Quartets*, *Time and the Rock*, and the *Cantos*. Read is as contem-

porary as any of them. But although he is a poet with a philosophy, he is not a philosophic poet. The difference, I believe, is
plain enough. He is a contemplative poet in the Wordsworthian
tradition; and one might wish that he believed enough in Wordsworth's blank verse to write his prose autobiographies if not in
blank, then in some other formal measure. (The modified Spenserian stanza of 'The Gold Disc' might have been useful.) But here
a strict adherence to the theory of organic form may explain
Read's refusal to write in sustained metre. The emotion, the image,
the perception all compose an experience in a rhythm which must
move according to its own laws. Here is not only Coleridge but a
trace of Imagism, and perhaps the ghost of T. E. Hulme. Meanwhile Sir Herbert Read remains one of the finest poets of our time,
and will continue so to remain after our time. Otherwise I should
not have written this Foreword.

Allen Tate

Acknowledgments

For permission to include in *Selected Writings of Herbert Read* material from books published by them grateful acknowledgment is made to the following: New Directions, Norfolk, Connecticut (for poems from *The Collected Poems of Herbert Read*. The following are reprinted with their permission; Nos 2 to 13, 16 to 21, 24 to 27, 33 to 38. All inquiries for reprint use of these poems in the United States should be referred to New Directions); Random House, Inc., New York ('In Defence of Shelley' from *The True Voice of Feeling*. Copyright 1953 by Herbert Read); Thames and Hudson, Ltd, London ('The Nature of Abstract Art' from *A Letter to a Young Painter*); Routledge and Kegan Paul, Ltd, London, and Schocken Books, Inc., New York ('The Politics of the Unpolitical' from *To Hell With Culture*); George Wittenborn, Inc., 1018 Madison Avenue, New York 21 ('Towards A Duplex Civilisation' from *The Grass Roots of Art*, in the series 'Problems of Contemporary Art'). Apart from new or hitherto uncollected essays and poems the remainder of the material in this anthology is taken from books published by Faber and Faber, Ltd, London, or Horizon Press, Inc., New York.

I. Poems

DAPHNE

1

Daphne so long attached
to my broken daydreams
with troubadors and bogomils
heresiarchs of all extremes

loosen your limbs and green tresses
from their botanical growth
redeem not your trembling flesh
nor the oval mouth

of your rapturous cry
stay rooted in black earth
but allow your mythical anguish
a miraculous rebirth

In your shade I am the dove
in your leaves the voice of love

2

The secret that you locked
in immobility
is evident in the tremors
of this intricate tree

from leaf to leaf a whisper
falls through the air
my taut intelligent ear
receives each syllable of despair

Slow virginal never torrential
rivers on a pergament map

19

your veins in many deltas
disperse a perpetual sap

septal pipes through which seep
osmotic fluids that never sleep

3

The god was young and terrible
with toad eyes and goat feet
his voice a gulp that tore a throat
rank with deceit

A hot breath burned her cheek
the hand that wrenched the saffron silk
released one breast that fell aslant
and white as milk

but she was free and fled down paths
where once she'd played with naked boys
as innocent as she — invincible prowess
added to the joys

of days of bland Olympian light
not broken by an earthly night

4

The palsy that possessed her limbs
immobilized each bone
impulsive energies
transformed the girdled zone

From hidden wells within her flesh
a green alchemic flood
began to climb along the veins
and chased the ebbing blood

right to the crimpled finger-tips
To tresses and coy fringes
it introduced a glaucous blush
and intermediate tinges

until her features seem to fade
into a shadow in a shade

5

The god clutched blindly at the twigs
grown lithe or brittle
caressed a branch smooth as a limb
and leaves more crisp and subtle

than any since enured by time
A piercing herbal scent
issued from the ribbed valleys
of her wild astonishment

His anguished digitals
bit into the mild bark
the cruel maculations
left their mark

as freckles of a darker green
mottling the trunk's mat even sheen

6

Sick with thwarted lust
Apollo sank on the cotted grass
that covered her groping roots
The blood that in a bolting mass

had pressed against his groins
passed like a veil across his eyes
and a calm occlusion
stifled the little cries

that pursed his bitter lips. How long he lay
we do not know
but when his eyes opened their vertical gaze
was filled with the moon's glow

against which the leaves of the laurel tree
trembled mockingly

7

Rooted Daphne remained: Apollo went
in quest of easier prey
Daphne was rooted but her senses
did not decay

but in the waving wilderness
found their surfeit
voices of innocence to celebrate
the god's defeat

her union with the green
organic wealth of trees
a dialogue with zephyrs
an intercourse with birds and bees

explicit signals of delight
sent out from leaves reflecting light

8

What Daphne lost in tears and blood
and frenzy of the flesh
you may imagine — I celebrate
the subtler mesh

of innocence and fear
She was not made
for lust and generation
and never sought the deceptive aid

of ogling eyes — in intercourse
her voice of silvery pitch
would penetrate the listening mind
low even inexplicably rich

and there was wedded to the ice
of images crystalline and precise

9

And yet there was no coldness there
but a radiance so intense

that those with whom she held debate
kept a silence

entranced as are astronomers
by a celestial interchange
of fire and frost — the voice of Orpheus
was not so strange

when he charmed the ravening beasts
Daphne enlightened a darker mind
and drove the shadow from the place
where love should be enshrined

I mean the love without a name
it is a love devoid of shame

10

Daphne is still alive
in the perpetual green
of the sacred wood
her druids keen

their holy hymns continuously — requiems
wuther in the hollow boles
of neighbouring oaks — lizards
coiled in puckered holes

emerge to guard the breathing leaves
from lesser worms
and lest her branches should be harmed
all brutal storms

hails and other elemental ills
are diverted by the clumpered hills

11

By love deceived or men rejected
we may frequent this sheltered grove
and listen to the canticles
about us and above

and some who well distinguish
Daphne's argent voice
may then decide that love is vain
in loveless life rejoice

Beyond the reach of sickly lust
and fretful strife
there is a stillness of the flesh
another mode of life

in which the still inquiring mind
a recompense for love may find

12

The stricken leaves that lingered
upon this pendant bough
have by now all fallen
low fallen low

The weasel and the ermine
make a secret lair
in Daphne's tawny roots
and all about the fragrant air

darting wrens and linnets
fill the endless day
with pretty cries and sonnets
that would seem to say —

the nymph that from Apollo fled
lives long after he is dead

THE WHITE ISLE OF LEUCE

Leave Helen to her lover. Draw away
before the sea is dark. Frighten with your oars
the white sea-birds till they rise
on wings that veer
against the black sentinels
    of the silent wood.

The oars beat off; Achilles cannot see
the prows that dip against the dim shore's line.
But the rowers as they rest on the lifting waves
hear the revelry of Helen and a voice singing
of battle and love. The rowers hear and rest
and tremble for the limbs of Helen and the secrets of the sacred
    isle.

THE FALCON AND THE DOVE

1

This high-caught hooded Reason broods upon my wrist,
Fetter'd by a so tenuous leash of steel.
We are bound for the myrtle marshes, many leagues away,
And have a fair expectation of quarry.

2

Over the laggard dove, inclining to green boscage
Hovers this intentional doom — till the unsullied sky receives
A precipitation of shed feathers
And the swifter fall of wounded wings.

3

Will the plain aye echo with that loud *hullallo!*
Or retain an impress of our passage?
We have caught Beauty in a wild foray
And now the falcon is hooded and comforted away.

THE SEVEN SLEEPERS

The seven sleepers ere they left
the light and colour of the earth
the seven sleepers they did cry
(banishing their final fears):

'Beauty will not ever fade.
To our cavern we retire
doom'd to sleep ten thousand years.
Roll the rock across the gap

Then forget us; we are quiet:
stiff and cold our bodies lie;
Earth itself shall stir ere we
visit Earth's mortality.

Beauty when we wake will be
a solitude on land and sea.'

FORMAL INCANTATION

O watery sun decline,
Defame the obdurate day,
Or the ashen slaves of Phoebus
Will find me with a golden key

And bid me unlock the casket, laid
Beneath the crumbling stairs,
Where Jason's fleece awaits the day
Medea's art recurs.

The pianola's notes resound
Through the damp rain-sodden rooms;
And I have naught I can repress
Against the anguish of the herbal flames

That flicker in the near zone
Of Hecate's naked plight.
O triune grace, I will not miss
Thee at the closure of night.

A NORTHERN LEGION

Bugle calls coiling through the rocky valley
have found echoes in the eagles' cries:
an outrage is done on anguish'd men
now men die and death is no deedful glory.

Eleven days this legion forced the ruin'd fields, the
burnt homesteads and empty garths, the broken arches
of bridges: desolation moving like a shadow before them, a
rain of ashes. Endless their anxiety

marching into a northern darkness: approaching
a narrow defile, the waters falling fearfully
the clotting menace of shadows and all the multiple
instruments of death in ambush against them.

The last of the vanguard sounds his doleful note.
The legion now is lost. None will follow.

THE IVY AND THE ASH

The ivy and the ash
cast a dark arm
across the beck.
In this rocky ghyll
I sit and watch
the eye-iris water move
like muscles over stones
smooth'd by this ageless action.

The water brings
from the high fell
an icy current of air.
There is no sun to splinter
the grey visionary quartz.
The heart is cool
and adamant among the rocks
mottled with wet moss.

Descend into the valley
explore the plain
even the salt sea
but keep the heart
cool in the memory
of ivy, ash
and the glistening beck
running swiftly through the black rocks.

KIRKDALE

I, Orm the son of Gamal
found these fractur'd stones

27

starting out of the fragrant thicket.
The river bed was dry.

The rooftrees naked and bleach'd,
nettles in the nave and aisleways,
on the altarstone an owl's cast
and a feather from a wild dove's wing.

There was peace in the valley:
far into the eastern sea
the foe had gone, leaving death and ruin
and a longing for the priest's solace.

Fast the feather lay
like a sulky jewel in my head
till I knew it had fallen in a holy place.
Therefore I raised these grey stones up again.

SUMMER RAIN

Against the window pane
against the temple of my brain
beat the muffled taps of rain.

Upon the scorch'd and mottled leaves
upon the blench'd and pented sheaves
the land receives

the liquid flood:
water like a blush of blood
returns to the parch'd rood.

The fox has left his fetid hovel
to lick the drenchéd blades of sorrel;
odours rise from thyme and fennel.

The worm in his retreat deep under
the earth's insipid crust
hearing a distant drumming thunder

blindly renews his upward undulation.
The soil respires as if in emulation
of living things. All elements their maculation

desire and achieve. A warm breath
issues from the nostrils beneath
the mask of death.

FELIX TRANSITUS

The valley and the crest
the heavy lid of night
the arch of bone
a head which on the breast
has fallen like a kite
wind-driven down.

The darkness of the earth
the sense of sinking deep
the blatant heart.
This stillness might be death
it is not sleep
it does not hurt.

An intercepted edge of lace
has printed on his brow
its faultless mesh;
and blood has left a trace
where lips unconscious now
once bruised the flesh.

THE INNOCENT EYE

Potential
mirror of gentle acts
agents of factual
joy

enjoy
deft engines

but shade yourself
against electric signs

that in the night
destroy the stars
and lurid phantoms
feature on hotel stairs.

Angelicos
diatoms
of senseful surfeit —
how can man deny you?

He should employ you
whenever
he wakes in the world
out of dusty fever

and with not worm
and weevil
for whom
God grows stavesacre

but with bird and lynx
enlarge his life
with crystal lens
and furtive lust.

THE THIRD

We two that live together
And love each other
Have no wandering thoughts
Beyond the present measure.

We love and work and subtly weave
Habitual chains: we wheel
Like birds above our focal hearth
Our fear-fring'd nest.

But always breaking through the screen
Of silence comes the warning note:
The world is not within us, we
In part are in some way without.

Peeping into our private room
We feel, not see, a Third:
The hollyhocks are parted and a face
Presses to the window and is gone.

Fine fingers I have felt
Like icy bands about my arms
Just when the impulse had been born
To demonstrate my tenderness.

The Person or the Thing has age
But is indefinite:
I would not care if I could force
Its sullen hand

And see an instrument of hate
Fall clattering to the ground
Or know that all it held was death
The Third to which we both are bound.

With death one day I shall pledge faith
And faithless be to you:
But who is this that treads between
The last bed and our own?

Is it the wind in the hollyhocks?
A trick of cloud and glass?
A nerve discordant round the bone?
A simple weariness?

Dear, do not let us hesitate
To shun the unbidden guest:
Resolv'd that all is distortion
Save life, and love, and death.

1945

They came running over the perilous sands
    Children with their golden eyes
Crying: *Look! We have found samphire*
    Holding out their bone-ridden hands.

It might have been the spittle of wrens
    Or the silver nest of a squirrel
For I was invested with the darkness
    Of an ancient quarrel whose omens
Lay scatter'd on the silted beach.
    The children came running toward me

But I saw only the waves behind them
    Cold, salt and disastrous
Lift their black banners and break
    Endlessly, without resurrection.

THE WELL OF LIFE

The waters of the well of life
Lie deep on a rock bed
Not fetched from running streams
But drawn at the well-head.

Two red-haired wives stand there
(Each has a lover)
One turns the wailing windlass
The other bends over

And dips a scoop into the well
To fill the pitcher at her side
The clouds are ghostly passengers
That on the stilled water ride.

The rooks are croaking in the elms
And men in the field labour
God bless these wives and their strong
Men's endeavour.

KALAMIS AND SOSANDRA

Above the lake the swallows dive
And fishes mock their flight:
Who is the goddess gave you birth
On some past starlit night?
Who cut the secret knot of life
And left a hollow where
The lion with the wounded paw
Impressed a seal of air
Invisible yet viable
The seed of my despair
That soon will sprout and climb and cling
Your ivy in my silver hair.

I do not wish another thing
But that you wear no new diguise
You have the wisdom of the young
And I the false youth of the wise
You hold a stylus in your hand
You have placed me on a pedestal
You have carved the torso and the head
Your gaze is on the genital.
A warm breeze blows across the lake
It is the season of the grape
The god the lion and the man
They have a single shape.

INBETWEENTIMES

Between the Winter and the Spring
between day and night
a no man's time a mean light
with cold mist creeping along the alleys
and the sun like a world withdrawn.

The shrill voices of surplus children
shake up the frosty dust
lamps are lit

and bleak shadows like bruises
rise under their golden eyes.

Through these cavernous streets
between a winter and a spring
between night and day
we wander our hearts lifted
above the shadows and the dust
secure in an alien light.

SEPTEMBER FIRES

Haulms burn
in distant fields.
Reluctantly the plumes of smoke
rise against a haze
of hills blue and clear
but featureless.

Our feet
crush the crinkled beech-leaves.
There is no other life than ours.
God is good to us this September evening
to give us a sun
and a world burning its dross.

Let us burn the twisted years
that have brought us to this meeting.
The crops are cull'd —
we can expect no other fruit
until another year
brings fire and fealty and the earth in barren stillness.

THE EVEN SKEIN

Ragged ends
are the world's ends: land in water, wind-woven branches,
sea-spray, star-fret, any atmosphere;
and everywhere
where mind meets matter, fray'd nerves

and tender fingers, feeling the stone's jagged edge;
ragged ends of love
that can never be complete,
secret meetings, interrupted speech,
broken handshakes
and the shuffle of reluctant feet
down alleys where the broken light
falls brokenly
on broken walls.

Ragged ends of life that has no aim
but plucks its flowers with a ragged stem
perhaps arranges them
in a bowl of clouded glass
where for a day or two
they stand exulting on console, sill or mantelpiece
then fade
into a dry and brittle ghost.

Ragged ends of time
that no time will knit together.
Death is the only even skein:
Death that is both ghost and gain.

TOURISTS IN A SACRED PLACE

A pallid rout stepping like phantoms
beneath the arching boughs,
have come with angel hands and wretched voices
to the valley and this choir of perish'd stones.

Valid was my anguish — as though a turbulent dove
had scatter'd the leafy silence.
Now in airless vistas, dim and blind my limbs will loiter
while the senses stray to vast defeats.

A rocking bell
peals in a grey tower.
The sound has broken down the strong defences
of age and innocence.

Cecily come with your virginal tremors
Cecily still the bell.
Your stresses are wet from the rushing river
a green weed clings like a vein on your breast.

Cecily, listen, the clangour is over
now only the burden of bees in the clover.
God and his angels have given you grace,
and stamp'd your mission on your naiad face.

EARLY ASTIR

Early, early I walked in the city:
The river ran its strength from misty valleys
And the sun lit the wings of stone angels.

Yarrol! Yarrol! I cried exultingly:
Passing dogs lifted wet noses
And housemaidens the blinds of their gables.

CRANACH

But once upon a time
the oakleaves and the wild boars
Antonio Antonio
the old wound is bleeding.

We are in Silvertown
we have come here with a modest ambition
to know a little bit about the river
eating cheese and pickled onions on a terrace by the Thames.

Sweet Thames! the ferry glides across your bosom
like Leda's swan.
The factories ah slender graces
sly naked damsels nodding their downy plumes.

A GIFT FOR SCARDANELLI

See: the field is empty ...
You came here by a curious detour

the hedges were trimmed but o-
ranges among the intricate thorns
glowed like torches. You expected to find
a temple of honey-coloured stone
and an old man crouched in the porch
listening to a marble-browed girl
that there discourses on the nature of love.

*April und Mai und Junius sind ferne
Ich bin nichts mehr : ich lebe nicht mehr gerne . . .*

The clouds are unanchored: they might
fall from the sky to cover you
I have brought you a basket of figs
and some fine linen
but alas
no white goat to slaughter
and fingers have faltered
that should have played the flute.

ANY CRUCIFIXION

O what is this encroaching midway
bird-bedraggled darkness but a hood
to hide your sense of loss of clenched dismay ?

And what the thin and crooked becks of blood
displayed to drain the delta of your pain
but lace upon the waled and woeful limbs
that led you to this spurious mound again ?

They are all gone. The jackal climbs
and watches from a mossy sill.
You are alone unendingly alone
and people slowly walking down the hill
bruise the myrtle on the calcined stone.

FLIGHT

The serial feathers
imbricated
conceal the struts

37

an extending
N: flex'd;
when taut

folding air
coiling the currents
never bending

till the body
seeks the level
of its rest.

TENEMENT

Third block
four up
the window shut
blank uncurtain'd

other windows
glint grin
all sinister
within

reflect
rainy clouds
uncertain tracery
of winter twigs

a wire sings
an insulator
clings
like a wren to the wall

MELVILLE

Melville fell
and the albatross
out of the rigging

38

Edam the moon
all angular else
mast and ropes

a feather fell
a claw
clutched the ladder

slipped
Melville fell
forty fathoms Melville fell

fathoms below the sea level

TECTIFORM

In this extensive gloom
foxes nest
under concrete ashlars

fallen like broken blades
half-in half-out
the tangled rusty steel

A raven rides
the rooftree settling down
angle of 63

ends flex'd gaunt
like accents
over the dark eyes of gutted sheds

The fox runs
over the vivid quitch burying
banks of black encaustic soil

the river is flowing clear

FERTILE FEATHERS

Feather & weather & the fertile zone
feature forever the mind of God

grace & gristle butcher-bird & bat
distribute the seed by splitting the pod

Mostly the swallow but sometimes the rook
risks the sun's anger by displacing a bud
but broaching the reef comes the gladstone-bag rampant
and restores to the egg its eye of bright blood

AILRED

awakes in the raw abbey
to the flare of rivulets
and the coal effort of the wren
the stript twigs are
veins of jet in the bruised flesh
of a dawn

articulate in the organic sighs
of rot, listless leaves, amused mice
and the massive
roll of drenched woods

otters advance
in silk sheaths splash oilily
into the cold current

Wherever the word is spoken
the Virgin is there to receive it
the moonstone a separate fire
on her bosom
watches an eye
open to the broken image
of the white hills and the high
scattered quails

BOWER BIRD

blest orange crest
Hunstein and Goldie
beak boy and olive-
brown breadwinner

bright basket and bough
black sap of berry
confused inclusion
of crumb and plunder

wispy tunnel
whiteleaf woe
he doles a shrill canticle
uptil a dry thorn

a fabric cone
and Christ why wonder
such telltale cumber
of hormone provender

SONNET

My hand that out of the silk subsiding waters
Reaches in despair
Might be some shipwrecked mariner's
And the cool soft breast it caresses
The curdled crest of a wave

But a heart beneath beats tranquilly
And her mind is wandering restlessly
Over the wide dominions of sense.

She is free: I know her voice will sing
Above the severed oaks: her steps
Will be light as she proceeds
Festively under a fate
Dark as falling assegai.

She is a nymph and she is free
And I am but a fettered ape.

SONNET

One day you will intuitively come
Home again driving westward

Into the burning sun: memory
a dusty screen that blinds the vision
You will wind through the narrow lanes
Over the frequent culverts where willows
Sprout in clumps. The marshes
Remember the marigolds and over the farm
The pines stretch agonized arms
It will be still and you will descend
Into an arena of yellow corn
That not a breath of wind stirs

And a rook if it should swerve in the sky
Will move the whole world momentously.

HERSCHEL GRYNSPAN

This beautiful assassin is your friend:
his action the delivery of love
with magnitude in the unblemish'd years
when hate and scorn and lust
are buried under the leaves of dread.

He lifts his hand in calm despair.
The gesture loses its solitary grace
and violence is answered by violence
until the sluggish tinder of the world's indifference
is consumed, consumed to the end.

Anger is now action. The white flame of justice
will dance wildly over Europe's dark marshes
until the morning air is everywhere
and clear
as on the hills of Hellas.

This beautiful assassin is your friend
walking and whispering in the night beside you.
His voice is the voice that made you
listen to secrets in the night around you.
The light of worlds beyond your world
beguiled you with hope of a harmony

wider than the anguish of our broken lives.
The wreckage of the day was hidden.

This beautiful assassin is my friend
because my heart is filled with the same fire.
We have sheltered under the same portico
listening to the silver voice of wisdom.

Our feet faltered among the fallen stones
where once the Vandals passed
and we found
under a vivid screen of leaves
the blood still warm from a martyr's wound.

A SHORT POEM FOR ARMISTICE DAY

Gather or take fierce degree
trim the lamp set out for sea
here we are at the workman's entrance
clock in and shed your eminence.

Notwithstanding, work it diverse ways
work it diverse days, multiplying four digestions
here we make artificial flowers
of paper tin and metal thread.

One eye one leg one arm one lung
a syncopated sick heart-beat
the record is not nearly worn
that weaves a background to our work.

I have no power therefore have patience
These flowers have no sweet scent
no lustre in the petal no increase
from fertilising flies and bees.

No seed they have no seed
their tendrils are of wire and grip
the buttonhole the lip
and never fade

And will not fade though life
and lustre go in genuine flowers
and men like flowers are cut
and withered on a stem

And will not fade a year or more
I stuck one in a candlestick
and there it clings about the socket
I have no power therefore have patience.

TO A CONSCRIPT OF 1940

*Qui n'a pas une fois désespéré de l'honneur, ne sera
jamais un héros.*
GEORGES BERNANOS

A soldier passed me in the freshly fallen snow
His footsteps muffled, his face unearthly grey;
And my heart gave a sudden leap
As I gazed on a ghost of five-and-twenty years ago.

I shouted Halt! and my voice had the old accustom'd ring
And he obeyed it as it was obeyed
In the shrouded days when I too was one
Of an army of young men marching

Into the unknown. He turned towards me and I said:
'I am one of those who went before you
Five-and-twenty years ago: one of the many who never returned,
Of the many who returned and yet were dead.

We went where you are going, into the rain and the mud;
We fought as you will fight
With death and darkness and despair;
We gave what you will give — our brains and our blood.

We think we gave in vain. The world was not renewed.
There was hope in the homestead and anger in the streets
But the old world was restored and we returned
To the dreary field and workshop, and the immemorial feud

Of rich and poor. Our victory was our defeat.
Power was retained where power had been misused

And youth was left to sweep away
The ashes that the fires had strewn beneath our feet.

But one thing we learned: there is no glory in the deed
Until the soldier wears a badge of tarnish'd braid;
There are heroes who have heard the rally and have seen
The glitter of a garland round their head.

Theirs is the hollow victory. They are deceived.
But you, my brother and my ghost, if you can go
Knowing that there is no reward, no certain use
In all your sacrifice, then honour is reprieved.

To fight without hope is to fight with grace,
The self reconstructed, the false heart repaired.'
Then I turned with a smile, and he answered my salute
As he stood against the fretted hedge, which was like white lace.

BOMBING CASUALTIES IN SPAIN

Doll's faces are rosier but these were children
their eyes not glass but gleaming gristle
dark lenses in whose quicksilvery glances
the sunlight quivered. These blench'd lips
were warm once and bright with blood
but blood
held in a moist bleb of flesh
not spilt and spatter'd in tousled hair.

In these shadowy tresses
red petals did not always
thus clot and blacken to a scar.

These are dead faces.
Wasps' nests are not so wanly waxen
wood embers not so greyly ashen.

They are laid out in ranks
like paper lanterns that have fallen
after a night of riot
extinct in the dry morning air.

A SONG FOR THE SPANISH ANARCHISTS

The golden lemon is not made
 but grows on a green tree:
A strong man and his crystal eyes
 is a man born free.

The oxen pass under the yoke
 and the blind are led at will:
But a man born free has a path of his own
 and a house on the hill.

And men are men who till the land
 and women are women who weave:
Fifty men own the lemon grove
 and no man is a slave.

BEATA L'ALMA

Beata l'alma, ove non corre tempo.
MICHELANGELO

1

Time ends when vision sees its lapse in
 liberty. The seven
sleepers quit their den and wild
 lament-
ations fill out voiceless bodies. Echoes only are.

You will never understand the mind's
 misanthropy, nor see
that all is foul and fit to
 screech in.
It is an eye's anarchy: men are ghoulish stumps

and the air a river of opaque
 filth. God! I cannot see
to design these stark reaches, these
 bulging
contours pressed against me in the maddening dark.

46

A blindman's buff and no distilling
    of song for the woeful
      scenes of agony. Never
        will rest
the mind an instant in its birdlike flutterings.

Could I impress my voice on the plas-
      tic darkness, or lift an
    inviolate lanthorn from
      a ship
in the storm I might have ease. But why ? No
      fellows

would answer my hullallo, and my
        lanthorn would lurch on the
      mast till it dipped under the
          wet waves
and the hissing darkness healed the wide wound of
      light.

A cynic race — to bleak ecstasies
      we are driven by our
      sombre destiny. Men's shouts
        are not
glad enough to echo in our groin'd hearts. We know

war and its dead, and famine's bleach'd bones ;
        black rot overreaching
      the silent pressure of life
        in fronds
of green ferns and in the fragile shell of white flesh.

2

New children must be born of gods in
    a deathless land, where the
    uneroded rocks bound clear
      from cool
glassy tarns, and no flaw is in mind or flesh.

Sense and image they must refashion —
    they will not recreate
  love: love ends in hate; they will
      not use
words: words lie. The structure of events alone is

  comprehensible and to single
    perceptions communic-
  ation is not essential.
      Art ends;
the individual world alone is valid

and that gives ease. The water is still;
    the rocks are hard and vein'd,
  metalliferous, yielding
      an ore
of high worth. In the sky the unsullied sun lake.

THE GOLD DISC

An Elegy

I will not tread the old familiar path
  Through watery meads and melancholy woods:
  My autumn air is cool, the stubble crisp
  And edged with frills of crystal frost: my moods
  Are for endurance stript — boughs would break
  Did leaves sustain a falling snow.
  Life's subtlest forms sink to evade
  Wintry storms: blizzards may blow
In vain against the bark, the shell, the seed beneath the sod.

Under a weather'd skin the blood will flow
  The faster in its tried and polish'd bed.
  If limbs have lost their agile fling
  It is because they leapt too far ahead
  Striving to gain precarious rest.

Grace is given when flesh and spirit run
In equal pace, two fettled mares
Yoked to a featherweight car. The race is won
On points of style and stateliness — the air is all.

The air is all and ageless — ageless too
The bubbling lymph that makes of man
An animal susceptible to love.
O, not the lust that since the world began
Spawned the race under hedge or roof,
But some remoter essence, drained from this,
That foregoes the natural aim, to weave
Legends of devotion or of mutual bliss —
The never defin'd, the always unrealiz'd pattern of our delight.

Why in this dry autumnal season
Should the Castalian wonder never cease ?
Why should nerves involuntarily twitch
That had settled to a serene and witless ease ?
A face in the amorphous crowd takes shape
Is framed in dark fire and fused
Like bright enamels on the vacant field
Of a mind that was wandering perhaps amused
By the vanity and the variety of an average mundane scene.

Is the response still electrically slick
Or is caution from the first a soft veil
That moderates the shock and restrains
A gesture whose configuration might fail
To register the shape (though not the size)
Of a nascent emotion ? Who can say ?
In a man imagination and mind
Blend to a unity: a woman may
Shift from mind to instinct, behave like a blind worm.

This instinct drives any one of us on
Like a boat before a wild and refluent wind.
If we are not wrecked on hidden sands or reefs
It is because we are guided by a mind
Bent on measuring distances and depths.
But caution breeds distrust: we are men

To the degree we adventure, lift eyes
From our immediate dead reckoning and then
Carry our load of longing to a haven unvisited.

Safe in this Thule or Trebizond
Sails furl'd and nibbling round the shore
We may then look over the dancing prow
And decide what we could not decide before:
Whether the new has a look of the old,
Whether the deck beneath our feet
Is more solid than the strand over there
Seductively shadow'd as it is for the sweet
Pleasures of love by palm-trees, acacias and rushes.

But we have to take account of crew and cargo
For one may mutiny and the other rot.
Those blustering fellows I have on board
Are restrain'd as they work by the thought
Of ultimate ease, all that wealth can buy.
Falter now and they will plot to kill
Their negative captain, scuttle the ship
Make for the shore and enjoy their fill
Of lust and leisure and the momentary whatever-you wish.

Between measure and mood, indecision and deed
We can hover a lifetime. I hover'd with you
And with you and with you — until I retir'd
With my stinking cargo and scowling crew.
I came back to port and now lie in dry dock
With the crew paid off and my hopes curtail'd
But it is odd that I feel no remorse
No sense of a mission that fail'd
As I savour the smoke of the burning leaves, and the acid decay.

But that, it will be said, was your physical cruise:
What of the spirit and its search for truth?
Have you found in old age some end
To the quest you began in your youth?
Yes: an end to the restless endeavour
To define what is within or without,
The scope of belief — of unbelief too

For in the end I have put all in doubt
God, man; earth, heaven: I live on in alert suspense.

I believe in my unbelief — would not force
One fibre of my being to bend in the wind
Of determinate doctrine. In doubt there is stillness
The stillness that elsewhere we may find
In the sky above us where the fix'd stars
Mete out infinity and space folds
To contain the secret substance of life
Which time in its tragic furnace moulds
To the forms of grief and glory, of vice and holiness.

But gently, lest the rhetoric steal
This mood of quietness. I will not preach
A private brand of pride or shame.
I too have heard the sounding rivers, the screech
Of amorous winds. But now the night is calm.
I listen to a music fraught with silence
To a solitude full of sound.
I have found the peace beyond violence
And gaze steadily into the gold disc that blurs all hard distinctions.

TIME & BEING

Wait while I shut the gate
    the wild wind is blowing
        and over the eastern wold
        the leaves of the trees and my tender thoughts
        are toss'd to the angry sea.

We will walk over the fields till we reach
    the bare top of the hill
        where the world spins round like a gambler's wheel
        and we and the sheep and the loose white stones
        must dance on its whirling rim.

Beneath this black and tortured thorn
    let us rest as we take our bearing
        you and I in a universe

where nothing is unless we utter
and out of our words comes a Word.

Nothing existed and something is born
like a lamb on the cold green grass
our Word is bloody and hardly can stand
bedraggl'd in wind and bitten by thistle
a bleat of distress.

But it is ours this weanling cry
not a thought but a poem
it came out of the womb where Nothing was
from the empty house of Being
in the time of another world.

Where the rafters are rough and the floors are bare
where the walls are blank and no vent
gives out on the wold or the sea
and the only sound is the sound we make
the dole of our wondering lips.

The curtains of the night are golden
the curtains of the day are gray
we are cast for the trembling labour
the shudder of pain as we slit the veil
or die in the caul.

II. Moon's Farm

A Dialogue for Three Voices

Note: *Moon's Farm* was originally written for broadcasting, and was produced for the British Broadcasting Corporation by Rayner Heppenstall on January 21, 1951.

Moon's Farm

A DIALOGUE FOR THREE VOICES

First Voice. A cave in the old quarry
a dry ditch and a tumbledown barn
such is all my shelter.
The black-faced sheep have gone
and with them the shepherds . . .
That was twenty winters ago.
Then came the men with axes
cut down the spinneys and plantations
lopped off the branches
    and carted the timber away
leaving this desolation
    at the head of the dale.

Oh, I can nestle in a ferny glen
or in the rafters of a fallen roof
    in myrtle bushes at the edge of the bog
But I grow weak
    I have no nourishment
        I languish like a mist at noon.

Once it was different.
That was in the time of the holy men
monks who came over the moor
    from the abbey by the sea
to build a monastery in the slender woods
    at the dale's mouth.
Their path
led up the dale and across the hills
and on the hills they had many sheep
and cattle in the meadows below the hills
They dammed up the beck

> to make fishponds
> and ran off a sluice
> > to drive the millwheel.

> They cared for me
> and built me in with woods and garths
> > with farmsteads and sheepfolds
> > > with chapels and graveyards
> even their dead
> > they gave to me.
> Now the broken stones of their buildings
> > lie under these grassy mounds and heather
> I am left
> > with birds and beetles for company
> > > and the little grey snails in the turf
> Even the foxes and badgers
> > have left this place
> There is no strength at all
> > left in the place.

SECOND VOICE. About here it must have been
> > but there is nothing left
> > > nothing left of Moon's Farm.
> There was a clump of pines
> > the last trees before the heather began
> And a stone trough
> > to gather the clear water from a rill
> It fell from a stone spout which must have been very old
> > fifty years ago they had given up carving such things
> > > from the solid stone
> > > (Took too much time, they said)
> Time, time
> > folk were already beginning to be aware of time
> > > even then.

FIRST VOICE. Not aware enough!
> When you live all the time in the same place
> Then you become aware of time.

SECOND VOICE. I begin to remember everything
> > but how it has changed!
> There were woods on the other side of the dale
> > and down there
> > > by the beck

56

was Moon's Farm.
Not a stone or stick of it left!
That's a mystery —
   how completely a solid structure
     like a farmhouse
can vanish in fifty years!
The stones they would carry off
   to make a new road
     miles away
But what happened to the trees ?
   there was even a stunted orchard
All gone.
All signs of human habitation
   rubbed off the landscape.
And yet
   there is still something. I still feel
     the spirit of the place.
FIRST VOICE. He is becoming aware of me.
SECOND VOICE. It was made up of so many things :
   the shapes of these hills
     and the changing shadows
   the cries of birds
     and the lapping of the stream over pebbles.
But more than that —
   a sense of glory and yes
     a sense of grief.
Glory in the present moment
Grief because it was all so momentary
   so fleeting
     so elusive.
And yet I am sure
   it was more than an illusion
some spirit did inhabit these hills
   some very ancient spirit.
The Roman legions passed this way
   the stones of their roads lie under the heather
Did they salute her as they passed ?
But there you are
   already personifying the thing
     imagining some wispy female.
The Romans were not so sentimental

their genius loci was masculine
    the devil of a fellow.
Hullo!
    there's someone coming up from the beck
    looks like an old beggar woman
        but what would she find up here?
She must have seen me from the other side
    and now comes to investigate.
But she takes her time.

FIRST VOICE. Now he has seen me.
    He is walking into my world with his innocent eyes
    He is looking straight into my hiding-place.

SECOND VOICE. Good morning!
    I did not expect to meet anybody up here. You surely
        don't live hereabouts.

FIRST VOICE. Indeed I do. I have always
    lived in this dale.

SECOND VOICE. Then perhaps you can help me. I too
    used to live in this dale
        but farther down.
    I left fifty years ago
        as a boy of ten
    I went far away
        into another country.
    Today, for the first time
    I have come back.
    I find everything changed.

FIRST VOICE. Oh yes: it has changed a lot
    in that long time.

SECOND VOICE. It is partly an illusion
    or *was* an illusion.
    You see: everything, yes, every thing
    is much smaller than I can remember.
    My childish eyes
        had magnified everything
    and now the world seems to have shrunk.

FIRST VOICE. When your possessions are small
    you enlarge them with wonder.
    My world
        remains always the same

SECOND VOICE. You speak like an educated woman

  yet you say
   you have never left the dale.
FIRST VOICE. I have never left the dale: my schooling
  was indeed simple.
SECOND VOICE. But apparently profound.
  I went to many schools
   and was no wiser in the end.
  I did not know, for example,
   that this dale would shrink.
  I thought I should find it
   as I had left it
    the people changed, of course
     most of them dead
      many gone away
  but I thought the place would be the same.
FIRST VOICE. It changes slowly.
  The trees are felled
   or brought down in a storm
  and no one plants new ones.
  The roofs fall in
   the stones crumble
    men go away in search of easier work.
  Only the hills
   remain
    in their old shape.
SECOND VOICE. And why have you been left behind
  apparently alone?
FIRST VOICE. I am not alone.
  I have a Father.
SECOND VOICE. A Father! And how old is he?
FIRST VOICE. You must ask him — I don't know.
SECOND VOICE. Is he about?
FIRST VOICE. Yes: he is always about.
  You will see him presently.
SECOND VOICE. Good! Are there any more in the family?
FIRST VOICE. That depends
  on what you mean by a family.
  Sometimes
   we have people to stay with us.
SECOND VOICE. For a holiday, no doubt.
FIRST VOICE. From time to time.

SECOND VOICE. Now I can see your Father
    he is coming down the hillside.
    But the sun is in his eyes
    he does not see us.

FIRST VOICE. Oh yes: he sees everything
    he can stare the sun out
    he can see in the dark.

SECOND VOICE. How extraordinary! You mean ...

FIRST VOICE. Hush! About such things
    he must tell you himself.

THIRD VOICE. Ah! I thought I would catch up with you
    here.

SECOND VOICE. But I came
    from the opposite direction.

THIRD VOICE. Yes: but I came to meet you.

SECOND VOICE. But I don't understand ...

THIRD VOICE. Never mind! The point is
    What are you going to do next?

FIRST VOICE. He means
    Where are you going to next?

SECOND VOICE. Does it matter to you?
    I am not trespassing, am I?

FIRST VOICE. You are not trespassing
    If you stay here.

THIRD VOICE. You surely have time enough.

SECOND VOICE. You mean
    you would like me to stay with you?

FIRST AND THIRD VOICES. For as long as you like.

FIRST VOICE. You would gradually recover
    the feeling of the place.

THIRD VOICE. You would gradually recover
    the sense of the past.

SECOND VOICE. Ah, that's just what I came for.
    I will gladly stay. I have the few necessary things
    in that rucksack.

FIRST VOICE. I will go to prepare a bed for you.
    I am afraid it will be a very simple one
    we have no house.

SECOND VOICE. It is very kind of you
    anything will do.

THIRD VOICE. We are what you would call tramps.

SECOND VOICE. Yes: but I don't see
    what you can possibly find to live on
      in a place like this.
THIRD VOICE. One needs less and less
    after a certain age.
SECOND VOICE. Yes: that is what I am beginning to discover.
THIRD VOICE. Until one needs nothing at all.
SECOND VOICE. You mean
    we die.
THIRD VOICE. That's right
    you will die.
SECOND VOICE. Tell me: were you too
    here fifty years ago?
THIRD VOICE. Yes, of course.
SECOND VOICE. You don't remember me, I suppose?
THIRD VOICE. I remember you perfectly well
    the boy at the Scarlets.
SECOND VOICE. Yes: that was the name of our farm.
  But surely
    you cannot recognize in my wasted features
      the boy of fifty years ago?
THIRD VOICE. There are some things that do not change
    the shape of the skull
    the cadence of the voice.
SECOND VOICE. But if you remember me so well
    why don't I remember you?
  I would say
    I had never seen you before.
THIRD VOICE. No: in those days
    you were not aware of me.
SECOND VOICE. So we might say
    you have the advantage over me.
THIRD VOICE. So we might say. But you will not forget me
    ever again.
SECOND VOICE. It's not likely. Meeting you like this
    in this lonely place.
  Can you tell me what the time is?
    it must be getting late . . .

                      (*A shrill scream.*)

What was that?
THIRD VOICE. A rabbit — perhaps, if we are lucky, a hare.

It is all we have to live on
    up here.
SECOND VOICE. I have heard wounded men scream like that.
    But I was asking you the time . . .
THIRD VOICE. I can still see you
        the day you nearly lost your life
            in the mill-dam.
SECOND VOICE. You were there!
THIRD VOICE. Yes: standing on the far bank
        watching the water-rats
    I saw how you were pulled out
        as good as dead.
SECOND VOICE. No wonder I didn't see you!
    And shortly after that narrow squeak
    I went away.
    That is why there was never any chance
        of getting to know you.
    You stayed in the dale
        I never came back
            until today.
THIRD VOICE. I stayed here.
SECOND VOICE. And perhaps that was wise of you. I wonder
    I wonder what I would have done
        had I stayed here
    what I would have become.
THIRD VOICE. We can only become what we are.
SECOND VOICE. True enough — 'Become what thou art!' — an oracle
    I have always believed in.
THIRD VOICE. So it made no difference
        going away?
SECOND VOICE. No essential difference, I suppose. And yet
        it is said we only learn by experience.
THIRD VOICE. And what did experience teach you?
SECOND VOICE. To discover myself
        perhaps only that.
THIRD VOICE. And other people?
SECOND VOICE. They remained mysteries
        except in so far as I got
            inside their skulls
    And even then
        it was pretty dark inside.

THIRD VOICE. But how did you discover yourself?
SECOND VOICE. Curiously enough
    in exploring other people.
I didn't discover that I was a male
    until I had known a female
I did not discover that I was an Englishman
    until I fought with a German
I did not discover that I was a European
    until I had lived in America.
Shall I go on?
THIRD VOICE. Yes: to the end.
SECOND VOICE. It has no end — yet.
I did not discover that I was alone in the world
    until I joined an army
I did not discover that I was brave
    until I had sheltered in a ditch with a coward
I did not discover that I was a liar
    until I met a man who never lied
        even to save his pride
I did not discover that I was sober
    until one night I got dead drunk
I did not discover that I could hate
    until I fell in love.
A mass of contradictions
    you will say.
THIRD VOICE. There is no unity in human character
Only God and the Devil are consistent.
    But go on.
SECOND VOICE. I did not discover that I was a peasant
    until I became a poet
I did not discover that I was miserly
    until I became rich
I did not discover that I was strong
    until God had forsaken me.
THIRD VOICE. Until you had forsaken God.
SECOND VOICE. No: it did not happen like that
    I did not deliberately forsake God.
    Rather I clung to Him
        like a child to its mother's skirts.
    But the garment was whisked away
        I fell to the ground.

THIRD VOICE. It may have been
    God wanted you to stand alone.
SECOND VOICE. Alone? I have been alone
     all these years.
   At first I was proud to be alone
   I found I could stand without a hand
    clutching at the finger of God.
   I was defiant and cried: God is dead.
   But then
    I grew less certain
   It was not that I believed in a resurrection of the dead
                              God.
   But it became obvious
    that for some people he was still alive.
   I could not convince them that he was dead
    and when they looked at me
     it was with eyes of pity
      as for someone who had lost a father or a son.
   I scorned their pity
    but I no longer despised their belief.
THIRD VOICE. You did not try
    to find your lost God?
SECOND VOICE. No. If God is still alive
   he is with us now
  staring us in the face
    His face is the sky
    His eyes are red berries in yon hedge
     or the glittering quartz in this stone.
    His voice is that bird
     crying in the gorse bush
     or the water
      lapping over the pebbles in the beck.
   If God exists
    he must be both immanent and ubiquitous
   What sort of God would play hide-and-seek?
THIRD VOICE. It takes two to play such a game.
SECOND VOICE. Yes: man is just as necessary to God
    as God to man.
   God depends for his existence
    on our recognition of Him.
   God is reborn

in every woman's womb.

THIRD VOICE. God exists but for a moment.

SECOND VOICE. The moment of our attention
    — or do you mean
that time will still exist
  when God is dead?

THIRD VOICE. That is what I mean.

SECOND VOICE. You are a very strange old man
    to talk so confidently
      about God and Fate.
I did not expect to find a man like you
  in such a lonely place.

THIRD VOICE. In such a lonely place
  no man would stay
  who had not made his peace
    with the eyes in the berries
      and the voice in the beck.

SECOND VOICE. Yes: most of us ignore them
    run away from them
      and think we have escaped
        their obstinate questionings.
Oh, I too ran away from them
  and have managed fairly well to forget them!
And that is how we begin to deceive ourselves
that, at any rate, is how I
  began to deceive myself
    began to 'avoid the issue' as we say . . .
Avoid the issue!
To be honest I ought to say
    that that is how I began to practise hypocrisy . . .
Hypocrisy
  is perhaps rather a strong word for it
Let me call it dissimulation
I had a habit
  no, not a habit — an innate disposition
to identify myself with the other person.
Sometimes it worked
  and sometimes it didn't.
I could not identify myself with very poor people
  nor with very rich people
    their upbringings had been so different.

But if a Christian began to talk to me
    assuming that I was a Christian
        I did not disabuse him
or if an aggressive patriot began to talk to me
    assuming that I would be willing to destroy a whole city
        with a single bomb
again I did not disabuse him.
It was not cowardice — on some other occasion
I would freely express
    an unorthodox opinion.
It may sometimes have been indolence — what I call
    my lazy larynx
        (for I have always felt
           the effort of talking).
Such is my physical disposition . . .
Voices
    how they expose us
      how they form our thoughts
A man's mind
    is an echo of his voice — or rather
      of his voices.
THIRD VOICE. Voices?
SECOND VOICE. Yes: we have two voices
      the instictive voice that flows like water from a spring
        or blood from a wound
      and the intellectual voice that blares like a fanfare
        from some centre in the brain.
THIRD VOICE. I have only one voice
    but it is new every day.
SECOND VOICE. Like the sun. But the ancient man who said
    that the sun was new every day
had spent his life seeking himself.
But the same ancient man said
    that though you travel in every direction
      you will never find the boundaries of the self
        so deep is the logos of it.
And that is the truth I have discovered. In the end
    I came back here
      to the scene of my birth and infancy.
I thought I might find the truth about myself here
but I don't see the end of my search yet!

So deep is the logos!

THIRD VOICE. The logos? Now that
    is not a word we use here.

SECOND VOICE. If I could tell you what such a word means
    I should be at the end of my task!

It is the most mysterious word.
    in the history of human thought.

'In the beginning was the Word
    and the Word was with God
        and the Word was God' . . .

I began to puzzle over that sentence
    when I was still a child

and I think most Christians have wondered
    why such a strange ambiguous word
        Word itself

should stand at the beginning of their Gospel.

Perhaps it is because the word

is the only link that exists between the known and the unknown
    between man and the cosmos.

If man had not been able to utter the word God
    he would never have conceived the idea of God

And so God was first manifested to man in speech
    and in the poetry inherent in speech
        in the logos.

That is perhaps fairly obvious

but the more I have pondered on this fact
    the more I have realized the predicament into which we
        as men

    are thrown by this dependence on logos.

For two things could happen
    and did happen.

In the beginning there was the cosmos
    (or nature as we more politely call it)

and in the midst of the cosmos
    and part of it
        was man

        growing aware of his environment.

He slowly perfected words to express his predicament.

But then the word became God
    the instrument that had enabled man to express the idea of
            an outer cosmos

was identified with the idea to be expressed.
Men then worshipped
   not the cosmos of which they were a part
     but the idea of the cosmos which they could
           separate from themselves as a word
and make absolute as an idea.
But that was not the end.
Eventually
   and not so long ago
man conceived the notion that his kind
in inventing the word
   the logos
had invented God.
The idea of God
   had not arisen from man's experience of the world
     but had been an original intuition of the mind
       an idea divinely inspired
         a glimpse of some transcendental realm of being
where time does not exist.
THIRD VOICE. I cannot conceive of such a realm.
SECOND VOICE. Nor I.
I have always felt perfectly satisfied
   with a natural outlook on life.
By this I do not mean
   the outlook of what is called natural science.
Materialists of that kind
   stand this side of the logos.
They assume
   that their words and signs are fixed and measurable
                         entities
   that with their words and signs
     they can explain the cosmos.
That is childish
   or perverse.
But it is merely a higher childishness
   to go to the opposite extreme
     that is to say
       beyond the natural function of the logos
to assume the autonomous reality
   of a realm with which we cannot communicate
     except by means of the logos.

In the begining was the word
 and in the end are many words
  nets to catch the butterfly truth.
THIRD VOICE. Truth! so that is what you are looking for!
 You thought you would find the truth up here?
SECOND VOICE. I'm sorry — truth
 is a word I did not mean to bring into our conversation
  it is an evil word I have sworn not to use.
 Truth
  is that for which men kill each other.
 I limit my search to myself
 I know that my self is different from all other selves
  and that what I discover
   is not going to be the envy of anyone else.
THIRD VOICE. But if you discover the truth
 you will be the envy of the world.
 You must therefore avoid the truth
  even the truth about yourself.
SECOND VOICE. Well, if I do discover the truth about myself
 I must keep it to myself.
 It will be my secret.
THIRD VOICE. What is the good of a secret
 known only to yourself?
SECOND VOICE. Perhaps I should say
 the secret of my strength,
  strength is the knowledge of one's limits
  and that knowledge
   helps a man to endure his fate.
 The man that knows himself
  can almost foresee his fate.
THIRD VOICE. Is that any consolation?
SECOND VOICE. Consolation? — not exactly.
 But it gives to life
  the excitement of a game of chance.
 There a man goes
  spinning out the thread of his destiny
   millions more are doing the same thing.
 The threads cross
  and turn
   and cross again
 and the pattern that emerges we call history.

A crazy pattern
  but the only one that exists. . . .

THIRD VOICE. And when the thread is cut?

SECOND VOICE. Why, then the pattern changes
  but so infinitely little
    it makes no difference.

THIRD VOICE. But the thread is your individual life:
  it makes a difference to you.

SECOND VOICE. No so long as I remain
  aware of the beauty of the pattern.

THIRD VOICE. You are sitting on the edge of the moor.
  Beyond the moor is the sea
    the unknown
  We are standing on the edge of the world
    and what do we see
      as we look over the edge?

SECOND VOICE. Our human eyes see very little
  the stars and the planets
  worlds beyond worlds
    universe without end.

THIRD VOICE. You don't know
  that it is without end.

SECOND VOICE. I know nothing
  beyond what my eyes
    or my eyes aided by clever instruments
  tell me.
  I can guess a little.

THIRD VOICE. Yes, but at the end of your guessing
  what do you see?

SECOND VOICE. Nothing
  I cannot see anything beyond the evidence of my senses.
  There may be something
    an unending Thing
    Nothing or Something
  I do not know.

THIRD VOICE. And you do not fear
  anything?

SECOND VOICE. Fear? Why should I be afraid?

THIRD VOICE. You are not afraid of the unknown?

SECOND VOICE. I do not think the unknown is a subject
  to inspire one with feelings of any kind.

Before such an unconceivable concept
    my mind is merely blank.

THIRD VOICE. Blank?
Have you then no curiosity?

SECOND VOICE. Of course — unending, restless, curiosity.
    But my curiosity
        nibbles away at the edge of the known
        it does not take a leap into nothingness.
It looks back at the wide and solid expanse of the known
    looks back
        and is lost in wonder.

THIRD VOICE. Wonder?

SECOND VOICE. That is another of my pet words. Wonder
        is the antidote to fear
        the essence of courage.
We say we are lost in wonder
    as though it were a forest
        or a sea.
But wonder invades us like the warmth of the sun.
Our very consciousness expands when we discover
    some corner of the pattern of the universe
        realize its endless implications
        and know ourselves
            to be part of that intricate design.

THIRD VOICE. But surely that discovery
    is the beginning of humility?

SECOND VOICE. No: humility is for human relationships
    an attitude of man to man.
But when I discover the same geometrical proportions
    in the human body and in a flower
        or a crystal
    in a cathedral
        and in a planetary system
then I am not humble.
Nor am I proud, for it is no effort of man
    that has created such correspondencies.
I am excited by such a thought
perhaps my heart beats more quickly
    or my eyes dilate
        for I am filled with wonder.

THIRD VOICE. But the day will come

      when your heart will stop beating
    and your eyes will no longer
      be aware of any of these wonders.
SECOND VOICE. Yet death
      is the greatest wonder of all.
That life can be extinguished
      is a fact as wonderful as the fact
        that it can be conceived.
The chance that you or I
      or any particular person
is born
      is an infinite one
and with the thought of the infinitude of that chance
      we should be ready to accept
        the finiteness of death. It is
          simply
our fate.

                              (A Silence

FIRST VOICE. You did not hear me return
      but I have been standing behind you
        listening.
    Your bed is ready.
SECOND VOICE. Thank you: I will come along presently. You were kind
    to listen patiently to all this nonsense.
FIRST VOICE. I did not mean to interrupt
    but I thought you had finished.
THIRD VOICE. It was the word Fate
    that made us pensive.
SECOND VOICE. It is a word that seems to end all argument.
    There is no appeal against fate
    and no sense in discussing it.
THIRD VOICE. Not if you imagine it as an enemy. But it isn't!
    It has been said
    man's character is his fate.
FIRST VOICE. Man is more than his fate.
    Man is moulded in a womb
    and dissolved in earth
    His foundations are two tombs
    He is like earth uprisen.
SECOND VOICE. I think I agree. A character can be uprooted.

We are proud
  of our upright posture
  of our legs that can carry us out of this dale
    into the wide world.
Men are proud of the machines that carry them over the seas.
  through the air.
But they carry their character with them
  and their character is their destiny.
But
  our characters are sometimes seduced.
If I am sitting in an aeroplane above the Atlantic
I have surrendered my fate to the pilot of the plane.
It might be said
  only a man of my character would fly across the Atlantic
but the same anonymous chances
  follow me on land and by sea.
It is not in man's character to desert his home —
That is what one calls
  tempting Fate
and tempting Fate does not mean
  that we act as if we accept our fate
it means acting in defiance of our fate.
I do not mean
  that restlessness cannot be our fate.
Man was once a nomadic animal
  and traces of the nomad
    linger in his groins.
But we have perfected ourselves in stillness.
FIRST VOICE. In suffering and in joy.
SECOND VOICE. Yes: I meant to imply suffering and joy.
  Fate is not ameliorative.
  But who can separate
    beauty and terror
      suffering and joy?
  I remember a valley in Greece.
  I came to it
    when the light was failing.
  The rocky hills were purple
    the sky a thin icy green
      fading eastward to a slatey grey.
  There was a huge mound, partly excavated

to reveal colossal stones
    the foundations of a fortress.
In the hillside was a tomb
    the tomb of a legendary king
        faultlessly shaped and tense
        like the inside of an eggshell.
I viewed it by the light
    of a fire of withered thyme ...
When I emerged
    it was dark in the valley and I felt around me
        the nameless terror that had penetrated
            the lives of that ancient king
            his adulterous queen
                and all their melancholy issue.
Their fates had overtaken them
    in that place
        more than three thousand years ago
and man had not dared to build again
    not on such a site of horror.
But I knew then
    that man's fate is not like a seed
    carried hither and thither by the wind
not like spawn on a restless tide
But is the creation of generations of men
    men who have lived in one place
        and absorbed its mysteries.
FIRST VOICE. Mysteries?
SECOND VOICE. Perhaps there are no mysteries of time or place
    but there are mysteries of life.
    A mystery
        is what is hidden, and it is Life
        not God
            that loves to hide.
    It is Life
        not God
            that is mysterious.
    The Greeks were right again: it is Life
        that plays the game of hide-and-seek
    The rhythm of the seasons
        is the interplay of Life and Death. In the person of
                                                    Persephone

74

it is Life itself
    that disappears for a wintry season.
But hiding involves a hiding-place. In Eleusis
    you can still see the pit
    down which Persephone sank
        to Pluto's dark realm.
All the ancient myths
    are precisely located. And today we have no myths
because we have no sense of place.
Our beliefs
    are like untethered balloons
    they drift into the clouds
        into the transcendental inane.
I would sooner men worshipped a tree or a rock.
THIRD VOICE. And yourself
    what have you worshipped?
SECOND VOICE. Ah! you have some right
    to ask me that question
        for it embarrasses me.
The truth is
    I have never been able to worship anything
        not even myself.
Worship is an act of adoration
    the complete surrender of the self to some Other
        to some Otherness.
It must be a great relief
    to get rid of that burden sometimes
        to feel utterly empty
        like a room that has been swept and made bright
            ready for a new occupant
to return to a body that has been renewed in ecstasy!
It is an illusion, of course
    but one of the desirable illusions.
FIRST VOICE. Have you then lived without illusions?
SECOND VOICE. Never for a moment.
I have lived with the illusion
    that I was in love
with the illusion
    that my loved ones loved me
with the illusion
    that I could give happiness to other people

as you would give a rose to a young girl
with the illusion
    that other people would see the world with my eyes
      and love the things that I love
with the illusion
    that my words would open men's hearts
      and give them understanding.
For fifty years I have lived
    in successive states of illusion
      and I am still not completely
disillusioned.

THIRD VOICE. What illusions remain to you?

SECOND VOICE. The illusion that it is not yet too late
    for any of these illusions to be re-established.
The illusion
    that a voice in the wilderness echoes in some green valley
the illusion that the wind
    or a bird
will take up the seed I have scattered on stony ground
    and drop it in a fertile field
the illusion
    that bitterness is dissolved in the serenity of old age
the illusion
    that I shall die a happy man.

THIRD VOICE. And at the time of your death
    what could make you happy?

SECOND VOICE. To die without fear and trembling.

THIRD VOICE. You are describing a state of happiness.
    You do not tell us
    what would ensure such a state.

SECOND VOICE. I am not sure that I know.
I suppose at the end I shall come to another Place
    it might be this dale-head
    it might be my white bedroom
    it might be a busy street.
I might die in pain
    in weariness
      or in despair.
But if at the last moment
I could see some perfect form
    it might be this fern at my feet

or a sparrow flickering past my window
or a painting on the wall
or some poet's vision of eternity
   like a great Ring of pure and endless Light
   all calm, as it was bright . . .
Granted that I could at the last moment
see some bright image
  I should die without fear and trembling.
It is when we look into the abyss of nothingness
  infinite nothingness
that we lose courage
  and die swearing
    or die praying.

FIRST VOICE. Yes: men should hold on to tangible things.
  Stay with me in these hills and glens
  where the birds cry lovingly to their young
    and the waters are never silent.
THIRD VOICE. Die to the day and its trivialities
  Die to the sense of time.
FIRST VOICE. Or to the sense of place
  to the place of generation and birth.
THIRD VOICE. Live with the sun by day
  and with the stars by night.
FIRST VOICE. Live with your eyes and ears
  and the exercise of your subtle fingers.
THIRD VOICE. Live in the moment of attention.
FIRST VOICE. Live in the presence of things.

                            (A silence

SECOND VOICE. It is getting dark.
  I can hardly see you.
FIRST VOICE. Yes: it is dark now.
  I shall lead you to your bed.
SECOND VOICE. You said it was down by the beck, didn't you?
FIRST VOICE. It is not far.
THIRD VOICE. And the way up and the way down are the same.
  I go up the hill.
FIRST VOICE. My Father will be with us again tomorrow.
SECOND VOICE. As boys we used to come here
    to gather wild daffodils.
  At Moon's Farm the pump was in the kitchen
    a well of clean crystal water.

And there was an old clock
   standing opposite the kitchen door.
It had a robin
   or perhaps it was a wren
painted on its white face
   but the fingers never moved
It was always 12.25 at Moon's Farm.
12.25 is God's time.

III. Literary Criticism

The Personality of the Poet[1]

Many writers, especially novelists, have written in accordance with some theory of the nature of personality, and an enquiry into such working theories would be of great interest. But that is an aspect of the subject which I should like to exclude from the present enquiry, which is to be concerned not so much with personality, as objectively conceived by the writer, as with the writer's own personality — the subjective nature of personality, the part it plays in the process of writing: what, briefly, we might call the creative function of the personality. This is, perhaps, a vague subject, but its very vagueness is the excuse I offer for dealing with it. If we can introduce a few definitions into this twilight, a good service to criticism will have been rendered. As it is at present, this word 'personality' is tossed about, a more or less meaningless counter, from critic to critic. There is scarcely a literary judgement made anywhere in recent times that does not resolve itself into a statement such as: 'The work of so and so is good because it is the perfect expression of his personality.' This is not an exaggeration. I take the first book that comes to my hand. It is Volume I of the Cambridge Shakespeare, with a general Introduction by Sir Arthur Quiller-Couch. There I find this passage — three birds for a single stone:

'... who can doubt that every true man, small or great, leaves some print of himself on his work, or indeed that he *must* if his work be literature, which is so personal a thing. As Sir Walter Raleigh puts it: "No man can walk abroad save on his own shadow." Yes, but as another writer, Mr. Morton Luce, well comments: "An author may be — perhaps ought to be — something inferior to his work." '

That reminds me of another passage, from *The Sacred Wood* of Mr. T. S. Eliot:

---

[1] *Form in Modern Poetry* (London, 1932), pp. 6–34.

'Poetry is not a turning loose of emotion, but an escape from emotion; it is not the expression of personality, but an escape from personality.'

'But, of course,' adds Mr. Eliot, 'only those who have personality and emotions know what it means to want to escape from these things'; and earlier in the same essay he has explained his meaning in these words:

'The point of view which I am struggling to attack is perhaps related to the metaphysical theory of the substantial unity of the soul: for my meaning is, that the poet has, not a "personality" to express, but a particular medium, which is only a medium and not a personality, in which impressions and experiences combine in peculiar and unexpected ways. Impressions and experiences which are important for the man may take no place in the poetry, and those which become important in the poetry may play quite a negligible part in the man, the personality.'

I do not quote these passages as texts, to attack or commend, but merely as illustrations of the use of the word 'personality' in modern criticism, and of the evident concern which critics have for its significance or otherwise. It will, however, be realized that the point of view of Mr. Eliot is a very exceptional one, and in fact a protest against a universal reliance on a vague concept. Mr. Eliot might hold that the notion of personality is *inevitably* vague; at least he does not attempt to define it. I think, however, that the attempt will be worth while.

We cannot hope to arrive at a definition of personality without encroaching to some extent on the science of psychology. Some of my readers will be uneasy at the prospect. Nevertheless, this is where I take my stand, even against my best friends in criticism, such as Mr. Eliot himself. I believe that criticism must concern itself, not only with the work of art in itself, but also with the process of writing, and with the writer's state of mind when inspired — that is to say, criticism must concern itself, not only with the finished work of art, but also with the workman, his mental activity and his tools. If that is not admitted, no really useful progress can be made in this essay. But assuming we are agreed on the sphere of criticism, then I cannot conceive how the critic can avoid a dependence on general psychology. It may be said that psychology is a very doubtful science, and that none of its conclusions is established; but that is to set up as a better psychologist than the psychologists themselves. If we depart a single pace from the

The Personality of the Poet

consideration of the work of art in isolation from all personal questions we involve ourselves in psychological considerations. It might be possible, for example, to plunge into the quarrel of Romantics and Classics with nothing in our armoury but an objective measuring-rod. An infallible distinction might be found in the use of the letter 'p', in feminine rhymes and false quantities; it would be infallible, but it would be dull. We should separate the sheep and goats, but the really interesting question — why some people are goats, and others sheep — that question would be left unsolved.

That is why, as a critic, I am tempted to seek an alliance with psychology, but I should like to distinguish between a general *entente* and a treaty of obligations. As a literary critic — that is to say, as a scientist in my own field — I insist on maintaining my territorial rights when I enter into treaty with another science. I accept just as much as seems relevant to my purpose, and I reject anything that conflicts with the evidence of my own special sensibility. But actually, if the literary critic will approach psychology without prejudice, he will find certain important conclusions which are generally accepted by psychologists themselves, and which he can apply with great profit to his understanding of literature.

I will take as an example, because it is relevant to the enquiry I am making, the theory of the mind as developed by the psychoanalysts, particularly by Freud. I am aware that there are certain fundamental aspects of psycho-analysis which are hotly disputed by psychologists in general — particularly that part of the theory which supposes the existence of an unconscious mind, or unconscious region of the mind. Now it happens that this particular hypothesis is the one which the literary critic is likely to be most tempted to adopt. Let him use every caution, for as one psychologist has warned us: 'All usages of the term "unconscious" that imply that it is an entity, such as saying that ideas are *in the unconscious*: or that the unconscious is dynamic, show a thoughtless or uncritical attitude — or ignorance.'[1] Freud himself, as we shall see, is not guiltless in this respect. I think, however, before we begin to criticize Freud, or even to use any of his terms, we should make sure that we know the meaning of them. It so happens that in a recent essay[2] Freud himself has given a concise résumé of his theory. He writes:

[1] Henry Herbert Goddard, 'The Unconscious in Psycho-analysis', *Problems of Personality* (1925), p. 300.
[2] *The Ego and the Id* (Eng. tr. 1927).

'The division of mental life into what is conscious and what is unconscious is the fundamental premise on which psycho-analysis is based; and this division alone makes it possible for it to understand pathological mental processes, which are as common as they are important, and to co-ordinate them scientifically. Stated once more in a different way: psycho-analysis cannot accept the view that consciousness is the essence of mental life, but is obliged to regard consciousness as one property of mental life, which may co-exist along with its other properties or may be absent.'

Then Freud shows how we are compelled to adopt the concept of the 'unconscious':

'We have found — that is, we have been obliged to assume — that very powerful mental processes or ideas exist which can produce in the mind all the effects that ordinary ideas do . . . without themselves becoming conscious . . . this is the point at which psycho-analytic theory steps in with the assertion that such ideas cannot become conscious because a certain force is opposed to them, that otherwise they could become conscious, and that then one would see how little they differ from other elements, which are admittedly mental. The fact that in the technique of psycho-analysis a means has been found by which the opposing force can be removed and the ideas in question made conscious renders this theory irrefutable. The state in which the ideas existed before being made conscious is called by us *repression*, and we assert that the force which instituted the repression and maintains it is perceived as *resistance* during the work of analysis. . . . We see, however, that we have two kinds of unconscious — that which is latent but capable of becoming conscious, and that which is repressed and not capable of becoming conscious in the ordinary way. . . . That which is latent, and only unconscious in the descriptive and not in the dynamic sense, we call *preconscious*; the term unconscious we reserve for the dynamically unconscious-repressed. . . .'

That is a long quotation, but it is essential to use these terms — 'conscious', 'preconscious', and 'unconscious' — and to use them in an accepted sense. The words as used by Freud have been subjected to criticism and he has not been afraid to revise his terms and make them more precise.

Freud says, in the work from which I have been quoting, that 'in every individual there is a coherent organization of mental processes, which we call his *ego*'; and this may serve as the *pre-*

liminary definition of 'personality' of which I am in search. This ego is identical with the conscious flow of our thoughts, the impressions we receive, the sensations we experience. Also, from this ego, this *coherent organization* of mental processes, according to Freud, proceed the repressions 'by means of which an attempt is made to cut off certain trends in the mind not merely from consciousness, but also from their other forms of manifestation and activity'. Freud, following another Austrian writer, Georg Groddeck, further claims that the conduct of the ego throughout life is essentially passive — we are 'lived', as it were, by unknown and uncontrollable forces. But presumably these forces are inherent, differentiated in each individual — being, in fact, that reserve of instincts and passions which normally we repress, but which are never securely under the control of our conscious reason. To this reserve Freud gives the name 'Id', for it is the impersonal aspect of the 'Ego'.

Near to the word 'personality' we have another word, often used interchangeably with it, sometimes contrasted with it — I mean the word 'character'. This concept, too, we can bring into relation with the general scheme of Freudian psychology. Character can be explained as a disposition in the individual due to the repression of certain impulses which would otherwise be present in the personality; it is therefore something more restricted than personality. Character, which always has such a positive aspect, is really the result of certain fixities or negations imposed on the flow of consciousness. A flood only gains character and direction when it is confined between banks.

Before trying to show how the mind of the poet is related to these several concepts, let me draw confirmation of the rightness of Freud's general analysis of the mind from an unexpected quarter, a work first published nearly fifty years ago and neglected until recently revived by Dame Ethel Smyth. *The Prison*, by H. B. Brewster, is a philosophic dialogue of great force and originality, and there I found this definition of the personality:

'We live in a web of associated memories; our general map — the chart thanks to which we know more or less clearly where to put what, recognize analogies, form classes, make order out of chaos and accumulate experience — is a network of memories. And one of ourselves, the loudest voiced one, the one we usually think of when we say *I*, corresponds to the spot on that map where the most frequent and familiar memories cross each other, as the railroads of a country at its capital.'

It will be perceived how nearly this definition approaches Freud's conception of the ego as 'a coherent organization of mental processes'. Much more in Brewster's dialogue might be related to Freud's psychology; for example, that state of mind which Brewster opposes to the personality is nothing but Freud's unconscious 'id'.

It would be easy to give many further illustrations from literature which would give support to our preliminary definition of personality, but as they are so often bound up with, and even confused with, the notion of 'character', we must first make a clear distinction between the two. The word 'character' derives from the Greek word meaning an engraved sign, a distinguishing mark; and in common usage it always implies a man moulded to a pattern, firm, consistent, dependable. Again, the use of the word for that literary form known as 'the character' and practised by Theophrastus, Vauvenargues, and others, gives the same meaning: a consistent type. Descriptive psychologists adopt this same conception; the definition of Münsterberg may be quoted as typical. Character, he says, 'is the power to keep the selected motive dominant throughout life.' The difficulty about such a definition is that some 'power' — force, will or energy — is implied, for which there is no adequate theory of causation. The psycho-analysts have supplied this, and again I think their hypothesis is the most suggestive one for our purposes. They regard inhibition as the basis of character, and a definition which we may accept as representative is that of Dr. Roback, which reads: '[Character is the result of] an enduring psycho-physical disposition to inhibit instinctive impulses in accordance with a regulative principle.'[1] Now there are various words in that very condensed definition which need explanation. Inhibition I have already referred to, but if we do not care to accept it in its psycho-analytical sense, I think it will do for our definition if we merely regard the 'disposition to inhibit' as the 'will to hold in check', in the ordinary moralistic sense. Again, the phrase 'instinctive impulses' need not be given any but its normal meaning — there are many instincts besides the sex instinct, and if any one instinct is more in question than another, I think it is probably the gregarious instinct. There is a passage in that penetrating analysis of the character, Meredith's

---

[1] 'Character and Inhibition', *Problems of Personality*, p. 118.

The Egoist, which describes this aspect of the problem very well:

'Within the shadow of his presence,' Meredith writes of Sir Willoughby Patterne, 'he compressed opinion as a strong frost binds the springs of earth, but beyond it his shivering sensitiveness ran about in dread of a stripping in a wintry atmosphere. This was the ground of his hatred of the world; it was an appalling fear on behalf of his naked eidolon, the tender infant Self swaddled in his name before the world, for which he felt as the most highly civilized of men alone can feel, and which it was impossible for him to stretch out hands to protect. There the poor little lovable creature ran for any mouth to blow on; and frost-nipped and bruised, it cried to him, and he was of no avail! Must we not detest a world that so treats us? We loathe it the more, by our measure of our contempt for them, when we have made the people within the shadow-circle of our person slavish.'

This does not mean that the man who avoids the herd will thereby form his character; you do not inhibit an instinct by avoiding its activity. But the man who maintains a certain integrity in the midst of the herd, that man is by way of forming his character. Dr. Roback quotes very appositely Goethe's couplet:

> *Es bildet ein Talent sich in der Stille:*
> *Sich ein Charakter in dem Strom der Welt.*

'A talent is formed in solitude; a character in the stream of the world'[1] — a sentiment which I would ask the reader to remember because I am presently going to suggest that this difference between the conditions necessary for the formation of a character and for the formation of what Goethe calls a talent and what I am here calling a personality, corresponds precisely with the difference between rhetorical and lyrical literature, which is the difference often loosely implied in the terms 'classical' and 'romantic' literature.

But first I must draw attention to the final clause in Dr. Roback's definition of character: it is 'an enduring disposition to inhibit instinctive impulses *in accordance with a regulative principle*'. That, of course, implies that there is an element of self-determination in character. It is obvious that characters vary

---

[1] Stendhal has said the same thing: '*On peut tout acquérir dans la solitude, hormis de caractère.*' (*De l'Amour*, Fragments Divers, 1.)

enormously in value, and I think a little consideration will show that the differences in value are due to differences in intelligence. A man without any intelligence, a lunatic, is a man most decidedly without any character. A man with a perverse intelligence, like Don Quixote, is a deformed character, a caricature of the real thing. Another negative aspect to remember is, that character once formed is not affected by experience. It is possible for groups of men to endure, over lengthy periods, the same experiences (I am thinking particularly of the experiences of war) and to emerge at the end of it with their characters not in the least changed. Character is in fact armour against experience; it is not in itself deflected by experience. From whatever direction we approach it, we get the notion of fixity; and once a man's character is determined, it is hardly possible to speak of his moral or spiritual development. A character is 'set', 'hardboiled' as the slang phrase vividly expresses it. Not even the emotions will dissolve it, or move it. The emotions indeed are irrelevant to character; they are waves which break themselves in vain against its base. History is full of examples of men of character who have exercised their justness and firmness in spite of the emotional claims of friendship and love.

Character, in short, is an impersonal ideal which the individual selects and to which he sacrifices all other claims, especially those of the sentiments or emotions. It follows that character must be placed in opposition to personality, which is the general-common-denominator of our sentiments and emotions. That is, indeed, the opposition I wish to emphasize; and when I have said further that all poetry, in which I include all lyrical impulses whatsoever, is the product of the personality, and therefore inhibited in a character, I have stated the main theme of my essay.

One problem absorbs me above all others: it is what I will call *the intermittency of genius*. Why, more often than not, does a poet blossom out in his adolescence and early manhood, and then wither to pedantry and dullness? Why does inspiration work fitfully and often at intervals of many years? Why, to put these questions in concrete terms, did Milton cease writing poetry for twenty-five years? Why did a poet like Gray write only one poem of supreme excellence? Why, for a brief decade did the great poetic genius of Wordsworth pour out its richness, and then lapse into comparative poverty? One could ask a hundred questions of this kind, but the reader is not to imagine that I am going

88

to provide a universal key to answer them all. I think, however, that this problem of the relations of personality to character does provide the right setting for such questions, and if psychology can solve *its* problem, then with the aid of psychology we shall be on the way to solving our own literary problem.

It would be too simple a solution to say that, character and personality being so opposed, inspiration will flow so long as the personality does not harden into character. In psychology you have always to reckon with the phenomenon of compensation. If you suppress one instinct, you revive another; we are infinitely complex machines, so that a check on one action is apt to release the spring of another action. The man of character may have repressed the conscious functioning of certain instincts; he cannot, however, prevent them from forcing their way underground into the preconscious and unconscious states described by Freud. The physical potentiality of the instincts remains in the body, though their surface workings may be suppressed. What is suppressed in consciousness may be found active in the imagination, which might be identified with the preconscious of Freud's phraseology. Dr. Jung confirms this supposition, remarking that 'the unconscious feeling of the intellectual is peculiarly fantastic, often in grotesque contrast to an exaggerated, rationalistic intellectualism of the conscious. In contrast to the purposefulness and controlled character of conscious thinking, the feeling is impulsive, uncontrolled, moody, irrational, primitive, archaic indeed, like the feeling of a savage.'[1] Along these lines, I think, we might explain the art of certain intellectual types of the present day — I mean, in literature, the writings of the 'Surréalistes' in France, of Franz Kafka in Germany, and even the later writings of Mr. James Joyce; and in painting, the art of men like Paul Klee and Max Ernst. Let me interpose here this axiom of criticism: by explaining the nature of a work of art, we do not explain it away. Art always rises superior to its origins. It is an entity of direct appeal; we do not, in the process of appreciation (no process but an immediate insight) unfold the process of creation.

To return to my main argument: this phantasy proceeding from the unconscious as a balance or compensation for instincts repressed in the interests of character, may be identified with *fancy*; and this I think fits in well, not only with the modern types of art and literature already mentioned, but generally with the

[1] 'Psychological Types', *Problems of Personality*, p. 300.

distinction between fancy and imagination in the literature of the past. For the sake of a tidy correspondence, it ought to be possible to relate *imagination* to the preconscious, and this I think can be done without much difficulty. But I must avoid, if only for lack of space, the endless controversy which revolves round these two words; I have, besides, on another occasion discussed the relationship which exists between the intellect and fancy.[1]

But now we must enlarge our description of *personality*. As a preliminary I have suggested that the term might be identified with Freud's 'Ego' — a coherent organization of mental processes. But the coherence of this organization is not to be confused with the fixed organization of a character — any more than the coherence of a work of art is to be confused with the concision of a machine. The nature of this coherence is very well defined in an essay on personality by Mr. Ramon Fernandez.[2] He has been discussing Nietzsche's conception of personality which he finds wanting in just this element of coherence.

'To be coherent', he explains, 'does not mean that one *feels oneself* the same, nor *that one acts* in the same way in all circumstances, but rather that one is ready to meet every circumstance when once a certain inward perspective has been established; it does not mean that one never changes, but that the changes of the world always find you ready to select your own point of view . . . the more complicated the personality grows, the more unstable it becomes, and the more it submits to the influence of the mind. . . . The ideal personality would be that of a man who showed himself ever capable of adapting his being to the movements of his thought, and whose thought would be ever in accord with the universal; who, in such conditions, considering himself with stern impartiality, would accept gladly that idea which for the moment may take the lead; because thought which ceaselessly renews itself will make him — in Emerson's phrase, "live always in a new dawn", but at the same time it will prevent him from falling into incoherence, being guaranteed by its own laws.'

Such a conception of personality is admittedly based on the most exact, the most complete and fearless revelation of a personality that we possess: Montaigne's Essays. I perhaps need quote[3] only one of a hundred passages in which this notion is put forth. It is a sufficiently famous one:

[1] *English Prose Style*, chap. ix.   [2] *De la personnalité* (1928), pp. 86-7.
[3] From the translation by E. J. Trechmann (Oxford, 1927), p. 266.

The Personality of the Poet

'What I do I do thoroughly, as a matter of habit, and make one step of it; and I seldom take any step that steals away and hides from my reason, and that is not very nearly guided by all my faculties in agreement, without division or inner revolt. My judgement takes all the blame or all the praise for it; and the blame it once takes it takes always, for almost from birth it has been one: the same inclination, the same direction, the same strength. And in the matter of general opinions, I have since my childhood occupied the position I had to hold.'

It will be seen that in both authors we have the idea of a free disposition which is that of the sensations and memory — the sensual being — and that this being is given coherence, is defined or outlined, by a judgement which is innate. The ego is a synthesis of the sensations, is generated by conscious experience, by that inward perspective which Montaigne exercised so freely for our delectation. The judgement is not imposed on the sensations from without, as if by an external agency — that is the process of repression which results in character; judgement emerges from the history of our sensations, is elected by them, and the coherence of personality is indeed the coherence of a natural process; not the coherence of an arbitrary discipline.

Mr. Fernandez's book, from which I have just quoted, has much more to offer us that is suggestive; its only fault, in my opinion, is that it tends to confuse the coherence of the personality with the fixity of the character; at least, it does not clearly mark off the functions of character. But speaking of the restricted, the too limited notion of personality in Corneille, he gives us a perfect description of character — he describes it as 'the tragic conformity of a man to his definition' — Freud would say 'to his "ego-ideal" '. The personality knows no such definitions, no such ideal; it is an active process of thought, a balance of relations maintained between our various feelings and sentiments. From this process, this play of thought, comes a certain act of belief, the *illative* act described by Newman. The nature of belief in general is not a subject to embark on now.[1] I would merely suggest that the reality of the personality — its operative efficiency — is dependent on a belief in the existence of the self, a belief that may have little support in objective evidence, but is made possible by that insight into the future, that belief in the con-

[1] It was the subject of a very adequate enquiry by the Reverend M. C. D'Arcy, S.J. (*The Nature of Belief*, London, 1931.)

91

tinuity of experience, which is the will to live. This is obviously a state of mind very different from that involved in character: the whole difference between blind compulsion to an external and arbitrary ideal, and an organic coherence intuitively based on the actual world of sensation.

I should like for my last illustration to pass from Mr. Fernandez to a friend of his whose work he has criticized so intelligently: I mean Marcel Proust. Proust's great work rivals Montaigne's in the deliberate light it throws on this problem of personality.

'Frequent discussions with Marcel Proust,' writes Mr. Fernandez (p. 23), 'who would adopt instantaneously no matter what point of view, have revealed to me that man dehumanizes himself by excess of affectivity at least as much as by excess of rationality. . . . To wish to introduce unity into the life of sensation and affectivity, by separating out one's sentiments and giving them a structure without ever leaving the level of concrete life, was not that precisely to put oneself in quest of a personality?'

Proust was very much occupied by this problem of personality and gave most attention to the very aspect of the problem that I now wish to consider here — I mean the extent to which the personality depends on the memory, and particularly on the memory of sensations. There is a famous excursus, coming almost exactly in the middle of Proust's long epic, which is a key to the author's whole philosophy of art and life. He has just related how, in a moment of complete physical collapse, there comes to him, by an instinctive act of recollection, the living image of his grandmother; and it is only at this moment, more than a year after her burial, that he becomes conscious that she is dead. This causes Proust to reflect that 'at whatever moment we estimate it, the total value of our spiritual nature is more or less fictitious, notwithstanding the long inventory of its treasures, for now one, now another of these is unrealizable, whether we are considering actual treasures or those of the imagination' — or those actually of the memory. Then Proust goes on to make this very significant, and for his work, quite essential analysis of the personality:

'For with the cloudiness of memory are closely linked the heart's intermissions. It is, no doubt, the existence of our body, which we may compare to a jar containing our spiritual nature, that leads us to suppose that all our inward wealth, our past joys, all our sorrows, are perpetually in our possession. Perhaps it is equally inexact to suppose that they escape or return. In any case, if they

92

remain within us, it is, for most of the time, in an unknown region where they are of no service to us, and where even the most ordinary are crowded out by memories of a different kind which preclude any simultaneous occurrence of them in our consciousness. But if the setting of sensations in which they are preserved be recaptured, they acquire in turn the same power of expelling everything that is incompatible with them, of installing alone in us the self that originally lived them.'[1]

Mr. Fernandez is very critical of this passage and therefore of Proust's method in general. He does not deny its acuteness, nor its significance — for Proust. But far from being the key to Proust's genius, he regards it as a confession of Proust's weakness. Mr. Fernandez's criticism at this point would be much clearer if it were combined with a distinction between personality and character; as it is, the inadequacy of Proust's analysis is impugned against such notions as the integrity of our sentiments, our ideals, our spiritual progress.

'If Proust is to be believed,' Mr. Fernandez writes, 'not only can man not guarantee his sentiments, and consequently his acts, and consequently man must be an eternal failure, but also he must renounce the consolation of feeling that he progresses despite this discontinuity and this intermittent blindness. . . . It is the problem of spirituality, of the value of the ideal, of the future and of human progress, that is set by the Proustian analysis of the intermissions of the heart. . . . If the intermissions of the heart and their corollaries represent the depths of human nature, the supreme experience of our ego, then the spiritual life must be ranged in its entirety in the category of the imagination, and the intelligence is the highest point of human development to which we may pretend . . . the victory of the intelligence would mark the defeat of the spirit.'

But is so much implied in Proust's analysis? It is, I think true that, as Proust says elsewhere, the respect for moral obligations, faithfulness to friends, the achievement of a task, the observance of a discipline, have a surer foundation in blind habits than in the momentary and ardent flights of our sensibility. But is this not equivalent to saying that character as we have defined it is formed by the inhibition of the instinctive life — that, put inversely, the full and free life of the personality must be sacrificed

[1] Marcel Proust, *Cities of the Plain*, translated by C. K. Scott Moncrieff, vol. i, p. 219.

in the interests of any fixed ideals, whether of morality or the imagination? But does this mean that no alternative progress is possible for the personality? That is the momentous question to which we are finally driven, and which I will now try to answer.

It may have been noticed how closely Proust's analysis agrees with Freud's. It is the phenomena of the mind in its conscious, unconscious, and even preconscious phases of repression and censorship, that Proust is describing in words not far removed from the scientific vocabulary of psycho-analysis. But I doubt very much that Proust had any exact knowledge of psycho-analysis; at many points we must regard his work as a confirmation, or an anticipation, of the observations of Freud. Proust speaks of the heart, and Freud of the mind; but these are interchangeable concepts.

I will not carry the parallel any further. But I do wish to point out how closely Proust's description of the intermissions of the heart can apply to that other parallel phenomenon — the intermissions of genius, or inspiration, to which I have already referred. We all have our moments of inspiration, and perhaps they differ, as between an ordinary mortal and a genius, only in the degree of their intensity. Poets have not often described their creative experiences, but there is one account, quoted by Mr. Percy Lubbock in his Introduction to the *Letters of Henry James*, that is quite unique in the beauty and fullness of its revelation. Henry James began one night to feel his way towards a novel which he had in mind, and among the working notes for this novel were found some pencilled lines from which I should like to quote the essential passage:

'Infinitely interesting — and yet somehow with a beautiful poignancy in it that makes it strange and rather exquisitely formidable, as with an unspeakable deep agitation, the whole artistic question that comes up for me in the train of this idea . . . of the donnée for a situation that I began here the other day to fumble out. I mean I come back, I come back yet again and again, to my only seeing it in the dramatic way — as I can only see everything and anything now; the way that filled my mind and floated and uplifted me when a fortnight ago I gave my few indications to X. Momentary side-winds — things of no real authority — break in every now and then to put their inferior little questions to me; but I came back, I come back, as I say, I all throbbingly and yearningly and passionately, oh mon bon, come back to this way that is clearly the only one in which I can do anything now, and that will open out to me more and more, and that has overwhelming reasons pleading all beautifully in its breast. What really happens is that the closer I get to the problem of the application of it in any particular case the more I get *into* that application, so that the more doubts and torments fall away from me, the more I know where I am, the more everything spreads and shines and draws me on and I'm justified of my logic and my passion. . . . Causons, causons, mon bon — oh, celestial, soothing, sanctifying process, with all the high sane forces of the sacred time fighting, through it, on my side! Let me fumble it gently and patiently out — with fever and fidget laid to rest — as in the old enchanted months! It only looms, it only shines and shimmers, *too* beautiful and too interesting; it only hangs there too rich and too full and with too much to give and to pay; it only presents itself too admirably and too vividly, too straight and square and vivid, as a little organic and effective Action. . . .'

Referring to this confession, Mr. Lubbock says: 'It is as though for once, at an hour of midnight silence and solitude he opened the innermost chamber of his mind and stood face to face with his genius.' I think, in the consistent phraseology I have tried to adopt, we might say that in such a mood of creative activity, the author stands face to face with his personality. He stands fully conscious of the wavering confines of his conscious mind, an expanding and contracting, a fluctuating horizon where the light of awareness meets the darkness of oblivion; and in keeping aware of that area of light and at the same time watching the horizon for a suggestion of more light, the poet induces that new light into his consciousness; as when, at twilight, no stars are visible to a casual glance, but shine out in answer to a concentrated stare. Such lights come, of course, from the latent memory of verbal images in what Freud calls the preconscious state of the mind; or from the still obscurer state of the unconscious, in which are hidden, not only the neural traces of repressed sensations, but also those inherited patterns which determine our instincts. But it is not inspiration alone — not the sudden ingress of light — which makes the poet; that is only the intermission which, if isolated, leads to an easy despair. The essential faculty is an awareness of one's own personality, and the capacity to cultivate its inherent activities 'without division or inner revolt', as accurately described by Montaigne. Montaigne was not a poet, though he might have been an inspired novelist. But that is beside the point; what distinguishes one kind of artist from another is not their states of mind, their mental machinery, but a difference in the distribution of sensational development — the difference, that is to say, between a poet and painter is a difference between verbal-aural and plastic-visual sensibility; a difference of material, not of method. And that, it seems, is another way of saying with Mr. Eliot that 'the poet has, not a "personality" to express, but a particular medium, which is only a medium . . . in which impressions and experiences combine in peculiar and unexpected ways'.

It looks, therefore, as though the one thing an artist must avoid is the fixity of character. This conclusion is forced on us from still another point of view. A man of character is generally distinguishable as a man of action. Or as Keats wrote in a letter to his friend Bailey (22nd November 1817):

'Men of Genius are great as certain ethereal Chemicals operating on the Mass of neutral intellect — but they have not any individuality, any determined Character — I would call the top and head of those who have a proper self Men of Power.'[1]

If we say that there is a fundamental opposition between the artist and the man of action, the statement is acceptable enough. At least, it would fit typical artists like (to mention only poets) Shakespeare and Blake. It would explain the sudden withering of Wordsworth's genius: he acquired a character. But what of Milton and Goethe? Well, of Milton we can say that he was a poet of one kind in his youth, that he then became a man of action and was silent for twenty-five years, and then became a poet once more, but of a different kind. Of Goethe I cannot speak with any confidence, but I suspect that a complete analysis might reveal a real poet and a real personality, but a somewhat fictitious character. Finally — to repeat a suggestion I have already made — may we not perhaps explain the dreary quarrel of romantic and classic as an opposition between two kinds of art, springing respectively from personality and from character? It is an explanation that would work out very well in practice. We have only to think of Dryden and of Dr. Johnson, and to compare them with Shakespeare and Keats.

The only objection which I can foresee to this theory of personality in literature is the one raised in a general way by Mr.

[1] *Letters* (Oxford, 1930), p. 72.

The Personality of the Poet

Fernandez: it does not account for the moral and intellectual development in a poet like Shakespeare. Between *Romeo and Juliet* and *Measure for Measure*, between *Hamlet* and *The Tempest*, there is a vast difference which we can only call, in Nietzsche's phrase, a transvaluation of all values. But the poet and his poetry remain the same. The medium, the material — all pedantry apart — is one. But then must we conclude, because a man of character is an admirable spectacle, in his fixity of demeanour and directness of action, a type to be envied and imitated, that therefore this other type of man, this mobile personality of which poets are made, can show no compensating virtues? Must we not rather conclude that the virtues of personality inhere in its very mobility?[1] For though thought by its own nature is capable of logical development, it can be informed by the whole personality, and therefore made real, only when that personality is free to adapt itself to the movements of thought. Thought and personality go hand in hand, and their goal, whether confessed or not, is that state of vision or inspiration which all great spirits have attained.

[1] Its 'negative capability', as Keats called it in a letter to his brothers (28th December 1817):

'I had not a dispute, but a disquisition, with Dilke upon various subjects; several things dovetailed in my mind, and at once it struck me what quality went to form a man of achievement, especially in literature, and which Shakespeare possessed so enormously — I mean *Negative Capability*, that is, when a man is capable of being in uncertainties, mysteries, doubts, without any irritable reaching after fact and reason. Coleridge, for instance, would let go by a fine isolated verisimilitude caught from the Penetralium of mystery, from being incapable of remaining content with half-knowledge.' (*Letters*, Oxford, 1930, p. 77.)

Psycho-analysis and Literary Criticism[1]

(i)

Any attempt to raise literary criticism above the vague level of emotional appreciation through the incorporation of scientific elements is sure to meet with opposition, not only from the great majority of critics, who depend on their emotions, but also from more serious people who imagine that the prescribed boundaries of decent critical activity are being broken down. To the former set we can only present our weapons; with the latter we must reason, and our task is all the more difficult for the lack, in England, of any scientific tradition. Our critics have, as a rule, resorted to nothing more distant from their subject than common sense. Perhaps the only successful attempt of a more ranging kind was that of Coleridge, who did consciously strive to give literary criticism the rank of a mental science by relating it to what he called 'the technical process of philosophy'. Unfortunately, what this technical process amounted to in Coleridge's day was a very innate kind of metaphysical speculation, speculation rather dim across an interval of more than a hundred years. We have become more empirical, and the general effect of the growth of science has been to discredit transcendental reasoning altogether.[2] Traditional criticism, therefore, in so far as it can claim to be fundamental, is a structure whose very foundations have perished, and if we are to save it from becoming the province of emotional dictators, we must hasten to relate it to those systems of knowledge which have to a great extent replaced transcendental philosophy. Physics, demanding as it does such impressive modifications of aspect and attitude, provides the most general background for all subsidiary efforts, but for the literary critic

---

[1] *The Criterion*, III, No. 10 (London, January, 1925).

[2] I imply 'in the general mind'. That empirical science can ever dispense with all aprioristic processes is a vulgar error to which the general tenor of this book is opposed.

psychology gains an intimate importance because it is so directly concerned with the material origins of art.

The critic, in approaching psychology, will not be altogether disinterested: he will merely raid it in the interests of what he conceives to be another science, literary criticism. This science — if it is permissible to call it a science — really covers a very wide field indeed. It is the valuation, by some standard, of the worth of literature. You may say that the standard is always a very definitely aesthetic one, but I find it impossible to define aesthetics without bringing in questions of value which are, when you have seen all their implications, social or ethical in nature. There is no danger, therefore (or very little danger), in the direction of a too inclusive conception of the critic's function: danger, and death, is rather to be found in the narrow drift of technical research, the analysis of the *means* of expression and so on. But it is a proper complaint against literary criticism in general that it has reached no agreed definition of its boundaries, and until it does it has no serious claim to be considered as a science. It is only because I want to distinguish one kind of literary criticism from another, even as you distinguish astronomy from astrology, or chemistry from alchemy, that I resort to a pretence of science. That distinction established, there is no need to carry the pretence any farther: it is not necessary, I mean, to simulate the vocabularies of science.

Another consideration meets us at the outset of this inquiry, and the more one realizes it the more it appears to put the whole utility of our discussion in doubt. I mean the very obvious difference in the subject-matter of our two sciences: psychology is concerned with the processes of mental activity, literary criticism with the product. The psychologist only analyses the product to arrive at the process: art is, from this point of view, as significant as any other expression of mentality. But of no more significance: its significance does not correspond to its value as literature. The psychologist is indifferent to literary values (too often, alas, even in his own work), and may even definitely deplore them, especially when they represent the trimming of subjective phantasies under the influence of some objective standard or tradition. But in any case the psychologist has found and will always find a large body of material in the imaginative literature of all epochs: that side of the question is so obvious that I shall pay no more attention to it. But whether in the nature of things it is possible for such psychology to add anything positive to the principles of literary criticism is more in doubt. Analysis involves the reduction of the symbol to its origins, and once the symbol is in this way dissolved, it is of no aesthetic significance: art is art as symbol, not as sign. Alfred Adler, whom I have found, for my purpose, one of the most suggestive of the psycho-analytical school, has recognized this, pointing out that '*the attraction of a work of art arises from its synthesis,* and that the analysis of science profanes and destroys this synthesis'.[1] This is perhaps *too* respectful an attitude; there is no need to make a mystery of art. But it is an easy and an unprofitable task to translate into crude terms of sexual phantasy a poem like William Blake's 'I saw a Chapel all of Gold'. One might as well confess that the impossibility of avoiding such a translation is a serious defect in the psychological critic; for him the naïve acceptance of such a poem is impossible; here at least there is no beauty without mystery. Luckily for the critic, few poets are so artless as Blake, and meaning and intelligence tend to be remote in the degree that they are profound.[2]

I have perhaps laid sufficient emphasis on the general limitations of the psychological method in criticism. Before I begin with my main task, which is to explore the uses of psycho-analysis to literary criticism, let me deal with one of its misuses. It perhaps concerns literature rather than criticism, but we must all realize by now that no good artist exists who is not, at every point of his career, firstly a good critic. The work of art emerges within a field of critical perceptions. But, criticism apart, the author who imagines that he can start from psycho-analysis and arrive at art is making a complete mistake. No literature, not even a novel, can arise out of a schematic understanding of the phenomena of life. Art has only one origin — inspiration. It is true that art is itself a schematic construction; an order imposed on the chaos of life. As such it has its own delicate and individual laws. But to conceive art as the illustration of science, or even as the embodiment in tangible fiction of aprioristic views of the universe, is surely a

---

[1] *Individual Psychology* (English edition, 1924), p. 268.

[2] When this remoteness occurs, as in the case of Shakespeare's *Hamlet*, then I think it inevitably follows that any explanation that psychology can offer for the complicated strands of poetic creation tends to quicken our general sensibility. Reasoning and mechanism do not lose their value because we follow step by step the processes of their operation; and a poetic process is exactly analogous. It is where you have, not a dynamic process, but a static symbol, that analysis is without any critical significance, and may be positively destructive of the aesthetic effect. I shall return to this point in dealing with Dr. Ernest Jones's study of *Hamlet.*

final sort of degradation, a use of the imagination more finally discredited than any it is possible to think of.

That is not to say that the study of psycho-analysis is entirely without object for the would-be novelist or poet. It might at least help him to realize, more quickly and more reasonably than the normal man would realize from his own experience, such facts as the subjectivity of love,[1] and the general law of determinism in which all our emotions and ideals are bound. Again, the novelist cannot in his plot ignore with impunity what we might now call the psycho-analytical probabilities. Then surely, it might be said, the examination of such probabilities is an opportunity for the critic well versed in psycho-analysis. But it does not follow. Here, admittedly, is the opportunity of the psycho-analyst, straying from his strict domain, eager to show what fools these artists be. But the literary critic will ignore this obvious use of psycho-analysis, if only for the sufficient reason that to a critic of any worth these psychological defects in a work of the imagination will appear as literary defects. You cannot write well — you cannot, as we say, 'create' your atmosphere — without a 'germ of the real'. Any psychological unreality will, in the end, be apparent in some insincerity of style or method.

In the endeavour to discover the critical utility of psycho-analysis I will, merely for dialectical reasons, formulate three questions.

I. What general function does psycho-analysis give to literature?

II. How does psycho-analysis explain the process of poetic creation or inspiration?

III. Does psycho-analysis cause us to extend in any way the functions of criticism?

I ask the first question, apart from its intrinsic interest, to make sure from both points of view — that of psycho-analysis and that of criticism — that we have the same subject-matter in mind. I ask the second question — again apart from its intrinsic interest — to make sure that we have a common conception of what 'creative' literature is. We can then, without fear of misconstruction, deal with the third question — which is the question I have all the time been leading up to.

To most questions in psycho-analysis there are three answers —

---

[1] Cf. Jacques Rivière, 'Notes on a Possible Generalization of the Theories of Freud' (*The Criterion*, vol. i, no. iv, pp. 344–5).

those respectively of Freud, Jung, and Adler — and as a mere ex-
propriator in this territory I take the liberty to lift my material
from whichever quarter suits me best. Perhaps in this matter of
the general function of literature Jung is the only one of the three
to work out a theory in any detail. Freud and Adler do not seem
to press the question beyond its individual aspect, to which I shall
come in my second question. Jung's theory springs from that
general principle of contrasted attitudes which is really the
characteristic method of his psychology — the contrasted attitudes which he calls introversion and extraversion, a fundamental
division of the self which may be traced in every activity and
which we may variously paraphrase as the opposition between
subject and object, between thought and feeling, between idea
and thing. Now Jung's theory is that living reality is never the
exclusive product of one or the other of these contrasted attitudes,
but only of a specific vital activity which unites them, bridges the
gulf between them, giving intensity to sense-perception and effective force to the idea. This specific activity he calls *phantasy*,
and he describes it as a perpetually creative act. 'It is the creative
activity whence issue the solutions to all unanswerable questions;
it is the mother of all possibilities, in which, too, the inner and the
outer worlds, like all psychological antitheses, are joined in living
union.'[1] Jung further differentiates *active* and *passive* phantasy —
the latter a morbid state which we need not stop to consider here.
Active phantasy he describes as owing its existence 'to the propensity of the conscious attitude for taking up the indications or
fragments of relatively lightly-toned unconscious associations, and
developing them into complete plasticity by association with
parallel elements'.[2] Now although Jung remarks that this active
phantasy is 'the principal attribute of the artistic mentality' he
nowhere seems to have pressed home the conclusions which are
surely latent in his theory, namely, that the poetic function is
nothing else but this active phantasy in its more-than-individual
aspect. The poet, in fact, is one who is capable of creating phantasies of more than individual use — phantasies, as we should say,
of universal appeal. Thus art has for psycho-analysis the general
function of resolving into one uniform flow of life all that springs
from the inner well of primordial images and instinctive feelings,
and all that springs from the outer mechanism of actuality —

[1] *Psychological Types* (English edition, London, 1923), p. 69.
[2] Ibid., p. 574.

doing this, not only for the artist himself, from whose own need the phantasy is born, but also, by suggestion and by symbol, for all who come to participate in his imaginative work.

And here at last the processes of psycho-analysis and literary criticism run together. 'Whether the actual social validity of the symbol', says Jung, 'is more general or more restricted depends upon the quality or vital capacity of the creative individuality. The more abnormal the individual, i.e. the less his general fitness for life, the more limited will be the common social value of the symbols he produces, although their value may be absolute for the individuality in question.'[1] Now 'the social validity of the symbol' is a phrase which I confess I would willingly annex for literary criticism, for it is to some such concept that any thorough critical activity leads us, and though I think the 'symbol' in literature (we should never call it that) is something more precise, more deliberate, something more intelligent than the normal unconscious symbol of psychology, yet, if psycho-analysis can help us to test its social validity, then it can in this respect be of some use to literary criticism.

(ii)

I come to the individual aspect: do we gain any further light from the psycho-analysis of the creative mind? How does the modern psychologist define inspiration, and does his definition bear any correspondence to our critical concepts? It is the general problem of the psychology of genius which I shall deal with in the next essay. But it will, I think, be worth while to examine here one or two relevant aspects of the question. I think that in the mind of every artist (though I think particularly of the literary artist) there are two contrary tendencies. In one direction he is impelled to shuffle off conscious control and to sink back into his primitive mind, where he knows he can find a fresh elemental imagery, a rich though incoherent phantasy. It is the disjointed fortuitous world of dreams — day-dreams. In the other direction he is impelled to establish strong affective tendencies — ideals of moral beauty, of plastic form, of order and architecture. These resolve themselves into some kind of unity and form the goal towards which, consciously or unconsciously, the artist's life is turned. You get the harmony of perfect art when the two forces achieve a balance. I think this is all a matter of psychological

---

[1] *Psychological Types*, p. 380.

observation, but it has a direct bearing on what we may call the central problem of literary criticism — I mean the question of romanticism and classicism. There is, therefore, a peculiar echo of reality in these words of André Gide, written from a purely literary standpoint, in reply to an inquiry on classicism:

'It is important to remember that the struggle between classicism and romanticism also exists inside each mind. And it is from this very struggle that the work is born; the classic work of art relates the triumph of order and measure over an inner romanticism. And the wilder the riot to be tamed the more beautiful your work will be. If the thing is orderly in its inception, the work will be cold and without interest.'[1]

It is this riot within that we ordinarily call inspiration, and a good deal of attention has been devoted to its description by modern psychologists. By some it is assumed to be a function of the unconscious mind, which is credited with autonomous activity, with powers of incubation and elaboration. Most people will be familiar with Poincaré's account of his own experiences in mathematical discovery (*Science et méthode*, chap. iii), where he describes how some sudden illumination would come to him after a period during which conscious application to the problem had been abandoned. Poincaré attributed these sudden illuminations to the unconscious workings of the mind, but he did not advance any explanation of the actual process. In general, psychologists explain sudden illumination or inspiration as due solely to a fortuitous entry into activity of ideas which are immediately associated and seized upon in their happy combination.[2] What really happens may perhaps be described in the following way: you have in the first place the prevailing affectivity, the latent ideal of form or thought; what forms this ideal, what brings it into being, I shall explain in a moment. You have, next, the bringing into activity fortuitously of some image or memory which until the moment of inspiration had lain latent in the unconscious mind; this fortuitous image is as it were criticized by the excited interest; it is selected or rejected; and if selected it is developed and transformed by the ever prevalent affectivity. If the affective tendency is suddenly and strongly roused, then you get a state of emotion, bringing with it an intensity of awareness to all the images and

---

[1] 'Réponse à une enquête de la Renaissance sur le classicisme,' 8 Janvier 1921. (*Morceaux Choisis*, p. 453.)
[2] Cf. E. Rignano, *The Psychology of Reasoning* (London, 1923), p. 129.

ideas that follow in the wake of the first fortuitous image. This is the state of ecstasy. Images seem to leap from their hiding-places all fully equipped for the service of the ideal or affective tendency. But even in this state of animation or ecstasy I believe that a good deal of selection and rejection of images still goes on. However, normally a creative act occurs when the exact word or image is found. And the full creative process is but a summation of many of these primary creative moments.

The concept of inspiration must have arisen as soon as mankind began to distinguish between spirit and matter, that is to say, in prehistoric times. Life itself was then explained as matter animated by spirit, and inevitably the spirit became associated with the breath, that warm and invisible emanation of the body which ceased at death. This dynamic relationship, which was actual enough for body and soul, was also used for all other spiritual visitations; so that when a man spoke with the voice of God, it seemed that the very breath of God had entered into his mortal frame. All the Hebrew prophets were regarded as being thus breathed into, or inspired. It was, therefore, natural enough at a later stage of development to transfer this concept to the poet, for the poet, like the prophet, seemed to speak with a more than human voice. Either the gods inspired him, or, if his utterance was too pagan, then a more sinister but still external agent was evoked — a daimon or genius. Even at its most rational extreme, the classical world could still play with the idea of a muse, whose more than human accents fell into the attentive ear of the poet.

The classical conception of inspiration or possession is beautifully illustrated by Plato, whose description of the poet in *Ion* is the final elaboration of the primitive metaphor:

'For all good poets, epic as well as lyric, compose their beautiful poems not by art, but because they are inspired and possessed. And as the Corybantian revellers when they dance are not in their right mind, so the lyric poets are not in their right mind when they are composing their beautiful strains; but when falling under the power of music and metre they are inspired and possessed; like Bacchic maidens who draw milk and honey from the rivers when they are under the influence of Dionysus but not when they are in their right mind. And the soul of the lyric poet does the same, as they themselves say; for they tell us that they bring songs from honeyed fountains, culling them out of the gardens and dells of the Muses; they, like the bees, winging their way from flower to flower. And this is true. For the poet is a light and winged and holy thing, and there is no invention in him until he has been inspired and is out of his senses, and the mind is no longer in him: when he has not attained to this state, he is powerless and is unable to utter his oracles.'[1]

It is not part of my intention to trace the history of this conception from the time of Plato — to a certain extent that has already been done by Erwin Panofsky.[2] All I would like to note here is that whilst the theory of inspiration persists in some form, at certain periods it tends to become exclusively religious. Saint Thomas Aquinas and the scholastics in general did not conceive art, whether in poetry, painting, or sculpture, as anything more than skill; and such inspiration as there was in the artist was in no way to be distinguished from spiritual grace. The only possible exception was demonic possession, and any form of inspiration that did not conform to the prevailing notion of Christianity probably perished as heresy or witchcraft. The attitude of the rationalists of the seventeenth and eighteenth centuries was essentially the same; the concept of inspiration was contrary to common sense and was generally condemned (in religion no less than in art) as a pernicious form of *enthusiasm*. It was only with the romantic revival that the concept was once more reinstated, and began to be seriously investigated.

Since the eighteenth century, inspiration has lost its religious significance and become almost exclusively an aesthetic term. One might almost say that the historical distinction between classicism and romanticism is determined by this concept. The classicist, and the naturalist who has much in common with him, refuse to see in the highest works of art anything but the exercise of judgement, sensibility, and skill. The romanticist cannot be satisfied with such a normal standard; for him art is essentially irrational — an experience beyond normality, sometimes destructive of normality, and at the very least evocative of that state of wonder which is the state of mind induced by the immediately inexplicable.

Classicism and romanticism are in the end temperamental attitudes, a contradiction which no argument can resolve. But whilst hitherto romanticism has had to rely on subjective convictions,

---

[1] Jowett's translation.
[2] *Idea*, Studien der Bibliothek Warburg, v, 1924.

and has thus earned a certain disrepute in philosophy and the science of art, it can now claim a scientific basis in the findings of psycho-analysis. That psycho-analysis itself rests under the same shadow of subjectivism is an accusation which must be dismissed, for however tentative its theoretical structure may be, the ground-work is a mass of correlated facts from which the main features clearly emerge. That the theory, even in its basic form, has a direct bearing on the problems of artistic creation has already been observed by Freud, and Freud himself has in various places made the first approach to a solution.

Freud's study of neurosis in general soon brought the phenomena of art within the scope of his researches. He found, for example, a similarity between the phantasies which obsessed his patients and the phantasies which the artist put forth as works of the imagination. There was, however, this difference: in one case the phantasies remained mental and led eventually to a nervous breakdown; in the other case they were projected and objectified and the mind remained stable. Art, therefore, was conceived as a way back from phantasy to reality. Freud does not, of course, ignore the question of aesthetic values, and is far from suggesting that every sublimation of phantasy is a work of art. The artist has the additional ability (which Freud calls 'mysterious') of so moulding the objective form of his phantasies that the result gives a positive pleasure, which pleasure is independent of the phantasy and due to the physical proportions, the texture, the tone, the harmony, and all the other specific and objective qualities which we recognize in a work of art. The only explanation he has to offer of this objective power in the work of art is that the technique of the artist is in some way a means of breaking down the barriers between individual egos, uniting them all in some form of collective ego. He suggests that the purely formal or aesthetic elements in a work of art constitute a sort of pleasure-premium or preliminary seduction which, once it operates on our sensibilities, permits the liberation of a secondary and superior kind of enjoyment springing from much deeper levels. 'I believe', he says, 'that the aesthetic pleasure produced in us by the creative artist has a preliminary character, and that the real enjoyment of a work of art is due to the ease it gives to certain psychic tensions.'

More recently Freud has elaborated his anatomy of the mental personality, and though he does not, in this part of his work, make any direct references to the aesthetic problem, some of his observations are suggestive. As formulated in his *New Introductory Lectures* (1933), we have now to regard the individual as being divided into three levels or degrees of consciousness, called the ego, the super-ego, and the id. These divisions can only be schematically represented as definite; actually they shade off into one another. The super-ego in particular is not to be imagined as something separated from the id by the ego; some of its characteristics are derived directly from the id. The id is 'the obscure inaccessible part of our personality; the little we know about it we have learnt from the study of dream-work and the formation of neurotic symptoms, and most of that is of a negative character, and can only be described as all that the ego is not. We can come nearer to the id with images, and call it a chaos, a cauldron of seething excitement. We suppose that it is somewhere in direct contact with somatic [i.e. physical or bodily] processes, and takes over from them instinctual needs and gives them mental expression, but we cannot say in what substratum this contact is made. These instincts fill it with energy, but it has no organization and no unified will, only an impulse to obtain satisfaction for the instinctual needs, in accordance with the pleasure-principle. The laws of logic — above all, the law of contradiction — do not hold for processes in the id. . . . There is nothing in the id which can be compared to negation, and we are astonished to find in it an exception to the philosopher's assertion that space and time are necessary forms of our mental acts. In the id there is nothing corresponding to the idea of time, no recognition of the passage of time, and (a thing which is very remarkable and awaits adequate attention in philosophic thought) no alteration of mental processes by the passage of time. . . . It is constantly being borne in on me that we have made far too little use for our theory of the indubitable fact that the repressed remains unaltered by the passage of time. This seems to offer us the possibility of an approach to some really profound truths. . . . Naturally the id knows no values, no good and evil, no morality. The economic, or, if you prefer, the quantitative factor, which is so closely bound up with the pleasure-principle, dominates all its processes.'

We must leave on one side the significance of the other two divisions of the mental personality — the ego and the super-ego — though their application to the sphere of criticism is not far to seek. The ego is the main agent of what Freud calls the reality-principle and its tendency is to synthetize the lawless products of the id — to bring together and unify the basic mental processes. It is in the ego that the work of art receives its formal organization, just as it is in the super-ego that it receives its moral or social aim. The super-ego is 'the representative of all moral restrictions, the advocate of the impulse towards perfection — in short, it is as much as we have been able to apprehend psychologically of what people call the "higher" things in human life.'

The work of art, therefore, has its correspondences with each region of the mind. It derives its energy, its irrationality and its mysterious power from the id, which is to be regarded as the source of what we have called 'inspiration'. It is given formal synthesis and unity by the ego; and finally it may be assimilated to those ideologies or spiritual aspirations which are the peculiar creation of the super-ego. The old metaphor underlying the word 'inspiration' is to this extent confirmed: that out of the darkness of that region of the mind we call the id, come these sudden promptings of words, sounds, or images from which the artist constructs his work of art. It is not for me to discuss at present *how* that construction is effected — to what extent, for example, it comes into consciousness ready-made. It is sufficient to note that Freud has provided a psychological explanation of the fact of inspiration. In another connection (he is discussing the phenomenon of mysticism) Freud suggests that under certain conditions 'the perceptual system becomes able to grasp relations in the deeper layers of the ego and in the id which would otherwise be inaccessible to it.' We might elaborate the metaphor and picture the regions of the mind as three superimposed strata in which a phenomenon comparable to a 'fault' in geology has taken place. As a result, in one part of the mind the layers become discontinuous, and exposed to each other at unusual levels; the sensational awareness of the ego being brought into direct contact with the id, and from that 'seething cauldron' snatching some archetypal form, some instinctive association of words, images, or sounds, which constitute the basis of the work of art. Ideas, and all the rational superstructure of the mind, can be conveyed by the instruments of thought or science; but those deeper intuitions of the mind, which are neither rational nor economic, but which nevertheless exercise a changeless and eternal influence on successive generations of men — these are accessible only to the mystic and the artist, and only the artist can give them material representation, though naturally the mystic may be, and often is, one kind of artist — a poet.

If this be a correct description of the process of poetic creation, then the part that may be played by suggestion or self-hypnosis in the encouragement of such states is obviously considerable, and I think that in time a complete technique of inspiration may be evolved. That this will result in a vast increase in the number of poets need not be feared, for nothing ever comes out of the unconscious mind that has not previously been consciously elaborated or sensibly felt: the product of the unconscious mind will always strictly correspond with the quality of the conscious mind, and dull or undisciplined intellects will find as ever that there is no short cut to genius.

It will be observed that there is nothing exceptional or peculiar in this description of the creative process: it is just what occurs in any man's mind when he is suddenly endowed with a 'bright idea'. Where then must we seek for an explanation of the abnormality of the artist? Obviously, I think, in the nature of the ideal or affective tendency to which his whole creative life is subservient.

Freud and his disciples would trace back the formation of the abnormal mentality of the artist to the period of infancy. 'Analysis of this aspiration' (for ideal beauty), says Dr. Ernest Jones, 'reveals that the chief source of its stimuli is not so much a primary impulse as a reaction, a rebellion against the coarser and more repellent aspects of material existence, one which psychogenetically arises from the reaction of the young child against its original excremental interests.'[1] The repression of such tabooed interests may indeed contribute to the details of aesthetic activity, but this particular hypothesis seems far too limited in conception, and far too poorly supported by facts, to account for the variety and profundity of aesthetic expression in general. The less specialized theory of Adler seems to offer a clearer explanation. According to the principles of 'individual psychology', 'every neurosis can be understood as an attempt to free oneself from a feeling of inferiority in order to gain a feeling of superiority.'[2] The feeling of inferiority usually arises in the family circle, and the compensatory feeling of superiority is usually a phantasy so absurd in its high-set goal of god-likeness that it remains in the

---

[1] *Essays in Applied Psycho-Analysis* (1923), p. 262.
[2] Alfred Adler, *The Practice and Theory of Individual Psychology* (English edition, London, 1924), p. 23.

unconscious; it is repressed by the communal standards of logic, sympathy, and co-operation. This buried sense of superiority is present in most of us, but the artist takes the goal of godlikeness seriously and is compelled to flee from real life and compromise to seek a life within life;[1] and he is an artist in virtue of the form and ideal perfection which he can give to this inner life. The neurotic fails to create a formal phantasy, and lapses into some degree of chaos. Now it is worth observing, as a confirmation of the truth of this theory, that the most general period for the formation of the superiority-complex coincides with the most general period for the outburst of the poetic impulse. I mean the time of the awakening of the adolescent sexual instincts, the time of the withdrawal of parental protection, the period of intense conflict between instinctive desires and social control. I think there can be no doubt that the artist is born of this conflict. Freud himself lends support to this view. He says: The artist 'is one who is urged on by instinctive needs which are too clamorous; he longs to attain to honour, power, riches, fame, and the love of woman; but he lacks the means of achieving these gratifications. So, like any other with an unsatisfied longing, he turns away from reality, and transfers all his interest, and all his libido too, on to the creation of his wishes in the life of phantasy.' And Freud goes on to explain how the artist can, by the expression and elaboration of his phantasies, give them the impersonality and universality of art and make them communicable and desirable to others — 'and then he has won — through his phantasy — what before he could only win in phantasy: honour, power, and the love of woman'.[2]

The essential point to notice is that psycho-analysis seems to show that the artist is initially by tendency a neurotic, but that in becoming an artist he as it were escapes the ultimate fate of his tendency and through art finds his way back to reality. I think it will be seen now where psycho-analysis can be of some assistance to the critic — namely, in the verification of the reality of the sublimation of any given neurotic tendency. The psycho-analyst should be able to divide sharply for us, in any given artistic or pseudo-artistic expression, the real and the neurotic. There is much in literature that is on the border-line of reality: it would be

[1] Ibid., p. 8.
[2] Sigmund Freud, *Introductory Lectures on Psycho-Analysis* (English edition, London, 1922), pp. 314–15.

useful for the critic to be able to determine by some scientific
process the exact course of this border-line. Again I would
suggest that in all probability the critic could determine this
border-line by general critical principles; but psycho-analysis
might be a shorter path to the test; and in any case it would supply
collateral evidence of a very satisfactory kind. Psycho-analysis
finds in art a system of symbols, representing a hidden reality,
and by analysis it can testify to the purposive genuineness of the
symbols; it can also testify to the faithfulness, the richness, and
the range of the mind behind the symbol.

(iii)

There still remains the third question that I propounded: Does
psycho-analysis modify in any way our conception of the critic's
function? The clear difference in subject-matter, already defined,
makes it unlikely that we shall find any fundamental influence. It
is merely a question of what kind of attitude, among the many
possible to the critic within the strict limits of his function,
psycho-analysis will stress. It does not, so far as I can see, amount
to anything very definite — anything more precise than a general
admonition to tolerance. Human activities are shown to be so
interrelated, so productive of unrealized compensations, that any
narrowly confined application of energy and intelligence results in
a distortion of reality. Hence the futility of a purely categorical
criticism — which may be illustrated by reference to 'the Hamlet
problem'. During the past two hundred years an extensive body
of criticism has accumulated around Shakespeare's cryptic
masterpiece. The difficulty, for the critics, is to account within
the canons of art for Hamlet's hesitancy in seeking to revenge his
father's murder. Dr. Ernest Jones has given a fairly complete
summary,[1] which I will summarize still further, of all the various
theories advanced at different times. There are two main points of
view: one, that of Goethe and Coleridge, finds a sufficient explanation of the inconsistencies of the play in the temperament of
Hamlet, whom they regard as a noble nature, but one incapable
of decisive action of any kind — 'without that energy of the soul
which constitutes the hero', as Goethe expresses it. The second
point of view sees a sufficient explanation in the difficulty of the

[1] 'The Problem of Hamlet', *Essays in Applied Psycho-Analysis* (London,
1923), pp. 1–98.

task that Hamlet is called upon to perform. Both these theories have been decisively refuted, time and time again, from the very facts of the play, and finally criticism has manœuvred itself into a paradoxical position, boldly asserting that the tragedy is in its essence 'inexplicable, incoherent, and incongruous'. This is the position taken up with so much force by the late J. M. Robertson. 'Robertson's thesis' (I quote from Dr. Jones's summary) 'is that Shakespeare, finding in the old play "an action that to his time discounting sense was one of unexplained delay, elaborated that aspect of the hero as he did every other", "finally missing artistic consistency simply because consistency was absolutely excluded by the material"; he concludes that Hamlet is "not finally an intelligible drama as it stands", that "the play cannot be explained from within" and that "no jugglery can do away with the fact that the construction is incoherent, and the hero perforce an enigma, the snare of idolatrous criticism".' All this can be said, and said intelligently, and with a convincing absence of emotional prejudice. But it leaves us curiously dissatisfied. We cannot dismiss so easily the personal intensity of expression throughout the play, and such intensity, such *consistent* intensity, gives the play a unity which the old academic criticism has failed to perceive. It seems that here is a case of an instrument not large enough, or not exact enough, to measure the material in hand.

Where literary criticism fails to account for its problem, what can psycho-analysis do? Dr. Jones has shown that it will claim to do a great deal, and he has elaborated in his study of Hamlet a psychological explanation of the peculiar problems of the play. He sees in Hamlet's vacillation the workings of a typical 'complex' — the Oedipus complex, as it is called by the psychoanalysts. That is to say, the mental peculiarities of Hamlet, expressed throughout the play with such vividness and actuality, can be explained as the consequences of 'repressed' infantile incestuous wishes, stirred into activity by the death of the father and the appearance of a rival, Claudius. With the use of this hypothesis Dr. Jones can explain, and explain very plausibly, all the difficulties and incoherences of the action; and he finds in the play such an exact delineation and such a rich wealth of supporting detail that he cannot but conclude that in writing *Hamlet* Shakespeare was giving expression to a conflict passing through his own mind. There is a certain amount of biographical confirmation of this further hypothesis in the circumstances of the com position of the play, but not facts enough, alas, to be of much use to any solution of the problem.

It would be interesting to follow this application of psycho-analysis to literary criticism into further detail, but perhaps I have indicated enough of Dr. Jones's theory and method to show the possibilities of this new approach to the problems of literature. Whether Dr. Jones's explanation is tenable or not, it does provide what is at present the only way out of a critical impasse, and for that reason alone it merits serious consideration. At the very least it points to a defect in our critical methods, for the failure of literary criticism to deal with *Hamlet* is largely due to its approach to the problem along too narrow a front: we must always be pre-pared for literature refusing to fit into our critical categories. Criticism is a process of crystallization, of the discovery and elaboration of general concepts; but we must be prepared for the voyage of discovery leading us into strange and unfamiliar tracts of the human mind.

That is one way in which psycho-analysis supplies a corrective to the narrowness of criticism. I find still another, tending to the same end. I have referred before to the eternal opposition of the classic and the romantic: to this blind difference under the in-fluence of which even the best of critics race into untenable dog-matisms. Can psycho-analysis resolve this difficult conflict and supply us with a common standpoint?

I think it can — particularly the psycho-analysis associated with the name of Jung. Jung has devoted his best work to the analysis of psychological types. As I have mentioned before, he distinguishes between two fundamental types, the extraverted and the introverted, determined according to whether the general mental energy of the individual is directed outwards to the visible, actual world, or inward to the world of thought and imagery. These two fundamental types are further subdivided into types determined by the functions of thinking, feeling, sensation, and intuition, but the psychological types so determined do not form hard-and-fast categories into which the whole of humanity can be classified: they are merely indications of extensive divisions which merge one into another. But in our particular sphere they do supply a scientific basis for the description of literary types. You will find, for example, that the romantic artist always expresses some function of the introverted attitude, whilst the classic artist always expresses some function of the extraverted attitude. Now

114

this suggests that the critic, like the psychologist, should take up a position above the conflict, and although his own psychological state may lead him to sympathize with one school or the other, yet as a scientific critic he must no longer be content with a dog-in-the-manger attitude. Again, he must broaden the basis of his criticism: he must see the romantic and classic elements in literature as the natural expression of a biological opposition in human nature. It is not sufficient to treat the matter one way or the other as a question of intellectual fallacy; it is a question, for the individual, of natural necessity; but criticism must find its general basis in a science of mankind.

I would like to indicate, in conclusion, what I think might be a fruitful direction for further work in the application of psycho-analysis to literature. Recent theories explain memory, and indeed most of the characteristics of mind, on a basis of physiological 'traces' left by experience. Experience may be individual or collective, and what happens individually must also happen collectively, and those instincts and experiences incidental to the struggle for adaptation and existence leave their traces on the mind when, and in so far as, it functions collectively. The accretion of innumerable traces ensures a set response to environment. A given physical structure of the brain results in certain inevitable forms of thought, and these Jung, following Burckhardt, calls primordial images. Such images eventually crystallize as myths and religions,[1] and psychology has already devoted a good deal of attention to the relation of such myths and religions to the unconscious processes of which they are the expression. Sometimes these collective ideas or primordial images find expression in literature, which, from an evolutionary point of view, has been regarded as a rational mythology.[2] Jung quotes from a letter of Burckhardt's these very suggestive sentences:

'What you are destined to find in *Faust*, that you will find by intuition. *Faust* is nothing else than pure and legitimate myth, a great primitive conception, so to speak, in which every one can divine in his own way his own nature and destiny. Allow me to

---

[1] This process, however, should not be held to exclude the possibility of the specific origin of myths. The opposition between psycho-analysts and ethnologists on this score is largely fictitious. The origin of the myth may be a plain event devoid of psychological significance: the elaboration of this event into a mythical structure, often over a period of many years, even centuries, may all the same be a process for which we should seek an explanation in psychology.

[2] Cf. Th. Ribot, 'La littérature est une mythologie déchue et rationalisée', *Essai sur l'Imagination Créatrice* (Paris, 1900), p. 114.

make a comparison: What would the ancient Greeks have said had a commentator interposed himself between them and the Oedipus legend? There was a chord of the Oedipus legend in every Greek which longed to be touched directly and respond in its own way. And thus it is with the German nation and *Faust*.'[1]

This train of thought, allied to what we know of the possibilities of psycho-analysis in dealing with myths, seems to suggest the further possibility of relating the types actualized by the poetic imagination to their origin in the root-images of the community. In this way criticism would possess still another basic reality on which it could ground the imaginative hypotheses of art. Whether criticism, under the guidance of psycho-analysis, could go still further and indicate the needs of the collective mind, is perhaps too venturesome a suggestion to make. But with the advance of reason we have lost the main historic content of the collective mind: the symbols of religion are no longer effective because they are no longer unconscious. We still, however, retain structural features of the mind that cry for definite satisfaction. The modern world is uneasy because it is the expression of an unappeased hunger. We need some unanimity to focus the vague desires that exist in the collective mind. Will the psychologist unite with the critic to define and to solve this problem?

[1] C. G. Jung, *Psychology of the Unconscious* (English edition, 1918), p. 490.

Swift[1]

(i)

There is a general difficulty in any critical approach to Swift's work which this note is only intended to raise, not to solve: the temerity of any purely literary judgement. If we make a distinction between contingent literature and absolute literature — between authors who only write when there is a public and external stimulus and authors whose stimulus is subjective, who write because they enjoy writing as a free and creative activity — then we shall see that the whole of Swift's work is contingent. He is, on a grand scale, an occasional writer; even *Gulliver's Travels*, the most absolute of his works, is determined by his political experience; it is a final judgement on humanity, — not the abstract humanity of history and philosophy, but the mass of human beings contemporary with the author. All that Swift wrote is empirical, experiential, *actuel*. It is impossible to detach it from circumstances; we must consider each book or pamphlet in relation to its political intention. It is true that the world has refused to do this in the case of *Gulliver*, but the world's appreciation of *Gulliver* is not critical, not exact. We cut the slings and blunt the arrows of that angry onslaught; we dull the deadly mirror with the moist breath of our complacency.

Nevertheless, though none of Swift's works can be separated from its historical occasion, historical considerations cannot usurp aesthetic judgement. Nor are we at liberty to assume that Swift himself would have resented the application of a purely literary standard to his writings. In a 'Letter to a Young Gentleman lately enter'd into Holy Orders', Swift laid the greatest emphasis on literary accomplishment. In that pamphlet occurs his famous 'true definition of style' — 'proper Words in proper Places'; and there he urges the study of the *English* language —

[1] *Times Literary Supplement*, 1926, 1929, 1935.

'the neglect whereof is one of the most general Defects among the Scholars of this Kingdom'. After warning the novice against pedantry and vulgarity, he selects two especial defects for mention:

'The first is the Frequency of flat unnecessary Epithets, and the other is the Folly of using old threadbare Phrases, which will often make you go out of your Way to find and apply them, are nauseous to rational Hearers, and will seldom express your Meaning as well as your own natural Words. . . . When a Man's Thoughts are clear, the properest Words will generally offer themselves first, and his own Judgement will direct him in what Order to place them, so they may best be understood. . . . In short, that Simplicity without which no human Performance can arrive to any great Perfection, is nowhere more eminently useful than in this.'

All this shows a high literary conscience; and the same quality is betrayed in the very interesting references to the composition of *Gulliver's Travels* which occur in his letters to Ford.[1] On 19th January 1723–4, he writes: 'My greatest want here is of somebody qualified to censure and correct what I write, I know not above two or three whose Judgement I would value, and they are lazy, negligent, and without any Opinion of my Abilityes.' Then in a letter of 20th November 1733, referring to Motte's edition, he writes: 'Had there been onely omissions, I should not care one farthing; but changes of Style, new things foysted in, that are false facts, and I know not what, is very provoking. . . . Besides, the whole Sting is taken out in severall passages, in order to soften them. Thus the Style is debased, the humor quite lost, and the matter insipid.' Other references to the composition of *Gulliver* show that it was first written in rough draft, then amended, and finally completely transcribed by the author.

Swift's literary conscience thus established, we might next inquire whether he considered himself as primarily a writer, as an author rather than a clergyman or a politician; whether he considered himself as of the same 'trade' as his cousin Dryden or his friends Pope and Gay. Such an inquiry touches on one of the mysteries of Swift's life — his attitude towards religion in general and his holy orders in particular. That difficult problem must for the present be evaded, though incidentally a sentence in a letter

---

[1] *The Letters of Jonathan Swift to Charles Ford*, edited by David Nichol Smith (Clarendon Press, 1935).

to Ford of 22nd June 1736 should be noted: 'I have long given up all hopes of Church or Christianity.' The problem can be evaded because a career as author is not inconsistent with a career in the Church — both ends can be pursued concurrently, as many careers testify (Newman's, for example). If we are charitable, and assume that Swift took orders for more than worldly motives; if we make the still more generous assumption that his political activities were based on a disinterested idealism; even then we can still ask: Did Swift consider himself as first and foremost an author? Was his highest ambition literary — was he, not merely a clergyman, but also, in the medieval sense of the word and in Julien Benda's modern sense, a clerk?

It is at any rate illuminating to reconstruct Swift's life from this point of view — to regard him as essentially what we should call an 'intellectual', and to see in his various strivings nothing but the desire of an intellectual to secure himself an economic competency and an assured position on which he could base a life of disinterested intellectual activity — a life of scholarship, as he would probably have called it. It will be remembered how much he hankered after the post of Historiographer Royal, and how scornful he was when it went to an obscure (though competent) archaeologist. In a letter to Lord Peterborough, written in 1711 when his political career was yet full of promise, Swift said: 'My ambition is to live in England, and with a competency to support me with honour', and there is no reason to doubt the sincerity of that modest ambition. But some of his letters to Ford, written with more obvious sincerity, are still more revealing. Later in this same year 1711 he wrote:

'Now to your former Letter, where you say the Publick requires my Leisure. The Publick is a very civil Person, and I am it's humble Servant, but I shall be glad to shake hands with it as soon as I can. . . . You are in the right as to my Indifference about Irish affairs, which is not occasioned by my Absence, but contempt of them; and when I return my Indifference will be full as much. I had as lieve be a Beau in Dublin as a Politician, nay, I had as lieve be an Author there; and if ever I have any thoughts of making a Figure in that Kingdom, it shall be at Laracor. I will talk Politicks to the Farmers, and publish my Works at Trim.'

Later, in 1719, when his high ambitions for place and power had been disappointed, when he was irrevocably condemned to a deanery in Dublin, he wrote to his friend a little more ruefully, but still in the same strain:

'You know I chuse all the sillyest Things in the World to amuse my self, in an evil age, and a late time of life, ad fallendam canitiem quae indies obrepit. Little trifling Businesses take up so much of my time, that I have little left for speculation, in which I could gladly employ my self, for my Eyes begin to grudge (that I may speak in Royall Style) me reading, and the Pen is not half so troublesom. But instead of that, I do everything to make me forget my self and the World as much as I can.'

About a month later he confesses to Ford that 'it would be an admirable Scituation to be neither Whig nor Tory. For a Man without Passions might find very strong Amusements.' A Man without Passions — party passions, national passions, religious passions — that is the definition of the true clerk, the intellectual, the scholar. One can admire Swift only this side idolatry and still regret that this 'indifference', this sublime rational sentiment, had been his earlier in life. For he found that 'the turn of Blood at fifty' disposed him strongly to fears; he had lost his equanimity, as Wood's halfpence were soon to prove. But in the midst of his fears he was struggling for serenity, and through the course of *Gulliver's Travels* we see him gradually achieving it. They were finished, revised, and transcribed in his country cabin at Quilca, among the bogs and rocks. His last Voyage was to a race 'whose grand Maxim is, to cultivate *Reason*, and to be wholly governed by it'. 'Neither is *Reason* among them a Point problematical as with us, where Men can argue with Plausibility on both sides of a Question; but strikes you with immediate Conviction; as it needs must do where it is not mingled, obscured, or discoloured by Passion and Interest.' But it was a man already broken in health, weary of nerve, and empty of love, who made this discovery; leaving us to wonder that in such extremity such a masterpiece could be written.

(ii)

The prodigious success that awaited *Gulliver's Travels into several Remote Nations of the World* on its first appearance towards the end of the year 1726 came as a great surprise to both author and publisher. The publisher's hasty shifts have been revealed in recent years by various ingenious bibliographers;

they have compared page with page, line with line and word with word, and in the end shown not only that three editions were published within a few weeks but that each of these editions was wholly or partly reset, and that Benjamin Motte, the publisher, unable to meet the demand single-handed, was compelled to utilize the services of more than one printing-house.[1] The first edition, apparently of several thousand copies, seems to have been sold out in about a week. The second edition was published about the middle of November, and the third possibly early in December. Two further editions were published by Motte in 1727, and still another in 1731; and in addition to these there had been two Irish editions and a serial publication in *Parker's Penny Post*. But it is of no account to pursue this enumeration; what matters is the revelation of the immediateness and completeness of the popularity of this extraordinary book.

Swift himself was not the man to lose his head over such good fortune; fourteen months after the event, in a letter to his publisher, he remarks in his detached way that 'the world glutted itself with that book at first, but now it will go off but soberly; but I suppose will not be soon worn out'. Not so soon, nor so soberly, as is suggested. *Gulliver* has sold year in year out; it stands with the Authorized Version and *The Pilgrim's Progress* as one of the three great precipitants of modern English usage, and rivals *Robinson Crusoe* in the amplitude of its secular appeal. It will perhaps be profitable to enquire into the causes which underlie this popularity — and this literary appeal; for the first step in any analysis is to realize a distinction here. There have always been two classes: those who are like the old gentleman who went to his map to search for Lilliput (or, more subtly, the bishop who hardly believed a word of it) and those who are like Pope and Arbuthnot and from the first see what the author is driving at. We shall not be far wrong if we ascribe the popularity of the book to the first class, and its position in English literature to the second. For of the first class are all children — of all sizes, ages, and epochs — who are open to be beguiled, innocently or ignorantly, by a tale of adventures. It is such as these, whose numbers are legion, that have kept the printing presses busy with these *Travels*: no other proposition is tolerable. For once to look into the dark pain and dreadful bitterness which lie beneath the

[1] A full account of all that concerns the Motte editions of *Gulliver's Travels* has been given by Mr. Harold Williams in the *Library* for December 1925.

verisimilitude of *Gulliver* is to resign the cloak of innocence and
the mask of ignorance. Those who have found themselves so
naked as this in the world are, for good or ill, too few to ensure
the popularity of a book.

The critic, of course, must plunge into this harsher element,
though he need not stay there: he will find a critical problem in
the very popularity of Gulliver. We want to know what the
elements are that in this book appeal so infallibly to some instinct
within us. It is obvious, of course, that we like to be beguiled — to
be taken out of ourselves, to forget ourselves in another world of
fancy. It is a mental playtime, the daydream of our senses, and
there is physical ease and rest in the process. But what in *Gulliver*
secures this effect? That is the first question to ask, and it is
decidedly to the point in any literary enquiry. For it will be found
that effects of this kind are purely effects of style. In *Gulliver* we
shall find two such distinctive features: the expression is direct
and unobstructed, and the development of the narrative is continuous. As for the first of these, Johnson went to the heart of the
subject, as he so often did in anything that concerned the technique of writing, when he wrote:

'His style was well suited to his thoughts, which are never
subtilized by nice disquisitions, decorated by sparkling conceits,
elevated by ambitious sentences, or variegated by far-sought
learning. He pays no court to the passions; he excites neither
surprise nor admiration; he always understands himself: and his
reader always understands him: the peruser of Swift wants little
previous knowledge: it will be sufficient that he is acquainted
with common words and common things; he is neither required
to mount elevations, nor to explore profundities; his passage is
always on a level, along solid ground, without asperities, without
obstruction.'

This is the perfect definition of a popular style, whose essence,
apart from the unqualifiable merit of grammatical righteousness,
lies in that simplicity which Johnson elsewhere characterized in
the remark, 'the rogue never hazards a metaphor'. The appeal that
is latent in all poetry and eloquence is an appeal to a higher and
a rarer sensibility; and it was just this appeal which Swift could
afford to neglect. He could venture in this way because he was
supported by that other feature of his style — the economy and
coherence of the narrated action. Of this Johnson's famous remark was, 'when once you have thought of big men and little

men, it is very easy to do all the rest'. But that is a spiteful sally, unworthy of its author. The actual performance is more wonderful, and amounts to an extraordinary logic in which, once a few premises are granted, a whole fabric of history is created, seemingly accurate in its verisimilitude and action. Logic here becomes a substitute for imagination. In imagination the writer moves from a foundation of experience to a fictive evocation whose touchstone is the original experience: the process is logical in a way. But in *Gulliver* Swift's whole erection is based on fictive elements; and the verisimilitude is not due to his selection of the various elements, but to the way in which many particulars are deduced from a few general premises. The make-believe is not one of fancy, but of effect: we are gulled by the implacable machinery of the narration, and our interest is not at all an interest of passion or surprise (to use Johnson's words), but rather of curiosity and constructiveness.

In such a manner we can explain the popularity of *Gulliver*; for these elements — of simplicity, of make-believe, of 'constructive' rather than of 'creative' elaboration — are the elements which appeal to any mind irrespective of its sensibility or, in a certain sense, its intelligence. But *Gulliver*, of course, does not owe its singular position in the history of English literature to any such adventitious causes: they were quite beside the author's intention in writing the book, and have nothing to do with its implications. Of Swift's purpose we are assured in unequivocal terms that it is solely to vex the world. 'Drown the world! I am not content with despising it, but I would anger it, if I could with safety.' In these words he exposed his spleen to Pope towards the end of 1725, just about the time he was 'finishing, correcting, amending, and transcribing' his *Travels*. And it was in this splenetic mood that the book was born, though it is possible that it was conceived in a happier state. The first hint of the project goes back to 1714, the year of the Scriblerus Club; and there is now no doubt that the actual writing was begun by the spring of 1721.[1] The date is significant; for it was at this time that the drama of his relations with Stella and Vanessa was drawing him into a condition of insupportable anguish, and the state endured until it reached its climax in the death of Vanessa, which was in 1723. We may well believe that the circumstances of her death

[1] See Mr. Harold Williams' Introduction to the text of the first edition published by the First Edition Club, 1926.

left Swift in mental anguish greater than any caused by the dilemma of her love for him during her life. The tremendous distraction of Wood's halfpence and *The Drapier's Letters* came mercifully at this juncture and occupied his mind the greater part of the succeeding year. This incident over, Swift turned once more to the *Travels*, to prolong them and deepen them into that darkness of despair which is their final quality.

It is to the precise definition of this quality that we must now turn. It has commonly been described as irony; and Swift himself gave countenance to the term:

> *Arbuthnot is no more my friend*
> *Who dares to irony pretend*
> *Which I was born to introduce,*
> *Refin'd it first, and shew'd its use.*

And Mr. Charles Whibley, in his essay on Swift (the Leslie Stephen Lecture for 1917), which is perhaps the most understanding of modern interpretations of the man, strongly underlines this quality, describing Swift as 'a great master of irony — the greatest that has ever been born in these isles. Great enough to teach a lesson to Voltaire himself, and to inspire the author of *Jonathan Wild*'.

There exist in the English language a group of terms which, though precise enough when pondered sufficiently, describe subtle variations of temper, and are therefore frequently confused in writing. These are satire, sarcasm, irony, cynicism, and the sardonic. It is not suggested that it is possible to define Swift's quality by any one of these terms: it would be possible to find in his writings specimens of them all. But if we consider *Gulliver*, and *Gulliver* is the most significant of all his works, we find in it an obvious consistency of mood which must be designated by a single term. Mr. Whibley (like Swift himself) would say irony. But there has been a general tendency to reject this term as too smooth, too suave in its connotation, to fit the savagery of *Gulliver*. Accordingly, the common voice has taken up cynicism. But one of the most convincing passages in Mr. Whibley's essay is devoted to a refusal of this term and to a refutation of the charge implied in it:

'Now the cynic may be defined as one who looks upon life and morals with an indifferent curiosity, whose levity persuades him to smile upon the views of others, and to let them go to destruction each his own way. Of this kind of cynicism Swift was wholly innocent. He may be absolved also of that cynicism which the dictionary defines as "captious fault-finding". The heart that was torn by *saeva indignatio*, to use a phrase from the epitaph he composed for himself, was no cynic's heart. The truth is that he was a born idealist, with no desire either to snarl or to smile at life. The master-passion of his mind was anger against injustice and oppression.'

This is valid criticism, and the only comment necessary is in the nature of a limitation of the word 'idealist'. For there are idealists of fancy and idealists of fact; idealists who would make the world consonant with their abstractions, and idealists who begin with a knowledge of cause and effect, and whose vision is a progressive sense of the issue of trial and error. These latter are better called rationalists; and reason was a very real term with Swift. The grand maxim of his beloved Houyhnhnms was 'to cultivate reason, and to be wholly governed by it'. The whole basis of the positive part of *Gulliver*, as implied, for example, in the criticisms of the King of Brobdingnag, is rational in the extreme. But this rational idealism was, from a cause which we shall proceed to investigate, brought to nothing by the prevalent pessimism of its author's mind.

Of satire and sarcasm there is, of an incidental kind, more than enough in *Gulliver*. These elements, we may again conjecture, go back to the early days of the conception; they come earliest in the book, and Arbuthnot and Pope were right in considering them the weakest part of it. The College of Projectors is the most obvious case in point. But if we reject satire and sarcasm as of no real account, and have disposed of cynicism, must we after all fall back on irony, or is there hope in the final term of our list — the sardonic?

All these terms have been clearly defined in Mr. Fowler's *Dictionary of Modern English Usage*. The definitions are there arranged in a tabular form, giving separately the motive or aim, the province, the method or means, and the audience, which each word should connote. Of satire the motive is given as 'amendment', the province as 'morals and manners', the method as 'accentuation', and the audience as 'the self-satisfied'. Similarly, sarcasm has for aim 'inflicting pain', for province 'faults and foibles', for method 'inversion', and for audience 'victim and by-stander'. These definitions are obvious in their rightness, and the definition of cynicism only shows how justly Mr. Whibley has dismissed it from the province of Swift's writings. Its motive is 'self-justification', its province 'morals', its method 'exposure of nakedness', and its audience 'the respectable'. The motive is sufficient to exempt Swift here, however near the method be to that of *Gulliver*. The definition of irony is even more decisive, but, on the other hand, it is perhaps the least adequate of any in Mr. Fowler's table. The motive is given as 'exclusiveness', the province as 'statement of facts', the method as 'mystification', and the audience as 'an inner circle'. It is the motive again that defeats any application to Swift; but in this case the audience too is in adequate — or, if not inadequate, too ample. There was, indeed, an inner circle, but it was contracted nearly to a point.

We look finally at the definition of the sardonic. It has for motive 'self-relief', for province 'adversity'; its method is 'pessimism', and its audience 'self'. There is no evidence that the author of this definition had Swift in mind when he made it; but the conjunction of the two brings with it a sense of illumination, and the use of the word in this connection cannot ever again escape us. *Gulliver* responds in all its particulars when once it is considered as the release of a mind from the strain of an intense emotion. It is, perhaps, only too easy to be sentimental about Swift's curious love affairs. The facts are far from complete, and in the absence of facts, to sentimentalize is the easiest course. But the reality of Vanessa's passion is inescapable; and this passion was insinuated, with Swift's complicity, into the rather base and inhuman tyranny of his love for Stella. It is doubtful if any useful analysis can be made of the complex state of Swift's mind at this juncture; what might, by such means, be reduced to a pettiness in his character might equally well be revealed as a tragedy. Signs are not wanting of both possibilities; but, on either supposition, that mind had as issue from its intolerable strain the sardonic pages of *Gulliver*.

The application of these terms cannot be exclusive, and the more precise we make them the less generally can they serve us. But if it be admitted that the special quality of *Gulliver* is sardonic, and that this quality arises out of the special stress of mind under which the work was composed, then it is still possible that the term 'irony' might be of use in the description of a more normal condition of the same mind. The sardonic, that is to say, might presuppose the ironic. This is only true, however, if we abandon

the special definition of irony which has been quoted; and this is
legitimate because that definition has a special application to
literature, being, in fact, the definition of a *genre*. But there is a
wider connotation of the word which implies the general sentiment of mockery; and from this sense Swift can hardly be
exempted. It would not generally be considered necessary so to
exempt him; irony is a fashionable mode, and has to-day an esteem
such as it also had in the eighteenth century. It is in this sense the
hall-mark of an insincere age; and though Swift is the last man to
be accused of a lack of sincerity, yet this provocative display of
indirectness is the counterpart of a certain defect of character.
This we may illustrate by reference to another age, when a sensitive nature might more honestly express its consciousness of this
defect. The following extract is from Renan's intimate account of
the life of his sister Henriette — a work surcharged with a kind
of beauty totally foreign to the previous century:

'Sa religion du vrai ne souffrait pas la moindre note discordante.
Un trait qui la blessa dans mes écrits fut un sentiment d'ironie
qui m'obsédait et que je mêlais aux meilleures choses. Je n'avais
jamais souffert, et je trouvais dans le sourire discret, provoqué par
la faiblesse ou la vanité de l'homme, une certaine philosophie.
Cette habitude la blessait, et je la lui sacrifiai peu à peu. Main-
tenant je reconnais combien elle avait raison. Les bons doivent
être simplement bons; toute pointe de moquerie implique un
reste de vanité et de défi personnel qu'on finit par trouver de
mauvais goût.'

Any ironic attitude implies a sense of superiority, which is
perhaps the same thing as the 'exclusiveness' of Mr. Fowler's
definition. And though a sense of superiority may be well grounded
in fact, it seldom takes the form of 'ironic philosophy' without involving the possessor of it in a certain vulgarity of sentiment
hardly consistent with the right kind of superiority. Renan
achieved the right kind precisely for the reason for which his
detractors despise him. He came to recognize, as he so frankly
states in this passage which we have quoted, that the good is
simply good, and is not enhanced by oblique or indirect expression. Perhaps in his intimate moods even Swift recognized something of this — the *Journal to Stella* is the best evidence of certain
moments of simple goodness; but his general lack of equanimity
and directness is bound up with a certain weakness in his character
which he was continually betraying. This is the unmeasured

vanity of his ambitions and the insistent rancour of his disappointment:

'My greatest misery', he wrote to Bolingbroke in 1729, 'is recollecting the scene of twenty years past, and then all of a sudden dropping into the present. I remember, when I was a little boy, I felt a great fish at the end of my line which I drew up almost on the ground, but it dropped in, and the disappointment vexes me to this very day, and I believe it was the type of all my future disappointments.'

We might have sympathized more fully if the fish had been a less appropriate metaphor; but it is the type of the very worldly success which Swift always had in mind. Wealth was the immediate object of his desire, and if he could not obtain it by direct means he would have its equivalent in another way:

'All my endeavours from a boy, to distinguish myself, were only for want of a great title and fortune, that I might be used like a Lord by those who have an opinion of my parts — whether right or wrong, it is no great matter, and so the reputation of wit or great learning does the office of a blue ribbon, or a coach and six horses.'

This is from a letter to Pope, and there is no reason to doubt the essential truth of the confession. Even this prostitution of his talents might in a sense be condoned if we could be sure that success would have brought him the happiness he longed for; but the innate parsimony of his character forbids that assumption.

There is no evidence to show that Swift entered the Church with any other purpose than the calculating purpose of a careerist. Once committed to that way of life, he seems to have decided that what he could not gain by the talents appropriate to his calling (which he did not possess) he might gain by political intrigue. But at the height of his influence — and no man ever went higher — he found himself waiting in vain for his reward and a bishopric. The dilatoriness of his patrons need not, perhaps, be ascribed to the highest motives — it may be that Swift had made himself too useful a tool to be dispensed with, or too dangerous a one to be released. But it is also conceivable that Harley and Bolingbroke had more judgement than they were credited with, and more respect for the Church; and that they hesitated to confer the dignity of a see on one whose character they knew too well. They, or other advisers of the Queen, may have considered that the author of the *Tale of a Tub*, though endowed with wit, was lacking in learning.

And this is the plain truth, if by learning we mean the appropriate mind.

Swift could write quizzically of Dr. George Berkeley, as he did in an otherwise kindly letter of recommendation to Lord Carteret; but if he had had more of Berkeley's humility he might have had some of his success. Berkeley is one of the contrasts that best illuminate Swift; for Berkeley had qualities of imagination and speculative intelligence which were totally wanting in the genius of Swift. It was this lack which justified to some extent Dryden's observation, which I shall deal with presently, that Swift was no poet. Whether we consider him as a writer or as a prospective bishop, this is a drastic limitation. It is not that it implies a lack of intellectual energy (Swift was inventive enough), but it does qualify the nature of that energy, making it operative on a lower plane and with a narrower range. The poet, who in this sense is not confined to verse, sees beyond his 'separate fantasy'; he perceives the 'clear universe of things around', and from this perception he derives a sense of sublimity and an eloquence to which Swift was a total stranger.

There is a very significant passage, in one of the letters to Pope which has already been quoted, in which Swift owns La Rochefoucauld as his 'favourite' — 'because I found my whole character in him'. This is not the only reference to La Rochefoucauld in Swift's correspondence; and from another passage it would seem that he had made Vanessa read his favourite. This direct connection is worth emphasizing; for, though Swift pretended to base his view of human nature on his own observations, it is possible that his mortification was soothed by no other influence so agreeable as the disconsolate philosophy of the French maxim-writer — a philosophy which, like Swift's, was derived from the limited field of Court intrigues and politics rather than from the world at large. Now La Rochefoucauld has his perfect foil and critic in Vauvenargues; and what Vauvenargues wrote of La Rochefoucauld very perfectly fits the case of Swift:

'Le duc de La Rochefoucauld a saisi admirablement le côté faible de l'esprit humain; peut-être n'en a-t-il pas ignoré la force; peut-être n'a-t-il contesté le mérite de tant d'actions éblouissantes, que pour démasquer la fausse sagesse. Quelles qu'aient été ses intentions, l'effet m'en parait pernicieux; son livre, rempli d'invectives contre l'hypocrisie, détourne, encore aujourd'hui, les hommes de la vertu, en leur persuadant qu'il n'y en a point de véritable.'

This is merely an introduction to a note in which Vauvenargues does full justice to the real greatness of La Rochefoucauld. He does, however, add a qualification relating to the latter's style: La Rochefoucauld 'n'était pas peintre, talent sans lequel il est bien difficile d'être éloquent' — and with Vauvenargues, elegance is the sign of true greatness (*grandeur d'âme*). It is to Vauvenargues's very character, indeed, that we should go for a further contrast; for Vauvenargues in his unhappy life suffered disappointments quite comparable with Swift's, but from his state there issued one of the most equable and courageous views of life that has ever found expression. Vauvenargues tried to show that the *grandeur d'âme* which was for him the greatest of realities was something as natural as bodily health: it was the power to be superior to one's misfortune and the power to control other men by virtue of one's patience, deeds, or counsels. The error of Swift's philosophy lies in the uniformity and perfection of its pessimism; and the best answer to the misanthropy of *Gulliver* is to be found in these lines of Vauvenargues:

'Les inégalités de la vertu, les faiblesses qui l'accompagnent, les vices qui flétrissent les plus belles vies, ces défauts inséparables de notre nature, mêlée si manifestement de grandeur et de petitesse, n'en détruisent pas les perfections. Ceux qui veulent que les hommes soient tout bons ou tout méchants, absolument grands ou petits, ne connaissent pas la nature. Tout est mélangé dans les hommes; tout y est limité; et le vice même y a ses bornes.'

Style is the touchstone of all these matters; and though Swift's style cannot be sufficiently praised for its vigour, clarity, and economy, yet it must be recognized that here too Swift has the limitations that belong to his character. Johnson was again percipient in a matter of technique. 'For purposes merely didactic' this style is the best of all. 'But against that inattention by which known truths are suffered to lie neglected it makes no provision; it instructs, but it does not persuade.' Vauvenargues would say it lacks eloquence — not that eloquence of words, which is better called invective, and in which Swift excelled, but the eloquence of ideas and sentiments. In this sense 'l'éloquence vaut mieux que le savoir'.

'Tout ce qu'on a jamais dit du prix de l'éloquence n'en est qu'une faible expression. Elle donne la vie à tout: dans les sciences, dans les affaires, dans la conversation, dans la composition, dans la recherche même des plaisirs, rien ne peut réussir sans elle. Elle se joue des passions des hommes, les émeut, les calme, les pousse, et les détermine à son gré : tout cède à son voix; elle seule enfin est capable de se célébrer dignement.'

Eloquence in this sense is mind's highest reach and widest conquest. It is the creative energy of life itself, manifested on those frontiers which we call variously religion, philosophy, and poetry. But in all these forms eloquence was denied to Swift; and without eloquence he was at the mercy of his passions. For a time he could temporize, and so give us *Gulliver's Travels*; but the disruptive forces could not for ever be held in check; and then, as Thackeray said, 'thinking of him is like thinking of an empire falling'.

(iii)

That the author of *A Tale of a Tub* and *Gulliver's Travels* should also be a considerable poet upsets the neat classifications of the literary historian; and even his contemporaries were not willing to admit his claim. On this subject every one knows Dryden's famous remark, repeated by Johnson: 'Cousin Swift, you will never be a poet.' This was justly inspired by a certain Pindaric Ode written to the 'Athenian Society', which begins in this strain:

> *As when the deluge first began to fall,*
> *That might ebb never to flow again,*
> *When this huge body's moisture was so great,*
> *It quite o'ercame the vital heat;*
> *That mountain which was highest, first of all*
> *Appear'd above the universal main,*
> *To bless the primitive sailor's weary sight;*
> *And 'twas perhaps Parnassus, if in height*
> *It be as great as 'tis in fame,*
> *And nigh to Heaven as is its name;*
> *So, after the inundation of a war,*
> *When Learning's little household did embark,*
> *With her world's fruitful system, in her sacred ark,*
> *At the first ebb of noise and fears,*
> *Philosophy's exalted head appears. . . .*

There is no sensible quickening of this pedestrian pace any where else in the Ode, which is long and desperately wearisome; there is not a single line with which a partisan of Swift could challenge Dryden's judgement. But the Ode was written by a young man of twenty-four; the Pindaric style was imposed upon him by the fashion of the time; and had he never written in another style, he would never have outlived Dryden's damnation.

But we cannot be sure that this side of Swift's genius is properly appreciated even now, with the whole bulk of his verse before us. That bulk is considerable (more than 1,000 pages of the Oxford edition edited by Mr. Harold Williams), and there is no doubt that Swift was a poet in his own estimation. In the estimation of others he has not fared so well. Goldsmith was willing to place him for poetic genius in the same rank as Milton, Dryden, and Pope; but the more representative estimate for the eighteenth century is that of Johnson:

'In the Poetical Works of Dr. Swift there is not much upon which the critick can exercise his powers. They are often humorous, almost always light, and have the qualities which recommend such compositions, easiness, and gaiety. They are, for the most part, what their author intended. The diction is correct, the numbers are smooth, and the rhymes exact. There seldom occurs a hard-laboured expression, or a redundant epithet; all his verses exemplify his own definition of a good style, they consist of *proper words in proper places*.'

The only critic who has since dared to qualify this Johnsonian estimate is Taine, whose nationality perhaps secured for him the necessary detachment. Taine, it is true, is still impeded by a certain presupposition about the nature of poetry: but who, among the critics of a romantic age, is free? 'Ce qui manque le plus à ses vers c'est la poésie. L'esprit positif ne peut ni l'aimer ni l'entendre; il n'y voit qu'une machine ou une mode, et ne l'emploie que par vanité ou convention. . . . Je ne me rappelle pas une seule ligne de lui qui indique un sentiment vrai de la nature; il n'apercevait dans les forêts que des bûches et dans les champs que des sacs de grain.' But if he could fall into this error (which we shall comment on presently) Taine could in return appreciate those aspects of genius which transcend academic distinctions, and cry out his admiration in these magnificent terms:

'Mais, dans les sujets prosaïques, quelle vérité et quelle force! Comme cette mâle nudité rabaisse l'élégance cherchée et la poésie artificielle d'Addison et de Pope! Jamais d'épithètes; il laisse sa pensée telle qu'elle est, l'estimant pour elle-même et pour elle seule, n'ayant besoin ni d'ornements, ni de préparations, ni d'allongements, élevé au-dessus des procédés métier, des conventions d'école, de la vanité rimailleur, des difficultés de l'art, maître de son sujet et de lui-même. Cette simplicité et ce naturel étonnent en des vers. Ici, comme ailleurs, son originalité est entière et son génie créateur; il dépasse son siècle classique et timide; il s'asservit la forme, il la brise, il y ose tout dire, il ne lui épargne aucune crudité. Reconaissez la grandeur dans cette invention et dans cette audace; celui-là seul est un homme supérieur qui trouve tout et ne copie rien.'

Magnificent? But not altogether true. For this picture of a giant breaking through all bonds, scorning all obstructions, master of his subject and of himself, is a romantic half-truth. In reality, before he can be master of himself and of his subject this giant must forge new chains. He cannot break an old form without finding himself under the necessity of creating a new one; and the grandeur and audacity of the poet Swift lies not in his lack of all convention, but in his discovery of his own. He found the Pindaric style uncongenial to the substance of his inspiration; for him it had no meaning and no sympathetic appeal. If he had meekly accepted Dryden's reproof he would never have written another verse. But he realized that although he might not be a poet in Dryden's sense, the poetry within him was too real to be refused expression.

Dryden died when Swift was only thirty-three. It is just possible that he may have seen 'Mrs. Frances Harris's Petition', which is one of the first of Swift's poems in an original manner. If so, it is difficult to believe that in his wise tolerance he would not have recognized its kinship with Chaucer, whom he praised so greatly. Mrs. Harris is as vivid as the Wife of Bath, and the verses in which she lives are a miracle of humorous invention. It must be admitted that we never find in Swift that 'rude sweetness of a Scotch tune' which Dryden rather grudgingly allowed to Chaucer, but in the poems which we would make the basis of an apology for him, the very accents of human speech are imposed upon the rhythm, giving it an actuality in which mere sweetness is transcended. It is doubtful whether Dryden would have admitted this quality into his poetic code, for with all his tolerance he reverted always to certain abstract categories against which he judged present performances. Of his English predecessors he was always ready to insist 'the times were ignorant in which they lived'. Of much of Shakespeare that we habitually admire, he would remark: 'What a pudder is here kept in raising the expression of trifling thoughts.'

Dryden's is the finest expression in English criticism of what we may term a traditional classicism. But there is another type of classicism, not necessarily an alternative type, which must be briefly delineated before we can justify Swift's right to the name of poet. We would call it a natural classicism, and it arises precisely from that effort to find new forms to match new substances for which Swift is notable. Dryden's abstract categories of verse were based on the best classical models; the problem was, how to mould our rough island speech into these golden numbers. But it is possible to conceive another kind of abstraction which is based on the inherent qualities of the poetic substance: the form is inherent in the substance, and the problem is one of elucidation.

There is no evidence that Swift ever posed the problem in this categorical manner, but the moral of 'The Battle of the Books', if it has one, tends in this direction. Ancient and Modern are terms conveying no necessary virtue; all alike must be submitted to a clear judgement, and the same judgement prevails in the act of composition. It is the presence of judgement, with the purpose of fitting form to substance, that determines the classical quality of the poet's work. The first instructions which Swift gives to 'a young beginner' in that ironic masterpiece, 'On Poetry — a Rhapsody', are meant seriously enough:

> *Consult yourself; and if you find*
> *A powerful impulse urge your mind,*
> *Impartial judge within your breast*
> *What subject you can manage best;*
> *Whether your genius most inclines*
> *To satire, praise, or humorous lines,*
> *To elegies in mournful tone,*
> *Or prologue sent from hand unknown.*
> *Then, rising with Aurora's light,*
> *The Muse invoked, sit down to write;*
> *Blot out, correct, insert, refine,*
> *Enlarge, diminish, interline;*
> *Be mindful, when invention fails,*
> *To scratch your head, and bite your nails.*

There can be no doubt that Swift found in himself a powerful impulse to write verse, and though at first, as we have seen, he attempted a form not suited to his genius, he soon abandoned these artificial exercises. The forms that he then adopted he made essentially his own. In his introduction to the essay which he devoted to Swift's verse[1] the late Dr. Elrington Ball remarked that 'no exact prototype is to be found for Swift's style of versification. It has been described as Hudibrastic, but the influence of Samuel Butler was only partial. In its construction Swift laid under contribution all classes of metrical composition from the Elizabethan age to his own, ephemeral songs and ballads no less than the standard writings of poets and dramatists.' We have already quoted Johnson's testimony to the technical perfection of Swift's verse, and indeed that has never been in question. It is the substance which we are called upon to justify.

Goldsmith said that Swift was the first poet who dared to describe nature as it is with all its deformities, and to give exact expression to a turn of thought alike dry, sarcastic, and severe. It was for this courage that he placed him in the same rank as Milton, Dryden, and Pope. This shows that the poet of 'The Deserted Village' had none of the prejudices about the nature of poetry which have distinguished many other poets and critics in the presence of Swift's verse. The assumption of such people is that poetry connotes but one half of life — things of beauty, sentiments of pleasure, innocence of experience. This is the attitude represented by *The Golden Treasury*, a justly famous anthology which has nevertheless done more to prevent a catholic appreciation of English poetry than any other single book or influence. Its sub-title 'Of the best Songs and Lyrical Poems' is always ignored; 'Lyrical' is silently equated with 'poetical'. There is an ironic justice in the fact that the only poem in the volume which reflects in any realistic manner the darker aspects of life should contain the lines:

> *Make no deep scrutiny*
> *Into her mutiny.*

But that is just what Swift was bent on doing. His whole life was one long mutiny — mutiny against the darkness of fate, the injustice of men, the baseness of our natural instincts, the indignity of our bodily functions — and his work is a deep scrutiny into these depths. It is possible to say that Swift's reaction to life was morbid. Mr. Ellis Roberts once expressed this point of view in an

[1] F. Elrington Ball, Litt.D., *Swift's Verse*, An Essay (London, Murray, 1929).

interesting essay which he published with a selection of Swift's poems.[1] He said:

'In this matter Swift exhibits all the signs of an enormous neurasthenia. To the neurasthenic anything which comes regularly and in routine is liable to become intolerable. Not all of life, fortunately, will so change its character. Different sufferers will become victims of different fears. . . . With Swift it was, at last, always this one thing. The boudoir, the closet, the double bed . . . his fancy only has to stray to one of them — and it strayed far too often — and he writhes helpless, indignant, outraged, in pangs which make him for ever of the company of those artists who pace, like the damned souls whom Vathek saw on the fiery and reverberating pavements of hell, each with his hand over his heart, and each with a heart of burning flame.'

Mr. Roberts in another place in his essay says of Swift that 'he does not delight in filth, as Rabelais: nor has he the curiosity, intellectual, sombre, enragedly humorous, into sexual life which marks Mr. James Joyce's work; Swift's attitude is one of plain, simple, immediate reaction'. Both these statements are true in intention, and so far illuminating; their fault is that they conjure up, in a slight degree, the romantic giant of Taine's invention. They do not, that is to say, sufficiently convey the cool deliberateness of Swift's pen. The man who wrote 'A Beautiful Young Nymph Going to Bed', 'The Progress of Marriage', 'The Lady's Dressing Room', 'Strephon and Chloe', and other such grim pieces was certainly indignant, but he was not helpless. He was always, in Taine's words, 'maître de son sujet et de lui-même.' If he had a tendency to be neurasthenic (and what man of sensibility is free from it?), then it is more than likely that in his poetry he purged himself of this anguish. But is it possible, the reader of *The Golden Treasury* may ask, to dignify with the name of poetry such dross of a diseased sensibility?

To this question we must answer, that the relations of art to life are so intricate that they do not permit of a neat separation into categories. It is impossible to define art by its substance; it is impossible to define it by its form. All we can say is that substance determines form, and that if from the substance we can proceed to the form, then the work of art is in being. The power needed

---

[1] Jonathan Swift, D.D., *Miscellaneous Poems*, edited by R. Ellis Roberts; decorated with Engravings on Wood, by Robert Gibbings (The Golden Cockerel Press, 1928).

to pass from substance to form, from matter to essence, is the specific creative impulse, an intense awareness of sensibility in the individual. The direction of this power is arbitrary; that is to say, it depends on the particular environment or constitution of the individual, and one might as well complain of the varieties of colour given by the light of the sun, as of the varieties of art reflected by the mind of man.

In Defence of Shelley[1]

(i)

Shelley has always had his enemies. For the most part they have been what we might call political enemies. Caring little for literature as such, these critics of the poet have fastened on his social and ethical ideas and have seen in them a subversive influence to be opposed with all powers of law and tradition. With such critics we are not really concerned; they no longer count in the controversy, for Shelley has been universally acknowledged as a poet, and his poetry is part of our culture. To dethrone Shelley it is no longer sufficient to prove his atheism or his anarchism, or any other alleged form of intellectual perversion; the critic must destroy his reputation as a poet, trusting that then he will silently disappear from our Parnassus carrying with him his dangerous load of mischief.

A frontal attack on that poetry would not be very effective. You may say that this poem or that poem is bad, but however many reasons you bring forward to support your opinion, an opinion and a personal opinion it remains. Your audience will simply register their disagreement, and continue to admire the poetry in their own way. But if somehow you can imply that it is rather bad form to admire Shelley's poetry, that it is the mark of an inferior taste, of muddled thought and vulgar sensibility, then you will set up a sort of fashionable inhibition far more powerful in its effect and far wider in its range. People will not like Shelley's poetry because they will not read it. His reputation will die of neglect.

The first necessity, therefore, will be a position of moral and intellectual superiority; a consequent air of condescension. Coleridge first suggested these tactics, but with the safeguard of his infinite humility and understanding:

---

[1] *In Defence of Shelley and Other Essays* (London, 1936), with later additions.

138

'I think as highly of Shelley's genius — yea, and of his *heart* — as you can do. Soon after he left Oxford, he went to the lakes, poor fellow! and with some wish, I have understood, to see me; but I was absent, and Southey received him instead. Now — the very reverse of what would have been the case in ninety-nine instances of a hundred — I *might* have been of use to him, and Southey could not; for I should have sympathised with his poetics, metaphysical reveries, and the very word metaphysics is an abomination to Southey, and Shelley would have felt that I understood him. His discussions — tending towards atheism of a certain sort — would not have scared *me*; for *me* it would have been a semi-transparent larva, soon to be sloughed, and through which I should have seen the true *imago* — the final metamorphosis. Besides, I have ever thought that sort of atheism the next best religion to Christianity; nor does the better faith I have learnt from Paul and John interfere with the cordial reverence I feel for Benedict Spinoza.'[1]

There is a generosity about Coleridge's sympathy which is very disarming; but there is also a fatal quality of pity. There is an assumption that Shelley was weak, or stumbling, or even blind, and that he, Coleridge, could be *of some use* to him. But this, as we shall see, is an entirely gratuitous assumption. Such as were Shelley's opinions at this time (in 1815) they were opinions honestly arrived at, and held by the poet with no essential variations to the day of his death.

It is difficult to find any excuses for the insufferable superiority of Matthew Arnold. His essay on Shelley, a review of Dowden's *Life*, is even from a literary point of view about as poor a piece of work as Arnold ever perpetrated. Its very style is infected with prejudice and disdain. In matter it is little more than a summary of Dowden's volumes, ending with that sublime sneer: *What a set!* Arnold, we are made to feel, had formed an ideal image of Shelley, a Shelley suggested by Hogg's description of the poet which Arnold had written down the first time he read it, and had always borne in his mind: 'Nor was the moral expression less beautiful than the intellectual; for there was a softness, a delicacy, a gentle-

[1] This is quoted from a letter of Coleridge's by Hogg (*Life*, ch. xiv). The same gist is given in a conversation with Coleridge recorded by J. H. Frere (see the Nonesuch *Coleridge*, p. 481). 'Shelley was a man of great power as a poet, and could he only have had some plane whereon to stand, and look down upon his own mind, he would have succeeded. There are flashes of the true spirit to be met with in his works. Poor Shelley, it is a pity I often think that I never met with him. I could have done him good . . .' etc.

ness, and especially (though this may surprise many) that air of profound religious veneration that characterizes the best works and chiefly the frescoes (and into these they infused their whole souls) of the great masters of Florence and of Rome.' Dowden, in his blind and blundering way, had shattered this image — had forced upon us 'much in him which is ridiculous and odious'. The image, Arnold tried to persuade himself, still subsisted; but 'with many a scar and stain; never again will it have the same pureness and beauty which it had formerly'. In the bitterness of his disillusion Arnold resorts to strong words — words whose force is not mitigated by their foreignness. 'It is a sore trial for our love of Shelley. What a set! what a world! is the exclamation that breaks from us as we come to an end of this history of "the occurrences of Shelley's private life". I used the French word *bête* for a letter of Shelley's; for the world in which we find him I can only use another French word, *sale*.'

Such righteous indignation sounds merely comical today, but we have no reason to doubt its sincerity. To recover the background of moral snobbery from which it proceeded would need a considerable effort of imagination; and it would be an effort wasted. Arnold, to do him justice, did not let his moral prejudice altogether obliterate his literary judgement. In the essay from which I have quoted, he excuses himself from dealing with Shelley's poetry for want of space — warning us, however, that the poetry would not get off unscathed. 'Let no one suppose that a want of humour and a self-delusion such as Shelley's have no effect upon a man's poetry. The man Shelley, in very truth, is not entirely sane, and Shelley's poetry is not entirely sane either.' And then he ends by repeating, from his essay on Byron, that trumpery phrase of which he was evidently so proud, about the beautiful and ineffectual angel 'beating in the void his luminous wings in vain'.

I have said that we find Arnold's attitude comical today; but perhaps I should have said that we find the expression he gave to his attitude comical. For if we were all agreed that the whole pother raised by Arnold could now be dismissed as one of the minor absurdities of the Victorian age, there would be no need for this essay in defence of Shelley. But Arnold's attitude has been repeated in our time by no less a critic than Mr. T. S. Eliot, in a lecture given at Harvard University in 1933.[1] In Mr. Eliot's

[1] *The Use of Poetry and the Use of Criticism* (London, Faber, 1933), 87–102.

case we shall find that the overt emphasis is not so much on the poet's morals, as on his ideas. Naturally the ideas cannot be separated from the morals, nor either from the poetry; but, before a modern audience, a master of critical strategy could not fail to concentrate his attack on the ideas.

Mr. Eliot's main charge against Shelley is one of intellectual incoherence. Incidentally he reveals a pretty strong distaste for the poet's personality, which is perhaps a logical consequence of the main charge. At the risk of some distortion I must give a summary of the whole indictment. 'The ideas of Shelley', Mr. Eliot begins, 'seem to me always to be ideas of adolescence. . . . And an enthusiasm for Shelley seems to me also to be an affair of adolescence. . . . I find his ideas repellent; and the difficulty of separating Shelley from his ideas and beliefs is still greater than with Wordsworth. And the biographical interest which Shelley has always excited makes it difficult to read the poetry without remembering the man; and the man was humourless, pedantic, self-centred, and sometimes almost a blackguard. Except for an occasional flash of shrewd sense, when he is speaking of someone else and not concerned with his own affairs or with fine writing, his letters are insufferably dull.' So far the items in the charge are almost the same as Arnold's, only a little more restrained in formulation. But after a page or so of concessions, Mr. Eliot returns to his main point: 'But some of Shelley's views I positively dislike, and that hampers my enjoyment of the poems in which they occur; and others seem to me so puerile that I cannot enjoy the poems in which they occur.' This leads to a discussion of the now famous problem of Belief and Poetry, and to the conclusion, in respect of Shelley, that 'when the doctrine, theory, belief or "view of life" presented in a poem is one which the mind of the reader can accept as coherent, mature, and founded on the facts of experience, it interposes no obstacle to the reader's enjoyment, whether it be one that he accept or deny, approve or deprecate. When it is one which the reader rejects as childish or feeble, it may, for a reader of well-developed mind, set up an almost complete check. . . . I can only regret that Shelley did not live to put his poetic gifts, which were certainly of the first order, at the service of more tenable beliefs — which need not have been, for my purposes, beliefs more acceptable to me.'

I propose, by way of answering this general charge against Shelley, to establish two points: the maturity and permanent worth of his best poetry, and the irrelevance of that mare's-nest of Belief, first introduced into the discussion of poetry by Dr. I. A. Richards. Incidentally I shall suggest that Shelley's ideas do not deserve the scorn heaped upon them by Mr. Eliot, whose attitude, in common with Coleridge's and Arnold's, is based on simpler if obscurer psychological reactions. In these reactions more poets and perhaps greater poets than Shelley are involved — Goethe, for example, of whom Mr. Eliot writes: 'it is perhaps truer to say that he dabbled in both philosophy and poetry and made no great success of either.' It will be found, I fancy, that it is the nature of the poet that is involved — not the actual recognition or definition of poetry itself in specific instances. When beliefs do not enter into the question — as in the case of Landor or of Keats — then I think Mr. Eliot and I would find a complete measure of agreement.

(ii)

Obviously my first concern must be to vindicate the high value of Shelley's poetry. It is curious that all these detractors of the poetry make vague but generous gestures of acceptance which are at variance with their detailed statements. To Coleridge Shelley is 'a man of great power as a poet'; Arnold speaks of 'the charm of the man's writings — of Shelley's poetry. It is his poetry, above everything else, which for many people establishes that he is an angel.' As for Mr. Eliot, though he confesses that he never opens the volume of his poems 'simply because I want to read poetry, but only with some special reason for reference', yet, as we have seen, Shelley's poetic gifts 'were certainly of the first order'. Not a critical judgement, but some moral asceticism, would seem to be the basis of Mr. Eliot's disdain. He does, it is true, accuse Shelley of 'a good deal which is just bad jingling', but he admits that *The Triumph of Life*, though unfinished, is a great poem. He admits to liking the last stanza of *Prometheus Unbound*. But this is about as far as his direct statements about the poetry go; for the rest, he is 'thoroughly gravelled', not by the poems themselves, but by the 'shabby' ideas expressed in them.[1]

At first Shelley's own attitude towards poetry as an art, and

[1] Under the influence of Leone Vivante, Mr. Eliot has now 'a new and more sympathetic appreciation' of Shelley: see his Preface to Signor Vivante's *English Poetry* (London, Faber, 1950). But this must not be taken as an approval of Shelley's general philosophy, but merely of 'recurrent insights which turn up again and again in Shelley's poetry'.

towards his own poetry in particular, seems to be decidedly treacherous. As early as 1813, when engaged on his first considerable poem, *Queen Mab*, we find him taking up an attitude which implies a certain contempt for the formal aspects of poetry. At the same time, from the very beginning, what we might in our modern fashion call an indifference to pure poetry is combined with what we would least expect — an avoidance of didactic poetry. Writing to Hogg in the year mentioned, Shelley says: 'My poems will, I fear, little stand the criticism even of friendship; some of the latter ones have the merit of conveying a meaning in every word, and all are faithful pictures of my feelings at the time of writing them. But they are, in a great measure, abrupt and obscure — all breathing hatred of despotism and bigotry; but, I think, not too openly for publication. One fault they are indisputably exempt from, that of being a volume of fashionable literature.' This would seem to be a fair confession of didacticism, but a few weeks later, writing to the same correspondent, he makes a much more positive statement to the contrary effect: '*Queen Mab* will be in ten cantos, and will contain about twenty-eight hundred lines; the other poems contain probably as much more. The notes to *Queen Mab* will be long and philosophical; I shall take that opportunity, which I judge to be a safe one, of submitting for public discussion principles of reformation, which I decline to do syllogistically in the poem. A poem very didactic is, I think, very stupid.' This distinction between poetry which is philosophical and yet at the same time not didactic deserves more examination than it has been given by critics of Shelley; it is important for our conception of Shelley's life and personality, as well as for any exact judgement on his poetry. Considering the strength of Shelley's moral and political views, it is a great proof of his instinctive sense of the limits of the art that he never for a moment thought of using poetry as an instrument of propaganda. Even as late as 1819 he could write (in a letter to Peacock): 'I consider poetry very subordinate to moral and political science, and if I were well, certainly I would aspire to the latter, for I can conceive a great work, embodying the discoveries of all ages, and harmonizing the contending creeds by which mankind have been ruled.' And this, in spite of the intervening *Defence of Poetry* in which he deepened and yet clarified his philosophy, remained his feeling to the end; for in his last letter to Peacock, written in the year of his death, he confesses 'I wish I had something better to do than furnish this jingling food for the hunger of oblivion, called verse, but I have not; and since you give me no encouragement about India I cannot hope to have'. In a footnote Peacock informs us that Shelley had expressed a desire to be employed politically at the court of a native prince.

In his last years in Italy Shelley used to wear a ring inscribed with the motto: *Il buon tempo verrà* — The good time will come; or, as he himself interpreted it: 'There is a tide both in public and in private affairs, which awaits both men and nations.' Shelley was by nature an optimist. During his short life he had more than a normal share of suffering, and often expressed his disillusionment with mankind. But in his political philosophy he remained an optimist, and his poetry is inspired by the intensest faith in life.

In this respect he stood apart from most of his fellow romantics. Romantic philosophy, as expressed at its source by Schelling, and as interpreted in England by our greatest romantic philosopher, Samuel Taylor Coleridge, was not optimistic. It was deeply tinged by that reaction to the contemplation of human existence which takes the form of dread or anxiety, and from it developed, during the course of the nineteenth century, the two pessimistic creeds of nihilism and existentialism. Shelley was untouched by this turbid stream of thought. He knew Coleridge and had read even some of his prose works. He possessed some of the works of Kant, though there is no evidence to show that he had ever read them. There is no need, however, to pursue such negative evidence, for Shelley's real interests are not in doubt. His mind was fed, if not formed, by Plato among the ancients and by Godwin among his contemporaries. It was reinforced, as time went on, by the Neo-Platonists, by Bacon, Hume, Berkeley, Spinoza, and above all by Rousseau, whose name he held sacred, whose imagination had, he said, 'divine beauty', and whom he was to make the central figure in his last poem. All these thinkers contributed in some degree to that blend of idealism and rationalism which makes up Shelley's philosophy.

We must remember that Shelley's life only lasted thirty years. His mind developed precociously, but from his school-days until 1815, that is to say, until his twenty-third year, it merely absorbed and reflected the ideas of others — notably those of William Godwin. The decisive change that came about in 1815 was due, no doubt, to the accumulation of emotional and financial worries during the previous twelve months. Shelley was finding the world a tougher place than Godwin had led him to expect it to be; and incidentally Godwin himself with his insatiable demands for financial aid was one of the agents of disillusion. But the greatest agency in this change in Shelley had been the passionate experiences of that year: his desertion of Harriet, his love for and elopement with Mary Godwin, and all the melancholy consequences of that defiance of social conventions. Life itself was in doubt, for in the Spring of 1815 a physician had told Shelley that he was dying rapidly of consumption; abscesses had formed in his lungs and he suffered acute spasms. But relief was at hand. At the beginning of this same year Shelley's grandfather had died, and Shelley's financial worries suddenly came to an end. In the calm that succeeded the storm of 1814, and with the security provided by a settlement with his father, Shelley was able to retreat into solitude, and in this solitude not only was his health restored, but he succeeded in coming to an intellectual settlement with himself. The immediate result was *Alastor, or the Spirit of Solitude*, a poem in which Shelley's original philosophy first makes a tentative appearance. I say 'tentative' because the philosophy as such is clothed in allegory, and Shelley himself felt bound to explain the poem in a Preface. He draws a contrast between those 'unseeing multitudes' who are selfish, blind, torpid, morally dead, and the 'adventurous genius' who is 'led forth by an imagination inflamed and purified through familiarity with all that is excellent and majestic, to the contemplation of the universe'. This genius imagines to himself a Being or Power, all wonderful, wise and beautiful. 'He seeks in vain for a prototype of his conception. Blasted by his disappointment, he descends to an untimely grave.'

Alastor is not a very optimistic poem, you might conclude. But actually it is inspired by the strongest faith in the beauty and goodness of the universe, and in the love and joy which can be realised by communion with Nature.

> *By solemn vision, and bright silver dream,*
> *His infancy was nurtured. Every sight*
> *And sound from the vast earth and ambient air,*
> *Sent to his heart its choicest impulses.*
> *The fountains of divine philosophy*
> *Fled not his thirsting lips, and all of great,*
> *Or good, or lovely, which the sacred past*
> *In truth or fable consecrates, he felt*
> *And knew.*

It may be said that there is nothing very original about this philosophy, and indeed, *Alastor* was written under the immediate influence of Wordsworth's *Excursion*, which had been recently published. But there are original notes, not only in the verse, but also among the ideas expressed by the verse. A more precise formulation of these ideas is to be found in a series of moral and philosophical essays which belong to the same period as *Alastor*. These are important because they show that most of the ideas that were to be embodied in his later and greater poems, and in *A Defence of Poetry*, were already taking shape in Shelley's mind.

The critical slander which accuses Shelley of intellectual adolescence, muddled thinking and obscure writing can hardly be based on a reading of these essays. Although they suffer from their incompleteness, they are remarkable by-products of a few weeks' poetic activity in a man's twenty-fourth year. In so far as they are complete, they are acutely and logically reasoned; and even as fragments they must strike any unprejudiced reader as the expression of a curious and vital intelligence.

From the essay 'On Life' we may take a statement of Shelley's revised philosophical position from which he was never to depart. 'I confess', he says, 'that I am one of those who am unable to refuse my assent to the conclusions of those philosophers who assert that nothing exists but as it is perceived'; and he goes on to describe an 'intellectual system', whose main outlines he no doubt owed to Berkeley. I will quote the most significant paragraph:

'It is a decision against which our persuasions struggle, and we must be long convicted before we can be convinced that the solid universe of external things is "such stuff as dreams are made of". The shocking absurdities of the popular philosophy of mind and matter, its fatal consequences in morals, and their violent dogmatism concerning the source of all things, had early conducted me to materialism. This materialism is a seducing system to young and superficial minds. It allows its disciples to talk, and dispenses them from thinking. But I was discontented with such a view of things as it afforded; man is a being of such high aspirations, "looking both before and after", whose "thoughts wander through eternity", disclaiming alliance with transience and decay; incapable of imagining to himself annihilation; existing but in the future and the past; being, not what he is, but what he has been and shall be. Whatever may be his true and final destination, there is a spirit within him at enmity with nothingness and dissolution. This is the character of all life and being.... Such contemplations as these, materialism and the popular philosophy of mind and matter alike forbid; they are only consistent with the intellectual system.'

Alastor, according to Shelley's own Preface, was designed to show the dangers of an exclusive concentration on such an intellectual system. He had discovered that the intellectual faculties — the imagination, the functions of sense — 'have their respective requisitions on the sympathy of corresponding powers in other human beings'. And so arose Shelley's doctrine of sympathy or love, to take a central place in his philosophy. It is beautifully outlined in one of the prose fragments of 1815:

'*Thou* demandest what is love? It is that powerful attraction towards all that we conceive, or fear, or hope beyond ourselves, when we find within our own thoughts the chasm of an insufficient void, and seek to awaken in all things that are, a community with what we experience within ourselves. If we reason, we would be understood; if we imagine, we would that the airy children of our brain were born anew within another's; if we feel, we would that another's nerves should vibrate to our own, that the beams of their eyes should kindle at once and mix and melt into our own, that lips of motionless ice should not reply to lips quivering and burning with the heart's best blood. This is Love. This the bond and the sanction which connects not only man with man, but with everything which exists. We are born into the world, and there is something within us which, from the instant that we live, more and more thirsts after its likeness.'

This aspect of his philosophy was to receive its supreme expression in *Epipsychidion*, written at Pisa six years later:

> *True love in this differs from gold and clay,*
> *That to divide is not to take away.*
> *Love is like understanding, that grows bright,*
> *Gazing on many truths; 'tis like thy light,*
> *Imagination! which from earth and sky,*
> *And from the depths of human fantasy,*
> *As from a thousand prisms and mirrors, fills*
> *The Universe with glorious beams, and kills*
> *Error, the worm, with many a sun-like arrow*
> *Of its reverberated lightning....*[1]

[1] This quotation is repeated in a fuller context on p. 171 below.

147

Shelley's philosophy of love, which caused so much dismay in his lifetime, is still too unorthodox, and most people would say too impracticable, to be acceptable even now, when the science of human relations and the blinder drift of public manners have led to more tolerance of what is vulgarly known as 'free love'. But there is nothing vulgar about the philosophy expounded in *Epipsychidion*. The only comparable work, by which it was much influenced, is Plato's *Symposium*, and the one is as pure and noble in conception as the other. Shelley himself compared his poem to the *Vita Nuova* of Dante, and he suggested that both poems were 'sufficiently intelligible to a certain class of readers without a matter-of-fact history of the circumstances to which (they) relate'; and to a certain other class both poems must, he said, 'ever remain incomprehensible, from a defect of a common organ of perception for the ideas which (they) treat'. What Shelley meant by love in this poem is not in doubt — in his own words it is 'the bond and the sanction which connects, not only man with man, but with everything which exists'. But like Plato and Dante, Shelley was ready to insist that such love is not necessarily ethereal, but should be embodied in our human relationships.

> *We — are we not formed, as notes of music are,*
> *For one another, though dissimilar;*
> *Such difference without discord, as can make*
> *Those sweetest sounds, in which all spirits shake*
> *As trembling leaves in a continuous air?*

The poet, especially an original poet like Shelley, is always conscious of the limited effect of all his work. '*Prometheus* was never intended for more than five or six persons,' he wrote in a letter to Gisborne, and for a poet with 'a passion for reforming the world' this is a bitter realization. It would be an intolerable realization were there no compensations in prospect; and what is in prospect is a matter of faith — of faith in one's appeal to a jury 'impanelled by Time from the selectest of the wise of many generations'. It will be noticed that this jury is of the wise, and not merely of the sensitive; and Shelley uses the word deliberately. For whilst avoiding like the plague the didactic use of poetry, Shelley is far from that theory of pure poetry, which would exempt poetry from any useful effect whatsoever. Poetry might after all be an essential process in the great work of regenerating mankind

— a preparation of the mind for the seeds of moral and political science, which otherwise might fall on rocky ground. The image is not a very noble one, but there are one or two statements of Shelley's which will give it a full idealistic force: for example, this from the Preface to *Prometheus Unbound*: 'For my part I had rather be damned with Plato and Lord Bacon, than go to Heaven with Paley and Malthus. But it is a mistake to suppose that I dedicate my poetical compositions solely to the direct enforcement of reform, or that I consider them in any degree as containing a reasoned system on the theory of human life. Didactic poetry is my abhorrence; nothing can be equally well expressed in prose that is not tedious and supererogatory in verse. My purpose has hitherto been simply to familiarise the highly refined imagination of the more select classes of poetical readers with beautiful idealisms of moral excellence; aware that until the mind can love, and admire, and trust, and hope, and endure, reasoned principles of moral conduct are seeds cast upon the highway of life which the unconscious passenger tramples into dust, although they would bear the harvest of his happiness.'

In a cancelled passage from the Preface to *Adonais* Shelley introduces the notion of 'sympathy', which we may find useful: 'If I understand myself, I have written neither for profit nor for fame. I have employed my poetical compositions and publications simply as the instruments of that sympathy between myself and others which the ardent and unbounded love I cherished for my kind incited me to acquire.' But the most explicit statement of his aims comes in the *Defence of Poetry*, there given a generalization and philosophical dignity which make the essay the profoundest treatment of the subject in the English language. The essay opens with a distinction between reason and imagination which is the fundamental distinction for the whole of this question, and which is a proof, if any were required, of the precision with which Shelley used his terms. The two modes of mental action are distinguished as 'mind contemplating the relations borne by one thought to another, however produced', and as 'mind acting upon those thoughts so as to colour them with its own light, and composing from them, as from elements, other thoughts, each containing within itself the principle of its own integrity'. Reason is analysis, or 'the enumeration of quantities already known'; imagination is synthesis, or 'the perception of the value of those quantities, both separately and as a whole. Reason respects the differences, and imagination the similitudes of things. Reason is to the imagination as the instrument to the agent. . . .'

Poetry is then defined as the instrument of the imagination, as distinct from science, which is the instrument of the reason. But poetry acts in a way peculiar to itself; 'it awakens and enlarges the mind itself by rendering it the receptacle of a thousand unapprehended combinations of thought.' These combinations of thought are due to that principle of sympathy already referred to, which is not only the mode of action typical of poetry, but also of morals. This identification of poetry and morality must be dealt with separately, but for the moment we will keep to the poetic process, which is further defined as an enlargement of the circumference of the imagination 'by replenishing it with thoughts of every new delight, which have the power of attracting and assimilating to their own nature all other thoughts, and which form new intervals and interstices whose void forever craves fresh food. Poetry strengthens the faculty which is the organ of the moral nature of man, in the same manner as exercise strengthens a limb.'

This dynamical, this almost physical conception of poetry, is extended in other directions which show how closely Shelley observed the psychological nature of his own activity. The ranging, gathering, accumulative character of the poetic process is not its only function; the materials poetry attracts to itself must be controlled, and a desire is therefore engendered in the mind to reproduce and arrange these materials 'according to a certain rhythm and order which may be called the beautiful and the good'. But such rhythm and order can only be engendered in the unconscious mind. 'Poetry is not like reasoning, a power to be exerted according to the determination of the will. A man cannot say, "I will compose poetry". The greatest poet even cannot say it; for the mind in creation is as a fading coal, which some invisible influence, like an inconstant wind, awakens to transitory brightness; this power arises from within, like the colour of a flower which fades and changes as it is developed, and the conscious portions of our natures are unprophetic either of its approach or its departure.' Nevertheless, and this is an observation which a less scrupulous psychologist might have omitted, 'the frequent recurrence of the poetical power . . . may produce in the mind a habit of order and harmony correlative with its own nature and with its effects upon other minds.'

The *Defence of Poetry* is an uncompleted essay, and it would be unreasonable to complain that it leaves many problems of poetry undiscussed. We miss, in particular, Shelley's observations on the technique of poetry. In a sense he was singularly uninterested in the subject, being content to take over the prevailing diction, which was, indeed, the reformed diction of Coleridge and Wordsworth. But there is little evidence that he had their reforming zeal, and if it suited his purpose he was just as ready to take over the technique of Spenser or Milton. He refers to *Adonais* as 'a highly-wrought *piece of art*', which is curiously suggestive of the attitude against which Wordsworth had revolted. On the other hand, in the *Defence of Poetry* he admits innovation as a necessary principle in verse. 'An observation of the regular mode of the recurrence of harmony in the language of poetical minds, together with its relation to music, produced metre, or a certain system of traditional forms of harmony and language. Yet it is by no means essential that a poet should accommodate his language to this traditional form, so that harmony, which is its spirit, be observed. The practice is indeed convenient and popular, and to be preferred, especially in such composition as includes much action: but every great poet must inevitably innovate upon the example of his predecessors in the exact structure of his peculiar versification.' And what he meant by this last phrase he had explained on a previous page, in a passage which shows how innately sound his poetic practice was — being based, as all true poetry must be based, on the material qualities of language. 'Language, colour, form, and religious and civil habits of action, are all the instruments and materials of poetry. . . . But poetry in a more restricted sense expresses those arrangements of language, and especially metrical language, which are created by that imperial faculty, whose throne is curtained within the invisible nature of man. And this springs from the nature itself of language, which is a more direct representation of the actions and passions of our internal being, and is susceptible of more various and delicate combinations, than colour, form, or motion, and is more plastic and obedient to the control of that faculty of which it is the creation. For language is arbitrarily produced by the imagination, and has relation to thoughts alone; but all other materials, instruments, and conditions of art, have relations among each other, which limit and interpose between conception and expression.' He then contrasts poetry, in this respect, with the arts of sculpture, painting, and music, and concludes that such arts can never equal poetry as an expression of the immediacy of thought.

Such a clear perception of the nature of poetry does not necessarily imply an ability to put precept into practice, and since the precepts were a late product of his short life, we must be prepared for much immature prentice work. For Shelley began publishing whilst still a boy at school, and in spite of his hero Godwin's opinion that early authorship was detrimental to the cause of general happiness, during the rest of his life his productions were sent to the press with almost indecent haste. Shelley always had the itch to see himself in print, and as heir to a fortune, if not in actual possession of money, he could always find a ready publisher. His collected poems, in the standard Oxford edition, make a volume of a thousand pages. How much of this bulk Shelley himself would have suppressed it would be presumptuous to guess; but any true friend of Shelley would willingly unload half of it into oblivion, and even some proportion of the rest he would only keep, as Mr. Eliot keeps the lot, for reference. A decisive change came in the year 1816, a year in which Shelley wrote very little, in which his poetic faculty seemed to lie fallow, numbed by domestic anxieties — the hostility of the Westbrooks, the intransigence of Godwin, ill-health, the lack of money. At the end of that year came Harriet's suicide, from which he sought some relief in the concentration of composition — the result being *The Revolt of Islam*, a poem of 4,818 lines. There was concentration only in the act, not in the issue. To follow Shelley's development of his theme is like following the course of a mighty river, from mouth to source: at first everything is wide, even and aqueous, but as we proceed the stream narrows and the surface breaks, flowing with a more obvious force and music — an image perhaps suggested by the subject-matter of *The Revolt of Islam*. Shelley tells us in his Preface that his object was 'to enlist the harmony of metrical language, the ethereal combinations of the fancy, the rapid and subtle transitions of human passion, all those elements which essentially compose a Poem, in the cause of a liberal and comprehensive morality. . . . For this purpose I have chosen a story of human passion in its most universal character, diversified with moving and romantic adventures, and appealing, in contempt of all artificial opinions or institutions, to the common sympathies of every human breast. . . . The Poem therefore . . . is narrative, not didactic. It is a succession of pictures illustrating the growth and progress of individual mind aspiring after excellence, and devoted to the love of mankind. . . .' The very phrases — a succession of pictures, ethereal combinations of the fancy — do not promise a coherent form; and when Shelley further informs the reader that he has chosen the Spenserian stanza because he was enticed 'by the brilliancy and magnificence of sound which a mind that has been nourished upon musical thoughts can produce by a just and harmonious arrangement of the pauses of this measure', that reader should not be surprised to find a poem whose action is dissipated in incident, whose theme is lost in a jungle of imagery. We seem to drift aimlessly always in some kind of boat or bark, upon some torrent or flood; and it is only in the last line of the poem that we find a haven, uncertain of the way we have come, indifferent, after so much wandering, to our destiny:

> *Motionless resting on the lake awhile,*
> *I saw its marge of snow-bright mountains rear*
> *Their peaks aloft, I saw each radiant isle,*
> *And in the midst, afar, even like a sphere*
> *Hung in one hollow sky, did there appear*
> *The Temple of the Spirit; on the sound*
> *Which issued thence, drawn nearer and more near,*
> *Like the swift moon this glorious earth around,*
> *The charmed boat approached, and there its haven found.*

This last stanza is representative enough of all the five hundred odd which compose the poem; Shelley uses his measure with mastery, and where he fails, in comparison with Spenser, is not in the mere manipulation of words, but in their choice. Spenser was very particular about his words; even pedantic. Shelley confesses, in his Preface, to an indifference on this very point: 'Nor have I permitted any system relating to mere words to divert the attention of the reader, from whatever interest I may have succeeded in creating, to my own ingenuity in contriving to disgust them according to the rules of criticism. I have simply clothed my thoughts in what appeared to me the most obvious and appropriate language. A person familiar with nature, and with the most celebrated productions of the human mind, can scarcely err in following the instinct, with respect to selection of language, produced by that familiarity.' There is obviously some oblique reference here — perhaps to Wordsworth's Preface to his Poems published in 1815. But though Shelley is right, in so far as he is relying on the subconscious origination of appropriate language (according to the theory he was, as we have seen, to state explicitly in *A Defence of Poetry*), yet there is in this passage a certain uneasiness, a certain anticipation of criticism, which is a confession of self-criticism. In a letter replying to Godwin's criticism of the poem, Shelley says: 'The poem was produced by a series of thoughts which filled my mind with unbounded and sustained enthusiasm. I felt the precariousness of my life, and I engaged in this task, resolved to leave some record of myself. Much of what the volume contains was written with the same feeling — as real, though not so prophetic — as the communications of a dying man.' Shelley, we might say, always wrote with one eye on posterity and the other on his tomb; and the feverish haste entailed by such an attitude leads to qualities which the most sympathetic critic cannot excuse. There is not a single long composition of Shelley which does not suffer from prolixity, from lack of those most precious qualities of precision and objectivity. At the same time we must not blame Shelley for failing to express qualities which were not in his nature; certain human features and faculties are antithetical, and we are asking for a monster if we look for them all in the same personality. Shelley, as we shall see later, was not what the psychologists call 'a visual type'; he was a transcendentalist, for whom words are never sufficient for the vision they must express.

This question, the fundamental one for the appreciation of Shelley's poetry, had better be discussed in relation to a more considerable poem than *The Revolt of Islam*. If I dismiss *The Revolt of Islam*, it is not because I think it can be ignored; it is a poem of many individual beauties, and even if the whole is 'sick with excess of sweetness', there is throughout a spirit of intellectual energy which lifts it into significance, making it a part, if only a prelude, of Shelley's great achievement. That achievement, in its strictly poetic aspects, is represented by *Prometheus Unbound*, written little more than a year after *The Revolt of Islam*, by *Epipsychidion* and *Adonais*, written the year before his death, and by various shorter odes and lyrics, all written in the last four years of his life. These three groups have certain characteristics in common, and possibly they merge into one another; but they have qualities which are distinct enough to justify a separate classification.

In concentrating on these three groups we shall be neglecting

certain works of which perhaps *The Cenci* is the only one which
must be explained away — other notable poems, such as *The
Witch of Atlas*, *Hellas*, and *The Triumph of Life*, I regard as conforming in every way to the characteristics of one or other of the
typical poems mentioned. But *The Cenci* is a different matter.
Byron called it 'sad work', and if not for the same reason ('the
subject renders it so') I agree with this judgement of a friend and
contemporary of the poet. For Shelley it was an experiment —
an attempt to be objective, *sachlich*. But he was writing against
the grain of his personality, and knew it. 'Those writings which I
have hitherto published', he tells Leigh Hunt in a Dedicatory
Letter, 'have been little else than visions which impersonate my
own apprehensions of the beautiful and the just. I can also perceive in them the literary defects incidental to youth and im-
patience; they are dreams of what ought to be, or may be. The
drama which I now present to you is a sad reality. I lay aside the
presumptuous attitude of an instructor, and am content to paint,
with such colours as my own heart furnishes, that which has been.'
It was a brave gesture, but doomed to failure. Far from the subject being the cause of this failure, it is its very horror which
compels a certain dramatic vitality, and makes it even possible to
act the drama with some effect. But as poetry, both in the limited
sense as blank verse and in the general sense as the creation of
poetic character and atmosphere, it does not begin to be a great
tragedy. It is a pastiche of Elizabethan drama, of Webster in
particular, and as a form has no originality and lacks that 'something wholly new and relative to the age' which Shelley recognized
in *Don Juan* and longed to possess. Even at its most forceful the
verse is wooden, unnatural.

> *How comes this hair undone?*
> *Its wandering strings must be what blind me so,*
> *And yet I tied it fast. — O, horrible!*
> *The pavement sinks under my feet! The walls*
> *Spin round! I see a woman weeping there,*
> *And standing calm and motionless, whilst I*
> *Slide giddily as the world reels. . . . My God!*
> *The beautiful blue heaven is flecked with blood!*
> *The sunshine on the floor is black! The air*
> *Is changed to vapours such as the dead breathe*
> *In charnel pits! Pah! I am choked! There creeps*

155

A clinging, black contaminating mist
About me . . . 'tis substantial, heavy, thick,
I cannot pluck it from me, for it glues
My fingers and my limbs to one another,
And eats into my sinews, and dissolves
My flesh to a pollution, poisoning
The subtle, pure, and inmost spirit of life!
My God! I never knew what the mad felt
Before; for I am mad beyond all doubt!
(More wildly) *No, I am dead! These putrefying limbs*
Shut round and sepulchre the panting soul
Which would burst forth into the wandering air!

There is worse ranting in Elizabethan drama, even in Webster. But we have only to compare the speeches of Shelley's Beatrice with those of Shakespeare's Isabella to see the difference between a literary conception of character and the lively representation of a human being. However justified the conventions of art may be, they must never contradict the purpose of a particular art-form, and the purpose of drama is, as Shelley realized, fundamentally realistic; it depends on the possibility of the audience participating in the emotional life of the characters. But this will never be achieved by merely negative precautions. 'I have avoided with great care in writing this play the introduction of what is commonly called mere poetry. . . . I have written . . . without an over-fastidious and learned choice of words . . . the real language of men in general. . . .' Thus Shelley may protest his good intentions, but he is once again really apologizing for his impetuosity; and in stripping that impetuosity of its concordant imagery, he was merely reducing the quality without restraining the quantity of his mode of expression. He was being unnatural, and when he had written *Epipsychidion*, the most natural expression of his genius that he ever gave, he realized it. 'The *Epipsychidion*', he wrote to John Gisborne, 'is a mystery; as to real flesh and blood, you know that I do not deal in those articles; you might as well go to a gin-shop for a leg of mutton, as expect anything human or earthly from me.'

That is the basis upon which I shall attempt to justify the poetry of Shelley — not condemn it as failing to achieve something which was not in the nature of the poet, but praise it for expressing, with an unsurpassed perfection, qualities which belonged to the poet and which are of peculiar value to humanity. But first I think it is necessary to establish the psychological type to which Shelley belonged.

(iii)

Anything like an exact psychological analysis of a poet who lived more than a hundred years ago is beyond the scope of literary criticism. The psychologist, on the basis of many anecdotes of his life, by a careful examination and classification of the imagery of his poetry, might be able to arrive at some definite conclusions. But for our present purpose it will be sufficient to establish certain general characteristics, and a knowledge of these may at least save us from the fatuity of blaming the poet for not possessing what it was not in his nature to possess.

If Shelley's life and writings are glanced at with a psychological eye, three significant features will at once be noticed:

(1) the occurrence, at intervals, of hallucinations of a morbid or pathological nature;

(2) an abnormal interest in incest motives;

(3) a general lack of objectivity in his normal mode of self-expression.

The psychologist will immediately form the hypothesis that all these features are related to a common cause, and he will seek to explain them by a general theory of the poet's personality and psychological development. We will first state the facts.

Shelley's liability to sudden and somewhat devastating hallucinations is attested by several of his contemporaries, but most clearly, and with some awareness of their significance, by his intimate friend Thomas Love Peacock. The first attack is fully recorded by Harriet Shelley, in a letter to Hogg dated 12th March, 1813:

'On the night of the 26th February we retired to bed between ten and eleven o'clock. We had been in bed about half an hour, when Mr S—— heard a noise proceeding from one of the parlours. He immediately went downstairs with two pistols which he had loaded that night, expecting to have occasion for them. He went into the billiard-room, when he heard footsteps retreating; he followed into another little room, which was called an office. He there saw a man in the act of quitting the room through a glass window which opened into the shrubbery; the man fired at

Mr S——, which he avoided. Bysshe then fired, but it flashed in the pan. The man then knocked Bysshe down, and they struggled on the ground. Bysshe then fired his second pistol, which he thought wounded him in his shoulder, as he uttered a shriek and got up, when he said these words: "By God, I will be revenged. I will murder your wife, and will ravish your sister! By God, I will be revenged!" He then fled, as we hoped for the night. Our servants were not gone to bed, but were just going when this horrible affair happened. This was about eleven o'clock. We all assembled in the parlour, where we remained for two hours. Mr S—— then advised us to retire, thinking it was impossible he would make a second attack. We left Bysshe and our man-servant — who had only arrived that day, and who knew nothing of the house — to sit up. I had been in bed three hours when I heard a pistol go off. I immediately ran downstairs, when I perceived that Bysshe's flannel gown had been shot through, and the window-curtain. Bysshe had sent Daniel to see what hour it was, when he heard a noise at the window; he went there, and a man thrust his arm through the glass and fired at him. Thank heaven! the ball went through his gown and he remained unhurt. Mr S—— happened to stand sideways; had he stood fronting, the ball must have killed him. Bysshe fired his pistol, but it would not go off; he then aimed a blow at him with an old sword which we found in the house. The assassin attempted to get the sword from him, and just as he was pulling it away Dan rushed into the room, when he made his escape. This was at four in the morning. It had been a most dreadful night; the wind was as loud as thunder, and the rain descended in torrents. Nothing has been heard of him, and we have every reason to believe it was no stranger, as there is a man . . . who, the next morning, went and told the shopkeepers that it was a tale of Mr Shelley's to impose upon them, that he might leave the country without paying his bills. This they believed, and none of them attempted to do anything towards the discovery. We left Tanyrallt on Sunday.'

This narrative would not survive present scrutiny, for it is full of highly suspicious circumstances. But its genuineness was suspected at the time, and Peacock himself made an investigation. 'I was in North Wales in the summer of 1813,' he relates, 'and heard the matter much talked of. Persons who had examined the premises on the following morning had found that the grass of the lawn appeared to have been much tramped and rolled on, but there were no footmarks on the wet ground, except between the beaten spot and the window; and the impression of the ball on the wainscot showed that the pistol had been fired towards the window, and not from it. This appeared conclusive as to the whole series of operations having taken place from within.' That Peacock realized the nature of the hallucination is shown by the comment which follows: 'The mental phenomena in which this sort of semi-delusion originated will be better illustrated by one which occurred at a later period, and which, though less tragical in its appearances, was more circumstantial in its development, and more perseveringly adhered to.'

Of this later affair, Peacock himself was a witness:

'In the early summer of 1816 the spirit of restlessness again came over him, and resulted in a second visit to the Continent. The change of scene was preceded, as more than once before, by a mysterious communication from a person seen only by himself, warning him of immediate personal perils to be incurred by him if he did not instantly depart.

'I was alone at Bishopgate, with him and Mrs Shelley, when the visitation alluded to occurred. About the middle of the day, intending to take a walk, I went into the hall for my hat. His was there, and mine was not. I could not imagine what had become of it; but as I could not walk without it, I returned to the library. After some time had elapsed, Mrs Shelley came in, and gave me an account which she had just received from himself, of the visitor and his communication. I expressed some scepticism on the subject, on which she left me, and Shelley came in, with my hat in his hand. He said: "Mary tells me, you do not believe that I have had a visit from Williams." I said: "I told her there were some improbabilities in the narration." He said: "You know Williams of Tremadoc?" I said: "I do." He said: "It was he who was here to-day. He came to tell me of a plot laid by my father and uncle, to entrap me and lock me up. He was in great haste, and could not stop a minute, and I walked with him to Egham." I said: "What hat did you wear?" He said: "This, to be sure." I said: "I wish you would put it on." He put it on, and it went over his face. I said: "You could not have walked to Egham in that hat." He said: "I snatched it up hastily, and perhaps I kept it in my hand. I certainly walked with Williams to Egham, and he told me what I have said. You are very sceptical." I said: "If you are certain of what you say, my scepticism cannot affect your cer-

159

tainty." He said: "It is very hard on a man who has devoted his life to the pursuit of truth, who has made great sacrifices and incurred great sufferings for it, to be treated as a visionary. If I do not know that I saw Williams, how do I know that I see you?" I said: "An idea may have a force of a sensation; but the oftener a sensation is repeated, the greater is the probability of its origin in reality. You saw me yesterday, and will see me to-morrow." He said: "I can see Williams to-morrow if I please. He told me that he was stopping at the Turk's Head Coffee-house, in the Strand, and should be there two days. I want to convince you that I am not under a delusion. Will you walk with me to London to-morrow, to see him?" I said: "I would most willingly do so." The next morning after an early breakfast we set off on our walk to London. We had got half way down Egham Hill, when he suddenly turned round, and said to me: "I do not think we shall find Williams at the Turk's Head." I said: "Neither do I." He said: "You say that, because you do not think he has been there; but he mentioned a contingency under which he might leave town yesterday, and he has probably done so." I said: "At any rate, we should know that he has been there." He said: "I will take other means of convincing you. I will write to him. Suppose we take a walk through the forest." We turned about on our new direction, and were out all day. Some days passed, and I heard no more of the matter. One morning he said to me: "I have some news of Williams; a letter and an enclosure." I said: "I shall be glad to see the letter." He said: "I cannot show you the letter; I will show you the enclosure. It is a diamond necklace. I think you know me well enough to be sure I would not throw away my own money on such a thing, and that if I have it, it must have been sent me by somebody else. It has been sent me by Williams." "For what purpose?" I asked. He said: "To prove his identity and his sincerity." "Surely," I said, "your showing me a diamond necklace will prove nothing but that you have one to show." "Then," he said, "I will not show it you. If you will not believe me, I must submit to your incredulity." There the matter ended. I never heard another word of Williams, nor of any other mysterious visitor. I had on one or two previous occasions argued with him against similar semi-delusions, and I believe if they had always been received with similar scepticism, they would not have been often repeated; but they were encouraged by the ready credulity with which they were received by many who ought to have known better. I call them semi-delusions, because for the most part, they had their basis in his firm belief that his father and uncle had designs on his liberty. On this basis his imagination built a fabric of romance, and when he presented it as substantive fact, and it was found to contain more or less of inconsistency, he felt his self-esteem interested in maintaining it by accumulated circumstances, which severally vanished under the touch of investigation, like Williams's location at the Turk's Head Coffee-house.

'I must add that, in the expression of these differences, there was not a shadow of anger. They were discussed with freedom and calmness; with the good temper and good feeling which never forsook him in conversations with his friends. There was an evident anxiety for acquiescence, but a quiet and gentle toleration of dissent.'

Delusions of persecution pursued Shelley to Italy. There is a story, which dates from 1818, of his having been knocked down in the post office at Florence by a man in a military cloak, who had suddenly walked up to him, saying: 'Are you the damned atheist Shelley?' This man was not seen by anyone else, nor ever afterwards seen or heard of; and Peacock classes this incident with the previous 'semi-delusions'. In 1822, the year of his death, the hallucinations recurred with unusual intensity. In June Shelley was busy writing *The Triumph of Life*. The composition of this poem, the perpetual presence of the sea, and other causes, relates Lady Shelley:

'contributed to plunge the mind of Shelley into a state of morbid excitement, the result of which was a tendency to see visions. One night loud cries were heard issuing from the saloon. The Williamses rushed out of their room in alarm; Mrs Shelley also endeavoured to reach the spot, but fainted at the door. Entering the saloon, the Williamses found Shelley staring horribly into the air, and evidently in a trance. They waked him, and he related that a figure wrapped in a mantle came to his bedside and beckoned him. He must then have risen in his sleep, for he followed the imaginary figure into the saloon, when it lifted the hood of its mantle, ejaculated "Siete sodisfatto?" and vanished.'

Another vision which occurred about this time is recorded by Williams in his diary published in Lady Shelley's *Shelley Memorials*:

'May 6. Fine. Some heavy drops of rain fell without a cloud being visible. After tea, while walking with Shelley on the terrace, and observing the effect of moonshine on the waters, he complained of being unusually nervous, and, stopping short, he grasped me violently by the arm, and stared steadfastly on the white surf that broke upon the beach under our feet. Observing him sensibly affected, I demanded of him if he was in pain; but he only answered by saying: "There it is again! there!" He recovered after some time, and declared that he saw, as plainly as he then saw me, a naked child (Allegra, who had recently died) rise from the sea, and clasp its hands as if in joy, smiling at him. This was a trance that it required some reasoning and philosophy entirely to wake him from, so forcibly had the vision operated on his mind.'

Still another vision occurred on June 6th. Shelley was heard screaming and when Williams went to the room, Shelley said he had not been asleep, had not screamed, but had seen Edward and Jane Williams come into the room, 'their bodies lacerated, their bones starting through their skin, their faces pale yet stained with blood; they could hardly walk, but Edward was the weakest, and Jane was supporting him. Edward said, "Get up, Shelley, the sea is flooding the house, and it is all coming down." Shelley got up, he thought, and went to his window that looked on the terrace and the sea, and thought he saw the sea rushing in. Suddenly his vision changed, and he saw the figure of himself strangling me; that made him rush into my room, yet, fearful of frightening me, he dared not approach the bed, when my jumping out awoke him, or, as he phrased it, caused his vision to vanish. All this was frightful enough, and talking it over the next morning, he told me that he had many visions lately; he had seen the figure of himself, which met him as he walked on the terrace and said to him, "How long do you mean to be content." '[1]

It is possible that these last two visions are of somewhat different type from the rest, but the evidence as a whole is sufficient to establish the fact that Shelley was suffering, during the last ten years of his life (and therefore during the whole of his effective poetic period) from a well-established kind of psychosis,[2] the 'paranoid' type of dementia praecox. Any further description of this psychological abnormality is not necessary — its character is sufficiently evident in the case presented by Shelley. We must now

---

[1] From a letter from Mrs. Shelley to Mrs. Gisborne, August 15th, 1822. Mrs. Julian Marshall, *Life and Letters of Mary Wollstonecraft Shelley*, 1889, ii, 11.

[2] In general I have preferred to use the term 'psychosis' rather than 'neurosis', following the distinction made by Freud. (*Collected Papers*, Vol. II.)

investigate the possible cause of the psychosis, but first I must describe the other significant features in Shelley's make-up.

Shelley's first attempt to deal openly with the incest motive was made in 1817, when he wrote *Laon and Cythna*, the original version of *The Revolt of Islam*. The poem was actually set up, and a few copies printed, before the publisher, Ollier, discovered that the lovers Laon and Cythna were represented as brother and sister. He was horrified and hastily stopped the publication, and then insisted on the poem being amended. Shelley put up the strongest resistance, but Ollier remained firm, so finally Shelley submitted, and the poem, with a few changes of sex, appeared as *The Revolt of Islam*. Undismayed by this experience, Shelley two years later returned to the theme in *The Cenci*. As Shelley was at pains to point out, it was the facts of the story which interested him, and which he proposed to present, abating the horror in an idealization of the characters, without any attempt to make them 'subservient to what is vulgarly termed a moral purpose'. For the present merely the fact that in two of his major works Shelley took incest as a motive is significant for our enquiry into his psychosis.

The third feature I mentioned, the general lack of objectivity in Shelley's mode of self-expression, is one which has its poetic as well as its psychological interest. But for the moment I confine myself to the latter aspect. It is a commonplace observation that most people's senses are unbalanced; one person will have keen visual sensibility, another keen aural sensibility; in others the sense of touch or smell will be developed at the expense of the rest of the senses. 'When I first knew Shelley', Hogg writes, 'he was alike indifferent to all works of art. He learned afterwards to admire statues, and then, at a still later period, pictures; but he never had any feeling for the wonders of architecture; even our majestic cathedrals were viewed with indifference. I took him into York Minster several times, but to no purpose; it was thrown away, entirely lost upon him. The insensible Harriet appeared to feel its beauty, until her admiration of the sublime structure was proscribed and forbidden by authority.' That Hogg was not in this matter in any way misrepresenting Shelley is shown by those very reactions to statues and pictures which Hogg refers to, and which still survive in Shelley's letters from Italy, and in his 'Critical Notices of the Sculpture in the Florence Gallery'. Most art criticism of the period is 'literary', but Shelley's notes show a complete unawareness of anything in the nature of what we should now call plastic values. A passage from a letter to Leigh Hunt (Sept. 8th, 1918) will serve as an illustration:

'Perhaps I attended more to sculpture than to painting, its forms being more easily intelligible than that of the latter. Yet, I saw the famous works of Raffaele, whom I agree with the whole world in thinking the finest painter. With respect to Michael Angelo I dissent, and think with astonishment and indignation of the common notion that he equals, and, in some respects, exceeds Raffaele. He seems to me to have no sense of moral dignity and loveliness; and the energy for which he has been so much praised, appears to me to be a certain rude, external, mechanical quality, in comparison with anything possessed by Raffaele, or even much inferior artists. His famous painting in the Sixtine Chapel seems to me deficient in beauty and majesty, both in the conception and the execution. He has been called the Dante of painting; but if we find some of the gross and strong outlines which are employed in the most distasteful passages of the *Inferno*, where shall we find *your* Francesca — where the spirit coming over the sea in a boat, like Mars rising from the vapours of the horizon — where Matilda gathering flowers, and all the exquisite tenderness, and sensibility, and ideal beauty, in which Dante excelled all poets except Shakespeare.'

In a letter to Peacock on the same subject, Shelley is even more outspoken about Michelangelo. 'He has not only no temperance, no modesty, no feeling for the just boundaries of art . . . but he has no sense of beauty, and to want this is to want the sense of the creative power of mind.' The odd thing is, that Shelley accuses Michelangelo of lacking precisely those qualities which a modern critic would see in the sculptor: majesty, creative power, moral dignity, idealization of the human type. One cannot help feeling that some other quality in the artist repelled Shelley — perhaps his extreme masculinity, which Shelley designated as 'a certain rude, external, mechanical quality'; or perhaps still obscurer aspects of Michelangelo's homosexuality.

It happens that a certain modern psychological theory will account for all these features in Shelley's personality, and though this theory will meet with a good deal of resistance, particularly from friends of Shelley, and will therefore seem very inappropriate to a so-called defence of Shelley, I shall put it forward, since I believe that the knowledge which comes from a complete understanding of a poet's personality is the best basis for the appreciation of his poetry. For it is not a belief in the ideas or dogmas of a poet that is essential for the reader's poetic 'assent', but rather a sympathy with his personality; and this is the sense in which I wish to amend Mr. Eliot's amendment of Dr. Richards's amendment of Coleridge's original suggestion.

The psychological theory I have in mind, known as 'the principle of primary identification', was first put forward by Dr. Trigant Burrow in two papers contributed to *The Psychoanalytical Review*[1]; there is an accessible discussion of it in Chapter XVI of Dr. John T. MacCurdy's *Problems in Dynamic Psychology*.[2] It is a theory which attempts to explain the origin of homosexual tendencies, and the consequences of the suppression of these tendencies, and as Dr. MacCurdy says, 'it is peculiarly significant that this, the most original and important contribution to psychoanalysis of recent years, has received no attention from Freud and his immediate followers.' I cannot do better than quote the summary of this theory as given by MacCurdy:

'While still *in utero*, the infant's "organic consciousness is so harmoniously adapted to its environment as to constitute a perfect continuum with it". The foetus has no knowledge of where he begins and the maternal envelope ends. He has no personality, no individuality, because these are the sum of consistent reactions to the environment which give the organism its psychic individuality or personality. Even for some months after birth the child is still without true individuality and, so far as consciousness is concerned, is still an extension of the mother, so to speak, for all his experience is gained through or with the mother.

' "Now during these early months of the infant's exclusive relationship with the mother, organic associations begin to be formed which mark the beginning of the awakening of consciousness. Let it be remembered though that since the child is still in the subjective, undifferentiated phase of consciousness, the associations of the first months of infantile life are entirely primary, subjective and unconscious, and that therefore its early associations, being subjective, non-conscious and undifferentiated, tend always toward the closer consolidation of the mother with itself, that is to say, they tend to the indissoluble welding together

[1] *The Genesis and Meaning of Homosexuality and its Relation to the Problem of Introverted Mental States* (vol. 4, no. 3) and *The Origin of the Incest-Awe* (vol. 5, no. 3).
[2] Cambridge University Press, 1923. Quoted with the kind permission of the Syndics.

of the infantile ego and the mother-image. Thus is strengthened from day to day the mental union — the psychic amalgamation between the mother and infant which establishes for him an organic bond in respect to feeling or consciousness subsequent to birth that is correlative with the organic correspondence prior to their separation at birth. It is his subjective continuity — this organic mental bond — which I call the *principle of primary identification*."

'. . . Such consciousness as [the infant] does enjoy is the subjective unity with his mother, hence his first efforts at objectivation follow the line of his mother's solicitation, namely, himself. So he regards his own body as a love-object, just as does his mother. With weaning he is thrown more back upon himself and his body becomes the constant and insistent object of his interest. Thus auto-erotism. "*Now auto-erotism or the love of one's own body is the love of that sex to which one's own body belongs and this, in psychological interpretation, is precisely homosexuality.*"

'By this argument unconscious homosexuality is merely an extension into adult life of the primary identification, and a psychoneurosis a state of heightened subjectivity correlated with the unconscious homosexuality which is simply one expression of it.

'. . . [Burrow] proceeds to examine the "sentiment of love" and finds that it consists in identification with the love-object. It is not hard to find evidence of the existence of this factor and Burrow adduces many examples from the vocabulary of love to prove it. Normally the biological sex urge leads the individual to direct his love capacity, his identification tendency, to one of the opposite sex, but the neurotic is so dominated by the primary identification that he cannot do this and so tends to identify himself, unconsciously at least, with one like himself, i.e., he is homosexual.

'Unconscious homosexuality is thus merely incidental to the psychoneurosis. A much more fundamental problem is the origin of repression, without which one would not get all the distortions and evasions which constitute symptoms. Repression in general is typified in the horror, the revolt, against incest, so Burrow sets himself to the task of relating this to his principle of primary identification.'

This outline is perhaps sufficient for our purpose, but there are some detailed consequences of the theory which fit in with the case of Shelley. For example, in describing the process of adaptation,

In Defence of Shelley

Dr. Burrow explains how it comes about that some individuals, and precisely those who do not succeed in completely adapting themselves, will show a lack of objectivity.

'Now the demands of the world of outer objectivity or of consciousness proper entail increasing outrage to this state of primary quiescence. . . . Thus our primary nature shrinks from the intrusion of those outer impressions which disturb its elemental sleep. And so it may be said that *Nature abhors consciousness.* But with the increasing importunities of reality there begins the gradual increase of outer objective consciousness. Slowly there is the establishment of that *rapport* between the organism and the external world, which constitutes individual adaptation. Observe that the process of adaptation is essentially outward-tending, away from the ego, that it is inherently a process of objectivation.'

It would follow, therefore, that a poet who had not successfully adapted himself to the external world, who was, at least unconsciously, still firmly bound to that state of consciousness which succeeds the primary identification with the mother — who was, that is to say, unconsciously homosexual — would be distinguished by a lack of objectivity in his attitude towards the outer world, and in his description of that attitude, that is to say, in his poetic diction. And such is precisely the character of Shelley's poetry.

A psychologist would probably be inclined to ask for more specific evidence of unconscious homosexuality in the actual imagery used by Shelley. I think enough to satisfy the psychologist could be found in Shelley's works — abundantly in the two prose romances, for example, which were his first published works, and even in his most deliberate poems, such as *Adonais.*[1] But any

[1] The symbol of the Eagle and the Serpent is a typical example of the kind of imagery that calls for some psychological explanation. It is used no less than four times by Shelley — in *Alastor*, II, 227-37; II, 324-5; *Prometheus Unbound*, III, ii, 72-4; and with great elaboration in Canto I of *The Revolt of Islam*:

> *For in the air do I behold indeed*
> *An Eagle and a Serpent wreathed in fight : —*
> *And now relaxing its impetuous flight,*
> *Before the aëreal rock on which I stood,*
> *The Eagle, hovering, wheeled to left and right,*
> *And hung with lingering wings over the flood,*
> *And startled with its yells the wide air's solitude.*
>
> *A shaft of light upon its wings descended,*
> *And every golden feather gleamed therein —*
> *Feather and scale, inextricably blended.*
> *The Serpent's mailed and many-coloured skin*
> *Shone through the plumes its coils were twined within*

167

such research I must leave to the psychologist. I would, however, like to point to the significance of a passage in one of Shelley's incompleted prose works, his *Speculations on Metaphysics*, the fifth section of which is an extraordinary anticipation of psychoanalysis. 'Let us reflect on our infancy', begins Shelley, 'and give as faithfully as possible a relation of the events of sleep.' And then he proceeds to give 'a faithful picture of my own peculiar nature relatively to sleep'.

'I distinctly remember dreaming three several times, between intervals of two or more years, the same precise dream. It was not

> By many a swoln and knotted fold, and high
> And far, the neck, receding lithe and thin,
> Sustained a crested head, which warily
> Shifted and glanced before the Eagle's steadfast eye.

> Around, around, in ceaseless circles wheeling
> With clang of wings and scream, the Eagle sailed
> Incessantly — sometimes on high concealing
> Its lessening orbs, sometimes as if it failed,
> Drooped through the air; and still it shrieked and wailed,
> And casting back its eager head, with beak
> And talon unremittingly assailed
> The wreathèd Serpent, who did ever seek
> Upon his enemy's heart a mortal wound to wreak.

> . . . in the void air, far away,
> Floated the shattered plumes; bright scales did leap,
> Where'er the Eagle's talons made their way,
> Like sparks into the darkness; — as they sweep,
> Blood stains the snowy foam of the tumultuous deep.

The description of the struggle continues for three more stanzas, and then the Eagle drops the Serpent, which falls to the sea, and makes its way to where a Woman, beautiful as morning, sits beneath the rocks. When the Woman sees the Serpent, she breaks into song — 'his native tongue and hers'—

> And she unveiled her bosom, and the green
> And glancing shadows of the sea did play
> O'er its marmoreal depth: — one moment seen,
> For ere the next, the Serpent did obey
> Her voice, and, coiled in rest, in her embrace it lay.

Possibly the psychologist will recognize in this imagery an archetypal pattern for which he has a ready interpretation — most probably some form of castration complex.* An eagle grasping a serpent is, of course, an emblem of fairly frequent occurrence; Mr. Hugh Sykes Davies tells me that the image is used by Homer. It is possible, therefore, that Shelley consciously selected it; but what is of significance is not so much the selection of the image, as the extraordinary vividness and detail which it assumes in Shelley's relation. Those qualities, we may assume, had a powerful subconscious motivation; and since this passage is one of Shelley's high poetic achievements, we are entitled to look for psychological explanations of all hyperaesthetic expression. There could be no clearer justification, if any were needed, of the psychological method in literary criticism.

* Cf. *The Riddle of the Sphinx*, by Géza Róheim. (London, Hogarth Press, 1934.)

so much what is ordinarily called a dream; the single image, unconnected with all other images, of a youth who was educated at the same school with myself, presented itself in sleep. Even now, after the lapse of many years, I can never hear the name of this youth, without the three places where I dreamed of him presenting themselves to my mind. . . .

'I have beheld scenes, with the intimate and unaccountable connexion of which with the obscure parts of my own nature, I have been irresistibly impressed. I have beheld a scene which has produced no unusual effect on my thoughts. After the lapse of many years I have dreamed of this scene. It has hung on my memory, it has haunted my thoughts, at intervals, with the pertinacity of an object connected with human affections. I have visited this scene again. Neither the dream could be dissociated from the landscape, nor the landscape from the dream, nor feelings, such as neither singly could have awakened, from both. But the most remarkable event of this nature, which ever occurred to me, happened five years ago at Oxford. I was walking with a friend, in the neighbourhood of that city, engaged in earnest and interesting conversation. We suddenly turned the corner of a lane, and the view, which its high banks and hedges had concealed, presented itself. The view consisted of a windmill, standing in one among many plashy meadows, inclosed with stone walls; the irregular and broken ground, between the wall and the road on which we stood; a long low hill behind the windmill, and a grey covering of uniform cloud spread over the sky. It was that season when the last leaf had just fallen from the scant and stunted ash. The scene surely was a common scene; the season and the hour little calculated *to kindle lawless thought*; it was a tame uninteresting assemblage of objects, such as would drive the imagination for refuge in serious and sober talk, to the evening fireside, and the dessert of winter fruits and wine. The effect which it produced on me was not such as could have been expected. I suddenly remembered to have seen that exact scene in some dream of long. . . .'

The account breaks off thus abruptly, and Shelley adds in a note: 'Here I was obliged to leave off, *overcome by thrilling horror*.'

We shall never know what 'thrilling horror', what 'lawless thought', was present in such vividness in Shelley's dream that he could not bring himself to relate the incident. We can only speculate that it was a scene connected with that 'horror' which had such a strong and inexplicable fascination for him — the horror of incest. Lest it be thought that a horror of incest would be inconsistent with the open treatment of the theme such as we get in *The Cenci*, here is a statement from MacCurdy, made without reference to Shelley, but in general reference to the kind of psychosis Shelley seems to have suffered from: 'According to Burrow's thesis, such an individual should have the greatest repugnance to incest and show the greatest capacity for "love". Yet he can entertain delusions of incest without evidence of any horror at the thought and is less capable of love, as that term is usually understood, than any other clinical type we know about.'

This brings us to the final evidence for assuming that Shelley lived in a state of heightened subjectivity due to his unconscious homosexuality — his attitude to love. We shall still rely on the psychology of Burrow, which provides us with a very satisfactory explanation of two types of love with which Shelley was much concerned. Love, in this psychology, is closely identified with that striving for unity which is the normal unconscious effort of the individual — of the individual who is fully adapted to his social environment, the normal individual who has completely repressed the desire for unity and can enter into objective sexual relations with another individual of the opposite sex on a basis of reciprocity and partnership. But in the case of the incompletely adapted individual, his essential subjectivity will demand a more generalized kind of unity, in which there is no separation of the individual from the world at large. Subjectivity implies a lack of interest in one's environment, and a consequent longing for community of thinking. To quote Burrow:

'It is but natural that having come suddenly into the franchise of consciousness, man should employ his liberty of action in the wanton aims of personal satisfaction, or in the tedious propitiations of vicarious conformities. But there is something deeper still, more native to man, than all this. It is expressed in the social merging of personalities into each other in the pursuit of the common good. It is that quality of man that ever goads him to search and strive to the utmost benefit of the race. It is this quality of harmoniousness and unity inherent in the social aims of man that is, it seems to me, the strongest principle of man's consciousness. This it is that men have called love. This, it seems to me, is the true affirmation of life and its prototype is the harmonious principle of the pre-conscious.'

In Defence of Shelley

That this theory corresponds in general to Shelley's attitude
to the subject will be at once obvious. But the extraordinary
completeness with which Shelley expresses the view that we should,
according to our hypothesis, expect him to express, can only be
demonstrated by further quotation. The *Epipsychidion* is, of
course, the supreme expression of his philosophy, and there
could be no better instance of how some understanding of the
psychology of a poet can aid us to an appreciation of his poetry;
and of how for the lack of such understanding so sensitive a reader
of poetry as Mr. Eliot can be 'thoroughly gravelled'. The lines
which troubled Mr. Eliot and which he quotes in his lecture, restored to their proper order and the omitted lines added, are
these:

> *I never was attached to that great sect,*
> *Whose doctrine is, that each one should select*
> *Out of the crowd a mistress or a friend,*
> *And all the rest, though fair and wise, commend*
> *To cold oblivion, though it is the code*
> *Of modern morals, and the beaten road*
> *Which those poor slaves with weary footsteps tread,*
> *Who travel to their home among the dead*
> *By the broad highway of the world, and so*
> *With one chained friend, perhaps a jealous foe,*
> *The dreariest and the longest journey go.*
>
> *True Love in this differs from gold and clay,*
> *That to divide is not to take away.*
> *Love is like understanding, that grows bright,*
> *Gazing on many truths; 'tis like thy light,*
> *Imagination! which from earth and sky,*
> *And from the depths of human fantasy,*
> *As from a thousand prisms and mirrors, fills*
> *The Universe with glorious beams, and kills*
> *Error, the worm, with many a sun-like arrow*
> *Of its reverberated lightning. Narrow*
> *The heart that loves, the brain that contemplates,*
> *The life that wears, the spirit that creates*
> *One object, and one form, and builds thereby*
> *A sepulchre for its eternity.*

There is nothing, I would submit, in such a poetic statement,
to gravel any unprejudiced reader; the doctrine is clear and

171

coherent, and, as I am attempting to show, based on — indeed, a consequence of — psychological realities. The question of the 'normality' of these realities I will deal with presently; but first, to present Shelley's doctrine in all its clarity, we must look again at the prose statement he wrote in 1815:

'*Thou* demandest what is love? It is that powerful attraction towards all that we conceive, or fear, or hope beyond ourselves, when we find within our own thoughts the chasm of an insufficient void, and seek to awaken in all things that are, a community with what we experience within ourselves. If we reason, we would be understood; if we imagine, we would that the airy children of our brain were born anew within another's; if we feel, we would that another's nerves should vibrate to our own, that the beams of their eyes should kindle at once and mix and melt into our own, that lips of motionless ice should not reply to lips quivering and burning with the heart's best blood. This is Love. This is the bond and the sanction which connects not only man with man, but with everything which exists. We are born into the world, and there is something within us which, from the instant that we live, more and more thirsts after its likeness. It is probably in correspondence with this law that the infant drains milk from the bosom of its mother; this propensity develops itself with the development of our nature. We dimly see within our intellectual nature a miniature as it were of our entire self, yet deprived of all that we condemn or despise, the ideal prototype of everything excellent or lovely that we are capable of conceiving as belonging to the nature of man. Not only the portrait of our external being, but an assemblage of the minutest particles of which our nature is composed[1]; a mirror whose surface reflects only the forms of purity and brightness; a soul within our soul that describes a circle around its proper paradise, which pain, and sorrow, and evil dare not overleap. To this we eagerly refer all sensations, thirsting that they should resemble or correspond with it. The discovery of its antitype; the meeting with an understanding capable of clearly estimating our own; an imagination which should enter into and seize upon the subtle and delicate peculiarities which we have delighted to cherish and unfold in secret; with a frame whose nerves, like the chords of two exquisite lyres, strung to the accompaniment of one delightful voice, vibrate with the vibrations of

[1] These words are ineffectual and metaphorical. Most words are so — No help! (Shelley's note.)

our own; and of a combination of all these in such proportion as the type within demands; this is the invisible and unattainable point to which Love tends; and to attain which, it urges forth the powers of man to arrest the faintest shadow of that, without the possession of which there is no rest nor respite to the heart over which it rules.'

Here, in language which only differs from a modern psychologist's in being poetic rather than technical, we have a clear description of the state of narcissism, that stage in the development of the individual when a growing self-consciousness becomes a growing self-love. Physically this state may be expressed in auto-erotic practices, but it can exist without auto-erotism, in fantasy alone. The clearest expression of this narcissistic attitude in Shelley's poetry (as Professor James Sutherland has pointed out to me) is in *Alastor*. I have already referred to the general theme of the poem, as outlined by Shelley in his Preface; it is the search for a 'prototype' (Shelley's word) who would make real or concrete his ideal conception of 'all that is excellent and majestic'. In the poem the Poet finds 'a veiléd maid' in 'the wild Carmanian waste' whose voice 'was like the voice of his own soul', and the music of it 'held his inmost sense suspended in its web' (11, 140–91). This is the 'antitype' of the passage quoted above, and the scene of their merger or identification, as described by Shelley in the poem, is not without erotic significance:

> Sudden she rose,
> As if her heart impatiently endured
> Its bursting burthen: at the sound he turned,
> And saw by the warm light of their own life
> Her glowing limbs beneath the sinuous veil
> Of woven wind, her outspread arms now bare,
> Her dark locks floating in the breath of night,
> Her beamy bending eyes, her parted lips
> Outstretched, and pale, and quivering eagerly.
> His strong heart sunk and sickened with excess
> Of love. He reared his shuddering limbs and quelled
> His gasping breath, and spread his arms to meet
> Her panting bosom: . . . she drew back a while,
> Then, yielding to the irresistible joy,
> With frantic gesture and short breathless cry
> Folded his frame in her dissolving arms.

173

In Defence of Shelley

Now blackness veiled his dizzy eyes, and night
Involved and swallowed up the vision; sleep,
Like a dark flood suspended in its course,
Rolled back its impulse on his vacant brain.

From narcissism the individual develops towards homosexuality (love of another like oneself) or towards heterosexuality, where objectivity may be completely developed. But, in Dr. MacCurdy's words, 'very frequently the alleged object of love is merely a lay figure; the subject is in love with his ideal of what the loved one should be. In such a case the union is happy just in so far as the object of attachment is capable of identifying himself or herself with the ideal. This type of love is narcissistic because what is loved is not another person at all but an autochthonous ideal. True objectivity occurs only when another person is loved as another personality and not only in so far as the object duplicates a fantasy of the lover. When a sexual object is credited with undue virtue (sexual overestimation), this is a product of narcissism, because the qualities in question do not reside in the object (or not in the degree represented) but are fantasies of the lover, things he would like to see and, therefore, does observe. Such an attachment may pass for true love, thanks to its loud protestations, but it is unstable. A puff of reality will blow it away.' It will at once be obvious how closely Shelley's love affairs correspond to this description. Not only in his explicit ideas, as expressed in his poetry, but also in the actions of his life, he reveals himself as a narcissistic type.

This, I think, is about as far as the literary critic can carry the psychological analysis of a poet. It has enabled us to establish beyond any reasonable doubt that Shelley belonged to a definite psychological type — a type whose consciousness is incompletely objectified, which is therefore evidently narcissistic, and unconsciously homosexual. Such unconscious homosexuality gives rise to a psychosis of which Shelley shows all the normal symptoms. It determines a line of moral conduct which Shelley exhibits in his life. It determines a quality of imagery and verbal expression which is present in Shelley's verse. It has as its concomitant a unity-complex which leads to the development of those social ideas of an anarchist tendency which are characteristic of Shelley's political thought. The chain of evidence is complete; it does not, so far as I can see, leave any room for argument.

174

In Defence of Shelley

But what still remains to be done is to give some estimate of the value of such a type. And by 'value' I mean the worth of such an individual to the social and intellectual life of the community at large. For it cannot be assumed that what is not normal is not valuable.

(iv)

Gibt es vielleicht — eine Frage für Irrenärtze — Neurosen der Gesundheit?
NIETZSCHE

One thing which modern psychology may claim to have established beyond question is the relativity of all human types; at least, the psychologist will tell you that any preconceived idea of normality will break down on the most superficial analysis. Dr. Burrow has called normality 'unconsciousness on a co-operative basis', and he for one is not deceived by the compromise it represents. But if not a reality in any absolute sense, this co-operative basis is an accepted fiction or illusion from which the neurotic finds himself excluded. The values of the actual situation are majority values — the conventional values of morality, conduct and taste. There is no evidence whatever that such values are, in any positive sense, biological or organic values — by which I mean values which promote the health and happiness of mankind in the only world of which we have any certain knowledge. If one is strong enough to detach one's self from the normal assumptions of society (thereby becoming, if only for the moment, neurotic[1]), then what, we may ask ourselves, is the value of this normal man — this man who has lost the joy of his childhood; this man who, clad in the triple armour of routine, convention and cant, goes through the paces of his hypocritical day; rising from a sleep in which the baffled forces of life have flickered phantasmagorically behind the screen of consciousness; immediately assuming the common mask, a shaven mask to which adheres, perhaps, a rudimentary whisker; then, having bathed and eased himself in shamefaced privacy, pursuing his daily course, donning his dull traditional clothing, fastening his senseless buttons, his starched

[1] Cf. Shelley:

> in truth I think
> Her gentleness and patience and sad smiles,
> And that she did not die, but lived to tend
> Her aged father, were a kind of madness,
> If madness 'tis to be unlike the world.

'The Sunset', a fragment of a poem written in 1816.

175

collar, his polished boots; greeting his friends with his usual grin; this pipe-sucking busybody, reading his newspaper which panders fulsomely to his unconscious sadism, his repressed homosexuality, his all-pervasive eroticism — need we follow him through the whole round of his visits, avocations and amusements? (Little man, he's had a busy day!) Not one moment of unchecked spontaneity, of whole-hearted participation in a life free, communal and unconfined. Everywhere the taboo, the code, the eternal vigilance of the unknown censor.

Against this mass self-deception, the neurotic is doomed to protest. It may be that in the process of his individual adaptation to life, his growth has been arrested; he has not, that is to say, completely dissociated himself from his original organic unity with his mother. He has not been fully weaned, he has not been completely *won* for society. Forcibly divorced from his mother, all the strength of his feeling has been transferred to the object of his mother's greatest regard — to himself. Social adaptation consists precisely in getting rid of this self-interest, this autosexuality; in sublimating it, as we say. But such adaptation is really a pretence; under the cover of our conventions we remain disparate, dissociated, resisting the organic wholeness of life. Only the neurotic refuses the compromise. Disparate as he may seem from the point of view of the normality we have achieved, actually he is nearer the source of life, the organic reality; his separateness is really an integrity of personality, an agreement of all the instinctive and affective life of the individual with the organic processes of life in general (the natural unity of our common life). 'If the neurotic regarded individually, or as the embodiment within himself of a societal lesion', writes Dr. Burrow, 'is an expression of separatism and pathology, the neurotic viewed organically, or as the embodiment within himself of the societal continuum, is no less an expression of confluence and health. If, in the first instance, he is himself the disorder that is his own separatism and unconsciousness, in the second he is the integration that is his own confluence and consciousness. It is this constructive aspect of the neuroses of which we have not yet taken account and of which we may take due cognizance only upon the basis of a wider, organismic interpretation of these disorders of the personality.'[1]

Our next step is to correlate, from this point of view, the neurotic and the artist. Actually this has already been done by Dr.

[1] *The Social Basis of Unconsciousness*, p. 153.

176

Burrow. 'The organic integrity of personality that is the composite life of man and that is organically inseparable from the unifying urge embodied in the impulse of mating, has its clearest intimations in the affirmations of the artist as in the frustrations of the neurotic.' The artist, that is to say, reveals an inward unity and concentration of personality in marked contrast with the extraneous dissipations and diversities of the average reaction-type: 'It is this unity of personality that is the source of the artist's creativeness as it is the inspiration of his genius. This composite quality of the sex life explains the gentler intuitions we often find in the personality of a man. There is undoubtedly the feminine in man though as yet he stands in fear of it. It does not wrangle or contend. It does not calculate success. The feminine in man is the artist in man.[1] It is because of this that there can be in the societal unity of the artist's intuitive instinct no place for the illusion that is called "the public". To him "the public" is but the collective repudiation of the common soul of man — a repudiation that corresponds to this same disavowal within the private soul of each of us. Unmoved by its clamorous demands, the artist feels within these manifestations of the public mind the common soul that underlies it, and senses within it the pain of denied needs identical with his own. This is the unfailing intuition of the artist.'[2]

The relevance of these distinctions to the case of Shelley will by now be evident. But before returning to Shelley I would like to refer to my previous discussion, in *Form in Modern Poetry*, of the distinction between personality and character in relation to the poetic process. When I wrote that essay I had not read any of Dr. Burrow's works; I was elaborating certain statements of Keats's, and in so far as I was going beyond my own experience, I was relying on my understanding of Freud. I feel now that the truth I was attempting to formulate is amply confirmed by Dr. Burrow (who was trained in the Freudian school) and given a more scientific basis. Literary critics like Mr. Eliot may refuse to be drawn into this discussion,[3] but it should now be obvious that such an attitude is merely an avoidance of the essential issue for modern criticism.

To return to Shelley. From the pathological point of view,

---

[1] Cf. Gerard Manley Hopkins: '. . . the things must come from the *mundus muliebris*.'

[2] Op. cit., pp. 218–19.

[3] 'Mr Herbert Read . . . pursues his speculations to a point to which I would not willingly follow him.' (*The Use of Poetry and the Use of Criticism*, p. 101 n.)

Shelley was a neurotic, in conflict with the social imposition of normality. But from a more general and human point of view, Shelley was a genius whose neurotic reaction, for all its distortion, represents an organic urge towards 'a completer oneness of life', 'a clearer, more conscious social order.' As much might be said of other poets — of Keats, for example. But just as, in Burrow's words, 'it is the distinction of the neurotic personality that he is at least consciously and confessedly *nervous*,' so the special value of Shelley is that he was conscious of his direction; he had, in the modern sense, but without expressing himself in modern terminology, analysed his own neurosis. He did not *define* his autosexuality; but he allowed the reaction full scope. That is to say, he allowed his feelings and ideas to develop integrally with his neurotic personality; and the élan of that evolution inevitably led to the formulation of 'a clearer, more conscious social order'.

In the light of this analysis, therefore, we must reconsider those 'shabby ideas' of his. For not for the first time in the history of human thought, the stone which the builders rejected may become the head of the corner.

(v)

It is not part of my intention in this essay to give any extensive account of Shelley's political and moral ideas; that has been done before, notably by Mr. John Shawcross in his Introduction to a selection of *Shelley's Literary and Philosophical Criticism* published in the Oxford Miscellany in 1909 and, in greater detail, by Professor Carl Grabo.[1] But it is necessary to say something in answer to the charge of incoherence, for that, as we have seen, is the main clause in Mr. Eliot's indictment.

Any intelligent mind, during the period of development or formation (a period which, in the most intelligent minds, lasts as long as life), is open to two kinds of influence. One is immediate, and is concerned with the temporary problems of the age we live in; the other is less urgent but more enduring, and is concerned with the permanent problems of human destiny. It is possible to adopt a superior attitude, and say that all the problems that matter were solved once and for all time by Aristotle, or by St. Thomas, or by Kant; and that all we need do at any particular stage of history

---

[1] *The Magic Plant: the Growth of Shelley's Thought.* (Chapel Hill, University of North Carolina Press, 1936.)

is to apply the eternal principles of one or other of these philosophers. It is a possible attitude but not a very helpful one; it involves the dogmatist in casuistry, for the immediate problems in
life are not necessarily the permanent ones. In our own day we shall
look in vain to the past for any solution of the peculiar problems,
ethical as well as economic, introduced into our society by modern
industrial and scientific methods of production. We are likely to
find more guidance in the works of Freud and Marx. It would be
equally foolish to seek the source of all wisdom in contemporary
philosophers, for wisdom, unfortunately, is not cumulative. It is
an insight given to but few individuals in the course of history;
and when not faced by new factors, we do well to hold on to the
truths tested by universal experience.

From the point of view of the present day, all this is very
obvious, if not platitudinous. But when we are considering a poet
of another age, such as Shelley, we do not necessarily bear this
distinction in mind. We can, if we are not sympathetic, judge him
by his immediate influences — the enthusiasms called forth by
the urgent problems of his age — and ignore the fact that he was
equally influenced by forces we readily accept as valid for all time.
The only legitimate demand we might make, perhaps, is that the
contemporary enthusiasms should not be the only enthusiasms.
We justly suspect the mind that feeds exclusively on a diet of
raw opinions. We demand balance, if not consistency. But no one,
so far as I am aware (certainly none of the critics I have mentioned),
has demonstrated even the inconsistency of Shelley's views.
There has been plenty of vague assertion, inspired by prejudice,
but no proof.

We can trace Shelley's intellectual development with fair ease.
He himself, in one of his early letters to Godwin (June 3, 1812),
gives us a somewhat picturesque summary: 'Until my marriage,
my life had been a series of illness; as it was of a nervous and
spasmodic nature, it in a degree incapacitated me for study.
I nevertheless, in the intervals of comparative health, read
romances, and those the most marvellous ones, unremittingly, and
pored over the reveries of Albertus Magnus and Paracelsus, the
former of which I read in Latin, and probably gained more knowledge of that language from that source than from all the discipline of Eton. My fondness for natural magic and ghosts abated
as my age increased. I read Locke, Hume, Reid, and whatever
metaphysics came in my way, without, however, renouncing

poetry, an attachment to which has characterized all my wanderings and changes. I did not truly *think* and *feel*, however, until I read *Political Justice*, though my thought and feelings, after this period, have been more painful, anxious, and vivid — more inclined to action and less to theory. Before I was a republican: Athens appeared to me the model of government; but afterwards, Athens bore in my mind the same relation to perfection that Great Britain did to Athens.' At Oxford (1810–11), we learn from Hogg, Hume's *Essays* was his favourite book; he also studied Locke with great care, and also 'certain popular French works that treat of man, for the most part in a mixed method, metaphysically, morally, and politically'. It was then that he began to read Plato, and 'was vehemently excited by the striking doctrines which Socrates unfolds'. From then onwards he read Greek continuously, and became very proficient in the language. 'Few were aware', says Hogg, 'of the extent, and still fewer of the profundity of his reading; in his short life, and without ostentation he had, in truth, read more Greek than many an aged pedant. . . . A pocket edition of Plato, of Plutarch, of Euripides, without interpretation or notes, or of the Septuagint, was his ordinary companion; and he read the text straightforward for hours, if not as readily as an English author, at least with as much facility as French, Italian, or Spanish.' During the last four years of his life, during the time he was writing his greatest poetry, he read Homer and Plato, Dante and Ariosto, Calderon and Goethe; he read them with continuous pleasure and deep understanding, and from these authors, if from any, he borrowed his 'shabby' ideas.

We might arrange his precursors in three groups: first Plato and other classical writers, such as Lucretius; then the philosophers of the Enlightenment, Locke and Hume, and their more platonic counterparts, Berkeley and Spinoza; and finally that school of philosophical radicalism which begins with Rousseau, includes Helvétius and Condorcet, and ends for Shelley with Godwin. It is possible to say that here we have mutually exclusive elements; there is little sympathy between Plato and Locke, for example. But we are not to imagine that Shelley accepted all these philosophers in equal measure. Plato was his touchstone, and to Plato he could assimilate what was most sympathetic in the others. But he was guided, of course, by his own intuition of the truth. 'As a poet and artist', Mr. Shawcross very rightly observes, 'Shelley is essentially a lover of order; in order he sees the principle of beauty, whether expressed in sensuous form or civic institution. It is against defective institutions that his attack on society is aimed — defective, because they fail to reflect outwardly the inner moral law.'

A captious critic might complain that the phrase I have used, 'his intuition of the truth', begs the question of coherence, but I should be willing if necessary to explain such a phrase in psychological terms. For my principle all the time is that an individual's coherence of thought is a reflection of his coherent personality — by which, of course, I do not mean a consistent character. We build our philosophy, our 'view of life', round our psychic elements — round our experience, if a plainer but a vaguer expression is preferred. Even Mr. Shawcross, who is innocent of my psychology, notes that 'no doubt in Shelley's aversion from the concrete and the complex we must seek an explanation of the remarkable influence which Godwin's writings exercised upon him'. In the same psychological facts we must seek an explanation of Plato's influence upon him. We may only be distinguishing between two kinds of philosophy, or, as Shelley expresses it in the first paragraph already quoted from *A Defence of Poetry*, between reason and imagination; but there is absolutely no necessity to regard one kind of logic or consistency (the consistency of a system within itself, the parts with the whole) as infallible, and preferable to another kind of logic (the consistency of a system as an interpretation of the materials of human nature and life). The first may be science and the second allegory; but both may be equally coherent, mature, and founded on the facts of experience.

The precise terms of Shelley's 'view of life' are never in doubt. That view may be idealistic, humanitarian and radical, but it is expressed, both in prose and verse, with a clarity which is not normally associated with a muddled mind. The notes to *Queen Mab*, the work of a youth of eighteen, are admirable in style, and show a mastery of exposition and dialectic which would be hard to match among the intellectual prodigies of the world. They deal with a dizzy range of subjects — astronomy, militarism, the labour theory of value, prostitution, the doctrine of necessity, atheism, Christian evidence, time, and vegetarianism. But however diverse the subjects, they are illuminated from one centre: a mind and personality of singular energy, purity and compassion. It was a mind, moreover, that was continually expanding and enriching

181

itself; and in the twelve years which were all that followed the
writing of *Queen Mab*, the progress is all in the direction of depth
and maturity. I have already paid my tribute to the philosophical
merit of the *Defence*; other prose works are fragmentary, but none
is despicable. Even the Irish tracts, which are not often referred to,
are good polemical writing; the speculations on metaphysics and
on morals, and the 'Essay on Christianity', are not to be considered as anything but random and interrupted efforts, but they
are acute and at times even eloquent. But the best of his philosophy is contained, of course, in his great poems, particularly in
Prometheus Unbound, *Epipsychidion* and *Adonais*. In these,
abstract thought finds such sensuous and harmonious expression
as only Wordsworth rarely rivals, and only Dante frequently
excels; there

> *Language is a perpetual Orphic song,*
> *Which rules with Dœdal harmony a throng*
> *Of thoughts and forms, which else senseless and shapeless were.*

The particular poetic quality which results from this perfect
fusion of thought and feeling we will examine presently; for the
moment I am only concerned to defend these poems as the expression of a coherent philosophy or 'view of life'. That philosophy Shelley embodied in the myth of Prometheus — the hero of
humanity struggling against the tyranny of ignorance and super-
stition. Demogorgon's final benediction is too well known to
quote, and even hostile critics submit to its supreme poetic power.
But the eminence of those verses should not distract us from the
more central exposition — Prometheus's speeches towards the
end of Act I, for example, and Asia's cosmic vision in Act II,
Scene iv, which I will quote:

> *There was the Heaven and Earth at first,*
> *And Light and Love; then Saturn, from whose throne*
> *Time fell, an envious shadow: such the state*
> *Of the earth's primal spirits beneath his sway,*
> *As the calm joy of flowers and living leaves*
> *Before the wind or sun has withered them*
> *And semivital worms; but he refused*
> *The birthright of their being, knowledge, power,*
> *The skill which wields the elements, the thought*
> *Which pierces this dim universe like light,*

In Defence of Shelley

Self-empire, and the majesty of love;
For thirst of which they fainted. Then Prometheus
Gave wisdom, which is strength, to Jupiter,
And with this law alone, 'Let man be free',
Clothed him with the dominion of wide Heaven.
To know nor faith, nor love, nor law; to be
Omnipotent but friendless is to reign;
And Jove now reigned; for on the race of man
First famine, and then toil, and then disease,
Strife, wounds, and ghastly death unseen before,
Fell; and the unseasonable seasons drove
With alternating shafts of frost and fire,
Their shelterless, pale tribes to mountain caves:
And in their desert hearts fierce wants he sent,
And mad disquietudes, and shadows idle
Of unreal good, which levied mutual war,
So ruining the lair wherein they raged.
Prometheus saw, and waked the legioned hopes
Which sleep within folded Elysian flowers,
Nepenthe, Moly, Amaranth, fadeless blooms,
That they might hide with thin and rainbow wings
The shape of Death; and Love he sent to bind
The disunited tendrils of that vine
Which bears the wine of life, the human heart;
And he tamed fire which, like some beast of prey,
Most terrible, but lovely, played beneath
The frown of man; and tortured to his will
Iron and gold, the slaves and signs of power,
And gems and poisons, and all subtlest forms
Hidden beneath the mountains and the waves.
He gave man speech, and speech created thought,
Which is the measure of the universe;
And Science struck the thrones of earth and heaven,
Which shook, but fell not; and the harmonious mind
Poured itself forth in all-prophetic song;
And music lifted up the listening spirit
Until it walked, exempt from mortal care,
Godlike, o'er the clear billows of sweet sound;
And human hands first mimicked and then mocked,
With moulded limbs more lovely than its own,
The human form, till marble grew divine;

183

And mothers, gazing, drank the love men see
Reflected in their race, behold, and perish.
He told the hidden power of herbs and springs,
And Disease drank and slept. Death grew like sleep.
He taught the implicated orbits woven
Of the wide-wandering stars; and how the sun
Changes his lair, and by what secret spell
The pale moon is transformed, when her broad eye
Gazes not on the interlunar sea:
He taught to rule, as life directs the limbs,
The tempest-wingèd chariots of the Ocean,
And the Celt knew the Indian. Cities then
Were built, and through their snow-like columns flowed
The warm winds, and the azure aether shone,
And the blue sea and shadowy hills were seen.
Such, the alleviations of his state,
Prometheus gave to man, for which he hangs
Withering in destined pain. . . .

This is the broadcloth of Shelley's verse, and better to be appreciated in the piece than in the pattern. Against its even goodness the songs and lyrics throw out their lustre. Shelley called this poem a lyrical drama; but actually it is an epic, the greatest expression ever given to humanity's desire for intellectual light and spiritual liberty. The hundred years since it was written is but a very short time in the history of that lone effort, and the day may yet come when this poem will take its commanding place in a literature of freedom of which we have yet no conception.

I must not, however, end this section of my argument on a vague exultant note. The riposte must reach its mark. 'We may be permitted to infer,' Mr. Eliot says, 'in so far as the distaste of a person like myself for Shelley's poetry is not attributable to irrelevant prejudices or to a simple blind spot, but is due to a peculiarity in the poetry and not in the reader, that it is not the presentation of beliefs which I do not hold, or — to put the case as extremely as possible — of beliefs which excite my abhorrence, that makes the difficulty. Still less is it that Shelley is deliberately making use of his poetic gifts to propagate a doctrine; for Dante and Lucretius did the same thing. I suggest that the position is somewhat as follows.' And then follows the charge of incoherence, immaturity, childishness, feebleness and shabbiness. But we cannot accept the suggestion (and it is only a suggestion: there is no demonstration). On the contrary, we affirm that Shelley's ideas were no more shabby and incoherent than those of Plato who was their chief inspiration; and that in so far as they were unplatonic, they showed a close parallel to the ideas of Lucretius, whom Mr. Eliot accepts. Retracing the steps of his inference, we must come to the conclusion that Mr. Eliot's objection to Shelley's poetry is irrelevant prejudice (for 'a simple blind spot' would not excite abhorrence); and such, I would suggest, is the kind of poetic approach of all who believe, with Mr. Eliot, that 'literary criticism should be completed by criticism from a definite ethical and theological standpoint'.[1] I do not deny that such criticism may have its interest; but the only kind of criticism which is basic, and therefore complementary not only to technical exegesis but also to ethical, theological, philosophical and every other kind of ideological criticism, is ontogenetic criticism, by which I mean criticism which traces the origins of the work of art in the psychology of the individual and in the economic structure of society.

(vi)

Shelley's central doctrine — I mean his doctrine of art and morality — is one of more than abstract philosophical interest; it is bound up with the texture of his poetry and the conduct of his life. The principle is simply one of identification; there is no question of the moral value of poetry because poetry and morality proceed from the same source. 'The functions of the poetical faculty are twofold; by one it creates new materials of knowledge and power and pleasure; by the other it engenders in the mind a desire to reproduce and arrange them according to a certain rhythm and order which may be called the beautiful and the good.' As thus stated, the identity might seem to be merely one of hedonist and aesthetic values; but Shelley's real meaning is much profounder. The following passage from *A Defence of Poetry* is a famous one, much quoted, but it should be re-read in the present context:

'Ethical science arranges the elements which poetry has created, and propounds schemes and proposes examples of civil

---

[1] T. S. Eliot, 'Religion and Literature', an essay contributed to *Faith that Illuminates*, edited by V. A. Demant (London, 1935).

and domestic life: nor is it for want of admirable doctrines that men hate, and despise, and censure, and deceive, and subjugate one another. But poetry acts in another and diviner manner. It awakens and enlarges the mind itself by rendering it the receptacle of a thousand unapprehended combinations of thought. Poetry lifts the veil from the hidden beauty of the world, and makes familiar objects be as if they were not familiar; it reproduces all that it represents, and the impersonations clothed in its Elysian light stand thenceforward in the minds of those who have once contemplated them, as memorials of that gentle and exalted content which extends itself over all thoughts and actions with which it co-exists. The great secret of morals is love; or a going out of our own nature, and an identification of ourselves with the beautiful which exists in thought, action, or persons, not our own. A man, to be greatly good, must imagine intensely and comprehensively; he must put himself in the place of another and of many others; the pains and pleasures of his species must become his own. The great instrument of moral good is the imagination; and poetry administers to the effect by acting upon the cause.'

We should note, in the first place, how closely this doctrine can be related to the modern psychological doctrine already imparted. 'Abstract truths are the personal relics of genius; their vindication in the concrete text of experience is the heritage of our common consciousness. . . . The source of genius is nuclear, original, essential. Moving amid the surface crusts of "types" which in their restriction of outer contact may only absorb or reflect the impressions about them, genius eradiates from the common centre of our societal organism sustained by an impulse that is cosmic. For this reason, it is the unalterable sentence of genius that it break with every accustomed adherence. It is its law that it raise itself out of habitual inertias and see straight and clear beyond all temporary immediacies, into the unfurbished truth of things.' When Dr. Burrow writes like this, he is merely repeating, in very different language, the truth which Shelley expressed with a more direct poetic intuition.

Expressed in these general terms, the moral aspect of Shelley's doctrine might seem harmless enough; 'the great secret of morals is love' — that may be taken as the central tenet in Shelley's philosophy, and his greatest poems are illustrations of its truth — illustrations rather than demonstrations, for Shelley had a horror of didactic poetry. The 'bold neglect of a direct moral purpose', he wrote, 'is the most decisive proof of the supremacy of Milton's genius.' Shelley's aim in all his poems is to administer to the effect by acting upon the cause — by which he means inducing in his audience a state of sympathetic response to the actions depicted in poetry. 'The imagination is enlarged by a sympathy with pains and passions so mighty, that they distend in their conception the capacity of that by which they are conceived; the good affections are strengthened by pity, indignation, terror, and sorrow; and an exalted calm is prolonged from the satiety of this high exercise of them into the tumult of familiar life; even crime is disarmed of half its horror and all its contagion by being represented as the fatal consequences of the unfathomable agencies of nature; error is thus divested of its wilfulness; men can no longer cherish it as the creation of their choice.' Or, as he otherwise expressed the same idea in his Preface to *The Cenci*: 'The highest moral purpose aimed at in the higher species of the drama, is the teaching the human heart, through its sympathies and antipathies, the knowledge of itself; in proportion to the possession of which knowledge, every human being is wise, just, sincere, tolerant and kind.' In this light we should receive a dramatic creation such as the figure of Beatrice; for, as he says, 'imagination is as the immortal God which should assume flesh for the redemption of mortal passion.' The significance of *The Cenci*, then, lies in the fact that Shelley wrote it without any didactic or philosophical purpose. He wished to illustrate, in the figure of Beatrice, that greatness of character is created by constancy in love, and he knew that this could be done only in dramatic action.

It may seem that Shelley's philosophy remains on a moral, even a mundane, plane, and does not attempt to answer those profounder metaphysical questions to which Coleridge and Wordsworth addressed themselves. But this is not true: the unfinished 'Triumph of Life' ends with the question 'What is life?' and it was a question of which Shelley was continuously conscious. And he did provide an answer. That love, which he declared the secret of morals, he also regarded as the guiding principle of the universe. Again, he was following Plato, and, more particularly, Dante. In the detail of his conception he is much nearer to Dante than to Plato, but as a confessed atheist he did not want to identify this 'unseen Power' with a divine agency. He therefore gives it an 'awful throne . . . in the wise heart', from which it springs to fold over the world its healing wings. This universal love is clearly and defiantly humanistic in character; its 'spells' are faculties within the titanic frame of man's imagination. In order to be

> *Good, great and joyous, beautiful and free*

it is necessary

> *To suffer woes which Hope thinks infinite;*
> *To forgive wrongs darker than death or night;*
> *To defy Power, which seems omnipotent;*
> *To love, and bear; to hope till Hope creates*
> *From its own wreck the thing it contemplates;*
> *Neither to change, nor falter, nor repent.*

These are Stoic virtues, human aspirations, and I see no evidence anywhere in Shelley's work which would justify any more transcendental faith. At the end of *Adonais* he writes:

> *From the world's bitter wind*
> *Seek Shelter in the shadow of the tomb.*

And though he uses words like 'Heaven' and 'Eternity', it is always in a metaphorical sense: they are attributes of the One, absolute, denied to the Many.

> *The One remains, the many change and pass;*
> *Heaven's light forever shines, Earth's shadows fly;*
> *Life, like a dome of many-coloured glass,*
> *Stains the white radiance of Eternity,*
> *Until Death tramples it to fragments.*

Resolute words, among the most immortal in our language; and they are followed by the relentless command:

> *Die,*
> *If thou wouldst be with that which thou dost seek.*
> *Follow where all is fled!*

'That which thou dost seek' is identified with the Spirit of Beauty:

> *That Light whose smile kindles the Universe,*
> *That Beauty in which all things work and move,*
> *That Benediction which the eclipsing Curse*
> *Of birth can quench not, that sustaining Love*
> *Which through the web of being blindly wove*

In Defence of Shelley

By man and beast and earth and air and sea,
Burns bright or dim, as each are mirrors of
The fire for which all thirst . . .

A fire, a white radiance, a transfused glory, a plastic stress, the splendours of the firmament of time — Shelley uses many such phrases to describe the immanent Spirit of the Universe, the ultimate Reality. They are concepts of the imagination, remote from revealed religion, but implying an endless resonance of love, beauty, and delight.

Shelley was one of those uncomfortable idealists who practise what they preach, and it is precisely the practical results of this doctrine from which the timid or the formal moralist recoils in horror or disdain. 'Bête!' 'sale!' cries Matthew Arnold. 'Blackguard!' cries Mr. Eliot. It is true that there was in his own day another voice that cried: 'You were all brutally mistaken about Shelley, who was, without exception, the *best* and least selfish man I ever knew. I never knew one who was not a beast in comparison.'[1] But that was the voice of one who, though he had been stretched on the rack of experience till he touched the extremes of iniquity and glory, and so should speak with profound authority, is admittedly not apt to quell a doctrinaire. There have been others who have forgiven Shelley out of their Christian sympathy, and a few who have dared to imply that a poet of such divine genius is above human laws. But none has attempted to justify Shelley in reason, and on the basis of psychological truth. That, however, is a task which may be attempted with the aid of those psychological considerations which I have brought forward.

The crux of the question is, of course, Shelley's treatment of his wife, Harriet. If Shelley had not so defiantly deserted her, if he had not so defiantly committed adultery with Mary Godwin, if the consequences of his action had not been so tragic, we should not have had so much righteous indignation about his character and conduct. Shelley's morals would have been confined to a polite essay and to his poetry, and we should have been free to admire the man and his work without distraction. But Shelley sinned against the most sacred clause in the social code of his time, and as a result has been vilified as a person and depreciated as a poet.

Until a few years ago, such judgements were made on a very

[1] Byron, in a letter to John Murray, August 3, 1822.

189

incomplete knowledge of the facts. It was not until Dr. Leslie Hotson discovered and published Shelley's letters to Harriet written at the time of his parting from her that the full evidence was made available. Dr. Hotson has marshalled that evidence, and presented it with a scholarly detachment from which emerges, on the facts simply, and all idealistic justification apart, a far more favourable view of Shelley's conduct than any that has hitherto prevailed.[1] The discovery attracted significantly little attention at the time, and now the world is prepared to relapse into its former superficial judgement, which has the sanction of all those forces, those 'habitual inertias', which maintain the social code in its hard complacency and fathomless hypocrisy.

I shall not recount the whole story again. A blunt statement of true circumstances would read somewhat as follows: In the year 1811, a harpy named Eliza Westbrook vamped a youth of nineteen into marrying her sister, a schoolgirl of sixteen. The youth had just been expelled from Oxford for 'atheism', was homeless, excited and impressionable, and was moreover the heir to a great estate. The schoolgirl was pretty, neat and witty, but completely under the control of the sister. There was a story of 'tyranny' at home and school, and a threat of suicide if not rescued. The youth, impetuous and romantic, proposed elopement; was eagerly accepted; and the harpy triumphed, even to the extent of fastening herself to the poor deluded couple.[2] The rest of the story is best told in a few excerpts from the letters of this youth, Shelley:

'1811 (*no date*). What have I said? I declare, quite *ludicrous*. I advised her to resist. She wrote to say that resistance was useless, but that she would fly with me and threw herself upon my protection. We shall have £200 a year; when we find it run short, we must live, I suppose, upon love! Gratitude and admiration, all demand that I should love her *for ever*. (*To Hogg*.)

'*March* 16, 1814. My friend, you are happier than I. You have the pleasures as well as the pains of sensibility. I have sunk into a premature old age of exhaustion, which renders me dead to everything, but the unenviable capacity of indulging the vanity of

---

[1] *Shelley's Lost Letters to Harriet*, edited with an Introduction by Leslie Hotson (London, Faber and Faber, 1930).

[2] Cf. Hogg: 'Harriet Westbrook appears to have been dissatisfied with her school, but without any adequate cause, for she was kindly treated and well educated there. It is not impossible that this discontent was prompted and suggested to her, and that she was put up to it, and to much besides, by somebody, who conducted the whole affair — who had assumed and steadily persisted in keeping the complete direction of her.' (Chap. XII.)

hope, and a terrible susceptibility to objects of disgust and hatred. (*To Hogg.*)

'(*The same*). Eliza is still with us. . . . I certainly hate her with all my heart and soul. It is a sight which awakens an inexpressible sensation of disgust and horror, to see her caress my poor little Ianthe, in whom I may hereafter find the consolation of sympathy. I sometimes feel faint with the fatigue of checking the overflowings of my unbounded abhorrence for this miserable wretch. She is no more than a blind and loathsome worm, that cannot see to sting. (*To Hogg.*)

'*July*, 1814 (*no date*). I repeat (and believe me, for I am sincere) that my attachment to you is unimpaired. I conceive that it has acquired even a deeper and more lasting character, that it is now less exposed than ever to the fluctuations of phantasy or caprice. Our connection was not one of passion and impulse. Friendship was its basis, and on this basis it has enlarged and strengthened. It is no reproach to me that you have never filled my heart with an all-sufficing passion; perhaps you are even yourself a stranger to these impulses, which one day may be awakened by some nobler and worthier than me; and you may find a lover as passionate and faithful, as I shall ever be a friend affectionate and sincere! (*To Harriet.*)

'*September* 15, 1814. You think that I have injured you. Since I first beheld you almost, my chief study has been to overwhelm you with benefits. Even now when a violent and lasting passion for another leads me to prefer her society to yours, I am perpetually employed in devising how I can be permanently and truly useful to you, in what manner my time and my fortune may be most securely expended for your real interests. In return for this it is not well that I should be wounded with reproach and blame: so unexampled and singular an attachment demands a return far different. And it would be generous, nay even just, to consider with kindness that woman whom my judgment and my heart have selected as the noblest and the most excellent of human beings. (*To Harriet.*)

'*September* 27, 1814. A common love for all that the world detests was once the bond of union between us. This you have been the first to break; and you have lost a friend whom you will with difficulty replace. Your contumelious language toward Mary is equally impotent and mean. You appeal to the vilest superstitions of the most ignorant and slavish of mankind. I consider it an insult that you address such cant to me. (*To Harriet*.)

'*? October* 3, 1814. I am united to another; you are no longer my wife. Perhaps I have done you injury, but surely most innocently and unintentionally, in having commenced any connexion with you. That injury, whatever be its amount, was not to be avoided. (*To Harriet*.)'

Such excerpts do not convey the whole story, but the full letters are there for any reader to consult. They must be supplemented by some estimate of the personality of Harriet, such as I have attempted for the personality of Shelley. But whatever conclusion we reached on the basis of the somewhat contradictory evidence, it would not affect the issue. Harriet may have been an angel in the house, with all the virtues of a good wife and an intelligent companion; or she may have been an extremely frivolous and tiresome schoolgirl, with a mania for self-destruction, incapable of passion as of understanding. In either case, she and Shelley were victims of life's most cruel joke (life, in this instance, being to a considerable extent personified in Eliza). Shelley, in his dilemma, might have kept the code and earned the approval of future moralists; but we do not know to what alternative tragedy he and Harriet would have drifted. Out of the fullness of his heart and the strength of his philosophy he chose to assert his individual liberty. He earned immediate opprobrium and more than a century of calumny; but he lifted himself out of a premature old age of exhaustion, into a brighter element of intellectual vitality, and into a new lease of poetic inspiration.

Earlier in his life, shortly before he was married to Harriet Westbrook, Shelley had upheld against Hogg the proposition that 'laws were not made for men of honour'. He then argued the case, as eloquently as any undergraduate, with appeals to Aristotle and Godwin. Three years later he had to argue the case in his own destiny, and deep within his own being he found that philosophy of love which is the theme of his greatest poetry. A superficial and a cynical mind will only see in such philosophical poetry a rationalization of Shelley's selfish instincts; but from our nearer and more sympathetic point of view we can have a deeper appreciation of a feeling too organic to be selfish, too magnanimous to be immoral, and too hopeful, in 'this cold common hell, our life', to be denied.

The particular quality of Shelley's poetry still remains to be defined. It is a quality directly related to the nature of his personality, and that is why I have taken so much trouble to describe that personality. Understanding the personality, we may more easily, more openly, appreciate the poetry.

Byron, who was a very honest critic, even of his friends, was the first to be aware of Shelley's *particular* quality. 'You know my high opinion of your own poetry', he wrote to Shelley, and added the reason: ' — because it is of *no* school.' To Byron all the rest of his contemporaries seemed 'second-hand' imitators of antique models or doctrinaire exponents of a mannerism. Shelley alone could not be so simply classified; his verse was too honestly original, too independently thought and wrought, to be accepted as 'fashionable literature'. For there are always these two types of originality: originality that responds like the Æolian harp to every gust of contemporary feeling, pleasing by its anticipation of what is but half-formed in the public consciousness; and originality that is not influenced by anything outside the poet's own consciousness, but is the direct product of his individual mind and independent feeling. The latter type is always long in winning recognition, and since Shelley's originality was essentially of this type, we need not be surprised that only a few of his contemporaries appreciated his poetry for its proper qualities.

The reaction of Keats is the most interesting, for he had perhaps a profounder understanding of the nature of poetry than any man of that age — profounder, I would say, than Byron and even profounder than Coleridge. We only discern this from the occasional statements made in his letters — there is unfortunately no formal essay to compare with Shelley's. Nor did Keats live to write poetry with which he was personally satisfied; we must not, that is to say, treat the poetry of Keats as an exemplification of his poetic ideals. A detailed comparison of the poetry of Keats and Shelley would not therefore be of great value. But Keats's reaction to Shelley's poetry, expressed in a letter to Shelley, is most definitely critical:

'... You might curb your magnanimity and be more of an artist, and load every rift of your subject with ore. The thought of such discipline must fall like cold chains upon you, who perhaps never sat with your wings furled for six months together.'

We cannot doubt the force of the impact which Shelley's poetry had made on Keats. The poetry had been felt, but felt as something strange or inadequate. And actually we can see that what is involved is a clash of personalities. There is no need to describe Keats's personality at length; but it was in no way parallel to Shelley's. Keats was not, of course, a normal type — no genius is; but compared with Shelley he was far more fully adjusted to his environment; physically more masculine and heterosexual; and though a sick man ('when I shook him by the hand there was death'), not a morbid one. Sensitive critics have even been considerably disturbed by what they regard as a deplorable strain of coarseness and vulgarity in his nature. Without going into any great detail, it will be obvious that the general mode of expression of such a personality would be very different from Shelley's; it would, by a process contrary to the one we have described in Shelley's case, show a tendency towards definiteness and objectivity. Now though much of Keats's poetry is anything but definite and objective, he was very conscious, as we have seen, of an intolerable hiatus between his personality and the poetic diction he had derived from traditional models and current fashions; and his whole effort, as expressed in his short but intense poetic development, is towards objective virtues.

The whole tendency of Shelley, on the contrary, is towards a clarification and abstraction of thought — away from the personal and the particular towards the general and the universal. Between the transcendental intellectualism of Shelley and the concrete sensualism of Keats there could be, and was, no contact.

The highest beauties of Keats's poetry are enumerative: a positive evocation of the tone and texture of physical objects. Even when describing an abstract conception like Melancholy, the imagery of physical sensation is dominant:

> *Ay, in the very temple of Delight*
> *Veil'd Melancholy has her sovran shrine,*
> *Though seen of none save him whose strenuous tongue*
> *Can burst Joy's grape against his palate fine . . .*

But the highest beauties of Shelley's poetry are evanescent and imponderable — thought so tenuous and intuitive, that it has no visual equivalent; no positive impact:

> *Life of Life! thy lips enkindle*
> *With their love the breath between them;*

In Defence of Shelley

And thy smiles before they dwindle
Make the cold air fire; then screen them
In those looks, where whoso gazes
Faints, entangled in their mazes.

Child of Light! thy limbs are burning
Through the vest which seems to hide them;
As the radiant lines of morning
Through the clouds ere they divide them;
And this atmosphere divinest
Shrouds thee whereso'er thou shinest.

Fair are others; none beholds thee,
But thy voice sounds low and tender
Like the fairest, for it folds thee
From the sight, that liquid splendour,
And all feel, yet see thee never,
As I feel now, lost for ever!

Lamp of Earth! where'er thou movest
Its dim shapes are clad with brightness,
And the souls of whom thou lovest
Walk upon the winds with lightness,
Till they fail, as I am failing,
Dizzy, lost, yet unbewailing!

In such a poem — and it is the supreme type of Shelley's poetic utterance — every image fades into air, every outline is dissolved in fire. The idea conveyed — the notional content — is almost negligible; the poetry exists in the suspension of meaning, in the avoidance of actuality.

In other words, such poetry has no precision, and the process of its unfolding is not logical. It does not answer to a general definition of any kind. It is vain to apply to it that method of criticism which assumes that the ardour of a verse can be analysed into separate vocables, and that poetry is a function of sound. Poetry is mainly a function of language — the exploitation of a medium, a vocal and sensuous material, in the interests of a personal mood or emotion, or of the thoughts evoked by such moods and emotions. I do not think we can say much more about it; according to our sensitivity we recognize its success. The rest of our reasoning about it is either mere prejudice, ethical anxiety, or academic pride.

Among his contemporaries, Shelley was perhaps nearest in poetic quality to Landor, whose *Gebir* was a lasting joy to him. A critical justification for this attraction would not be far to seek. The next nearest analogies are with Schiller and Goethe, both of whom Shelley read with enthusiasm; the influence of *Faust* has been traced in *The Triumph of Life*,[1] but between Goethe and Shelley there is a general sympathy of poetic outlook which is not explained by direct contacts. Other analogies, some of which I have already mentioned, are remoter: 'the gentle seriousness, the delicate sensibility, the calm and sustained energy' of Ariosto; and above all 'the first awakener of entranced Europe . . . the congregator of those great spirits who presided over the resurrection of learning; the Lucifer of that starry flock which in the thirteenth century shone forth from republican Italy as from a heaven, into the darkness of the benighted world' — Dante. All great poetry, said Shelley in the same reference to Dante, is *infinite*; and that is the final quality of his own poetry, the quality which lifts it into regions beyond the detractions of moralists and sciolists.[2]

Shelley is of no school; that is to say, Shelley is above all schools, universal in the mode of his expression and the passion of his mind. That passion, the force that urged him to abundant voice, was simple, almost single, in its aim. 'I knew Shelley more intimately than any man', wrote Hogg, 'but I never could discern in him any more than two fixed principles. The first was a strong, irrepressible love of liberty; of liberty in the abstract, and somewhat after the pattern of the ancient republics, without reference to the English constitution, respecting which he knew little and cared nothing, heeding it not at all. The second was an equally ardent love of toleration of all opinions, but more especially of religious opinions; of toleration, complete, entire, universal, unlimited; and, as a deduction and corollary from which latter principle, he felt an intense abhorrence of persecution of every kind, public or private.' Liberty and toleration — these words have a tortured history, and are often perverted for a moral purpose. But that was not Shelley's intention. 'The highest moral purpose

[1] F. Melian Stawell, 'Shelley's *Triumph of Life*' (English Association: *Essay and Studies*, vol. V, p. 105).
[2] The best elucidation of this quality in Shelley's poetry is Leone Vivante's, in the work already cited.

aimed at in the highest species of the drama, is the teaching the human heart, through its sympathies and antipathies, the knowledge of itself; in proportion to the possession of which knowledge, every human being is wise, just, sincere, tolerant and kind.' Inasmuch as the final quality of Shelley's poetry is infinitude, so the final quality of his mind is sympathy. Sympathy and infinitude — these are expansive virtues, not avowed in the dry air of disillusion, awaiting a world of peace and justice for their due recognition.

American Bards and British Reviewers[1]

 It is one of the conveniences of history, or perhaps one of the limitations of the human vision when we look down its long perspective, that to each nation is given one towering archetypal figure, one representative poet. Greece has its Homer and Rome its Vergil; England its Shakespeare and France its Racine; Italy its Dante and Germany its Goethe. It is one of my most confident beliefs that the United States already possesses a representative poet of this universal significance. I refer not, as might be anticipated, to Walt Whitman, but to Henry James. If you are inclined to protest that James is not a poet in the sense that Shakespeare or Dante were poets, I must beg to differ, here at the beginning of my discourse. Poetry, in this largest sense, transcends the technicalities of diction. If we who speak the English language are honest with ourselves, what does the poetry of a Greek, a Latin, a German or a French writer mean to us? We may speak a foreign language like a native, as we say; but do we, who live in another land, and daily absorb other sights and sounds, hear but a distant echo of the poet's own voice? Certain languages we even designate as 'dead', so how can we, who still dispute how a vocable was uttered by an ancient poet, pretend that we are conscious of the poetic subleties of these languages? No, in so far as our judgement of the universality of poetry rests on linguistic criteria, we must accept the verdict of the poet's own countrymen; at the same time affirming that by its very nature universality is a quality independent of locality, a question, not so much of the poet's utterance but of the width and depth of the vision or consciousness of which the living voice is but the mediating instrument.[2]

[1] Deliver as an Address to the National Poetry Festival, Washington, D.C., October 24th, 1962.
[2] How James himself felt about this question is clearly shown in a letter of September 7th, 1913, to his French translator, Auguste Monod: '. . . I confess that it is a relief to me this time to have so utterly defied translation. The new volume

I shall presently seem to contradict this confident assertion. I do not for one moment wish to deny the verbal or vocal nature of poetry: poetry is a physical and not a metaphysical phenomenon. If we are poets we know that we not only, as Wallace Stevens said, *read* poetry with our nerves: we *write* poetry with our nerves — or, to translate the metaphor into philosophical jargon, poetry is a process of perceptual apprehension, not one of a conceptual realization. But these definitions by no means exclude the works of Henry James — rather, Henry James compels us, by the very range and inclusive splendour of his perceptual apprehensions, to enlarge our conception of poetry itself. Where else, in American literature, if not in the sensitive consciousness of a Maggie Verver or Milly Theale, are we to find any such deep aesthetic awareness of the terror and beauty of the human predicament, any comparison with the poetic exercise of these powers in a Shakespeare or a Dante? In Henry James America already has a great universal poet, received, as all such poets are, with mistrust and incomprehension during his life-time, but now at last emerging solidly into the light of universal acclaim.

Such poetry is not quotable. You may say that Shakespeare's genius is represented by certain verbal touchstones, by 'the temple-haunting martlet' or by the crow that 'makes wing to the rooky wood'. But James had his touchstones, too, though they are of another character. I do not refer to the poetic perfection of his titles — symbols that condense into a concrete image the whole nature of a tragic experience, nor to the innumerable phrases, as isolated and as memorable as the temple-haunting martlet and the rooky wood, that overflow from those 'full vessels of consciousness', those characters that reflect the author's own 'lucid higher intention'. To quote such merely felicitous phrases as touchstones of poetry would be unfaithful to what I conceive to be the modern poet's own higher intention, which is precisely not to rely on the musical phrase in poetic composition, but on certain larger units which are qualities of perception — on what James himself called, with reference to the kind of sensibility he prized, an inordinate capacity for *being* and *seeing*. These qualities of perception modify

will complete that defiance and express for me how much I feel that in a literary work of the least complexity the very form and texture are the substance itself and that the flesh is indetachable from the bones! Translation is an effort — though a most flattering one! — to *tear* the hapless flesh, and in fact to get rid of so much of it that the living thing bleeds and faints away!' (*Letters to A. C. Benson and Auguste Monod*, edited by E. F. Benson, London, 1930, pp. 117–18.)

the formal structure of the writing, and in this way the style becomes idiomatic. James's own style is idiomatic in this sense — the Jamesian parenthesis, Ezra Pound has recently suggested, *is* an American form.[1]

I won't insist further on this distinction, but will assume that our vision has been adjusted to nearer views of smaller objects, which is perhaps the distinctive characteristic of the modern mind. We are then confronted with a different difficulty — the confusing variety of what now presses on our organs of perception. Our consciousness is subjected to two pressures which Wallace Stevens at the conclusion of his essay on 'The Noble Rider and the Sound of Words', defined as the reality that presses into the mind and the imagination that presses back against the reality — 'a violence from within that protects us from a violence without'. Modern American poetry has been born of this clash of forces. We have to determine whether it has found a state of equilibrium poetic in its effect.

As a critic who divides his attention between poetry and painting I am apt to indulge in comparisons that do not necessarily have any logical justification. American painting (sculpture and architecture, too, but I try to simplify the situation) achieved its independence only comparatively recently, and then with a passionate conviction that threatens to exhaust itself too quickly. That independence was not a spontaneous act of revolt. Equally it was not the final ripening of a native tradition. There were some decisive historical events, accidental in their origins, such as the sojourn here, under the stress of war, of foreign artists and animators like Andre Masson and André Breton. But, whatever the nature of the intrusive catalyst, the transformation that then took place, between the years 1940 and 1945, was complete: a new American painting emerged with its own easily recognized characteristics, and was destined to revitalize the art of painting throughout the world.

In our time nothing of the same kind has happened to American poetry. The comparable poetic assault took place a hundred years ago and its 'commando' was Walt Whitman. In the interval Americans may have lived down Walt Whitman — they may have shot him in the back, but so far as the rest of the world is concerned, his soul still goes marching on, and whether we are Frenchmen or Englishmen, Spaniards or Germans, we still tend to iden-

[1] *Paris Review* (no. 28, 1962), p. 26.

tify anything that may be distinctively American in American poetry with Whitman. And *only* with Whitman, the one pioneer as Lawrence called him. 'No English pioneers, no French. No European pioneer poets. In Europe the would-be pioneer poets are mere innovators. The same in America. Ahead of Whitman, nothing. Ahead of all poets, pioneering into the wilderness of un-opened life, Whitman. Beyond him, none. His wide, strange camp at the end of the great high-road.' Lawrence wrote this in 1924, and then he could add: 'Because Whitman's camp is at the end of the road, and on the edge of a great precipice . . . there is no way down. It is a dead end.'[1]

So it has proved, in the sense intended by Lawrence. Lawrence was looking for a great leader, by which he meant a great moralist, 'a great changer of the blood in the veins of men.' But if Whitman was a dead end it was for the very good reason that the American poets who came after him no longer responded to the forced rhetoric of the pioneer. This is not because the American poet has turned off the open road, to evade the moral issue that engaged not only Whitman, but also Hawthorne, Poe, Longfellow, Emerson and Melville; it is because the whole scene or circumstance has changed. It we cared to elaborate Lawrence's rather banal meta-phor, we might say that the pioneering days being over, there is now no escaping the sophistications of a closed society, in which the road is no longer open, but winds in diminishing circles round a golden calf. The moral issue remains, inseparable from the human predicament. The best American poets are preoccupied with it, but they have discovered that Whitman's rhetoric, Lawrence's too, is too brutal for the task of redemption.

After Whitman, so far as we have registered any direct impact on our translantic consciousness, came Ezra Pound. But Pound left America and came to Europe — came in the costume of a troubadour and when he was shamed out of it, went to school with Gautier and Remy de Gourmont, Laforgue and Hume. Pound, from London, served as foreign correspondent to *Poetry*, the American review whose foundation fifty years ago we are now celebrating. But the more he reported from England or France or Italy, the more evident it became that he was no longer on the road, following where Whitman had led. 'Have I a country at all?' was to be his tragic cry. 'Not that I care a curse for any nation as such or that, as far as I know, I have ever suggested that I was

[1] *From Studies in Classic American Literature, 1924.*

trying to write U.S. poetry. . . ."[1] He deflected, and, great poet
though he be, was lost to America; and what he might have been,
William Carlos Williams became. I do not mean that Dr. Williams
merely stepped into some place in the ranks vacated by the poet
from Idaho — I shall return to him presently. But Pound, in so
far as he remained a stylistic preceptor, was as exotic and as
irrelevant as Tu Fu or Fenellosa, which fact Williams realized at
least as early as 1920. This is not to deny Pound's influence, even
on such an indigenous poet as Williams himself. Indeed, one has
only to read Pound's letters to Harriet Monroe, between 1912
and 1916, to see how perceptively and severely he formulated the
rules of the game at the decisive moment. Without his repeated
insistence that poetry should be as well written as prose, that
language is made out of concrete things, without his call for
objectivity and concentration, for seeing and being — without
this relentless campaign for purity and integrity, American poetry
would never have been what it is today. Pound wrote from Europe,
he had become a European, if not a Confucian; but he was
preaching virtues that are universal.

At this stage in the argument it would be invidious not to make
some observations on Thomas Stearns Eliot, as authentically from
St. Louis as Ezra Pound from Idaho. Eliot came to England in
1914 and came to stay. He stayed to become the most universally
acclaimed poet of our age — but in the becoming in what sense
did he remain an American poet? Admittedly I have not yet
defined what we mean by the Americanness of an American poet,
but all Williams's animadversions on 'exoticism' were applied
equally to Eliot as to Pound. It is perhaps an embarrassing choice
for the American critic, but if he believes in the Americanness of
American verse, then he must renounce Pound and Eliot, con-
signing them to some international limbo. He may, I think vainly,
try to make some distinction between the early Eliot, the poet of
Prufrock and Other Observations (1917), and the poet of the *Four
Quartets* (1944), but the quarter of a century that intervenes is an
advance from exoticism to universality, and I fail to detect anywhere, apart from the subject-matter of some of the earlier poems,
any idiomatic element that could be described as specifically
American. Indeed, we may conclude that Eliot's influence on the
poetry of the United States has been, not only away from Whit-

[1] See letter to William Carlos Williams of 11 September, 1920. (*Letters*, pp. 223,
222.)

man (not to mention Emerson and Longfellow) but towards a traditionalism altogether opposed to the American ethos and idiom.

I see that I can no longer avoid some attempt at a definition of this idiomatic element, as it strikes an observer from abroad. An idiom, any dictionary will tell us, is something one makes one's own, something peculiar to one's speech and, by extension, to the language of a people or a country. As a word it has close connections with 'idiot', but that is perhaps irrelevant. What is *not* irrelevant is that it represents a deviation from a standard, from an accepted mode of expression. The idiomatic is therefore very unclassical, and one does not expect to find idiomatic expressions in a classical language, or in a poet using a classical language. From this point of view there is certainly such a thing as classical English and poets like Dryden, Gray, Tennyson, and Bridges have made deliberate use of it; its use in America has been recommended by an American critic, Yvor Winters.

Classical conventions are metrical rather than verbal, systems of scansion that may be quantitative or syllabic or accentual. In this sense I do not find anything idiomatic in American verse. I know that there is a supposition, prevalent since Wordsworth first formulated it, that the diction of poetry can correspond in some close manner to the rhythms of speech, and that American speech rhythms being different from British speech rhythms, the difference would constitute a new kind of poetry. But Byron neatly disposed of this solecism — Wordsworth

> *Who, both by precept and example, shows*
> *That prose is verse, and verse is merely prose;*
> *Convincing all, by demonstration plain,*
> *Poetic souls delight in prose inane. . . .*

Conversational rhythms may or may not be poetic; if they are poetic the poet imitates them, not because they are conversational, but because they are exceptional. I do not wish to labour an obvious point, but in so far as we make a distinction between poetry and prose, we are making a distinction between two kinds of rhythm, a normal rhythm which is the rhythm of prose and is based on the rhythm of speech; and an abnormal rhythm which is the rhythm of poetry and is based on a heightened, an intensified, or, if you like, a regularized modification of speech rhythm. To say, with Ezra Pound, that poetry must be at least as well written as prose does not mean that it must imitate prose: it means that poetry has laws which are at least as strict as those of prose.

What I am trying to suggest, as tactfully as possible, is that the whole concept of a linguistic idiom, as distinct from a personal idiom, is an illusion. The idiom of Robert Burns, to take an extreme example, is different from the idiom of Lord Byron, but the fact that the one wrote in Scots dialect while the other wrote in King's English is poetically irrelevant.

> *Thou'll break my heart, thou bonnie bird*
> *That sings upon a bough;*
> *Thou minds me o' the happy days*
> *When my fause luve was true.*
>
> *Though my many faults defaced me,*
> *Could no other arm be found,*
> *Than the one which once embraced me*
> *To inflict a cureless wound?*

These two verses, the first written by Burns, the second by Byron, differ in idiom, but not in diction; but it is the diction that determines the poetry. The idiom of Donne differs from the idiom of Milton, a vast difference, but they speak the same language. The difference in their speech rhythms, if it existed, was determined by physical constitution, psychological temperament, social origins and education. When Dr. Williams tells me that 'the iamb is not the normal measure of American speech' I must retort that neither is it the normal measure of British speech. When he suggests that 'the key to modern poetry is *measure*, which must reflect the flux of modern life', he is either asserting a truism, that modern poetry must suit modern tastes, or he is merely re-affirming my own contention, that the individual poet must find a measure that matches his own sensibility, his individual awareness of the visible world. But it will be *his* sensibility, *his* measure, and not one dictated by some undefined and indefinable national ethos.

When Kenneth Rexroth, interpreting William Carlos Williams, asserts that '. . . his poetic line is organically welded to American speech like muscle to bone, as the choruses of Euripides were welded to the speech of the Athenians in the market place', we are again asked to accept a truism that none of us doubts, namely, that the poet, whatever his language, must continually renew the expressive vitality of his verse by returning to what Wordsworth called 'a selection of the real language of men in a state of vivid sensation'. It is possible to maintain that the English now spoken in the United States is more 'real' in this sense than the English spoken in the East End of London or the West Riding of Yorkshire, though that remains a matter of opinion. What is not a matter of opinion, and is freely acknowledged by this British reviewer, is that the ears of the American poet are more open to these variations, these demotic phrases and expressions, than those of the majority of contemporary British poets! The comparatively greater richness in the texture of modern American poetry is no doubt explained by this closer attention to demotic speech. But have we not learned from the classic case of Wordsworth that poetry, English poetry, to the degree that it is 'classic' — I use the word again because Kenneth Rexroth calls Williams 'the first American classic' — to that degree the poet refines the demotic ore, tempers it to some mode or measure that is essentially English?

When I examine the verse of William Carlos Williams, this first American classic, and have in my mind's eye and ear the late verse of *The Desert Music* and *Journey to Love*, I find what is to my judgement indubitably classical verse. There is a test piece which I do not insist on too strongly, for I should be using the word 'classic' in an ambiguous sense, which is a version from the Greek of the first Idyll of Theocritus.

> *The whisper of the wind in*
> *that pine tree,*
> *goatherd,*
> *is sweet as the murmur of live water;*
> *likewise*
> *your flute notes. After Pan*
> *you shall bear away the second prize.*
> *And if he*
> *take the goat*
> *with the horns,*
> *the she-goat*
> *is yours; but if*
> *he choose the she-goat,*
> *the kid will fall*
> *to your lot.*
> *And the flesh of the kid*
> *is dainty*
> *before they begin milking them....*

What is there demotic, or American, about these beautiful cadences? Is it not the very language of Wyatt, of Campion, of Gray or Landor — to mention some of the purest of our English poets? And when we turn the pages and come to 'Asphodel, That Greeny Flower', the poem which W. H. Auden has rightly called 'one of the most beautiful love poems in the language' (he did not say 'in the American language') we find verse of such pellucid brightness, of such simple human and passionate sentiment, that no sense of time and place ever obtrudes between the ear and the music, between the poet and his audience. This is universal poetry, and the language is English.

I must admit a personal predilection for the poetry of William Carlos Williams. It may be that American in the grain as he is, and English as I am (in this context I refuse to call myself British), we share the same idiosyncrasies. But any critic's point of view, if he be honest, is determined by physical facts, by constitutional elements that are also responsible for the psychological facts. The voice of the poet has the timbre of his body, and that, as I have already suggested, is the only sense in which we should use the word 'idiom'. But if, in our examination of contemporary American poetry, we are thrown back on the psychological facts, what then do we find?

We find certain poets who, from a distant view, are typically American. We find Hart Crane, Wallace Stevens, Robert Lowell and John Berryman, the American poets currently most admired and imitated by the younger British poets. Have these four anything in common that is distinctively American? Having rejected the claim to an exclusively American idiom, can we perhaps admit in its place an exclusively American psyche?

Waldo Frank has said that the poetry of Hart Crane is 'a deliberate continuance of the great tradition in terms of our industrialized world' — the great tradition that 'rose in the Mediterranean world with the will of Egypt, Israel and Greece, to recreate the individual and the group in the image of values called divine'. Crane himself, in his short but highly significant essay on 'Modern Poetry', affirmed that the function of poetry in a Machine Age is identical with its function in any other age; and that 'its capacities for presenting the most complete synthesis of human values remain essentially immune from any of the so-called inroads of science'. The point is not that poetry should absorb the machine, but that it should '*acclimatize* it as naturally and casually as trees, cattle, galleons, castles and all other human associations of the past . . .'. Otherwise poetry 'has failed of its contemporary function'. Those who go to Hart Crane for a justification of an American idiom will be disappointed. They will find instead a traditionalist, his verse grounded on the practice of early English prosody, in some sense specifically Elizabethan, a traditionalist aware that (to quote his own words) 'the most intense and eloquent current verse derives sheerly from acute psychological analysis, quite independent of any dramatic motivation'.

There you have the description, if not the definition, of what a British reviewer might admit as the quality most distinctively American in American verse, the revealed tension between analysis and motivation, reality and imagination; and it is highly significant that Crane himself found the source of this quality in Whitman — 'The most typical and valid expression of the American *psychosis* seems to me still to be found in Whitman', he wrote in this same essay — 'He, better than any other, was able to coordinate those forces in America which seem most intractable, fusing them into a universal vision which takes on additional significance as time goes on.' Earlier in the essay he had quoted Coleridge's definition of genius as 'the power of acting creatively under laws of its own origination', and he concludes that Whitman was a revolutionist beyond the strict meaning of this definition, 'but his bequest is still to be realized in all its implications.'

May I therefore suggest, not only that Crane himself did his best to realize Whitman's bequest, but also that what is distinctive in American poetry since Crane's death has been a continuation of this attempt to find a valid expression of the American psychosis? Before I ask for agreement I must, of course, make some attempt of my own to define the American psychosis, or rather, to make a significant choice among the many diagnoses of this psychosis made by American critics and psychologists. Professor Blackmur has reproved Crane for using this word 'psychosis' and both he and Professor Winters have a poor opinion of Crane's transcendentalism. But somehow Crane survives their criticisms. We remember Dr. Williams's protest, that 'it isn't what (a man) *says* that counts as a work of art, it's what he makes, with such intensity of perception that it lives with an intrinsic movement of its own to verify its authenticity'. Words that remind me incidentally of one of Henry James's definitions of lyric poetry — 'stoney-hearted triumphs of objective form'.

Critics, alas, cannot do without a philosophic sounding-board: it is the only thing that makes us resound at all, for in the physical presence of the poem, or the picture, we can but register our sensations. The great intelligence — yes, that too is necessary; but it is a crudity of sensibility to imagine that the poet's or the painter's intelligence functions as an acceptable philosophy. What philosophy did a great painter like Turner profess? For that matter, what philosophy did our greatest poet profess? Some critics have tried to derive a philosophy from Shakespeare's works, but they have only succeeded in revealing a great confusion.

I think we should respect Crane's brief excursion into the definition of modern poetry because even if it does not measure up to the logician's standards of consistency or profundity, it does indicate the poet's own intention more nearly than any critical analysis from the outside. His use of the word 'psychosis' may not be clinically correct, but Crane obviously thought that it was adequate to describe the alienation caused by the machine, and the title of his greatest poem 'The Bridge' was chosen deliberately as a psychological symbol.

But what separate shores was this symbolical Bridge meant to connect? The last section of the poem is entitled 'Atlantis' and it is headed by a quotation from Plato: 'Music is then the knowledge of that which relates to love in harmony and form'. Substitute, without any violence to Plato's meaning, the word 'poetry' for 'music' and Crane's message becomes clear:

> *O Thou steeled Cognizance whose leap commits*
> *The agile precincts of the lark's return;*
> *Within whose lariat sweep encinctured sing*
> *In single chrysalis the many twain, —*
> *Of stars thou art the stitch and stallionglow*
> *And like an organ, Thou, with sound of doom —*
> *Sight, sound and flesh Thou leadest from time's realm*
> *As love strikes clear direction for the helm.*

I am reminded of another great spirit of our time, Simone Weil, who also made use of this same symbol, the bridge. 'The bridges of the Greeks. We have inherited them but we do not know how to use them. We thought they were intended to have houses built up on them. We have erected skyscrapers on them to which we ceaselessly add storeys. We no longer know that they are bridges, things made so that we may pass along them, and that by passing along them we go towards God.'

The Bridge, by connecting imagination and reality, heals the dichotomy in man's mind — the mind can then advance along Whitman's Open Road, and that is precisely what Crane affirms, in that section of his poem called 'Cape Hatteras', where the 'joyous seer' is invoked by name, and where

> *Vast engines outward veering with seraphic grace*
> *On clarion cylinders pass out of sight*
> *To course that span of consciousness*[1] *thou'st named*
> *The Open Road — thy vision is reclaimed!*

Crane, like James, had a complete and consistent awareness of a particular world of appearances, the world of Manhattan, of subways and sidewalks, of derricks and cables, of docks and piers, of the sleepless river and the encircling sea; of the 'lovely and herded men' lost in this inorganic wilderness, this waste land. There is no poet of London, or indeed of Paris or Rome or any other great city (unless it is Bert Brecht of Berlin) who has had such a comprehensive vision — again a vision and not a theory — of our specifically modern predicament, that is to say, of our alienation. If the poetry of the American psychosis had been carried no further, it would, in Crane's work, remain a unique achievement in contemporary poetry. But Crane was to be followed by other poets, distinctively American in their concern for acute 'psychological analysis'.

At this point I would like to remind you once more that I am trying to present, not my personal point of view, but that of British viewers in general. My own vision is slightly myopic —

---

[1] With the word 'consciousness' we return to Henry James and his conception of the poet's function, what he called the generality and comprehensiveness of the poet's impulse. James, according to Dr. Dorothea Krook — believed 'that art concerns itself to render the world of appearances; that these appearances exist only in the consciousness, indeed, *are* the content of the consciousness, of human observers; that the world of art therefore is a beautiful representation of the appearances present to a particular consciousness under particular conditions, and the artist's overriding task is accordingly to exhibit in the concrete, with the greatest possible completeness and consistency, as well as vividness and intensity, the particular world of appearances accessible to a particular consciousness under the specific conditions created for it by the artist'. . . . In this wider consciousness any distinction between the poet and the novelist disappears, as I said at the beginning of this lecture. Any definition of artistic consciousness, as James himself said, 'makes but a mouthful of so minor a distinction, in the fields of light, as that between verse and prose'. (*The Ordeal of Consciousness in Henry James*, Cambridge University Press, 1962, p. 399.)

I do not see very clearly beyond the poets of my own generation — Pound, Eliot, Williams, Crane, Tate, and Marianne Moore. These are not the poets who most excite the younger generation in Great Britain. Wallace Stevens is an exception, because, owing to the accidents of publication, his work has had a delayed action. I suspect that what appeals to Stevens's admirers among the younger English poets is the sophistication of his work — an aspect of Stevens's work that has also attracted some of the younger American poets. Young English poets praise Stevens as 'a great master of lyrical meditation' — I quote from their reviews — as 'one of the most considerable poets of the last hundred years', 'one of the major poets of this century' — no other American poet has earned such hyperboles.

Stevens said many apparently contradictory things about poetry, and about his own poetry in particular (perhaps to keep pace with the changing nature of that poetry) but on one point he was firm — in his own words — 'the artist, the presence of the determining personality. Without that reality no amount of other things matter much.' His ideal artist was a painter, Cézanne, one who knew better than any of his contemporaries how to resist 'the pressure of external event or events on the consciousness to the exclusion of any power of contemplation'. The poetry of Stevens may be interpreted as, in this sense, a triumphant exclusion of the American scene — though not necessarily of what Crane called the American psychosis, which I am inclined to believe is not American at all. The alienation that creates the psychosis is a condition of man everywhere in our technological civilization.

It is a question, therefore, of creating a life of the imagination at least as forceful as the reality of the machine — the 'harde iron' of Miss Moore's poem, on which Stevens wrote a commentary, contrasting the mythical bird of Miss Moore's imagination with the real ostrich of the *Encyclopaedia Britannica* — the achieved or individual reality emerging as more potent than the bird of the ornithologist. Cézanne never painted an ostrich, and if he had done so, it would not have borne much resemblance to the ostrich in Miss Moore's poem. Cézanne strove to realize his sensations in front of nature. It was an effort of the imagination, but the images involved were given in contemplation: they were a penetration and correction of visual habits, perceptual conventions. But according to Stevens — and I believe he is accurately describing his own and perhaps Miss Moore's intention — the poem is what he calls a 'transcendent analogue' of the reality revealed to our perceptions. Reality is broken down into particulars in order that these particulars may be reassembled according to the heart's desire, the heart being, in Stevens's anatomy, an organ of 'affabulation'. I am not questioning this analysis of the poetic process — on the contrary, I agree that 'the venerable, the fundamental books of the human spirit are vast collections of such analogues'. But what have these analogues to do with the American scene, or the American idiom; what, indeed, have they to do with the American psychosis, except as abstract symbols of its complexity?

Stevens often refers to painters like Watteau and Fragonard as though he had a special sympathy for their charming, artificial fantasies. I believe that his own poetry, by intention, belongs to the same elegant tradition, with whimsicalities and satirical quirks for which Callot or Goya would be a more appropriate comparison. The habit of contemplation which he cultivated gradually led to a dulling of his 'perceptual apprehensions'; the analogues became metaphysically transcendent. But the metaphysics was no longer poetry; as Cowley was no longer Donne.

Randall Jarrell once pointed out that Stevens had the weakness — 'a terrible one for a poet' — of thinking of particulars as primarily illustrations of general truths, which is the inverse of the poetic process, which always requires the poet 'to treat the concrete as primary'.[1] Stevens anticipated the criticism, denying that 'abstraction is a vice except to the fatuous'. Mr. Jarrell had Goethe's saying in mind, that 'it makes a great difference whether the poet seeks the particular in relation to the universal or contemplates the universal in the particular. . . . [In the first case] the particular functions as an example, as an instance of the universal; but the second indeed represents the very nature of poetry. He who grasps this particular as living essence also encompasses the universal.' One British reviewer, Professor Frank Kermode, has dealt very effectively with Mr. Jarrell's objection, affirming that, Goethe's saying notwithstanding, there is such a thing as a poetry of the abstract.[2] Order itself, the enduring form if not the living essence of any art, is itself an abstraction. It is the am-

---

[1] *Poetry and the Age*, by Randall Jarrell (London, Faber & Faber, 1955), p. 130.
[2] *Wallace Stevens*, by Frank Kermode (Edinburgh and London, 1960).

biguity of the word 'abstract' that confuses this discussion; abstraction is always abstraction from particulars; conceptualization is the vice.

Goethe's text, used by Mr. Jarrell to reveal a possible weakness in Stevens, might serve equally well to indicate the strength of Robert Lowell. His poetry from its beginnings was always a poetry of particulars, of bright particular images, in which the poet encompasses the universals of our human destiny. In his poetry the minute particular, the 'terrible crystal' of Richard Watson Dixon, serves as the precipitative agent. The whole of the Lowell family, very particular people, their heirlooms and their habits, are sacrificed on this demanding altar of the universal. It is such sacrifices, efficiently performed, that inspire reverence. But Lowell is no innovator — least of all American poets can he be cast for the role of indigenous bard. His masters are European — Villon and Baudelaire, Rimbaud and Rilke. The texture of his verse is traditional, and reaches back perhaps fifty years for its historical links. Do I exaggerate? Let me try an experiment. I shall quote two passages, one from 'The Mills of the Kavanaughs', the other from a poem first published in London in 1913. You may, or you may not, detect the transition from one to the other:

So gazing, like one stunned, it reached his mind
That the hedge brambles overhung the brook
More than was right, making the selvage blind
The dragging brambles too much flotsam took.
Dully he thought to mend. He fetched a hook,
And standing in the shallow stream he slashed,
For hours, it seemed; the thorns, the twigs, the dead leaves splashed,
Splashed and were bobbed away across the shallows;
Pale grasses with the sap gone from them fell,
Sank, or were carried down beyond the shallows.
The bruised ground-ivy gave out earthy smell . . .
And now the mussed blue-bottles bead her float:
Bringers of luck. Of luck? At worst, a rest
From counting blisters on her metal boat,
That spins and staggers. North and south and west:
A scene, perhaps, of Fragonard — her park,
Whose planted poplars scatter penny-leaves,
White underneath, like mussels to the dark
Chop of the shallows.

There is perhaps more individuality in the last eight lines, which are Lowell's, but in tone and cadence, in image and atmosphere, they seem to form an organic continuity with the other lines, which come from 'The Daffodil Fields' of John Masefield. But while I was quoting these lines from Masefield's forgotten poem I was conscious also of the voice of Robert Frost; and where, indeed, in distilling the essence, shall we find any difference of accent or cadence, of measure or idiom, between the poetry of Masefield, Housman, Hardy or Edward Thomas and poets so essentially post- or anti-modernist (again I borrow a judgement from Mr. Jarrell) as Robert Lowell — or, to make a balance of names, John Berryman, Richard Wilbur, Delmore Schwartz and Randall Jarrell himself?

To describe Lowell as post- or anti-modernist is not to make a qualitative judgement. To deserve to be ranked with Hardy or even with Masefield (a poet unduly neglected by British critics) is no mean achievement. But it does not, of course, bring out the distinctive quality in Lowell's verse, which is a violence from within that seems to accept, as punishment, the violence from without. The masochism has, I believe, been noted before. There is no artifice here, no 'trancendent analogue', but rather a resentment too bitter for disguise:

> *I walk upon the flood:*
> *My way is wayward; there is no way out:*
> *Now how the weary waters swell, —*
> *The tree is down in blood!*
> *All the bats of Babel flap about*
> *The rising sun of hell.*

Violence it is, that almost overwhelms the poetry with its passionate excess. The same tendency is revealed in Robert Lowell's choice of models, 'the dark and against the grain,' as he calls them in his recent *Imitations*. I doubt if full justice has been done to this volume — certainly not by British reviewers. Forget for a moment that these poems are derivative in conception — that another poet in another language invented the occasion, found the image and the idea. Then consider Lowell's claim, that nothing like these poems 'exists in English, for the excellence of a poet depends on the unique opportunities of his native language', and if you admit this, as I think you must, then I think you must admit the thesis I have ventured to put before you —

that whatever its origin, whatever its occasion, English poetry is English, and that as American or British poets (Australian or Canadian) we seize the opportunities of a unique language, and succeed in creating a poetry to the extent that we exploit the singular music and expressiveness of that language.

Music *and* expressiveness — I use these words as if they were inevitable aspects of the same poetic reality, but it may be that the distinctive achievement of modern poetry is to have separated them, and to have made expressiveness the single criterion. Once again I would call attention to the parallel to be found in the plastic arts. There, in the past eighty or hundred years, a distinct style has been developed to which we give the name of expressionism, and the exponents of this style have quite deliberately renounced the ideal of beauty, which ever since the great age of Greek sculpture had been the universally accepted ideal of humanist art, and have substituted the ideal of *vitality*. 'Beauty, in the later Greek or Renaissance sense, is not the aim of my sculpture,' is the affirmation of one of our greatest contemporary artists, Henry Moore: 'for me a work must first have a vitality of its own.' The music or the measure of words, the modern poet seems to say, is not the aim of my verse; for me a poem must first have an intensity of its own. It would be difficult to find anywhere in the verses we have been discussing single lines or images to match Matthew Arnold's mauled touchstones, or even Mr. Allen Tate's brighter list. The modern poet seems to lack the very ambition to write of 'bare ruined choirs, where late the sweet birds sang'; such music is too sweet for his psychological muse. Instead he will show us 'a mother skunk with her column of kittens swill(ing) the garbage pail'.

I have spent too much effort in the past trying to justify expressionism in painting and sculpture to have the inconsistent desire to attack it in poetry. When a British reviewer praises American poets for 'coping openly with the quick of their experience, experience sometimes on the edge of disintegration and breakdown',[1] I recognize that he is praising poets for qualities which, in the past, I have praised painters and sculptors. But to praise Munch or Van Gogh, Kokoschka or Beckmann, has not led me to renounce Cézanne or Matisse, Bonnard or Chagall. Though beauty and vitality have been separate ideals in the plastic arts, they still preserve a certain equilibrium in the total

[1] *The New Poetry*, selected and edited by A. Alvarez (Penguin Books, 1962).

achievement. I am not sure that in poetry, despite the touch-stones to be found in an Eliot or a Frost, we can now make the same claim. The British reviewer I have just quoted, Mr. Alvarez, proudly asserts that modern poets have gone 'beyond the Gentility Principle'. It is possible, of course, that he is confusing gentility and grace.

It would seem that I am about to conclude with a defence of pure poetry. It is true that in the plastic arts my preference is given to the representation of pure form, to the kind of art we call 'abstract'. I agree with that great poet Mistral, whom Paul Valéry so greatly respected, that 'form alone exists — only form preserves the works of the mind'. I think Wallace Stevens meant the same by 'the idea of order', the 'blessed rage for order'. I admit that poetry is a formal aspect of language — that English poetry is the most expressive order of our English tongue. But what gives it vitality and beauty, in indissoluble unity, is a spiritual resonance proceeding from the organic substance and structure of our speech. American poetry in our time, indeed ever since the time of Whitman, has been a great poetry because it has renewed the spiritual vitality of the English language — 'made it new' as certain Irish writers — Shaw and Yeats — also in their time made it new. In an essay on 'The Argentine Writer and Tradition', Jorge Luis Borges, whose argument in respect of the Spanish poet in our time is the same as mine in respect of the English poet, reminds us that Gibbon in his *Decline and Fall of the Roman Empire*, observes that in the Arabian book *par excellence*, in the Koran, there are no camels; and Borges believes 'that if there were any doubt as to the authenticity of the Koran, this absence of camels would be sufficient to prove it as an Arabian work. It was written by Mohammed, and Mohammed, as an Arab, has no reason to know that camels were especially Arabian; for him they were part of reality, he has no reason to emphasize them; on the other hand, the first thing a falsifier, a tourist, an Arab nationalist would do is to have a surfeit of camels, caravans of camels on every page; but Mohammed, as an Arab, was unconcerned; he knew he could be an Arab without camels.' In the same way, and for the same reason, I believe that a poet can be an American without mentioning whatever you may choose as the American camel — perhaps Mr. Lowell's mother skunk.

The English language, the physical substance from which our poetry has been smelted, the linguistic ore of our eloquence, the formative matrix of our consciousness, of our imagery, of our intelligence, is greater than the demotic idiom of any of the numerous peoples that now speak this language. We often refer to the pure well of English undefil'd, but the well-worn metaphor is too static. My revision of it will be equally banal, but we might say that English was formed from many remote linguistic sources which as they gained force and definition became associated with personal names — Chaucer, Wyclif, Malory; Wyatt, Surrey, Skelton; Drayton, Daniel, Sidney — sources that met and became bright mountain becks and winding streams, that in Spenser and Marlowe are already headlong torrents soon to unite in the wide and irresistible river that flows on from Shakespeare and Milton. In that current we still have our only existence.

I have, I hope, made my meaning clear. As poets we do but diminish our stature and strength if we claim to steer a separate course. To be an English poet is a great honour, the greatest honour that is given to a poet and the envy of the poets of the whole world. We have most dignity, whatever our origins, if we acknowledge the long and vital tradition of our common language and strive, not to speak with a wayward accent, but as purely as our individual sensibility will allow. That, I believe, is what the best American poets have done. Their achievement is to have approached, more nearly than their British contemporaries, the grace, the realism and the intensity that were always the proper virtues of an English verse.

IV. Art Criticism

The Modern Epoch in Art[1]

The heart that beat for this world has been almost extinguished in me. It is as though my only bond with 'these' things were memory. . . . One relinquishes this world and builds into a region beyond, a region which can be all affirmation. The cool romanticism of this style without pathos is astounding.

PAUL KLEE, *Diary*, 1915

(i)

In discussing the origins of naturalism in the Middle Ages, Max Dvořák warned us against the folly of trying to fix a specific 'beginning' to anything so underground as the first growth of an artistic style. The modern movement in art, which in general is a reversal of the movement discussed with such brilliance by Dvořák (in his *Idealismus und Naturalismus in der gotischen Skulptur und Malerei*), offers no exception to this rule. Its origins are extremely obscure, and, like roots, proceed from different levels and contradictory directions. One cannot exclude either the revolutionary romanticism of a Blake or the revolutionary classicism of a David; Constable's scientific naturalism is certainly a factor, but so is the historical idealism of Delacroix (to Cézanne always 'le grand Maître'). The realism of Courbet and Manet; the expressionism of Van Gogh and Munch; the symbolism of Emile Bernard and Gauguin — all these precede and in some degree predetermine the specifically modern movements of fauvism, cubism, constructivism and surrealism. Perhaps we should abandon our biological analogies and think rather of the complex 'movement' of a chronometer; for historical 'time' seems to reduce, on analysis, to such an interlocking of gears and ratchets. It will be said that even the chronometer has a spring at the centre, but this is not necessarily true of the modern chronometer, which may be set and kept in motion by the simple alternation of night and day.

There is, of course, the further explanation offered by the theory of dialectical materialism. For night and day in our metaphor we

[1] Introduction to *History of Modern Painting: From Baudelaire to Bonnard* (Geneva, 1949).

219

may substitute rich and poor, bourgeoisie and proletariat, and in the circulation of élites see a sufficient motive power for all the stylistic changes of art. This is not an argument that can be ignored, for art never exists in a vacuum, but is inextricably entangled in the life of society as a whole. If we discover that the modern artist is relatively isolated from society we must not be led to suppose that such isolation is a characteristic of art itself — an island as such is only defined by reference to a neighbouring land-mass.

Nevertheless, economic facts and social movements can only have an indirect relation to the stylistic evolution of art. In the period that concerns us here, there is one broad economic development of the utmost significance — the gradual decline of private patronage due to the severe restrictions imposed on the accumulation of wealth. Private collectors still buy works of art in the open market — to that extent there are still patrons, if only through the medium of the art-dealer. But they no longer *command* the artist like the monastery or the guild, the court or the castle. The position has been so reversed that the contemporary artist must form the taste and recruit the public (through the intermediary of the art critic, in himself a modern phenomenon) on whose patronage he will then depend. The modern artist is miserably dependent on the media of publicity. That is his deepest humiliation.

There is another and a more limited sense in which the course of art is determined by economic factors. Scientific and industrial progress, particularly in the nineteenth century, threw out as by-products certain theories and inventions which had a direct impact on the technique and social significance of art. These have been too often discussed to need more than a passing reference. The formulation of a scientific theory of colour, which at first led to such aberrations as pointillism, has not had any permanent effect on artistic practice — the artist has discovered by now that he must rely on his sensibility and not attempt to particularize from laws of aesthetic effect. But more significant and more permanent in its influence on the development of art has been the invention of photography and of photographic methods of reproduction. The economic consequences of such inventions are serious enough — the public is provided with a cheap substitute for the plastic arts. It may not be aesthetically so satisfying, but it suffices for the low level of sensibility that seems to be a consequence of mass production and mass education. The effect on the artist has been even more profound, for it has relieved him of one of the social functions of art — that of 'visual aid'. It is true that certain subtleties of imaginative literature will still call for creative illustration; but for instruction and clarification it is better to provide an *Orbis sensualium pictus* by means of the camera. What has been effected is a clear distinction between *illustration* and *interpretation*. This may not seem so significant at first, but implied in it is the distinction between *image* and *symbol*, which, as we shall see presently, is fundamental to an understanding of the modern movement in art.

What in general may be admitted in this connection is that economic and social trends determine and give their fluctuating shades to broad movements of thought and opinion in every epoch. The work of art cannot escape the ambience of such intangible effluences (the philosophies and theologies of the period). To the extent that a work of art is romantic or classical, realistic or symbolic, it will certainly be beyond the personal control of the artist. Even the structure of the work of art (the style of composition) may be a matter of taste or fashion determined by social contacts. But there comes a point in the evolution of art at which all these imponderable forces are but external pressures which result, not in a consequential 'line of force', but in a leap into creative originality of a quite incalculable kind. The dialectical materialist may still claim that social factors have determined that anamorphosis, but the quantum in art, as in physics, may be discontinuous. A brief examination of the concept of *originality* will perhaps make my meaning clear.

(ii)

It has often been observed that if we have regard only for that quality we call 'sensibility', which would throughout history seem to be the essential element in art, that then no progress whatsoever is discernible between the cave drawings of the palaeolithic period and the drawings of Raphael or Picasso. Sensibility is not the only value in art — as successive civilizations develop their cultures they invariably dilute this basic sensibility with other values of a magical or logical nature — they *use* sensibility in social contexts, and it is the variations of context that seem to explain whatever changes occur in the history of art. There is, of course, a degree beyond which the sensibility cannot be forced or prostituted — the result is then the *rigor mortis* of academicism, or the moral rot of sentimentalism. The vitality of art would seem to depend on the maintenance of a delicate balance between sensibility and whatever intellectual or emotional accretions it derives from the social element in which it is embedded.

The process is, it will be seen, a dialectical one, and it is certainly one in which tensions and contradictions inevitably develop. One way in which a tension may be relaxed takes the form of a decline of sensibility, and the tension must be restored if art is to survive. What precisely happens in such a crisis is in dispute. The alternative suggestions are: (1) the artist retraces the historical development of his art and resumes contact with the authentic *tradition*; or (2) the artist resolves the crisis by a leap forward into a new and original state of sensibility — he revolts against the existing conventions in order to create a new convention more in accordance with a contemporary consciousness. We may admit that in doing so he merely recovers, in all its actuality, the original basic quality of art — aesthetic sensibility in all its purity and vitality. But the context is new, and it is the synthesis of an untrammelled sensibility and a new set of social conditions which constitutes, in the evolution of art, an act of originality.

We must guard against interpreting 'social conditions' in a sense narrowly economic or political. The artist's awareness of these conditions rarely assumes a politically conscious form, and certainly there is no correlation to be made between such consciousness in the artist and his degree of originality. Courbet, Pissarro, William Morris — these are the politically conscious artists and they have an important place in the history of modern art. But a more important place is taken by artists like Cézanne, Gauguin and Matisse, whose awareness of the social context of their work was never expressed in a political formula. It is only a primitive mind that can interpret the social context as Daumier's third-class railway carriage. The social context is the totality of our way of life, and its impact on the artist may be through a philosophy or a science, or even through a pair of old boots (Van Gogh) or a heap of rubbish (Schwitters).

From this point of view a renewed contact with tradition may have as much revolutionary significance as any originality in style or technique. The validity of a tradition depends on its retention

of the element of sensibility. We agree to find this element in the
paintings of Poussin; therefore, said Cézanne, let us go back to
Poussin and try to recover, in front of nature, the element that
made Poussin a great artist. Cézanne implied, not that the
modern artist should imitate Poussin's style (which was personal
to Poussin), but that a study of Poussin's art might lead to the
recovery of sensibility — to the re-animation of his (Cézanne's)
ability to 'realize' his sensations in the presence of nature.
'Nature' meanwhile had changed, because nature is but another
word for the social context already mentioned. *To renew one's
sensibility towards one's environment* — that is the method of both
the traditionalist and of the revolutionary. Nevertheless, there is
still a degree of originality which is not necessarily covered by the
phrase.

The sense of 'reality' is surely one of those conventions that
change from age to age and are determined by the total way of
life. Not only does the concept of reality differ as between a
mediaeval philosopher like St. Thomas Aquinas and a modern
philosopher like Bergson, but a similar difference also exists on
the average level of apprehension (the difference between anim-
ism and theism, between supernaturalism and materialism, and
so on). The 'reality' of a citizen of the Soviet Union is certainly
different from the 'reality' of a citizen of the United States. We
have now reached a stage of relativism in philosophy where it
is possible to affirm that reality is in fact subjectivity, which
means that the individual has no choice but to construct his own
reality, however arbitrary and even 'absurd' that may seem. This
is the position reached by the Existentialists, and to it corresponds
a position in the world of art that requires a similar decision. The
interpretation (or even the 'imitation') of reality was a valid
function for the artist so long as it was agreed that a general and
basic reality existed and was only waiting for revelation. Once
this sense of security is removed (that is to say, is destroyed by
scientific analysis) then philosophy and art are public auctions
in which the most acceptable reality commands the highest
price.

This may be a passing phase in philosophy and the world may
return to systems of faith and revelation in which art once more
resumes its interpretative function. But Existentialism is but the
latest phase of a development of thought that reaches back to
Kant and Schelling, and it is difficult (from a point of view inside

the stream) to see any other direction which philosophy can take (it already carries along with it the contradictions of Christianity and atheism). It is in this mental climate that contemporary art has shown a tendency to usurp the positivist rôle of philosophy and to present its own self-sufficient 'reality'. A certain type of modern artist claims to construct new realities ('réalités nouvelles'), and he will go so far as to assert that his construction is in no way determined even by such vague concepts as universal harmony or the collective unconscious, but is an act of creation in the almost divine sense of the word. Naturally such an artist has to use elements of form and colour which are common to all the arts, and the world has not shown any inclination to recognize his work as art unless it possesses some of the sensuous qualities of the traditional work of art.

The conclusion we are driven to is that originality is always conceptual, thematic, structural — never sensuous. There are new ways of thinking and doing — we call them inventions; there are new ways of stimulating the senses. But sensation itself can only be modified — coarsened or refined. It has the physical limitations of our animal frame; stretched on that frame the nerve breaks if forced beyond its expressive compass.

At the same time we must recognize, with the Marxists, the historic nature of human consciousness; and, with certain psychologists, the ambiguous nature of this evolutionary acquisition. In terms of art it gave us the symbol where hitherto there had been only the image. Man in his first unreflecting unity with nature needed only the image to project his sensations. Man as a self-conscious individual separated from the rest of creation needed a language of symbols to express his self-ness. The elaboration of that need gave rise not only to conceptual symbols like 'God' but also to a myriad of plastic symbols, some of them constant and archetypal, others temporary and even personal. If we could reconstruct the stages in human evolution which led from the eidetic, vitalistic art of the Palaeolithic period to the symbolic, geometric art of the Neolithic period, we should have a clear conception of the rise of not only human self-consciousness, ethical conscience and the idea of a transcendental God, but also of the origins of that polarity in art which has caused a rhythmic alternation of styles throughout the history of art, and which now exists as an unresolved dialectical contradiction. It is the *co*-existence of the image and the symbol, as norms of art, which explains the apparent complexity and disunity of the modern movement.

(iii)

The true understanding of art depends upon an appreciation of the nature and uses of symbolism. Symbolism is one of the two ways in which the human mind functions, the other being the direct experience of the external world (the 'presentational immediacy' of sense perception). Since language itself is already symbolism, and the complicated forms of thought depend on a system of symbols such as we have in the science of algebra, it is natural to assume that there is something primitive and ineffective about the presentational immediacy of sense perceptions. This is far from being the case. It is much more difficult to be faithful to our direct experience of the external world than to 'jump to conclusions' which are in effect symbolic references. The poet, said Gautier, is a man for whom the visible world exists; he wishes, by this definition, to exclude from art those secondary elaborations of perception involved in the use of symbols. As the poet is condemned to use the symbolism of language, the ideal would seem to be quixotic. (Nevertheless poetry continues to reveal a fundamental strife between imagism and symbolism.)

The special position of the visual artist may be illustrated by a quotation from Whitehead's *Symbolism: its Meaning and Effect* (1928). 'We look up and see a coloured shape in front of us and we say — there is a chair. But what we have seen is the mere coloured shape. *Perhaps an artist might not have jumped to the notion of a chair. He might have stopped at the mere contemplation of a beautiful colour and a beautiful shape.* But those of us who are not artists are very prone, especially if we are tired, to pass straight from the perception of the coloured shape to the enjoyment of the chair, in some way of use, or of emotion, or of thought. We can easily explain this passage by reference to a train of difficult logical inference, whereby, having regard to our previous experiences of various shapes and various colours, we draw the probable conclusion that we are in the presence of a chair.'

This clearly illustrates the difference between a perceptive experience (the immediate perception of an image) and the use of a symbol (the image plus its mental associations). Whitehead adds: 'I am very sceptical as to the high-grade character of the mentality required to get from the coloured shape to the chair.

P

H.R.

One reason for this scepticism is that my friend the artist, who kept himself to the contemplation of colour, shape and position, was a very highly trained man, and had acquired this facility of ignoring the chair at the cost of great labour.'

With this distinction in mind we can perhaps begin to understand what Cézanne meant by 'realizing his sensations'. We can understand what Van Gogh meant when he said that 'a painter as a man is too much absorbed by what his eyes see, and is not sufficiently master of the rest of his life'. (Letter 620.) Van Gogh's letters are full of descriptions of his intense concentration on what a philosopher like Whitehead would call 'presentational immediacy'. For example: 'I myself am quite absorbed by the immeasurable plain with cornfields against the hills, immense as a sea, delicate yellow, delicate soft green, delicate violet of a ploughed and weeded piece of soil, regularly chequered by the green of flowering potato-plants, everything under a sky with delicate blue, white, pink, violet tones. I am in a mood of *nearly too great calmness*, in the mood to paint this.' (Letter 650, written in Dutch.)

This 'mood of nearly too great calmness' is the mood of direct experience, of instinctual awareness in which the eidetic image is, as it were, preserved from the contamination of symbolism — from the need for further reference to other elements in our experience. It has been claimed that the capacity for realizing and retaining the image in a state of perceptive vividness is the quality that distinguishes the artist from other men, but in fact it is the distinguishing quality of one type of artist — the imagist. It was by his insistence on the strict purity of his perceptive experience that Cézanne restored to art some degree of primal rectitude.

At the other extreme of artistic practice the artist abandons himself freely to a symbolic activity. Whitehead has said that 'the human mind is functioning symbolically when some components of its experience elicit consciousness, beliefs, emotions, and usages, respecting other components of its experience. The former set of components are the "symbols", and the latter set constitute the "meaning" of the symbols' (p. 9). An artist of the symbolist type is creating a combination of forms and colours (or of sounds if he is a musician) which will convey a meaning, and in art this meaning always has an aesthetic or emotional tinge. Art of this kind may therefore be defined as 'the symbolic transfer of emotion', and

as Whitehead says, this definition is at the base of any theory of
the aesthetics of art — 'For example, it gives the reason for the
importance of a rigid suppression of irrelevant detail. For emotions inhibit each other, or intensify each other. Harmonious
emotion means a complex of emotions mutually intensifying;
whereas the irrelevant details supply emotions which, because of
their irrelevance, inhibit the main effect. Each little emotion
directly arising out of some subordinate detail refuses to accept its
status as a detached fact in our consciousness. It insists on its
symbolic transfer to the unity of the main effect' (p. 101).

This definition of symbolism agrees closely with those definitions of 'synthètisme' which were formulated by Emile Bernard
in 1888 and which, through the medium of Gauguin, were to
have a revolutionary effect on the whole development of modern
art. Bernard wrote:

'Puisque l'idée est la forme des choses recueillies par l'imagination, il fallait peindre non plus devant la chose, mais en la
reprenant dans l'imagination, qui l'avait recueillie, qui en con-
servait l'idée, ainsi l'idée de la chose apportait la forme conven-
able au sujet du tableau ou plutôt à son idéal (somme des idées)
la simplification que l'essentiel des choses percues et par consé-
quent en rejette le détail. La mémoire ne retient pas tout, mais
ce qui frappe l'esprit. Donc formes et couleurs devenaient
simples dans une égale unité. En peignant de mémoire, j'avais
l'avantage d'abolir l'inutile complication des formes et des tons.
Il restait un schéma du spectacle regardé. Toutes les lignes
revenaient à leur architecture géométrique, tous les tons aux
couleurs types de la palette prismatique. Puisqu'il s'agissait de
simplifier, il fallait retrouver l'origine de tout: dans le soleil, les
sept couleurs dont se compose la lumiere blanche (chaque couleur
pure de la palette y répondant); dans la géométrie, les formes
typiques de toutes les formes objectives.'[1]

This distinction between painting 'devant la chose' and 'en
la reprenant dans l'imagination' expresses neatly the two ways
open to the artist, and the further insistence on 'simplification'
(Bernard) or 'unity of the main effect' (Whitehead) points to
that characteristic in symbolic art which can involve a progressive
modification of the 'schema' in the direction of abstraction.
There is nothing in the paintings of Gauguin which would seem

[1] Quoted by Maurice Malingue, *Gauguin, le peintre et son oeuvre* (Paris, 1948),
p. 35.

to imply or justify the abstractions of a Kandinsky or a Mondrian; nevertheless, there is what Whitehead calls 'a chain of derivations of symbol from symbol' whereby finally the local relations, between the final symbol and the ultimate meaning, are entirely lost. Thus these derivative symbols, obtained as it were by arbitrary association, are really the results of reflex action suppressing the intermediate portions of the chain. By such a chain of derivations we could conceivably establish an association between such apparently disconnected symbols as Gauguin's *Yellow Christ* and Mondrian's *Boogie-Woogie*. Mondrian was fond of describing his art as 'a new realism', but it is clear from his writings that he had invented a new symbolism. Mondrian insists that art is a parallel experience, not to be identified in any way with our experience of the external world; but in Whitehead's words we would say that such parallelism is an illusion due to the suppression of intermediate links. The creation of a 'new' reality is not within the scope of our human, time-conditioned faculties.

(iv)

Let us now leave the realm of theory and try to trace what has actually happened in the evolution of art in the modern epoch. We shall not be able to leave ideas entirely out of account, because my main contention is that art has developed in stages that are parallel to the development of thought, and that both developments have intimate connections with social movements. Perhaps a few words will make clear to what extent the formal evolution of modern art has been 'conditioned' by social and economic forces.

I have already drawn attention to the relative isolation of the artist in modern society. The general effect of the industrial revolution on art has been a gradual exclusion of the artist from the basic economic processes of production. This development may be said to begin with the capitalist system itself; that is to say, with the accumulation of individual wealth. The way in which, from the fifteenth century onwards, the 'patron' gradually forces his own personality, even his own person, into the work of art has often been remarked. At first he is the pious donor, humbly kneeling in an obscure corner of the picture; but he gradually grows in size and importance until, in a painting like Holbein's *Virgin and Child with the Burgomaster Mayer and his family* (1526), he is painted on the same scale as the holy figures.

Man is as good as God — as a theme for the artist. This humanism gave rise to the development of schools of portrait painting and historical painting which for three centuries constituted the main substance of the plastic arts. But such a development left the artist in a precarious position — dependent, not on the social organism as such (his position during the Middle Ages), but on the patronage of a limited class within that organism. For most of this time he maintained vitalizing contacts with the general processes of production — in our sense of the word he was still an industrial artist who might on occasion turn his hand to the design of metalwork, furniture or tapestries. But by the time the industrial revolution was complete, the artist was cut off from even these subsidiary activities and had become parasitically dependent on his patron.

In such a situation the artist might react in several ways. He might become sycophantic, adopting the point of view of his patron, supporting the existing structure of society, supplying works of art designed to satisfy the tastes and flatter the vanity of his clients. Such, in general, is the bourgeois art of the eighteenth and nineteenth centuries. But such, also, is a situation that implies the progressive degradation of art. No longer drawing any inspiration or force from the organic wholeness of society, the art in such a situation becomes anaemic and sophisticated, and, in any spiritual sense, purposeless. The basis of patronage may spread more widely, as it did throughout the nineteenth century, but the result will only be an art measured to the mean capacities of *l'homme moyen sensuel*. Just as, according to the Marxists, capitalism contains in itself the seeds of its own inevitable destruction, so (more certainly, even) such a relation between the artist and society involves inevitable decadence.

The artist who resists such decadence may react in two distinct ways. If he is socially conscious, he may revolt against the social situation as such and become a revolutionary artist — that is to say, an artist who consciously uses his art to reform the social situation. That type of artist is rare — it implies a use of art in the service of preconceived *ideas* which the true artist cannot accept. Even Courbet, in a political sense probably the most revolutionary artist of the nineteenth century, held that 'the art of painting can consist only in the representation of objects visible and tangible to the painter' and that 'art is completely individual, and that the talent of each artist is but the result of his own inspiration and his own study of past tradition' (open letter to a group of prospective students, 1861). But the same social situation produces in the artist a state of mind in which he turns from what he regards as the false aesthetic values of the past to seek new aesthetic values more consonant with the developing social consciousness of his fellow-citizens. Constable was not politically minded, but when he wrote (Notes for his lectures at the Royal Institution, May 26, 1836) that art 'is *scientific* as well as *poetic*; that imagination never did, and never can, produce works that are to stand by a comparison with *realities*', he was expressing a revolutionary sentiment, a revolt against the art of Boucher which in its turn had been the expression of another and very different social situation. This attitude is still more clearly expressed in a note of June 16, 1836:

'I have endeavoured to draw a line between genuine art and mannerism, but even the greatest painters have never been wholly untainted by manner. . . . Painting is a science, and should be pursued as an enquiry into the laws of nature. Why, then, may not landscape be considered as a branch of natural philosophy, of which pictures are but experiments?'

On that 'experimental' note the modern epoch is announced, and never from that moment until comparatively recently has the artist relented in his experimental attitude. Exactly seventy years later we find Cézanne writing in almost the same terms as Constable (letter of September 21, 1906):

'Shall I ever reach the goal so eagerly sought and so long pursued? I hope so, but as long as it has not been attained a vague feeling of discomfort persists which will not disappear until I shall have gained the harbour — that is, until I shall have accomplished something more promising than what has gone before, thereby verifying my theories, which, in themselves, are easy to put forth. The only thing that is really difficult is to prove what one believes. So I am going on with my researches. . . .'[1]

Research, experiment — these words describe the efforts of all the great artists that fall within these seventy years — Millet, Courbet, Manet, Degas, Monet, Pissarro, Renoir, Rodin, Whistler, Seurat, Van Gogh — it is all a persistent attempt to correlate art and reality. It is the research, not of the absolute, but of the concrete, of the *image*, and behind it all is not only the divorce of the artist from the processes of production, but also the

[1] Trans. Gerstle Mack, *Paul Cézanne* (London, 1935), p. 390.

concurrent attempt to establish a philosophy of reality, a pheno-
menalism that owes nothing to divine revelation or universal
truths, but brings to the analysis of human existence the same
faculties that the artist brings to the analysis of nature. Constable,
Cézanne, Picasso — Hegel, Husserl, Heidegger; these names represent parallel movements in the evolution of human experience.

But this movement, in art, was not to remain unchallenged.
To the image as representation is opposed, as we have seen, the
symbol as interpretation, and there is no doubt that the 'synthètisme' of Bernard and Gauguin was a conscious reaction
against the scientific attitude in art. The theoretical basis of this
reaction was given in the definition of 'synthètisme' by Bernard
already quoted, but what that theory involved in practice was
first shown by Gauguin. We can best appreciate the antithetical
nature of the contradiction by considering what form and colour
meant respectively for Cézanne and Gauguin.

Both artists went through an impressionist phase, and their
divergence developed as they felt dissatisfaction with the results
of their practice of the impressionist technique. Both artists,
incidentally, found a meeting-place in Pissarro, who is the chief
point de repère for the whole revolution. What Cézanne learned
from Pissarro was of fundamental importance for his subsequent
development, but it did not affect the direction taken by that
development. Cézanne felt that the analytical methods of the
Impressionists had led to a certain dissolution of reality; they had,
as it were, realized the vitality of objects, the vibrancy of light,
the vividness of colour, at the cost of the essential nature of these
objects — their solidity — indeed, their reality. The analysis of
light and colour had led to a separation of colour and form, and
this Cézanne felt to be a betrayal of the painter's function. Without sacrificing the real advances made by the Impressionists, he
set himself the task of realizing and presenting the solid structure
of objects. He arrived at a method which he called 'modulation'
(as distinct from the Impressionists' 'modelling') in which volume
was represented by local colour changes. His own words must be
quoted:

'For progress towards realization there is nothing but nature,
and the eye becomes educated through contact with her. It becomes concentric through observation and work; I mean that in
an orange, an apple, a sphere, a head, there is a focal point, and
this point is always nearest to our eye, no matter how it is

affected by light, shade, sensations of colour. The edges of objects recede towards a centre located on our horizon.'[1]

This rather obscure passage is illuminated by a letter of December 23 of the same year:

'This I declare to be indisputable — I am very dogmatic: an optical sensation is produced in our visual organ which causes us to grade the planes represented by sensations of colour into full light, half-tones and quarter-tones (light does not exist for the painter). Necessarily, while we are proceeding from black to white, the first of these abstractions being a sort of point of departure for the eye as well as for the brain, we are floundering, we do not succeed in mastering ourselves, in ruling over ourselves. During this period — we go to the great masterpieces the ages have handed down to us, and we find in them a solace and a support.'[2]

One further question, for it is essential for an understanding of the origins of modern art to be quite sure that we first understand what Cézanne was after:

'Now the idea to be insisted on is — no matter what our temperament or power in the presence of nature — to produce the image of what we see, forgetting everything that has been done before. Which, I believe, should enable the artist to express his entire personality, great or small.

'Now that I am old, almost seventy, the sensations of colour which produce light are a source of distraction, which do not permit me to cover my canvas or to define the delimitations of objects when the points of contact are so tenuous, fragile; the result is that my image or picture is incomplete. Then again the planes are superimposed on one another, from which springs the Neo-impressionist system of outlining the contours with a black line, an error which should be opposed with all our strength. Now if we consult nature we shall find a way to solve this problem.'[3]

'I regret my advanced age, on account of my sensations of colour', — such was the recurrent complaint of Cézanne in his last years. He felt a certain opposition between the surface sensuousness of objects and their real nature — his eyes were, as it were, dazzled by the brilliance of light and colour. Light and colour were not the same thing as *lucidity*. ('I am becoming more

[1] Letter of July 25, 1904, trans. Gerstle Mack, op. cit., p. 380.
[2] Trans. Gerstle Mack, op. cit., p. 381.
[3] Trans. Gerstle Mack, op. cit., pp. 382–3.

lucid in the presence of nature, but — the realization of my sensations is always painful. I cannot reach the intensity which appears to my senses . . .') — (September 8, 1906). And then, in his final letter to Bernard, who significantly enough was the *agent provocateur* in this struggle for theoretical expression (significantly, because he played the same rôle for Gauguin), he says: 'I am progressing towards the logical development of what we see and feel by studying nature; a consideration of processes comes later, processes being for us nothing but simple methods for making the public feel what we ourselves feel, and for making ourselves intelligible.'

There were, therefore, in Cézanne's final phase, two stages in the production of a work of art: first, the realization of sensations, by which he meant a 'logical' analysis of percepts, of what the eye actually sees; second, processes by means of which this analysis could be presented to the public.

Cézanne was an extremely intelligent but simple man, and his efforts to explain his intuitive processes are not very clear. What in his stumbling way he seems to have grasped is the principle of the 'good *Gestalt*'. Without going further into the theory of perception than would be justified in a general essay of this kind, it is difficult to give a convincing account of this term, but the underlying idea is that visual perception itself only makes sense, only becomes coherent, by virtue of an organizing faculty within the nervous system. We should not be able to cope with the multiplicity of impressions which the eye receives were we not, at the same time, capable of organizing these impressions into a coherent pattern. In the words of a *Gestalt* psychologist: 'Perception tends towards balance and symmetry; or differently expressed: balance and symmetry are perceptual characteristics of the visual world which will be realized whenever the external conditions allow it; when they do not, unbalance, lack of symmetry, will be experienced as a characteristic of objects or the whole field, together with a felt urge towards better balance — the stimulations which under ordinary circumstances affect our eyes are perfectly haphazard from the point of view of the visual organizations to which they may give rise. The organism — does the best it can under the prevailing conditions, and these conditions will not, as a rule, allow it to do a very good job (good, from the point of view of aesthetic harmony). A work of art, on the other hand, is made with that very idea; once completed it serves as a source of stimulation specifically selected for its aesthetic effect.'[1]

Before Cézanne the principle of composition in painting was architectonic — the picture-space was 'organized' as an architect organizes his building, and inevitably questions of balance and symmetry were taken into consideration. Cézanne's paintings are analysed and criticized as if they conformed to this principle, and such a method does indeed 'work', though it ignores the essential virtue in Cézanne's compositions. For architectonic composition is *a priori*; it fits the objects of perception into a preconceived pattern, a system of perspective and elevation, which is not necessarily inherent in perception itself. A landscape by Claude or Turner is as artificial as a garden, and as much the result of intellectual preconceptions. But a landscape by Cézanne begins with no preconceptions — nothing but the direct contact of eye and nature, and the 'composition' is determined by what happens 'in the eye' — the automatic selection of a focal point, limitation of boundaries, subordination of details and colours to the law of the whole. The 'whole' is the *Gestalt*, but the psychologists recognize that the process does not end there — that there are 'good' and less good *Gestalts*. 'It is characteristic of a good *Gestalt* not only that it produces a hierarchical unity of its parts, but also that this unity is of a particular kind. A good *Gestalt* cannot be changed without changing its quality — in a masterpiece of painting no line, no form, no colour, can anywhere be changed without detracting from the quality of the picture.'[2]

I think there is no doubt whatsoever that Cézanne was trying to realize the good *Gestalt*. By intuitive processes he had hit upon a scientific truth which psychology subsequently discovered by experimental research. Cézanne, therefore, still remains within the characteristic development of nineteenth century art — as much as Constable he is an artist who regards landscape painting as a branch of natural philosophy. But Cézanne's natural philosophy was not destined to be understood by many of his followers, and it was largely on a misinterpretation of his purpose that cubism came into being (its subsequent development is another question). But before we discuss the influence of Cézanne let us return to the challenge to the scientific attitude in art made by Gauguin.

[1] K. Koffka, 'Problems in the Psychology of Art'. *Art: a Bryn Mawr Symposium*, 1940.
[2] Koffka, op. cit., 247–8.

(v)

One's first inclination is to treat Gauguin as an artist altogether inferior to Cézanne. We cannot doubt his integrity or his sincerity, and the sacrifices he made for his art were certainly as great as Cézanne's. The contrast between the two artists lies in the field of sensibility, of technical accomplishment. Certainly some hard things can be said about Gauguin's technique. He despised the whole business of what he called 'counting the hairs on the donkey'. He had been an Impressionist and had sat at the feet of Pissarro; but his reaction was violent. 'The impressionists study colour exclusively, but without freedom, always shackled by the need of probability. For them the ideal landscape, created from many different entities, does not exist. They look and perceive harmoniously, but without aim. Their edifice rests upon no solid base and ignores the nature of the sensation perceived by means of colour. They heed only the eye and neglect the mysterious centres of thought, so falling into merely scientific reasoning.'[1] Form was not to be found in nature, but in the imagination. 'It is well for young men to have a model, but let them draw the curtain over it while they are painting. It is better to paint from memory, for thus your work will be your own: your sensation, your intelligence, and your soul will triumph over the eye of the amateur.'[2] At every point Gauguin contradicts Cézanne, a fact understood better by Cézanne than by Gauguin. 'He never understood me,' said Cézanne. 'I have never desired and I shall never accept the absence of modelling or of gradation; it's nonsense. Gauguin was not a painter, he only made Chinese images.' To which Gauguin would have replied (in words he wrote to Daniel de Monfried): 'The great error is the Greek, however beautiful it may be. . . . Keep the Persians, the Cambodians, and a bit of the Egyptians always in mind.' (October, 1897.) Or: 'It is the eye of ignorance that assigns a fixed and unchangeable colour to every object. . . . Practise painting an object in conjunction with, or shadowed by — that is to say, close to or half behind — other objects of similar or different colours. In this way you will please by your variety and your truthfulness — your own. Go from dark to light, from light to dark. The eye seeks to refresh itself through your work; give it food for enjoyment, not dejection. . . . Let

---

[1] *Intimate Journals*, trans. Van Wyck Brooks (New York, 1936), pp. 132–4.
[2] Ibid., p. 71, 1936.

everything about you breathe the calm and peace of the soul. Also avoid motion in a pose. Each of your figures ought to be in a static position. . . . Study the silhouette of every object; distinctness of outline is the attribute of the hand that is not enfeebled by any hesitation of the will. . . . Do not finish your work too much. . . .' One could go on building up the contradictions, but they all amount to this: *the laws of beauty do not reside in the verities of nature.* The work of art is in some sense a suggestive symbol, stirring our emotions rather than stimulating our sensations.

Between these two points of view, these two distinct conceptions of art, there can be no compromise. Most of the contradictions and varieties of modern art spring from their antithetical opposition. No synthesis within the realm of art seems to be possible; it is not obvious why it should be desirable.

(vi)

The situation as it developed towards the end of the century was not, however, to remain a simple antithesis. If, for the sake of brevity, we describe the aim of Cézanne as the representation of the real, and that of Gauguin as the creation of beauty, there still remained another ideal of which Van Gogh became the leading exponent. Provisionally we might call it the expression of emotion, but the phrase needs a particular definition. The word *express*, however, inevitably recurs in all our attempts at definition, and Expressionism is the name which has been given to this tendency in modern art. 'To *express* the love of two lovers by a marriage of two complementary colours, their mingling and their opposition, the mysterious vibrations of kindred tones. To *express* the thought of a brow by the radiance of a light tone against a sombre background. To *express* hope by some star, the eagerness of a soul by a sunset radiance. Certainly there is nothing in that of stereoscopic realism, but is it not something that actually exists?' — these words of Van Gogh written at Arles in 1888 show the beginnings of a divergence of aim which in the years to follow was to modify profoundly the evolution of modern art.

Such a humanistic ideal in art was, of course, no new thing. It goes back to Rembrandt, if not farther, and in this tradition are such painters as Delacroix, Millet and Israels — all favourites of Van Gogh. Even Courbet and Manet contribute to the tradition, though their main significance lies elsewhere. Another quotation from Van Gogh's letters will serve to define this tradition and separate it from contemporary trends like Impressionism:

'What a mistake Parisians make in not having a palate for crude things, for Monticellis, for clay. But there, one must not lose heart because Utopia is not coming true. It is only that what I learned in Paris is leaving me, and that I am returning to the ideas I had in the country before I knew the impressionists. And I should not be surprised if the impressionists soon find fault with my way of working, for it has been fertilized by the ideas of Delacroix rather than by theirs. Because, *instead of trying to reproduce exactly what I have before my eyes, I use colour more arbitrarily so as to express myself forcibly.* Well, let that be as far as theory goes, but I am going to give you an example of what I mean.

'I should like to paint the portrait of an artist friend, a man who dreams great dreams, who works as the nightingale sings, because it is his nature. He'll be a fair man. I want to put into the picture my appreciation, the love that I have for him. So I paint him as he is, as faithfully as I can, to begin with.

'But the picture is not finished yet. To finish it I am now going to be the arbitrary colourist. I exaggerate the fairness of the hair, I come even to orange tones, chromes and pale lemon yellow.

'Beyond the head, instead of painting the ordinary wall of the mean room, I paint infinity, a plain background of the richest intensest blue that I can contrive, and by this simple combination of the bright head against the rich blue background, I get a mysterious effect, like a star in the depths of an azure sky.

'In the portrait of the peasant again I worked in this way, but without wishing in this case to produce the mysterious brightness of a pale star in the infinite. Instead, I think of the man I have to paint, terrible in the furnace of the full harvest, the full south. Hence the stormy orange shades, vivid as red hot iron, and hence the luminous tones of old gold in the shadows.

'Oh, my dear boy . . . and the nice people will only see the exaggeration as caricature.'[1]

The whole theory of expressionism, in its strength and weakness, is in this letter. Its strength lies in its humanism — in the

---

[1] Letter 520, from *Further Letters of Vincent van Gogh to his Brother.* 1886–1889 (London & Boston, 1929).

fact that art cannot be limited to the search for any absolute, whether of reality or beauty, but must ever return to the essential dignity of our common human qualities, our human nature. Its weakness lies in the imprecision of its terminology — in words like mystery and infinity which, when it comes to the point of translation into practice, into terms of form and colour, have no real meaning. There are no 'infinite' shades of blue, and brightness is no mystery — that, at least, would have been Cézanne's opinion. Gauguin would have been more in sympathy with this language, but he was not really interested in painting a postman, for example, 'as I feel him', but rather in using any suitable model for the creation of an independent aesthetic entity — a work of art that creates and contains its own emotional values and is not dependent on the evaluation of a human context. For Gauguin the work of art, as a symbol, must be detached from any particular occasion, just as a crucifix is detached from the Crucifixion.

Van Gogh had no immediate following in France. It was in the far North, in Scandinavia and later in Germany, that expressionism had its widest expansion. Here the dominant figure is the Norwegian Edvard Munch. Munch was born ten years later than Van Gogh (in 1863), and he may to some extent have been inspired by the Dutchman. There is certainly a close affinity of aim, and even of style, between the two artists. But a countryman of Ibsen's had really no need of external inspiration, and though Munch modified his style after his visits to France, he may be said to have been born with the desire to express himself forcibly. His scope, however, is not quite the same as Van Gogh's: it is more objective. It is true that he could write in his diary in 1889 words which are quite reminiscent of those we have quoted from Van Gogh's letter of the previous year: 'No more painting of interiors with men reading and women knitting! They must be living people who breathe, feel, suffer and love. I will paint a series of such pictures, in which people will have to recognize the holy element and bare their heads before it, as though in church.'[1] But in Munch's subsequent paintings, as in the work of the expressionist school generally, there is an element of despair, leading to remorseless analysis and masochism, which was not characteristic of Van Gogh. This Kierkegaardian morbidity in

[1] Quoted by J. P. Hodin, *Edvard Munch* (Stockholm — Neuer Verlag — 1948), p. 28.

Expressionism is a sufficient explanation of its failure to appeal more strongly to the Latin races. There is plenty of wonder in Expressionism, but little joy.

(vii)

By 1900 the three forces I have described — Realism, Symbolism and Expressionism — were ready to radiate into the new century. Their courses, however, were to be intricate and confused; only Expressionism developed with any logical consistency, though its inner despair was to destroy it. But meanwhile, in Kokoschka, Beckmann, Nolde, Heckel, Schmidt-Rottluff, Rohlfs, Soutine, Chagall and Rouault (not all of whom acknowledge the title of Expressionist) it produced artists of great talent and achievement.

The development of Realism has not been so uniform. In his last phase Cézanne, in his desire to emphasize the solidity of objects, had formed a style which is not merely architectonic in a metaphorical sense, but patently geometrical in a structural sense. The framework of the structure, perhaps a pyramid or a diamond, becomes dominant, and a considerable degree of distortion of the natural object is tolerated in order that the subject may conform to the perception of a 'good *Gestalt*'. Between 1907 and 1909 Picasso and Braque gave a further accentuation to this geometrical scaffolding and thereby affected what can only be described as a quantum-like jump into an altogether different type of art. Both Picasso and Braque were to retreat from their discovery, but it was taken up by Juan Gris, who did not, however, live long enough to pursue the new inspiration to its logical limits. This was done first by artists in the immediate vicinity (Marcel Duchamp, Gleizes, Delaunay, etc.), and almost simultaneously in other centres — Munich (Kandinsky, Klee), Moscow (Tatlin, Malevich, Gabo), Amsterdam (Mondrian) and London (Wyndham Lewis). This general tendency to abstraction, as we may call it, bore fruits of very various kinds, and became confused with such irrelevancies as machine-age romanticism. But at its best and purest — in, for example, the work of Mondrian, Gabo and Ben Nicholson — it undoubtedly expresses some profound need of the age. It may be derided as a flight from reality, but there are at least two possible defences; — it flies from a discredited reality to create a 'new reality', a realm of the absolute, of mystical purity; and in doing so it makes use of laws or elements that are fundamental to the structure of the physical universe. Whatever the explanation, the movement has shown vigour and tenacity for forty years, and the contempt of the critics and the neglect of the public have not sufficed to discourage its exponents.

A much more consistent use of Cézanne's discoveries was made by Henri Matisse. Matisse was not particularly interested in Cézanne's search for solidity, but he did take over Cézanne's insistence on a focal point in perception and consequently in composition — he too is an artist of the good *Gestalt*. But other influences were at work — Gauguin, perhaps, and certainly the discovery of Oriental art (more particularly in Matisse's case, of Persian art). This led Matisse to a complete breakaway from Cézanne's binding of colour to form. Colour is released, as in Gauguin's painting, to play its own dynamic and symbolic rôle. The result is a decorative pattern, but a pattern which still takes its organization from nature and the laws of perception. 'An artist must possess Nature. He must identify himself with her rhythm, by efforts that will prepare the mastery which will later enable him to express himself in his own language.' (Letter to Henry Clifford, February 14, 1948.)

'L'exactitude n'est pas la vérité' — this slogan of Matisse's has been the excuse in our time for much painting that is neither exact nor true. The exhaustion of the scientific impulse in art, which had lasted from Constable to Cézanne, put artists under the necessity of discovering a new principle of organization. Such new principles as have been discovered are either conceptual or instinctual. Cubism, the early 'metaphysical' paintings of Chirico, futurism (with some exceptions), constructivism, neo-plasticism, etc., — these are all attempts to impose a law of harmony on the visual perception of the artist. (A futurist such as Boccioni could announce the somewhat contradictory intentions of (*a*) 'opposing the liquefaction of objects which is a fatal consequence of impressionistic vision' and (*b*) 'the translating of objects according to the lines of force which characterize them' — thus achieving a new plastic dynamism, a pictorial lyricism. The short life of the futurist movement is probably to be explained by such inner contradictions.) A conceptual art is in effect a classical art, and it is not difficult to find a correspondence between Mondrian and Poussin, Gleizes and Sir Joshua Reynolds.

In general, however, the instinctual principle has prevailed in modern art since about 1910. Picasso has resolutely refused to treat cubism as a canon of art, external to the immediate intuitions of the artist. 'Mathematics, trigonometry, chemistry, psychoanalysis, music, and what not have been related to cubism to give it an easier interpretation. All this has been pure literature, not to say nonsense, which brought bad results, blinding people with theories. Cubism has kept itself within the limits and limitations of painting, never pretending to go beyond it. Drawing, design and colour are understood and practised in cubism in the spirit and manner that they are understood and practised in all other schools. Our subjects might be different, as we have introduced into painting objects and forms that were formerly ignored. We have kept our eyes open to our surroundings, *and also our brains.*' (Statement of 1923; my italics.)

There are one or two further remarks of Picasso's which serve to bring out the essentially instinctual nature of his activity. For example (from the same 'Statement' of 1923): 'Among the several sins that I have been accused of committing, none is more false than the one that I have, as the principal objective in my work, the spirit of research. When I paint, my object is to show what I have found and not what I am looking for.' Again, from his conversation with Christian Zervos, 1935: 'How can you expect an onlooker to live a picture of mine as I have lived it? A picture comes to me from miles away: who is to say from how far away I sensed it, saw it, painted it; and yet the next day I can't see what I've done myself. How can anyone enter into my dreams, my instincts, my thoughts, which have taken a long time to mature and to come out into the daylight, and above all grasp from them what I have been about — perhaps against my own will?'[1] These statements directly contradict everything for which Cézanne stood — his patient research for the form inherent in the object, his laborious efforts to reproduce this form with scientific exactitude. The result of such a new attitude was an explosive liberation of expression, not only in Picasso himself, but throughout the whole civilized world. It is part of my contention that a long process of germination has been taking place in the social consciousness of the same civilized world — Picasso is preceded by Hegel, Marx, Bergson, Freud, by revolutions in science, economics and social organization. But genius is the capacity to

[1] Quotations by Alfred Barr, *Picasso* (New York, 1946), Museum of Modern Art.

focus diversity — the ability to draw into a single burning point of light the discoveries and inventions of a whole generation. Picasso had this gift and his influence accordingly has been universal. It is safe to say that there has never been an artist who in his own lifetime has had so many imitators. Well may Picasso himself exclaim: 'To repeat is to run counter to spiritual laws; essentially escapism.'

(viii)

The general effect of the revolution in painting established by Matisse, Picasso, Braque and their immediate contemporaries was subjectivist in character, and the same generalization can be made of other arts (Proust, Joyce, D. H. Lawrence). This development in the arts had been supported by the new hypothesis of the unconscious first clearly formulated at the turn of the century by Freud. Again it must be emphasized that the causal connections are not necessarily direct. A writer like D. H. Lawrence may be tempted to justify the nature of his art by a direct appeal to psycho-analysis, but he is the exception rather than the rule. Subjectivism is a mental climate, announced more than a century ago by Kierkegaard and Hegel. It is a climate that has 'prevailed' for the past forty years, and though we may be rather tired of it, there is no sign of an immediate change.

A specific product of this prevailing climate has been the Surrealist movement. The Fauvistes had always imposed limitations on their spontaneity. They disclaimed any plan of campaign, any programme, but they always sought an 'objective correlate' for their sensations. The objectivity of this correlate was always determined by universal qualities which, in their sum, may be called Harmony. 'What I dream of', Matisse once wrote (*La grande revue*, December 25, 1908), 'is an art of balance, of purity and serenity devoid of troubling or depressing subject-matter, an art which might be for every mental worker, be he business-man or writer, like an appeasing influence, like a mental soother, something like a good armchair in which to rest from physical fatigue' — a naïve confession which nevertheless describes the normal function of art. The Surrealists rejected this 'bourgeois' conception of art in favour of an activity which should be fundamentally disturbing and essentially impure. The first Manifesto of the Surrealists was not published until 1924, but a very necessary preparation had been taking place during the previous ten or fifteen years, years in which the harmonic conception of art was gradually discredited. The chief instigator in this destructive movement was undoubtedly Duchamp, and the surrealists have always honoured him as their forerunner. But the futurists, along with Chirico, Picabia and the sculptor Archipenko also played their parts, and the foundation of the Dada group in 1916 (in Zürich) was the first conscious negation of the aesthetic principle in art. The way was then clear for a new principle, and it was announced by André Breton as *automatism* — 'pure psychic automatism, by which it is intended to express, verbally, in writing or by other means, the real process of thought. It is thought's dictation, all exercise of reason and every aesthetic or moral preoccupation being absent.'

Attempts have been made to find precedents for surrealism in the art of the past (Arcimboldi, Bosch, Goya), but they are mistaken, because however fantastic in their conceptions, these artists were always guided by aesthetic preconceptions. Surrealism is a completely revolutionary conception of art, and the only question is whether it is still 'art'. We should deny the term 'science' to an activity that refused to recognize the laws of induction; we have the same right to deny the term 'art' to an activity that rejects the laws of harmony. But the surrealists have not consistently practised what they have preached, and the colour harmonies of Miró, the balanced compositions of Ernst and Dali, the dynamic rhythm of Masson, constitute objective correlates of an aesthetic nature in spite of the artist's intention to rid himself of such categories. In fact, 'pure psychic automatism' only takes place in the unconscious (and we only become aware of it in emerging from a state of unconsciousness, that is to say, in dreams). As soon as we attempt to translate unconscious phenomena into perceptual images, the instinctive laws of perception intervene — we automatically project the good *Gestalt*, the composition that obeys aesthetic laws.

Nevertheless, an immense liberation of aesthetic activity was achieved by this subjectivist revolution. It is not possible to resist the *play* of artists like Miró and Klee — their work simply gives pleasure, and needs no theory to defend it. The work of other surrealists (as of certain expressionists), sometimes intentionally, sometimes unintentionally, is 'troubling or depressing subject-matter' and has its proper place in the case-books of the psychiatrists. One should not necessarily exclude from art the tragic aspects of life — it is perhaps Matisse's limitation that he has — but even in the tragic art of the past the intention was always to 'sublimate' the theme, to resolve the conflict, to create an overwhelming atmosphere of serenity.

(ix)

Und ich wiederhole: naturferne Kunst ist publikumsfremde Kunst. Muss es sein.

WILHELM WORRINGER

It has not been my aim in this essay to mention every artist of importance, or even to produce one of those charts in which every movement has its appropriate graph. The truth is obscured by such rigid complexities. It is the broad effects that are significant for my present purpose, and these are complex enough. If I have succeeded, the reader will be conscious of a stream which runs fairly consistently through a tract of time measuring about a century, widening as it approaches our present sea of troubles. But this stream is carrying down with it the sands and pebbles that have ineffectually opposed its progress. This silt accumulates as the river is about to attain its end, blocks the flow and creates a delta — the one stream becomes many separate streams. But here the metaphor breaks down, for the separate streams do not make their way fanwise to the ultimate sea; some turn inland again and are lost in the desert.

This diversion in modern art is due to the failure of the scientific attitude in art. It has not proved possible, or at any rate finally satisfying, to consider art as 'a branch of natural philosophy, of which pictures are but experiments'. In art, 'l'exactitude n'est pas la vérité.' 'We all know that art is not truth. Art is a lie that makes us realize truth, at least the truth that is given us to understand.' (Picasso.) Art is a closed system, and it is 'true' in the degree that its rhetoric convinces us, pleases us, comforts us. It has no spiritual mission; it is accused of having no social function.

The artists themselves have recognized their isolation. 'Uns trägt kein Volk,' cried Klee — the people are not with us. But it is useless to blame the artist for that isolation — as well blame the weathercock for not turning when there is no wind. (It is true, there is a kind of weathercock that does not turn because its hinges are rusty — the academic artist.) The climate of the age

(*Zeitgeist, usw.*) is the creation of a thousand forces, and perhaps the Marxists are right in giving priority, among these forces, to economic trends. But the failure of the Soviet Union, after more than forty years of strenuous effort, to produce a new art on the basis of a new economy, proves that the inspiration of the artist cannot be forced. We must wait, wait perhaps for a very long time, before any vital connection can be re-established between art and society. The modern work of art, as I have said, is a symbol. The symbol, by its nature, is only intelligible to the initiated (though it may still appeal mysteriously to the un-initiated, so long as they allow it to enter their unconscious). The people can understand only the image, and even this they distrust in its eidetic purity, for even their vision is conventional. It does not seem that the contradiction which exists between the aristo-cratic function of art and the democratic structure of modern society can ever be resolved. But both may wear the cloak of humanism, the one for shelter, the other for display. The sensi-tive artist knows that a bitter wind is blowing.

Surrealism and the Romantic Principle[1]

June, 1936. After a winter long drawn out into bitterness and petulance, a month of torrid heat, of sudden efflorescence, of clarifying storms. In this same month the International Surrealist Exhibition broke over London, electrifying the dry intellectual atmosphere, stirring our sluggish minds to wonder, enchantment and derision. The press, unable to appreciate the significance of a movement of such unfamiliar features, prepared an armoury of mockery, sneers and insults. The duller desiccated weeklies, no less impelled to anticipate the event, commissioned their polyglot gossips, their blasé globe-trotters, their old-boy-scouts, to adopt their usual pose of I know all, don't be taken in, there's nothing new under the sun — a pose which merely reflected the general lack of intellectual curiosity in this country. But in the event they were all deceived; their taunts fell on deaf ears, and though for a time there was no lack of the laughing jackass — an animal extinct in most parts of the world and even in this country generally emerging only from beyond the pale of the ineffectual Cheviots — in the outcome people, and mostly young people, came in their hundreds and their thousands not to sneer, but to learn, to find enlightenment, to live. When the foam and froth of society and the press had subsided, we were left with a serious public of scientists, artists, philosophers and socialists. Fifteen years have now passed by, bringing with them death, destruction, and the diaspora of another world war; but that serious public still remains.

From the moment of its birth surrealism was an international phenomenon — the spontaneous generation of an international and fraternal *organism* in total contrast to the artificial manufacture of a collective *organization* such as the League of Nations.

---

[1] Introduction to *Surrealism*, edited by the author (London, 1936).

Surrealism and the Romantic Principle

It would therefore be contrary to the nature of the movement to disengage, as some have suggested, a specifically English version of 'surréalisme'. We who in England supported this movement had no other desire than to pool our resources in the general effort. Nevertheless, an English contribution has been made to this effort, and its strength and validity can only be shown by tracing its sources in the native tradition of our art and literature. The evidences on which the claims of Surrealism are based are scattered through the centuries, the partial and incoherent revelations of permanent human characteristics; and nowhere are these evidences so plentiful as in England. My main purpose in this essay will be to present this English evidence, to unite it with the general theory of surrealism, and to reaffirm on this wider basis the truths which other writers, above all André Breton, have already declared.

In an Introduction which I contributed to the catalogue of the exhibition I asserted, in the cryptic and exiguous manner demanded by the occasion, that 'superrealism in general is the romantic principle in art'. It will be noted that I used a variation of the word 'surrealism'. When it first became essential to find an English equivalent for the original French word, I made an attempt to establish 'superrealism'. Pedantically, euphonically and logically I think I was right; 'superrealism' is not only simple to say, but self-explanatory to the meanest intelligence ('super' is slang, 'sur' is a purely grammatical affix). But I was defeated by that obscure instinct which determines word-formation in the life of a language, and for which I have the greatest respect. The very clarity of the term 'superrealism' was against it; the public wanted a strange and not too intelligible word for a strange and not too intelligible thing; and I bow to that decree. But I do not propose to abandon the word 'superrealism' altogether; I propose rather to make a distinction between superrealism in general and surrealism in particular, employing the first word for the tentative and historical manifestations of what has now become a conscious and deliberate artistic principle. And those tentative and historical manifestations of superrealism I shall identify with some of the essential characteristics of romanticism — but of romanticism understood in a certain strict and not too comprehensive sense.

No critic of experience will return to a discussion of the terms 'romanticism' and 'classicism' with anything but extreme reluctance; no subject has provoked so much weary logomachy since the scholastics argued themselves out on the question of nominalism. I only take up the discussion again (eating my own words in the process) because I think that surrealism has settled it. So long as romanticism and classicism were considered as alternative attitudes, rival camps, professions of *faith*, an interminable struggle was in prospect, with the critics as profiteers. But what in effect surrealism claims to do is to resolve the conflict — not, as I formerly hoped, by establishing a synthesis which I was prepared to call 'reason' or 'humanism' — but by liquidating classicism, by showing its complete irrelevance, its *anaesthetic* effect, its contradiction of the creative impulse. Classicism, let it be stated without further preface, represents for us now, and has always represented, the forces of oppression. Classicism is the intellectual counterpart of political tyranny. It was so in the ancient world and in the medieval empires; it was renewed to express the dictatorships of the Renaissance and has ever since been the official creed of capitalism. Wherever the blood of martyrs stains the ground, there you will find a doric column or perhaps a statue of Minerva.

Academic critics have not been unaware of this alignment, but have united, of course, to give living colours to the corpse they have embalmed. I have often praised Sir Herbert Grierson's clean handling of this problem; like Brunetière, whose main line of demarcation he follows, he is not altogether unsympathetic towards romanticism, but there is a question of values involved which must be challenged. A classical literature, he writes, 'is the product of a nation and a generation which has consciously achieved a definite advance, moral, political, intellectual; and is filled with the belief that its view of life is more natural, human, universal and wise than that from which it has escaped. It has effected a synthesis which enables it to look round on life with a sense of its wholeness, its unity in variety; and the work of the artist is to give expression to that consciousness; hence the solidity of his work and hence too its definiteness, and in the hands of great artists its beauty. . . . The work of the classical artist is to give individual expression, the beauty of form, to a body of common sentiments and thoughts which he shares with his audience, thoughts and views which have for his generation the validity of universal truths.

'Classical and romantic — these are the systole and diastole of the human heart in history. They represent on the one hand our need of order, of synthesis, of a comprehensive yet definite, therefore *exclusive* as well as inclusive, ordering of thought and feeling and action; and on the other hand the inevitable finiteness of every human synthesis, the discovery that, in Carlyle's metaphor, our clothes no longer fit us, that the classical has become the conventional, that our spiritual aspirations are being starved, or that our secular impulses are "cribb'd, cabin'd, and confined". . . ."[1]

The particular danger of this argument is due to its false dialecticism. A certain type of society is regarded as a 'synthesis', a natural order or balance of forces, a state of equilibrium; and any deviation from that standard is regarded as abnormal, degenerate or revolutionary. Actually such types of society merely represent the dominance of one particular class — the economic dominance and therefore the cultural dominance of that class. For the stability of such a society a certain uniformity of ideas and modes of expression is a fundamental necessity; and the less novelty these ideas and modes of expression show the better. This explains the constant return to the norms of classical art; for these norms (in architecture we call them the 'orders') are the typical patterns of order, proportion, symmetry, equilibrium, harmony and of all static and inorganic qualities. They are intellectual concepts which control or repress the vital instincts on which growth and therefore change depend, and in no sense represent a freely determined preference, but merely an imposed ideal.

The fallacy we are discussing is logical in its origin. It is a sophism by means of which two terms are conceived as dialectical opposites whereas actually they represent types of action and reaction. This is a very important distinction, and its neglect is the cause of much confusion. In dialectics the thesis and the antithesis are both objective facts, and the necessity for a resolution or synthesis is due to the real existence of a contradiction. But 'classic' and 'romantic' do not represent such a contradiction. They correspond rather to the husk and the seed, the shell and the kernel. There is a principle of life, of creation, of liberation, and that is the romantic spirit; there is a principle of order, of control and of repression, and that is the classical spirit. Naturally there is some purpose in the latter principle — the instincts are

[1] *The Background of English Literature* (London, 1925), pp. 266, 287–8.

curbed in the interest of some particular ideal or set of values; but on analysis it always resolves into the defence of some particular structure of society, the perpetuation of the rule of some particular class. To identify romanticism with revolt as Grierson does is true enough as an historical generalization; but it merely distorts the values involved if such revolt is conceived in purely literary or academic terms. It would be much nearer the truth to identify romanticism with the artist and classicism with society; classicism being the political concept of art to which the artist is expected to conform.

It may be as well to forestall at once the criticism that on this showing the artist is merely the individualist in conflict with society. To a certain extent, as I have shown elsewhere,[1] this is true; the mental personality of the artist may be determined by a failure in social adaptation. But his whole effort is directed towards a reconciliation with society, and what he offers to society is not a bagful of his own tricks, his idiosyncracies, but rather some knowledge of the secrets to which he has had access, the secrets of the self which are buried in every man alike, but which only the sensibility of the artist can reveal to us in all their actuality. This 'self' is not the personal possession we imagine it to be; it is largely made up of elements from the unconscious, and the more we learn about the unconscious, the more collective it appears to be — in fact, 'a body of common sentiments and thoughts . . . universal truths,' such as Grierson assumes to be the exclusive concern of the classical artist. But whereas the universal truths of classicism may be merely the temporal prejudices of an epoch, the universal truths of romanticism are coeval with the evolving consciousness of mankind.

It is in this sense, then, that surrealism is a reaffirmation of the romantic principle; and though poets and painters in all ages have clung to a belief in the inspirational and even the obsessional nature of their gifts, repudiating in deeds if not in words the rigid bonds of classical theory, it is only now, with the aid of modern dialectics and modern psychology, in the name of Marx and Freud, that they have found themselves in a position to put their beliefs and practices on a scientific basis, thereby initiating a continuous and deliberate creative activity whose only laws are the laws of its own dynamics.

Before passing on to a more precise examination of the romantic

[1] *Art and Society*, chap. VI.

principle as actually manifested in English art and literature, there is one further interpretation of the classic-romantic antithesis which is worth referring to, especially as it finds its justification in modern psychology — I mean the theory that the two terms correspond to the general distinction between 'extravert' and 'introvert' types of personality. The comparison is valid enough if it has reference to the personalities involved; what is questionable is the very existence of such a type as an extravert *artist*. To the degree in which he becomes extravert the artist, we would say, ceases to be, in any essential sense of the word, an artist. Now admittedly there is much in the process of producing a work of art which involves, or may involve, an objective attitude towards the materials the artist is using; only the automatic text or drawing is strictly speaking subjective, and though the surrealist insists on the significance of such automatic expression and makes it the basis of his own practice, he is far from asserting that all art must of necessity be produced under such conditions. What he does assert, however, is the absolute impossibility of producing a work of art by the conscious exercise of talents. The notion that a work of art can be created by observing a set of rules is only to be compared with the notion that a human being can be produced in a test-tube.

'Verbal and graphic automatism', Breton has said, 'only represents a *limit* towards which the poet or artist should tend.' The opposed limit is represented by all those 'arts of poetry', those academic discourses on painting, in which various ages have sought to codify for all time the laws of art. Between these limits we find the whole range of aesthetic expression, but it is towards the limit of automatism, and away from the limit of rational control, that we find the most enduring vitality, the words which live when the poet is dead, when even his name is forgotten —

A rose-red city half as old as time

— a single line surviving from the complete works of a poet, and surviving precisely by virtue of its irrationality.

It is very difficult to determine the factors which lead to the survival of any particular work of art. There is a considerable element of chance, even under modern conditions of publishing and propaganda. We know that contemporary judgement is very uncertain, very arbitrary; every age has its Ossians and there may still be Donnes to be redeemed from a neglected past. We ascribe this fickleness of public estimation to changes in sensibility, but sensibility itself does not change, only the control of it. The sensibility which appreciated the poems of Donne at the time of their first appearance was lively and direct; it needed the colossal irrelevance of a Johnsonian intellect and the general diffusion of a rational spirit to throw them into obscurity. The sensibility which we have now recovered and by virtue of which we once more appreciate the poetry of Donne is the identical sensibility for which his poems were written; and it is no gust of fashion which has re-established his fame, but a revival of poetic sensibility itself — the same revival which has once more placed Shakespeare at the utmost pinnacle of fame, which has given Blake his due eminence and has secured immediate recognition for Hopkins and Eliot. No doubt we are age-bound like the rest and our standards are relative to our circumstances; but it is difficult to imagine, in any form of society congenial to our elementary demands of economic security and intellectual liberty, any return to the standards which tended to exalt a Dryden or a Pope above Shakespeare.

Some recognition of the truth which I am affirming — the identity of art and romanticism — has been given by the philosophers of art; not by all philosophers, but particularly by those who have shown the greatest appreciation of art, or who have been, like Plato, great artists themselves. Plato's description of the poet in *Ion* is well known; I have quoted it before, but I think it should be read again in the present context. Socrates is the speaker:

'For all good poets, epic as well as lyric, compose their beautiful poems not by art, but because they are inspired and possessed. And as the Corybantian revellers when they dance are not in their right mind, so the lyric poets are not in their right mind when they are composing their beautiful strains; but when falling under the power of music and metre they are inspired and possessed; like Bacchic maidens who draw milk and honey from the rivers when they are under the influence of Dionysus but not when they are in their right mind. And the soul of the lyric poet does the same, as they themselves say; for they tell us that they bring songs from honeyed fountains, culling them out of the gardens and dells of the Muses; they, like the bees, winging their way from flower to flower. And this is true. For the poet is a light and winged and holy thing, and there is no invention in him until he has been inspired and is out of his senses, and the mind is no longer in him: when he has not attained to this state, he is powerless and is unable to utter his oracles.'[1]

It is pointless to observe that because of their irrational character Plato excluded poets from his ideal republic. Within the logic of his rational philosophy, this was inevitable; just as later it was inevitable that Hegel, for quite similar reasons, should come to the conclusion that 'the fair days of Greek art, as also the golden time of the later middle ages, are over'. Both philosophers held the view that a reflective, idealistic and ratiocinative culture was not merely desirable, but actually represented a higher stage in human evolution. They were both right in considering that the sensuous phenomena of art — the completely irrational basis of the imaginative faculty — are inconsistent with such a reflective culture. But what we now assert with the strongest conviction is our disbelief in either the inevitability or desirability of such a culture. The whole evidence of history, as well as of modern psychology, causes us to reject without hesitation such a fool's paradise of idealism. For good or for evil the instinctive and impulsive components of our being are irreducible and irreplaceable, and we ignore them or repress them at our peril. Not merely the neuroses of individuals result from such repression, but there is more and more reason to believe that the mass hysteria manifested, for example, in such a nation as Germany, is the collective aspect of general repressions. The only absolutely pacifist races (if any such still exist) are those which live in a golden age of hedonism such as, apparently, the Minoan civilization enjoyed for many centuries. Unfortunately we do not know enough about the Minoan civilization to relate its freedom from war to, for example, its freedom from morality; but we are beginning to know sufficient about our own civilization to be sure that war has no simple explanation in economic forces, but is most probably not unrelated to the frustration of certain primitive impulses during childhood, a frustration which is prolonged and reinforced by adult codes of morality. War is, in theory as in fact, the correlative of religion. The Christian religion in its Calvinistic rigour induced the bloodiest epoch in the world's history. Piety and asceticism are inevitably accompanied by masochism and sadism, and the more religion has been deprived of a ritualistic and occult indulgence of the senses, rationalizing itself in the form of moral

[1] Jowett's translation.

253

precepts and social conventions, the deeper the world has plunged into compensatory orgies of hatred and bloodshed.[1]

Those who have not experienced war at first hand may perhaps entertain illusions about its comparative evil; they may entertain the idea, that is to say, that even its modern intensity of horror is sanctioned by some nobler effects of heroism, of national awakening, of personal regeneration. Such a belief is a pestilential idiocy. There is in modern war neither grace nor dignity. It is mad and inconsequential in its inception; beyond the scope of human control in its conduct — a dreary shattering of human flesh in conditions of physical and mental disgust, a long agony which can only be ended in exhaustion. In spite of this truth, which must be evident to millions of people, we today contemplate a political situation (it would be more exact to say a psychological situation) whose inevitable outcome seems to be another world war even more stupid, more purposeless and more horrible than the last. Everywhere in all countries we meet apparently friendly and peaceful human beings; we exchange visits, books, ideas — not to insist too much on manufactures; we slowly build up an international understanding in which there is no thought of anything but mutual help and general well-being — an indivisible peace. Yet in a few days the face of the world may change. Bugles blow, klaxons screech, an immense machine begins to move and we find ourselves segregated, regimented, drafted into armies and navies and workshops. Bull-necked demagogues inject a poisonous propaganda into our minds and then the storm of steel breaks above us; our bodies become so much manure for an acid soil, and our ideas, our aspirations, the whole structure of our civilization, becomes a history which the future may not even record.[2]

The astonishing fact is that men can contemplate such a fate and remain passive. Nothing in the world is so disturbing as human docility. Man is indeed a wild animal tamed; broken in and made to trot obediently in a ring, to respond to every crack of the whip. He accepts the tips and the kicks, the doles and the charity of his indifferent and cynical masters. Only the fact that

[1] It is impossible to ignore the evidence on this question presented by Dr. Edward Glover in *War, Sadism and Pacifism* (London, 1933, new edn. 1947). Cf. also C. G. Jung, *Aufsaetze zur Zeitgeschichte* (Zürich, 1946), trans. *Essays on Contemporary Events* (London, 1947).

[2] This paragraph was written in 1936, before the Second World War. There is, alas, no reason to alter it now.

history shows that the goad may be driven too deep, that out of extreme suffering will come general revolt — only this melancholy thought saves us from complete despair.

· Underlying this condition of humanity are motives no less irrational than those which promote war-mindedness; the capitalist and the socialist no less than the militarist and the pacifist are moved by obscure instincts. Admittedly it is not a very obscure instinct that makes a man desire to triumph over his fellows, to enjoy a position of comparative wealth and ease, to command the admiration of the loveliest women — such desires are elementary and we are only ashamed of them in the degree of our sensibility and altruism. But the individuals who possess this altruism, this sensibility, are certainly not the priests and preceptors whose position and authority is assured by the social system of which they are an integral part. Nothing is simpler to demonstrate than the dependency, in every age, of the official codes of morality on the class interests of those who possess the economic power. The only individuals who protest against injustices — or who make their protest vocal — are in effect the poets and artists of each age, who to the extent that they rely on their imaginative capacities and powers, despise and reject the acquisitive materialism of men of action.[1]

I am not leaving it open for anyone to suggest that in this respect — in its adoption of a revolutionary political attitude, its protest against injustice and inhumanity — surrealism merely represents a sentimental movement of the heart. Surrealism is anti-rational, but it is equally anti-emotional. If you wish to reduce surrealism to its foundations you will find the only basic elements on which any useful structure can be built — the basic elements of natural science and psychology. The surrealist builds on that materialistic basis. But he builds. He creates. And he has his method of building, his craft of logic, his dialectic.

The philosophical justification of surrealism is to be found, if anywhere in the past, in Hegel. But it is a Hegel deprived for the most part of those elements which he would have considered of the greatest importance. Just as Marx, for his purposes, turned Hegel upside down, 'sloughed off' the mystical form of Hegel's dialectic, so the surrealist, for his purposes, subjects the philo-

---

[1] It is obvious that the few revolutionary priests who may be included (St. Francis of Assisi, Wycliffe, Huss) were in our sense of the word no less poets than priests.

sopher to the same indignity. If I am asked why, in this matter, we should return to Hegel rather than start our philosophy of art afresh, there are various answers to give — answers similar to those which have to be given in the field of political philosophy. One is that Hegel represents a convenient *crux* in philosophy: all previous philosophies seem to meet in him, to be sorted and smelted and reduced to the purest and least contradictory elements of human thought. Hegel is the great scavenger of philosophical systems; he cleans them up and leaves a tidy piece of ground on which we can build. More than that, he provides a scaffolding within which we can build — the scaffold of his dialectic.

This dreaded word *dialectic* — a word which the English-speaking public finds difficult to digest and which even our so-called socialists, with a few exceptions, would willingly forget — this word is actually the name of a very simple and very necessary process of thought. If we consider the natural world, we soon become aware that its most striking characteristic is not permanency, solidity or stability, but *continuous change* or development. Physicists now affirm that not merely the organic world, not merely this earth we live on, but the whole universe is undergoing a process of change. Dialectics is nothing more than a logical explanation of how such a change takes place. It does not suffice to say that 'it grows', or 'it decays', 'it runs down', 'it expands'; these phrases are vague abstractions. The change must take place in a definite way. Between one phase and another of that development there must intervene an active principle, and Hegel suggested that this principle was actually one of opposition and interaction. That is to say, to produce any new situation (i.e., any departure from an existing condition of equilibrium) there must previously exist two elements so opposed to each other and yet so related to each other that a solution or resolution is demanded; such a solution being in effect a new phase of development (temporary state of equilibrium) which preserves some of the elements of the interacting phases, eliminates others, but is qualitatively different from the previously existing state of opposition.

Such is the dialectical logic, elaborated by Hegel for idealistic purposes and brilliantly adapted by Marx for materialistic purposes. As an instrument of thought it enabled Marx to explain the evolution of human society from primitive communism to feudalism and through the various stages of capitalism; it enabled him, moreover, to predict the self-extinction of capitalism and the coming of the socialist state. But that is by the way. What I wish to stress now is that surrealism is an application of the same logical method to the realm of art. By the dialectical method we can explain the development of art in the past and justify a revolutionary art at the present time.

In dialectical terms we claim that there is a continual state of opposition and interaction between the world of objective fact — the sensational and social world of active and economic existence — and the world of subjective fantasy. This opposition creates a state of disquietude, a lack of spiritual equilibrium, which it is the business of the artist to resolve. He resolves the contradiction by creating a synthesis, a work of art which combines elements from both these worlds, eliminates others, but which for the moment gives us a qualitatively new experience — an experience on which we can dwell with equanimity. Superficial critics may pretend to be unable to distinguish such a qualitatively new state from an ordinary compromise, and it is to be feared that in practice most dialectical solutions are of this kind. But a true synthesis is never a reversion; it is always a progression.

That is the central core of the surrealist claim, and any attempt to discredit or criticize surrealism must present an adequate philosophical alternative; just as any criticism of dialectical materialism as embodied in the socialism of Marx must present an adequate philosophical alternative. At present any alternative in art worthy of our consideration is lacking.

To return for a moment to Hegel. He dealt with the subject of art at such length (in his *Aesthetik*) that one would expect to find there some approach to the dialectical interpretation of art which the surrealist now advances. Actually we no more find that than, in his other works, we find an anticipation of Marx. Everything, in his philosophy, is sacrificed to the necessity of making 'ideas', or states of self-consciousness, the supreme forces in creative development. As Marx observed in his Preface to the first edition of *Kapital*:

'My dialectic method is not only different from the Hegelian, but its direct opposite. To Hegel, the life-process of the human brain, i.e. the process of thinking, which, under the name of "the Idea", he even transforms into an independent subject, is the demiurgos of the real world, and the real world is only the external, phenomenal form of "the Idea". With me, on the contrary, the ideal is nothing else than the material world reflected by the human mind, and translated into forms of thought.'

With the surrealists, we might also say, the ideal is nothing else than the material world reflected by the human mind, and translated into images. But 'reflection' and 'translation' are not, for us today, such simple mechanical processes as perhaps Marx implies. For us the process is infinitely complicated: a passage through a series of distorting mirrors and underground labyrinths.

When Hegel generalizes his logic in relation to art, the result is not far from our present point of view. In one place he says:

'This universal need for artistic expression (Bedürfniss zur Kunst) is based on the rational impulse in man's nature to exalt both the world of his inner experience and that of nature into the conscious embrace of mind, as an object in which he rediscovers himself. He satisfies the demand of this spiritual freedom by making explicit to his *inner* life all that exists, no less than by giving correspondingly a realized *external* embodiment to the self made thus explicit. And by this reduplication of what is his own he places before the vision and within the cognition of himself and others what is within him. This is the free rationality of man, in which art as also all action and knowledge originates.' (*Aesthetik*, Introduction, III, i, d.)

But Hegel was not able to continue to treat art as an integral activity. In the name of the Idea he must differentiate between three types of beauty — the symbolic, the classical and the romantic. If in high hope that at least within his romantic category we shall find some anticipation of our theory we turn to that part of his work which deals with romantic art, we find that the terms do not apply to qualities of art in general, but denote specific arts; symbolic art being identified with architecture, classical art with sculpture, and romantic art with painting, music and poetry. In short, Hegel is only concerned to denote the degree of sensuousness in art — which is the negation of the degree in which the Idea, in all its immateriality, is adequately realized. And the Idea is, of course, precisely that mystical emanation of German idealism which the surrealists, no less than the Marxians, repudiate and reject.

It is my ambition some day to submit Hegel's *Aesthetik* to a detailed examination — to do for the realm of art on the basis of Hegel's dialectic something analogous to what Marx on the same basis did for the realm of economics. With such a philosophy of art one could then proceed to a complete revaluation of aesthetic values. I am convinced that the general body of existing aesthetic judgements are *conventional*. For the most part they consist of dogmas handed down by tradition or inculcated by education. They rarely have any real basis in personal experience. We pay lip-service, perhaps to Homer and Sophocles, perhaps to Virgil and Lucretius, Ariosto and Dante, Racine and Boileau, Shakespeare and Milton, and many other names in poetry and the other arts; but very few of these names represent for us *active influences*. I am not suggesting that the whole façade of our culture is false; but it has an architectonic completeness which is historical rather than actual. We look up at this façade and see a magnificent array of saints, all ordered in their appropriate niches; we recognize Homer, Dante, Shakespeare and several others; but for the most part we are ignorant of the identity of the figures and have to consult the guide-book. Our culture is altogether on the guide-book model; Shakespeare has four stars, Milton three, Donne and Blake one. We do not stop to ask on what system, and by whom, the stars were awarded. If we did, we should discover some dusty college of pedants, their noses buried in a profit and loss account of bibliographical data, critical overdrafts and vested interests. If we dared to travel without a guide, to trust our eyes and ears and our contemporary sensibility, the result would be catastrophic. Schoolmasters and professors would wander about helplessly like myopic men deprived of their glasses; textbooks would be irrelevant and teaching an impudent imposition.

Surrealism demands nothing less than such a revaluation of all aesthetic values. It has no respect for any academic tradition, least of all for the classical-capitalist tradition of the last four hundred years. It believes that as a general rule even men of genius during this period — and it has no difficulty in conceding genius where it is due — have been hampered and repressed by the conventions of their education and by their social environment. For poets like Dryden and Pope, for painters like Michelangelo and Poussin, and for many lesser artists, we can only have an angry and in no sense patronizing pity. The spectacle of the immense genius of Michelangelo, for example, caught in the toils of the moral and aesthetic conventions of his day, is a titanic tragedy. On the other hand the exaltation of conforming mediocrities in every age into a position of authority is a melancholy farce.[1] It is true that only a small proportion of them survive the inevitable ridicule of posterity, but there still remain on every classical Parnassus stuffed corpses that should be thrown on the dunghill.

That such a revaluation would be in effect merely a rehabilitation of romanticism is true enough, if the definition of romanticism I have already given is borne in mind. I would suggest, merely as examples of the tasks awaiting us, and merely in the restricted field of English literature, the following:

(1) *A fuller acknowledgment of the supreme poetic quality of our ballads and anonymous literature.* I do not refer to the actual work of recovering and editing the material; to that ghoulish activity it is time to cry halt. The ballads have become the happy hunting ground of academic competence; they must be rescued from such dead hands and be fully recognized as the most fundamental and authentic type of all poetry. Ballads are partly collective (if not in origin, at least in development) and to some degree automatic, and illustrate the intrinsic nature of surrealist poetry. I include in this category, not merely the familiar Border Ballads, but the popular ballads of more recent times (even Woolworth's Song Sheets) and the vast store of primitive poetry mostly still hidden in anthropological works.

(2) *Driving home the inescapable significance of Shakespeare.* To claim Shakespeare as an ally will be treated as an act of impudence by academic critics, but to justify our claim it is only necessary to point to the history of Shakespearean criticism. The rehabilitation of Shakespeare's genius, after the class and classical denigration of the seventeenth and eighteenth centuries, has been the work of specifically romantic critics, beginning with Coleridge and ending, for the moment, with Middleton Murry. Other critics have tinkered with his text — usually to little purpose — or have elaborated the historical background. But the poetic status of Shakespeare — his relative position among the poets of England and of the world — that depends on the romantic theory of poetry. It is impossible — the very attempt is absurd — to establish the genius of Shakespeare on any classical basis. He breaks all the academic rules.

A critic who would not be described as romantic — Professor Dover Wilson — published a few years ago a long book on a vexed

---

[1] For the perfect expression of the resentment of the mediocre talent in the presence of genius, see Aretino's letter to Michelangelo of November 1545.

question: the problem of Hamlet.[1] Most critics have been puzzled by the incoherency of this, the most famous of Shakespeare's plays — an incoherency which affects not only the action of the play, but also the character of the hero. Various solutions have been proposed, and Professor Wilson reviews them all and finds them wanting. He has great fun demolishing the clumsy or ingenious attempts which have been made to explain the inexplicable; and ends where they might all have begun — by accepting the inexplicable at its face-value, its value as inexplicableness, as irrationality. The heart of the mystery proves to be the mystery itself:

'In fine, we were never intended to reach the heart of the mystery. That it has a heart is an illusion; the mystery itself is an illusion; Hamlet is an illusion. The secret that lies behind it all is not Hamlet's, but Shakespeare's; the technical devices he employed to create this supreme illusion of a great and mysterious character, who is at once mad and the sanest of geniuses, at once a procrastinator and a vigorous man of action, at once a miserable failure and the most adorable of heroes. The character of Hamlet, like the appearance of his successive impersonators on the stage, is a matter of make-up.'

Not since Warton defended the irrational imagery of Milton has such light streamed into the dark cloisters of the academic mind! It is really a very significant event in the history of scholarship. Professor Wilson is not a stray wolf in academic robes — such do occasionally find their way into the fold. He is the authentic type, the adept of a modern apparatus of the most efficient kind. He moves his apparatus into position; sets it in motion to do its carding and sorting and tidy ordering and then discovers that it will not work. Abandoning his apparatus he approaches the work of genius with his naked eye, and is dazzled. Rest, rest, perturbed spirit.[2]

(3) *The exact relations between metaphysics and poetry.* 'e il pensamento in sogno transmutai' — Dante's line is the perfect description of a process which has yet to be given a full psy-

---

[1] J. Dover Wilson, *What Happens in Hamlet* (Cambridge, 1935).

[2] This critic's acknowledgment of the irrationality of Shakespeare's genius is not confined to this one instance. For example, what can he mean in saying that in *King Lear* Shakespeare 'has fashioned a mirror of art in which, more successfully than any man before or since, he has caught the whole of life and focused it to one intense and burning point of terror and beauty'? (*The Essential Shakespeare*, Cambridge, 1932, p. 127.) It is not in such terms that the academic critic is wont to award his marks.

chological explanation. We think we know how one kind of poetry originates — in inspiration, directly from the sensational awareness of the objective world, or no less directly from the promptings of the unconscious. But we have to admit — it is the only justification of the poetic elements in classical verse — that poetry may be generated by discursive reasoning or metaphysical speculation. In an early essay I described metaphysical poetry as 'felt thought', and I still think that no thought can become poetic unless it is apprehended in its mental configuration — we lack the equivalent of the more exact German word *Gestalt*. But what is still necessary is some explanation of why thoughts or ideas should evoke, not merely a metaphorical imagery, but a sensuous identification with visual images: thought transmuted into dream. Obviously it is some extension of the 'association of ideas' upon which psycho-analysis relies; the poet passes from the idea to the image unconsciously, and for reasons which might be revealed in analysis. But from our present point of view it is only necessary to affirm and prove that even in its most intellectual forms poetry acquires its poetic quality by a process which brings it into line with the irrational sources of lyrical and romantic poetry.

This fact has not been generally acknowledged by critics in the past, but one who enjoys great respect in quarters where the surrealists expect none had some inkling of the truth. 'Although poets often have unusual powers of reflective thought', wrote A. C. Bradley, 'the specific genius of a poet does not lie there, but in the imagination. Therefore his deepest and most original interpretation is likely to come by way of the imagination. And the specific way of imagination is not to clothe in imagery consciously held ideas; *it is to produce half-consciously a matter* from which, when produced, the reader may, if he chooses, extract ideas.'

Some further tasks of revaluation must be referred to more generally and quite briefly:

(4) *Lifting the moral ban.* Though something has been accomplished during the last twenty or thirty years, it is still true to say that poets like Shelley, Byron and Swinburne are judged by standards which must be repudiated. If we can agree that a poet's work is to be judged by purely aesthetic standards, as in general we judge a painter's work, then we can proceed to the task unimpeded by the irrelevant standards of morality. But if we prove incapable of such detachment — and I admit it is almost inhuman

to expect it — if, like Mr. Eliot, we believe that 'literary criticism should be completed by criticism from a definite ethical and theological standpoint', then a revaluation becomes all the more necessary. For the ethical and theological standpoint from which we should then judge Shelley would be much nearer to Shelley's ethics and theology than to the ethics and theology of the Church. And the moral shudder that the very name of Byron sends through our bourgeois homes would be intensified by our acclamation. Byron is not, in any obvious degree, a superrealist poet; but he is a superrealist personality. He is the only English poet who might conceivably occupy, in our hierarchy, the position held in France by the Marquis de Sade. The function of such figures is to be so positive in their immorality, that morality becomes negative by comparison. They show, by the more-than-human energy of their evil, that evil too, as Milton was compelled to admit, has its divinity. In short, they reveal the conventionality of all systems of morality. They prove that the most deeply rooted taboos, such as incest, can be thwarted by the individual will; and the courage they manifest in such defiance is so absolute that a figure like Byron becomes the unconfessed hero of humanity. How else explain the enduring fascination of Byron's personality? By all the rules which condemn such lives as worthless and without honour, he should long ago have sunk into an oblivion from which his poetry would not have rescued him. But it is safe to say that no statue in the temple of fame is so securely lodged as Byron's; irrational in his life, he is now the object of irrational devotion.

The case of Swinburne is no less interesting. Though the public is still kept in ignorance of the true nature of Swinburne's character — or wilfully or unwittingly keeps itself in such ignorance — it is no longer to be disguised that the best of Swinburne's poetry is precisely that part of it which most openly celebrates what most people regard as unnatural aspects of human passion — poems like 'Anactoria', 'Faustine' and 'Dolores'. Swinburne during his life was bullied into conformity and bad verse, and his fate is one more unforgivable crime committed in the name of the bourgeois God. It was a crime against beauty, against honesty, against life itself. It should be clearly understood that, in taking up such an attitude towards the case of Swinburne or Byron, there is no question of encouraging vice as such; unnatural behaviour is not in itself interesting or admirable, and is only made anything but dull and distressing by the active aggression of moralists. But Swinburne himself expressed the truth of the matter in a self-defence he was compelled to publish in 1866:[1]

'The question at issue is wider than any between a single writer and his critics, or it might well be allowed to drop. It is this: whether or not the first and last requisite of art is to give no offence; whether or not all that cannot be lisped in the nursery or fingered in the schoolroom is therefore to be cast out of the library; whether or not the domestic circle is to be for all men and writers the outer limit and extreme horizon of their world of work. For to this we have come; and all students of art must face the matter as it stands. Who has not heard it asked, in a final and triumphant tone, whether this book or that can be read aloud by her mother to a young girl? whether such and such a picture can properly be exposed to the eyes of young persons? If you reply that this is nothing to the point, you fall at once into the ranks of the immoral. Never till now, and nowhere but in England, could so monstrous an absurdity rear for one moment its deformed and eyeless head. In no past century were artists ever bidden to work on these terms; nor are they now, except among us. The disease, of course, afflicts the meanest members of the body with most virulence. Nowhere is cant at once so foul-mouthed and so tight-laced as in the penny, twopenny, threepenny or sixpenny press. Nothing is so favourable to the undergrowth of real indecency as this overshadowing foliage of fictions, this artificial network of proprieties. *L'Arioste rit au soleil, l'Aretin ricane à l'ombre.* The whiter the sepulchre without, the ranker the rottenness within. Every touch of plaster is a sign of advancing decay.'

Swinburne speaks the language of his age, but the case would be no different if we were to translate it into the more technical terms of modern psychology. The dilemma which faces all moralists is that the repression of instincts is apt to breed a worse disease than their free expression; incidentally it entails a feebler art.

(5) That last sentence may, however, need a certain qualification in this sense: that what is repressed may nevertheless find a disguised outlet. Without subscribing to the view that art is in every respect a sublimation of repressed instincts (for sublimation usually involves a conformity to collective ideals which completely submerges the individuality of the artist), one must nevertheless recognize — it is indeed one of our main theses —

---

[1] *Notes on Poems and Reviews* (London, 1866).

that art is closely linked with these same instincts. Actually it is a question of consciousness. If we are conscious of our instincts and repress them, then we act under duress and produce nothing but intellectual reactions. We try to be good and only succeed in being dull. But if we are not conscious of our instincts, and at the same time allow them to be expressed in a disguised form, then the result may well be interesting. I will return to the psychological aspect of the question presently; for the moment I want only to suggest that certain kinds of literature which are tolerated because they are described as mad or nonsensical — the Prophetic Books of Blake, the nonsense verse and tales of Lear and Lewis Carroll — are actually charged with this unconscious significance. Nothing would be so angrily resented as a revelation of the psychoanalytical significance of *Alice in Wonderland* — the work of a strongly repressed individual; but such significance is obvious and the resistance which its exposure would evoke is only a confirmation of its reality. In our opinion such significance only adds to the value of such literature, and in revealing it we have no other desire than to affirm its importance; that is to say, among the tasks of revaluation we include a reconsideration of all such literature. From our point of view, Lear is a better poet than Tennyson; Lewis Carroll has affinities with Shakespeare.

Many other tasks of revaluation will suggest themselves to the reader who has seized our point of view. I am sure, for example, that the whole field of English fiction must be reviewed, though I do not feel competent to make any proposals myself. It is possible that 'Monk' Lewis, Maturin and Mrs. Radcliffe should, relatively to Scott, Dickens and Hardy, occupy a much higher rank. For myself I find them all equally difficult to read. I prefer the *Arabian Nights*, or Franz Kafka. It seems to me that fiction, that is to say, the prose narrative, awaits a complete transformation. In so far as it is to justify itself as art, it must be transformed into poesy. For fundamentally there is no distinction between prose art and verse art; there is only the one verbal art which is poesy.

As for English Painting, there too we must insist on a complete revision of values. The pen is more irresponsible than the brush; we print things which we dare not depict. That is a crude aspect of the general truth that poetry is an art of wider scope and deeper significance than painting, and this will remain the truth even when the art of painting is completely emancipated from the prejudice of naturalism. But during the many centuries in which painting has been hampered by this prejudice, it is obvious that its close adherence to a standard of objective verisimilitude would give only a minor and exceptional scope to any superrealist elements. I would, of course, claim that the art of the Middle Ages, except in so far as occupied with the mass-production of ecclesiastical symbols, was wholly of a super-realist character; for before the age of reason art was supernatural. Between the superreal and the supernatural there is only a difference of age, of evolution. The supernatural is associated with the mysticism of a religious view of life. But both agree in rejecting the 'real' or the 'natural' as the only aspect of existence. Supernaturalism, it is true, implies a dualism of spirit and matter; whereas super-realism implies a monism or identity of spirit and matter. Nevertheless, there is sufficient resemblance in the two attitudes to give more than a surface resemblance to their arts. Medieval religion required the plastic realization of irrational concepts. An angel or a devil could not be copied from a living model; the artist was compelled to use his imagination. Medieval sculpture, and above all medieval manuscripts, offer a wealth of material which it would be only too easy to call surrealist. I do not draw on this material, because I respect the difference of intention. Nevertheless, as an example of what I mean, we find that a subject like 'Christ in Limbo' is often treated in a manner recalled by Picasso's etching 'Minotauromachia'.

Between the end of the Middle Ages and the beginning of the Romantic Movement, painting and sculpture in England were almost completely dead: a significant fact. Interest begins again with Gainsborough and Blake. Blake I will leave aside for the moment; I shall have something to say about him here in another connection, and I have written about him elsewhere. The early paintings of Gainsborough have a naïve spontaneity which brings them close to the Douanier Rousseau; as he increased in technical efficiency, he scarcely added to his aesthetic appeal. At least, his dullest works were done to rival the academic standards of Reynolds or to flatter the bourgeois desire for 'finish'. The same is true of Constable, and the history of Turner is actually the history of the emancipation of a great artist from the fetters of naturalism. Turner is certainly a subject for revaluation; from the first the victim of Ruskin's enthusiasm, and in our own day the blind spot of influential critics like Roger Fry, this painter actually transformed the topographical canvas which he had inherited into a veritable torch of sensational fury. A little dogged in spirit, he lacked the final courage to take leave of his senses — the vacation which every hard-working artist owes to himself. But he remains a very significant figure — far more significant than any of the French Impressionists, the compeer of Delacroix and Cézanne. There are other painters to be rescued from the dustbin of the nineteenth century: Samuel Palmer and John Martin; but the most serious task is a reconsideration of the Pre-Raphaelites. I doubt if any Englishman — at least, any Englishman still so near to them — can approach these artists with the freshness and freedom that Salvador Dali, for example, brings to their revaluation. But certain truths may be admitted. First, the Pre-Raphaelites were integral artists; like the surrealists, they had a philosophy of life which embraced painting, poetry, philosophy and politics. They were also convinced of the imbecility of most of their contemporaries, and reacted in the strongest possible way to the academic naturalism of the time. They were not afraid to experiment with their sensations; they acknowledged the primacy of the imagination. But they were incapable of a really comprehensive reaction — a revolution. They had no dialectic, no scientific method, no real energy. In a word, they were sentimentalists. They should have developed romanticism from the stage where Coleridge left it; instead, they developed nostalgia. They read the *Ancient Mariner* and Keats and Blake, and merely indulged in the easy path of repetition. They might have read instead the *Biographia Literaria* and even Hegel, and produced a more vital movement of thought. One has only to contrast Morris with Marx, contemporaries almost, to measure the failure of the Pre-Raphaelites and their followers.

Their followers degenerated into soulful weavers, mock-medieval craftsmen, bookbinders and harpists. English plastic arts had to wait for the inspiration of Picasso to show any real revival. In the last twenty years we have produced potentially great artists — Wyndham Lewis is the typical example — but they have suffered from a disastrous form of individualism. The English sin has always been eccentricity; by which I do not mean a lack of conformity, but simply a lack of social coherence. Surrealism, like Communism, does not call upon artists to surrender their individuality; but it does insist that artists have common problems to solve and common dangers to avoid, and that a certain coherence, even a certain mutuality, is one of the conditions of the efficacity of art.[1]

The fact that the surrealists inherited from the dadaists a certain scorn for the 'formalism' and 'purism' of the later stages of impressionism has led to some misunderstanding of their attitude towards the technique of art. Surrealists are opposed to any intellectualization of art — to any preference, that is to say, for rational as opposed to imaginative elements. Nothing, in their opinion, could be more futile and unnecessary than an art exclusively concerned with the rendering of some aspects of natural fact — effects of light, of space, of mass or solidity. This seems to them to be a purely mechanical or muscular preoccupation, and the result entirely without artistic interest. Was it not Monet who painted the same haystack in thirty-two different degrees of light? Well, there is always a haystack to be seen somewhere at whatever time and in whatever light you like. It does not seem worth recording at immense pains the passive mutations of such a banal object. It would be just as interesting to record the artist's reaction to thirty-two different degrees of toothache. Even the preoccupation of a Cézanne, though it invested nature with a structure that in actual appearance it lacks, and to that extent contributed a mental and even an imaginative element; and though this preoccupation led to the discovery of perfect relations between intellectual order and sensuous colour; yet even such an art is deceptive if it does not extend our sensibility on more than a sensational level. Cézanne himself seemed to realize this, and was not satisfied with his apples. The series of 'Baigneuses' which he painted at the end of his career marks the wider imaginative range of his genius. Seurat is a special case, too complex and too unresolved to dogmatize about — we must not forget that he died at the age of thirty-two; but obviously, in paintings like 'Le Cirque' and 'La Parade', he was creating a new world, a world of imagination or fantasy which owed no more than its primary elements to the world of objective vision. Since their day, painters not so great as Cézanne or Seurat have seized on one part of their achievement, and that the least interesting part, and have elaborated it into an exclusive method. They have made painting an ocular exercise; a decorative variation on the data of physical

[1] I restore the original reading of this sentence, and stand by it, insisting only on the proper meaning of the word Communism. I did not write Stalinism, nor even Marxist-Leninism. For a definition of Communism, see "Essential Communism", *Anarchy and Order* (London, 1954).

vision. Against such an art it was necessary to protest; and the best protest, which should have been final in its effect, was the invention of the collage by Picasso or Braque — the work of art made of any old pieces of string or newspaper but which, nevertheless, in spite of its complete lack of the fiddling kind of finesse that threatened to become the sole aim of painting, was undeniably a work of art. Max Ernst, taking rubbings from the surfaces of wood and other natural materials, went a step further and reproduced *mechanically* the actual effect of sensibility so much prized as a personal quality by bourgeois amateurs. In this manner the physique of art was seen in its proper proportions; not as a thing which could be dispensed with or despised, but as an instrument subordinate to the sovereign power of the imagination.

The surrealist, therefore, by no means denies or ridicules aesthetic values as such. To him, no less than to any other sensitive creature, there is good art and bad art, good painting and bad painting, *good surrealism and bad surrealism*. He has a scale of values and these values are aesthetic. But aesthetic values are not necessarily objective values — in painting they are not necessarily what the Germans call *malerisch* or painterly values: they do not belong so much to the paint as to the person. Like the pitch of a voice, the 'hand' in handwriting or even the gait in walking, they are the expression of a personality — a mentality. Dali's neat, tight Vermeerish *facture* has its aesthetic as well as Picasso's bold, plangent, viscous brushwork. There is no one style of using paint, no one criterion of perfection: the artist is using a medium to express certain sensations or ideas and he is not to be judged by the manner in which he uses the medium but by the success with which he conveys the sensations or ideas (I do not suggest that in practice there is any possibility of making the distinction). This is even true of so-called 'abstract' art, where the ideas are contained within the formal relations: are, that is to say, the direct expression of formal relations. The alternative which must otherwise be admitted is an art tending towards one uniform standard of perfection: a form of idealism contradicted by history no less than by common sense.

This explanation made, it will perhaps be seen how certain 'found objects' which are not the work of human artists, but the products of natural (or unnatural) forces, come to be cherished by surrealists. If I am walking along the beach and my eye catches a sea-worn and sun-bleached knot of wood whose shape and colour strongly appeal to me, the act of identification (which may in any case have a psychological explanation) makes that object as expressive of my personality as if I had actually carved the wood into that shape. Selection is also creation. Nothing is so expressive of a man as the fetishes he gathers round him — his pipe, his pens, his pocket-knife — even the pattern of his suit. Art in its widest sense is an extension of the personality: a host of artificial limbs.

To the plastic objects which we find by the aid of our eyes correspond, on another plane of consciousness, the images found in dreams. The direct use of dream imagery has not been frequent in the past, for the good psychological reason that the conscious mind is a jealous guardian of the secrecy of this world. But now we turn to the dream with the same confidence that formerly men placed in the objective world of sensation, and we weave its reality into the synthesis of our art. It is possible that in the integral dream — the dream as entire myth rather than as a series of fragmentary symbols — the work of synthesis is already done. In most dreams we find elements that are merely the casual residues of the day's anxieties; but we find also the day-world transformed, and occasionally this new reality presents itself to us as a poetic unity. But to make this distinction clear I will relate the history of an experiment.

Hitherto poets and critics have shown singularly little curiosity about the actual mechanism of poetic inspiration. There are, of course, many disjointed statements which throw light on the subject, such as Wordsworth's quasi-psychological description of emotion recollected in tranquillity, and Keats and Rilke have observed themselves to some profit. Not long before his death A. E. Housman disconcerted his academic cronies by confessing that inspiration was most often induced in him by a pint of beer; that in any case it had physical symptoms. My own suggestion is that poetic inspiration has an exact parallel in dream-formation. In what respect the two processes differ can only be shown by the analysis of a particular case of inspiration, which is what I propose to undertake. But first I must make sure that the reader has a clear picture of the process of dream-formation as described by Freud.

In his latest 'Revision of the Theory of Dreams'[1] Freud gives the following schematic summary of the process:

[1] *New Introductory Lectures* (London, 1933). Trans. W. J. H. Sprott. Chap. 1, p. 30 ff.

'The introduction: the wish to sleep, the voluntary withdrawal from the outside world. Two things follow from this: firstly, the possibility for older and more primitive modes of activity to manifest themselves, i.e., regression; and secondly, the decrease of the repression-resistance which weighs on the unconscious. As a result of this latter feature an opportunity for dream-formation presents itself, which is seized upon by the factors which are the occasion of the dream; that is to say, the internal and external stimuli which are in activity. The dream which thus eventuates is already a compromise formation; it has a double function; it is on the one hand in conformity with the ego ("ego-syntonic"), since it subserves the wish to sleep by draining off the stimuli which would otherwise disturb it, while on the other hand it allows to a repressed impulse the satisfaction which is possible in these circumstances in the form of an hallucinatory wish-fulfilment. The whole process of dream-formation, which is permitted by the sleeping ego, is, however, under the control of the censorship, a control which is exercised by what is left of the forces of repression.'

What is allowed to emerge as a dream — that is to say, what is remembered as a dream — Freud calls the dream-text or the *manifest* dream; but what the analyst suspects to lie beyond the dream, its motive force, these are the *latent* dream-thoughts. 'Their dominating element is the repressed impulse, which has obtained some kind of expression, toned down and disguised though it may be, by associating itself with stimuli which happen to be there and by tacking itself on to the residue of the day before.' The rest of Freud's description should be followed with close attention, because its bearing on the process of poetic inspiration is direct and immensely significant:

'Just like any other impulse this one presses forward towards satisfaction in action, but the path to motor discharge is closed to it on account of the physiological characteristics of the state of sleep, and so it is forced to travel in the retrograde direction to perception, and content itself with an hallucinatory satisfaction. The latent dream-thoughts are therefore turned into a collection of sensory images and visual scenes. As they are travelling in this direction something happens to them which seems to us new and bewildering. All the verbal apparatus by means of which the more subtle thought-relations are expressed, the conjunctions and pre-positions, the variations of declension and conjugation, are lacking, because the means of portraying them are absent; just as in primitive grammarless speech, only the raw material of thought can be expressed, and *the abstract is merged again in the concrete from which it sprang*. What is left over may very well seem to lack coherence. It is as much the result of the archaic regression in the mental apparatus as of the demands of the censorship that so much use is made of the representation of certain objects and processes by means of symbols which have become strange to conscious thought. But of more far-reaching import are the other alterations to which the elements comprising the dream-thoughts are subjected. Such of them as have any point of contact are *condensed* into new unities. When the thoughts are translated into pictures those forms are indubitably preferred which allow of this kind of telescoping, or condensation; it is as though a force were at work which subjected the material to a process of pressure or squeezing together. As a result of condensation one element in a manifest dream may correspond to a number of elements of the dream-thoughts; but conversely one of the elements from among the dream-thoughts may be represented by a number of pictures in the dream.'

This spate of quotation is already too long, but there are two further refinements in the process of dream-formation which are still relevant. The first is *displacement* or transference of accent. The individual ideas which make up the dream-thoughts are not all of equal value; 'they have various degrees of affective tone attached to them, and, corresponding to these, they are judged as more or less important, and more or less worthy of attention. In the dream-work these ideas are separated from their affects; the affects are treated separately. They may be transferred to something else, they may remain where they were, they may undergo transformation, or they may disappear from the dream entirely. *The importance of the ideas which have been shorn of their affect reappears in the dream in the form of the sensuous vividness of the dream-pictures*; but we notice that this accent, which should lie on important elements, has been transferred to unimportant ones, so that what seems to be pushed to the forefront in the dream, as the most important element in it, only plays a subsidiary rôle in the dream-thoughts, and conversely, what is important among the dream-thoughts obtains only incidental and rather indistinct representation in the dream.'

The other refinement in the process is, from our point of view, perhaps the most important of all. 'After these operations on the dream-thoughts the dream is almost ready. There is still, however, a more or less non-constant factor, the so-called secondary elaboration, that makes its appearance after the dream has come into consciousness as an object of perception. When the dream has come into consciousness, we treat it in exactly the same way that we treat any content of perception; we try to fill in the gaps, we add connecting links and often enough we let ourselves in for serious misunderstandings. But this, as it were, rationalizing activity, which at its best provides the dream with a smooth façade, such as cannot correspond to its real content, may be altogether absent in some cases, or only operate in a very feeble way, in which case the dream displays to view all its gaps and inconsistencies. . . .'

To trace the parallel between dream-formation and poem-formation it is necessary to analyse a particular poem, and of necessity such a poem must be one of my own (or otherwise I should have to conduct a long and searching analysis of another poet). The poem I shall take is actually based on a dream. On December 31, 1935, I was present at a family fathering in Yorkshire, and at midnight we celebrated the passing of the Old Year and the birth of the New Year by drinking a rum-punch (I am, it will be seen, about to confirm Housman's diagnosis). I retired to bed and dreamt a vivid dream. It was still vivid to me when next day I travelled by train back to London, and since, like several poets of my acquaintance, I have always found the rhythm of a train journey conducive to poetic composition, I began to transfer to paper the haunting images of my dream. The following poem was the result — I will explain the significance of the roman type presently:

> *The narrow labyrinth has light*
> *which casts our shadows on the wall*
> *as in extremity of flight*
> *I follow one whose face I have not seen.*
> *The walls are white*
> *and turn at intervals to make a screen*
> *on which our racing shadows rise and fall*
> like waves against the bleached cliff.
> *Anxious to make my mentor turn*
> *I lift my hands and make a pass*
> *which casts upon the facing wall*

> *a silhouette hovering like a baffled bird.*
> *But on he leads unmoved*
> *and fatally I follow till at last*
> *we leave the labyrinth and I find*
> *myself alone, upon a plinth.*
> *The houses in the square below*
> *stand newly built, brick-rough, bright*
> *bathed in some* Castilian *light.*
> *In the unpaved area a few children play.*
> *This must be a foreign land, I say,*
> *and gaze about with eager eyes.*
> *Then suddenly know that it is* Heaven
> *to which* Death *has led me in disguise.*

What I described in this poem was, of course, the *manifest* content of my dream; the *latent* content could only be elicited by analysis, and is of no immediate interest. But our poetic analysis of the poem should begin by asking to what extent I succeeded in conveying the manifest content. Is the poem efficient merely as the narrative of an experience? As far as the events of the poem are concerned, I think it is only towards the end that I myself am conscious of any failure. I fancy that in the dream the identity of the unknown figure was revealed to me, and that immediately I awoke — in the process of awaking — this identity slipped from me and I was left with a sense of being baffled. The notion of suddenly finding myself in a Heaven was present in the dream, but identifying the figure with Death was a subsequent rationalization; it did not, if I can trust my memory, occur to me until I began to write the poem.

Let us now examine the images in the poem. In the dream the labyrinth was real; an intricate maze always turning at right angles and full of an evenly diffused white light; the figure, clad rather like a harlequin in close-fitting tights, never turned. I made the pass by lifting my hands above my head and making a shadow on the wall in the manner of the shadow-game played by children; the image of the baffled bird — the fluttering shadow like a bird beating against a window-pane — *occurred to me in my dream*. In this it differs from the wave-image I have used to describe the shadows of our bodies on the walls of the labyrinth, which is a conscious image produced in the process of writing the poem; I would on that account call it a metaphor rather than an image. In a similar way the word 'Castilian', used to describe the peculiar light which was diffused over the square, is an epithet derived from my conscious experience; the nearest equivalent in my memory being certain effects of sunlight in Spain. I have not conveyed exactly enough the vivid impression I have of the effect of this dream-light on the houses; I have a distinct sensuous image of the porous quality of the brick into which the light seemed to soak, as if absorbed. The children in the square (it was a new square, not yet paved or laid out in any way, rough and uneven) seemed to be self-centred, detached, in a different perspective to the rest of the scene; an effect which Salvador Dali often conveys in his paintings.

It will be observed that there are several rhymes, but no regular rhyme system; these rhymes were not sought by me, but came unconsciously in the act of writing the poem. If I had sought for rhymes I should inevitably have been compelled to distort my narrative and my imagery, and to that extent to be false to my inspiration. And such, indeed, has always been my practice in writing poetry. I neither seek rhymes nor avoid them, for either attitude would involve a too conscious control of my expression — would defeat the desirable automatism. But this does not prevent me from recognizing that when there is no total inspiration — when a poet is writing line by line — the search for rhymes may lead to the discovery of surprising images. That is merely a different method of composition; a mosaic as opposed to a reflection. If a poet wishes to remain faithful to a myth — a myth presented to him integrally — he cannot afford to go off in pursuit of surface ornaments.

Perhaps the most important distinction which this analysis reveals is that between images and metaphors — a distinction which has already been made by Pierre Reverdy and which I have referred to before (Breton also quotes it in the First Surrealist Manifesto):

'L'image est une création pure de l'esprit.

'Elle ne peut naître d'une comparaison mais du rapprochement de deux réalités plus ou moins éloignées.

'Plus les rapports des deux réalités rapprochées seront lointains et justes, plus l'image sera forte — plus elle aura de puissance émotive et de réalité poétique . . .'

In my poem the metaphor of the waves against the bleached cliff, though to my mind accurate enough as description, has not the same force as the image of the baffled bird; and actually, of course, the whole content of the poem — labyrinth, square, light, children — is a series of images, but of images whose counterpart is not manifest, and which therefore we call symbols.

The metaphor may have its associational significance within the psychological unity of the poem; if it is purely intellectual in origin it is apt to stick out of the poem like an irrelevant ornament.

This type of poem, then, we might describe, to adopt Freud's terminology, as the manifest content of a dream whose latent thoughts have been turned into sensory images or visual scenes; the abstract, that is to say, is merged again in the concrete form from which it sprang.[1] Certain of the dream-thoughts have been condensed into images or symbols, whose latent significance resists any analysis, but which nevertheless, *and perhaps precisely on that account*, have extreme poetic force. Then, to disguise any gaps or incoherency, the conscious mind of the poet has worked over the poem, and given it that smooth façade which is generally demanded by the literary conventions of an age, and which in any case makes for ease of communication.

It is not every poem that has the integral character of a dream, but every authentic image is conceived in the unconscious; that is to say, the two realities of which Reverdy speaks, though more or less distantly separated, cohere as an image and gain their emotive power from the presence in the unconscious of a hidden connecting link. There is no need, in any poetic analysis, to reveal that repressed connection; the poetic reality lies in the evident power of the image, and is no stronger — indeed, may be much weaker — if its latent meaning is made manifest. The whole irrationality of art, and the surrealist defence of irrationality, is explained by the Freudian theory of regression. An unconscious impulse creates the poem no less than the dream; it provides,

[1] Compare Vico's theory of poetry, especially the following passage: '(So for us) the whole art of Poetry reduces itself to this, that anyone who wishes to excel as a poet must unlearn all his native language, and return to the pristine beggary of words; by this necessity he will express the feelings of his mind by means of the most obvious and easily perceived aspects of things; he will, by the aid of the senses and the imagination, paint the most striking and lovely images of things, manners and feelings; and just as anyone who wishes to be a philosopher must first purge himself of the prejudices of children and common people, so anyone who would write a poem must feel and think entirely according to the childlike and common views of the world. In this way he will become really imaginative, and will compose at once sublimely and in accordance with the popular understanding.' (*De Constantia Philologiae*, trans. by H. S. Davies.)

that is to say, the mental energy required for its formation. That impulse seeks in the poem, no less and no otherwise than in the dream, its desired satisfaction. The latent ideas or thoughts are turned into visual images, are dramatized and illustrated, are finally liberated in the hallucinatory reality of the poem.

That the actual choice of words — the poet's language as distinct from his imagery — is formed by a similar process of unconscious association, would seem to be a fair deduction from the evidence of psychoanalysis. In the degree that they are poetic such words are automatic associations of an aural rather than a visual nature. It may be that some poets search the dictionary of their conscious memory for the apt epithet, and in that way display an inventive wit; but such a faculty — the faculty of a Pope or a Dryden — is not the essentially poetic gift. The poetic image, to adapt a saying of Picasso's, is found, not sought. It emerges, perhaps not easily but at any rate directly, from the well of the unconscious. It may be elaborated or distorted by the exercise of conscious skill, but there is no evidence at all to show that as a result the poem ever gains in its specifically poetic power.

We are so uncertain of the limits of mental activity — its actual range and effectiveness — that even as materialists we must not exclude the possibility of hitherto unsuspected modes of operation. For example, psychoanalysis has already been compelled to admit the scientific possibility of thought-transference or telepathy. On the analogy of such 'occult' phenomena, it is possible that the mind of the poet or painter, during the course of its ordinary activity, picks up and transmits 'messages' in a wholly unconscious manner. I think it is possible that such 'messages' are always in the form of 'images' — that is to say, the ideas they deal with are not verbalized. In this way, for example, the 'residues' of the day's activity, in their least unimportant and unobserved details, are taken up and 'used' in the course of the dream activity. A pattern on a wall, a patch of lichen, or any abstract pattern which I have for a moment stared at, may in this way sink into my mind and determine the form of my unconscious images, which when called up in the activity of painting, emerge in this apparently inexplicable and illogical shape. That process is comparatively easy to understand; but in the contrary direction it is also possible that ideas, with which we may have been obsessed during the activity of thought, may, when conscious thought is for the time being superseded by instinctive modes of expression, so guide such expression that it corresponds to the latent thought. Salvador Dali relates how a splash of paint on his palette had assumed *unknown to his conscious mind* the shape of a distorted skull which he had consciously and vainly been trying to discover. It is another aspect of automatism; and all that it is necessary to admit is the superreality, the something-more-than-conscious naturalism, which encompasses all our actions. At this moment I have an intimation that I shall find in Blake a verse or a sentence bearing on this question. I take the book from the shelf, it opens at page 562 and I read:

> '. . . *Condens'd his Emanations into hard opaque substances,*
> *And his infant thoughts & desires into cold dark cliffs of death.*
> *His hammer of gold he seiz'd, and his anvil of adamant;*
> *He seiz'd the bars of condens'd thoughts to forge them*
> *Into the sword of war, into the bow and arrow,*
> *Into the thundering cannon and into the murdering gun.*
> *I saw the limbs form'd for exercise contemn'd, & the beauty of*
> *Eternity look'd upon as deformity, & loveliness as a dry tree.*
> *I saw disease forming a Body of Death around the Lamb*
> *Of God to destroy Jerusalem & to devour the body of Albion,*
> *By war and stratagem to win the labour of the husbandman.*
> *Awkwardness arm'd in steel, folly in a helmet of gold,*
> *Weakness with horns & talons, ignorance with a rav'ning beak,*
> *Every Emanative joy forbidden as a Crime*
> *And the Emanations buried alive in the earth with pomp of*
> *religion,*
> *Inspiration deny'd, Genius forbidden by laws of punishment,*
> *I saw terrified. I took the sighs & tears & bitter groans,*
> *I lifted them into my Furnaces to form the spiritual sword*
> *That lays open the hidden heart. I drew forth the pang*
> *Of sorrow red hot: I work'd on my resolute anvil:*
> *I heated it in the flames of Hand & Hyle & Coban*
> *Nine times . . .*'

Jerusalem, i, 9.

Thus Blake labours in hope that Enthusiasm and Life may not cease. In the whole of his writings I feel the presence of an instinctive dialecticism which is of the greatest interest. I know that some surrealists have important reserves to make about Blake; they are suspicious of his obscurity, which wears the too obvious mask of mysticism. I am equally suspicious; but I must

278

confess that the more I have studied Blake the more these mists have dispersed. It would be absurd to call Blake a materialist (it would be absurd to call the surrealist anything but a *dialectical* materialist); nevertheless, in works like *The Marriage of Heaven and Hell* and *Jerusalem* there is a realization of the fundamental contradictions of reality, and a movement towards a synthesis which is anything but idealistic.

From much the same point of view the metaphysical element in Shelley should be re-examined. In Shelley's case there is no doubt of the point of departure — a materialistic determinism of the most antitheist type. But it is generally assumed that Shelley abandoned his early antitheism and ended in the clouds of neo-platonic idealism. But actually he too arrived at a dialectical synthesis of the real and the unreal, actuality and hallucination, as the following quotation from his *Speculations on Metaphysics* will make clear:

'Thoughts, or ideas, or notions, call them what you will, differ from each other, not in kind, but in force. It has commonly been supposed that those distinct thoughts which affect a number of persons, at regular intervals, during the passage of a multitude of other thoughts, which are called *real* or *external objects*, are totally different from those which affect only a few persons, and which recur at irregular intervals, and are usually more obscure and indistinct, such as hallucinations, dreams, and the ideas of madness. No essential distinction between any one of these ideas, or any class of them, is founded on a correct observation of the nature of things, but merely on a consideration of what thoughts are most invariably subservient to the security and happiness of life; and if nothing more were expressed by the distinction, the philosopher might safely accommodate his language to that of the vulgar. But they pretend to assert an essential difference, which has no foundation in truth, and which suggests a narrow and false conception of universal nature, the parent of the most fatal errors in speculation. A specific difference between every thought of the mind, is, indeed, a necessary consequence of that law by which it perceives diversity and number; but a generic and essential difference is wholly arbitrary.'

In an essay of this kind I am mainly concerned with presenting the positive aspects of surrealism; all that necessary part of a critical activity which consists in removing misunderstandings and replying to criticism made on the basis of such misunderstandings may be left to more fugitive forms of publication. But one form of attack may be mentioned here because it is of a serious nature and because it will serve to introduce an aspect of surrealism which yet remains to be dealt with. During the London Exhibition Mr. J. B. Priestley was commissioned to write an article for an evening paper famous for its betting news. Now, that Mr. Priestley should be made to feel, as he confesses, 'not too comfortable', in fact, 'profoundly disturbed' by surrealism is exactly as it should be. But when he goes on to ascribe to the surrealists in general all kinds of moral perversion, he is merely indulging in the abortive vituperation of his kind:

> *As if a man should spit against the wind;*
> *The filth returns in's face.*

The surrealists, he said, 'stand for violence and neurotic unreason. They are truly decadent. You catch a glimpse behind them of the deepening twilight of barbarism that may soon blot out the sky, until at last humanity finds itself in another long night.' In that fuliginous perspective, and knowing what a man of Mr. Priestley's prejudices means by decadence, the surrealists might willingly stand. But that is not the end of Mr. Priestley's insinuations. 'There are about far too many effeminate or epicene young men, lisping and undulating. Too many young women without manners, balance, dignity — greedy and slobbering sensation-seekers. Too many people who are steadily lapsing into shaved and powdered barbarism. . . . Frequently they have strong sexual impulses that they soon contrive to misuse or pervert.'

Mr. Priestley no doubt feels none too comfortable on his bed of roses, and sympathy for the under-dog flows in a copious if somewhat muddled stream from his generous heart. But Mr. Priestley is not personally acquainted with the surrealists, in this country or any other; and as a novelist he ought to have enough penetration to realize that the least repressed of people are generally the most moral; or, as Huysmans puts it, 'au fond . . . il n'y a de réellement obscènes que les gens chastes.' As a matter of fact, the surrealists are no less aware than Mr. Priestley of undesirable elements in their midst; but they are not themselves to be identified with such elements. It is true that they cannot protest against the perversions of a moral code for which they have no respect. But they despise the kind of people who indulge in perversion just as much as they despise people who indulge in hypocrisy. They despise any kind of weakness, any lack of personal integrity. Their principle of liberty allows to each the free exercise of his natural propensities so long as this does not infringe the equal rights of others. On the subject of homosexuality, for example (a subject which the evening papers do not mention, though it is one of the most acute questions of the day), the surrealists are not in the least prejudiced; they recognize that inversion is an abnormal condition due to a certain psychological or physiological predisposition for which the individual is in no way responsible. But they protest when such individuals form a sodality or freemasonry for the purpose of imposing their special ethos upon the social and intellectual life of the day. It leads in particular to an intolerance for women which is certainly no part of the surrealist creed.

In short, the surrealists admit the disciplinary truth that, if you have to attack a diseased body for the purpose of healing it, your own body should be in a healthy state. The kind of insult which Mr. Priestley hurls at the surrealists is the kind of insult that used to be insinuated about the early Bolsheviks until the purity and disinterestedness of their lives could no longer be disguised.

The surrealist is opposed to current morality because he considers that it is rotten. He can have no respect for a code of ethics that tolerates extremes of poverty and riches; that wastes or deliberately destroys the products of the earth amidst a starving or undernourished people; that preaches a gospel of universal peace and wages aggressive war with all the appendages of horror and destruction which its evil genius can invent; that so distorts the sexual impulse that thousands of unsatisfied men and women go mad, millions waste their lives in unhappiness or poison their minds with hypocrisy. For such a morality (and these are merely its most general features) the surrealist has nothing but hatred and scorn.

His own code of morality is based on liberty and love. He sees no reason why the frailties of the human race should be erected into a doctrine of original sin, but he realizes that most men are born imperfect and are made less perfect still by their circumstances. Such evils and imperfections cannot wholly be eradicated in any conceivable span of human development. But it is his belief that the whole system of organized control and repression which is the social aspect of present-day morality is psychologically misconceived and positively harmful. He believes, that is to say, in the fullest possible liberation of the impulses and is convinced that what law and oppression have failed to achieve will in due time be brought about by love and fraternity.

The surrealist is not a sentimental humanitarian; the superrealism of his art has its counterpart in the realism of his science. He is a psychologist of the strictest type, and if he uses words like 'love' and 'fraternity', it is because his analysis of the sexual and affective and of the economic life of man has given him the right to use such words cleanlily, without the least surplus of sentimentality. Art, we conclude, is more than description or 'reportage'; it is a dialectical activity, an act of renewal. It renews vision, it renews language; but most essentially it renews life itself by enlarging the sensibility, by making men more conscious of the terror and the beauty, the *wonder* of the possible forms of being.

The renascence of wonder — I remember this as the title of an essay by Watts-Dunton, the friend of Swinburne. I should not be afraid to adopt such a grandiloquent phrase to describe the general aim of surrealism, as I conceive it. Just as curiosity is the faculty which drives man to seek out the hidden structure of the external universe, thereby enabling him to build up that body of knowledge which we call science, so wonder is the faculty which dares man to create what has not before existed, which dares man to use his powers in new ways and for new effects. We have lost this sense of the word 'wonderful' — it is one of the most outworn clichés in the language. But actually 'wonder' is a better and more inclusive word than 'beauty', and what is full of wonder has the most compelling force over the imagination of men. 'We cease to wonder at what we understand,' said Dr. Johnson, a man indifferent to the cost of complacency. It would have been much more to the point to have observed that understanding ceases when we cease to wonder; that, as Pascal, a less complacent man, observed, 'there are reasons of the heart of which Reason knows nothing'.

The Nature of Abstract Art[1]

I t is now more than half a century since the abstract movement in art made its first tentative appearance. It was for many years attacked by critics, ridiculed by the man in the street, ignored by collectors and museums, but in spite of all discouragement, amounting sometimes to persecution and often involving financial sacrifice, the number of artists practising some sort of abstraction has continued to increase and some of them enjoy a certain measure of popularity. As a movement abstract art is now a world-wide phenomenon and is not likely to disappear. Indeed, it may even be said that abstract art has become the academism of our time, and most young artists regard it as a perfectly natural mode of expression in painting and sculpture.

What is the explanation of this extraordinary revolution in art that has taken place in our time?

Let us first decide what we mean by the word 'abstract'. If we consult a dictionary we discover that it means 'separated from matter, practice, or particular examples, not concrete'; and that indeed was the original application of the word to works of art. It was used to describe paintings which had drawn from the particular concrete object in front of the artist an *essence* which in his opinion was nearer to the truth than any mechanical representation of its appearance. This intention to find an essential reality beyond the retinal image began with Cézanne, who felt that there was something false and impermanent about a direct visual impression such as the Impressionists had vainly tried to render. He wished to 'realize' (that is to say, reveal and clarify) the basic structure of things. Cézanne was concerned with his sensuous apprehension of the object in front of him, in all its concreteness. His desire was to be more realistic than his predecessors, and 'essence' he would have regarded as a question for philosophers, not artists.

[1] From *A Letter to a Young Painter* (London, 1962), there entitled "The Social Significance of Abstract Art" (pp. 233–54).

The next stage in the evolution towards abstract art is represented by Cubism. This movement was based partly on the structural simplicity of Cézanne's paintings, partly on the geometrical simplification found in African tribal sculpture, which was discovered around 1908 by Picasso and his friends. Picasso described African negro sculpture as 'raisonnable', which in French means having to do with conception rather than perception, in other words, with thought rather than vision. The artist begins with an idea and tries to give it visual form — the idea of a god, or of a ghost, or of an animal. Cubism was not inspired by the same motive, but it took the superficial aspects of negro sculpture (notably a flattening out of the surface planes), combined these with a sense of underlying structure which Cézanne had derived from the observation of nature, and the result was the style we call 'cubist'. But it was not yet abstraction. There was always a concrete object at the back of the artist's mind. When Picasso and Braque saw in what direction their experiments were leading, they drew back in alarm. 'There is no abstract art,' Picasso declared. 'You must always start with something. Afterwards you can remove all traces of reality. There's no danger then, anyway, *because the idea of the object will have left an indelible mark.*'

But all artists did not agree with Picasso. Juan Gris, who began to experiment alongside Picasso and Braque from 1911, soon saw other possibilities in Cubism. Briefly, he gradually abandoned the analytical and descriptive approach, to substitute a method that might be called synthetic and formal. There was no theoretical basis to his method, but he tended to use 'a series of unrelated, arbitrary, angular and modular relationships and proportions to carry out his Cubist displacements and his Cubist analysis of volumes with a feeling of greater explicitness and exactitude'.[1] Gris never abandoned the object, but he distorted it almost beyond recognition, and completed the picture-space by the use of geometrical areas of colour determined by the formal unity of the composition as a whole. He claimed to be able to reduce any given composition to purely geometric terms. Other artists — Gleizes, Delaunay, Mondrian — pursued the same geometrical aim; but there came a stage in their evolution when they said, in effect, why bother with an object? If the proportions are good and the colours harmonious, they in themselves will suffice for a work of

[1] John Golding, *Cubism: A History and an Analysis, 1907–14*, p. 131.

art. The *representation* of a concrete object, a *motif*, was irrelevant. The picture was, so to speak, its own *motif*, a thing of beauty and a joy for ever.

Thus abstract art was born — but only one kind of abstract art. At the same time that these developments were taking place in Paris, parallel developments were taking place in Munich. There art had followed the course of events in Paris — impressionism, post-impressionism, and even, under the direct influence of Paris, the first phases of cubism. But there was a separate current in Germany, coming from the North, the expressionism of Munch, Van Gogh, Rohlfs and Nolde, based on feeling rather than thought, using colour to express emotion in the most direct and brutal manner. But expressionism, too, was influenced by primitive African and Oceanic art, and to this extent shared one of the sources of cubism.

One day in 1908, Kandinsky, a Russian painter working in Munich, came back to his studio and saw on the easel a painting he did not recognize — glowing with colour, expressive in form, but representing nothing. It was one of his own expressionistic paintings which he had left on its side, and which he therefore did not immediately recognize. This experience was to Kandinsky an apocalyptic flash of illumination: the painting as it stood there in its incomprehensibility was more moving than it had been in its proper position. He began to experiment, using touches of colour and non-representational forms, to create 'symbols of inner necessity'. He combined these forms into paintings which he called 'improvisations', a word often used for musical compositions. Kandinsky was a friend of the composer Schönberg, and had often discussed with him the aims of their separate arts, as expressed in sound and in vision, and he had come to the conclusion that these aims were fundamentally the same, to express an inner emotional state — to find satisfaction for vague feelings in precise forms. But it was not until he saw his painting upside-down that he suddenly felt that this aim could be more perfectly realized if the painter was not concerned with the different and possibly irrelevant aim of representing a concrete object — a landscape or a portrait. The real landscape was in the soul.

We thus have two separate origins for two distinct types of abstract art. Critics have never been able to agree on the appropriate names for these types, but one is essentially *expressionist*, based on emotion, and the other is essentially *construc-*

tivist, based on formal intuition. The constructivist may argue that in the result his work of art involves the emotions and expresses an inner state of feeling; the expressionist may argue that in the result his work of art achieves formal relations and colour-harmonies without which there would be no aesthetic appeal. The public may conclude that the name does not matter so long as the result is a work of art.

In the course of the last fifty years there has been an intense development of these two types of abstraction, but though they sometimes constitute separate schools, such as *De Stijl* in Holland, or Action Painting in the United States, there is no decisive departure from the original types of abstraction.

It is sometimes suggested that the movement known in the United States as Action Painting is a new development because the artist is concerned not to express an inner state of feeling, but rather to extend the field of his physical awareness. His activity has no basis in emotion, but is rather an exercise as impersonal and as enjoyable as fencing or skating. But this, I believe, is a distinction without a difference: though the action painter may not have the intention to express emotion, nevertheless he generates it, and the result, from the spectator's point of view, may be equally effective. Every gesture we make, whether we are skating or painting with a brush, signing a letter or dribbling colours on to a canvas from a pierced can (the method sometimes used by Jackson Pollock) is 'expressive'. Expressive of what? Perhaps not of an 'inner necessity' such as Kandinsky felt, perhaps of nothing that could be described as spiritual or metaphysical; expressive just of the artist's personality, but of that personality seeking some security in the outer world, some communion with other people — a life-line, as it were, thrown out into a sea where there is no anchorage.

This brings us to the heart of the subject. We can trace the evolution of art towards abstraction step by step, and as a development it seems logical enough. A retrospective exhibition of one of the pioneers of abstract art (such as Piet Mondrian) will show how slowly and tentatively each step was taken. Between one painting and another, between the work of one year and the work of the next, there is a scarcely discernible difference. But slowly the natural object, a tree or a church, is modified. Lines are interrupted, shapes dissolve, colours are broken down and their constituent elements separated and purified; until over a period of five or six years we lose all sense of the original object, and what at first was entitled 'The Church at Domburg', becomes first 'Church Façade' (it is no longer possible to identify any particular church) and then perhaps 'Façade' (for even a church is no longer in evidence), and finally 'Composition', for there is no longer any trace of the object left.

But Picasso would say there is still the *idea* of the object, and that the composition could not have existed unless the church tower at Domburg had made an indelible impression on Mondrian's vision, on his mind. That is perhaps true of Mondrian's paintings up to about 1916, but then he began to experiment with lines and colour planes, not 'starting with something in reality', unless lines and colours are said to be 'reality'. In all the discussion of abstract art one continually falls into such semantic traps. By 'reality' Picasso meant a 'given' reality, trees and churches and other such environmental objects; but when, after 1916, Mondrian spoke of 'reality' he meant a 'created' reality, a reality that comes into existence, or is discovered for the first time by the artist when he establishes certain relations between lines and colours. In 1912–20 he wrote a long essay in dialogue form to make clear this distinction between 'natural reality' and 'abstract reality'.

That abstract art is a flight from reality is the usual supposition, but this Mondrian and all the pioneers of abstract art have fiercely denied. Historically it can be argued (this is the thesis of Wilhelm Worringer, whose essay on *Abstraction and Empathy* was published in Munich in 1908, the year of Kandinsky's apocalyptic experience) that the tendency to make art unnatural, geometric, abstract, is a tendency found in periods when, or in climates where, the environment is against man. He retreats from the brutal facts of life into a world of abstract harmony which does not remind him of these facts. Far from wishing to 'represent' life, his only desire is to forget it, and to find peace and security in a realm of transcendental fantasy.

Since our modern world fits this historical explanation only too well, it is logical to apply this hypothesis to modern abstract art. We live in an age of anxiety, of war and revolution; what could be more natural than to retreat into a world of beauty, expressed in rhythmical lines and harmonious colours, far from the madding crowd of visual impressions that assault our sensibilities if we look around us?

I believe that this is a superficial explanation for the appearance of abstract art in our time, but it is not an adequate explanation of its development and its present universal appeal. If abstract art were merely a flight from reality, it would be a negative thing, of little value to mankind. But all the evidence suggests that abstract art is a positive thing, dynamic and creative. Compared with the academic art of the nineteenth century, it is intensely dynamic, and inspires an almost religious devotion in its practitioners and disciples. What is the source of its positive appeal?

It is easy to invent metaphysical explanations — to say that abstract art is an expression of man's desire to be in tune with the universe. Mondrian often used that kind of explanation — for example: 'Plastic vision implies action; by plastic vision, we destroy the natural experience, and reconstruct that appearance abstractly. Our plastic vision so to speak corrects our habitual, natural vision — thus we reduce the individual to the universal with which we become united.' But Mondrian also used very practical explanations. He was fond of dancing, and the two last great paintings of his life, painted in New York, *Broadway Boogie-Woogie* and *Victory Boogie-Woogie*, are evidence of this passion. He found a parallel to abstract art in modern dancing, more particularly in modern dance steps.

In the old style of dancing, the music and the steps of the dance flowed into each other; the movement of the dance might be represented by a curved line. In modern dancing, according to Mondrian, one dances *against* the music. There is an opposition between the rhythm of the dance and the melody of the music, and the steps of the dance are no longer represented by a curved but by straight lines. This may be a fanciful comparison, but Mondrian meant to illustrate the fact that vitality itself comes from the balance of opposed forces: that art, like life, is the expression of a duality. The modern movement has discovered the essential dialectical character of art: the unity that is achieved by resolving contradictions. Rhythm and stability, direction and position, colour and shape, horizontal and vertical, form and expression — all these elements are opposed to each other within the unity of the work of art.

Such unity, a unity that is *in* art as it is *in* reality, is not an escape from chaos and anxiety, but is achieved by a refinement of vision, by what is in effect an extension of visual sensibility; and Mondrian believed that such a new vision was the basis for a new society. It is significant that the greatest admirers of Mondrian, as of the constructivist sculptors Gabo and Pevsner, are architects, for they perceive the connection between what we might call the constructive vision of the artist and the practical vision of the architect. Indeed, there is no distinction, except that of scale, between the work of a Mondrian and the work of an architect like Mies van der Rohe: both belong to what Mondrian has called 'a society based on the equation of the material and the spiritual, a society composed of balanced relationships'. Mies has used almost identical words: 'In its simplest form architecture is rooted in entirely functional considerations, but it can reach up through all degrees of value to the highest sphere of spiritual existence, into the realm of pure art.'

By concentrating on Mondrian and what is sometimes called 'pure' abstraction I may seem to have left the other kind of abstract art, abstract expressionism, without an explanation, but I do not think so. All these new tendencies in art have been ascribed, as Mondrian noted, to greater consciousness of the fourth dimension. I am not sure that many artists would be able to give an adequate account of the fourth dimension, but we are all conscious of the problems of time and space as revealed (but not solved) by modern physics, and artists have something to say about such problems. In one direction (the direction of Mondrian and Gabo) the solutions (they are not identical) are found *against* the music — the synthesis is found in a determined balance, in unified relationships. In the other direction (the direction of Pollock and De Kooning) the synthesis is found *without* music; that is to say, by an indeterminate leap into space itself, as if to discover there the nature of infinity. Action-painting might therefore be defined as a plastic speculation on the nature of infinity.

There is one further refinement to note before we have surveyed all the varieties of abstraction. Perhaps as an extension of action-painting, perhaps as a return to Picasso's belief that the artist 'must always start with something', and more precisely as a result of a new appreciation of Monet's 'immense and mysterious' renderings of water landscapes, a somewhat revised version of abstract impressionism has appeared, especially in the United States. The aim is not so much to remove gradually all traces of reality, in the manner of some of the early Cubists, but rather to give a direct rendering of the artist's immediate sensations in the presence of natural objects. Such immediate sensations are not realistic; Monet complained that the sun set too fast for him to render the 'instantaneity' of the effects he sought to render; and Kandinsky, after seeing one of Monet's Haystacks in 1895, described very accurately the effects that the abstract impressionists of to-day are still trying to achieve:

'. . . Suddenly, for the first time, I saw a "picture". That it was a haystack, the catalogue informed me. I could not recognize it. This lack of recognition was distressing to me. I also felt that the painter had no right to paint so indistinctly. I had a muffled sense that the object was lacking in this picture, and was overcome with astonishment and perplexity that it not only seized, but engraved itself indelibly on the memory and, quite unexpectedly, again and again, hovered before the eyes down to the smallest detail. All of this was unclear to me, and I could not draw the simple consequences from this experience. But what was absolutely clear to me was the unsuspected power, previously hidden from me, of the palette, which surpassed all my dreams. Painting took on a fabulous strength and splendour. And at the same time, unconsciously, the object was discredited as an indispensable element of the picture. . . .'

'The object was discredited' — that is the essential point, and the object remains discredited. The names of Mark Tobey and (in his recent work) Milton Reznik will perhaps indicate more precisely the type of abstraction to which I am referring.

In order to try and clear up this misunderstanding I shall now try to give a direct answer to some of the objections that have been raised against abstract art. The most general charge that can be brought against abstract art is that it fails to communicate any meaning. Francis Henry Taylor, who was for some years the Director of the Metropolitan Museum of Art in New York, expressed this point of view when he said: 'unless participation is allowed the spectator, (a painting) becomes a hopeless riddle and ceases to be a work of art at all.'

Forty years ago C. K. Ogden and I. A. Richards wrote a famous book called *The Meaning of Meaning*, dealing with problems of language and logic. A similar problem exists in the plastic arts.

Only the most simple people would suggest that the meaning of the picture is the story it tells — that a work of art should be the description of a scene or the narration of an event. Tolstoy, who was not a simple person, asserted that the value of the work of art lies in its truth, and Ruskin, though he had a different conception of the truth, argued in much the same way.

The Nature of Abstract Art

At this point we encounter a philosophical problem. Is understanding a rational process, the kind of discourse that should be confined to logical statements; or is it possibly an irrational process, the kind of discourse we can carry on only by the use of symbols?

The defender of abstract art believes that art is a form of symbolic discourse, and that, even when it is representational, its message is conveyed by form and colour rather than by the imitation of the things we see. He points out that other arts, such as music and architecture, do not necessarily imitate anything in nature, but communicate by abstract arrangements of sounds, intervals, proportions, and rhythms. There is no reason why an arrangement of lines and colours should not be abstract in the same way.

It is merely a convention, of limited historical significance, to maintain that the visual arts should communicate their meaning by imitating the arbitrary forms that nature has evolved. Music might just as logically be confined to the imitation of bird songs or thunder; architecture, to the imitation of caves and mountains.

The abstract work of art may be a riddle, but it is not hopeless nor is it meaningless: it is a symbol which may stand for the artist's deepest emotions and intuitions, and in which the spectator may find his own emotions and intuitions defined and illuminated.

I will now turn to a second charge that is often made against abstract art, especially that kind we call 'abstract expressionism' or 'action painting'. It is said that in such art there are no standards of imagery or technique. Anyone — even a child — can paint an abstract painting. Mere doodling may be offered as abstract art. Thus, it becomes impossible to tell a good abstract picture from a bad one.

What is a standard of imagery? Presumably, the visual images given in our perception of the external world. Again a philosophical problem is involved, for there is no standard image of the external world.

The image of the external world which we have at any moment is a convention, and varies from age to age. This is evident enough from the history of art — each period has its own method of constructing an image of the external world; there is little in common between an image of the Byzantine period and an image of the classical Renaissance.

The Nature of Abstract Art

The image of man, as a recent exhibition at the Museum of Modern Art showed, varies not only from age to age, but also from artist to artist. What is a standard image of man? The Chinese have one image, the Greeks have another. Some religions create an image of the ideal man; others, such as Islam, forbid the representation of such an ideal (for only God is perfect, and it would be presumptuous of man to consider himself capable of representing such perfection).

One kind of abstract artist, like the Islamic artist, believes there is an ideal of perfection, but that it is impersonal, that is to say, a question of quantitative harmony — the rhythmical succession of lines, the balance of areas, the harmonious unity of colours, the organic articulation of space. Another kind of abstract artist seeks an image that may, or may not, have such concrete qualities, but is essentially expressive of emotion, or has some inexplicable magical quality.

There are shapes that appeal to us for no rational reason — the graining of wood, the eroded pebbles in a stream, cloud formations, sunsets, blots of ink, flotsam from the sea. The Chinese and Japanese take great irregular pieces of rock and erect them in their gardens because they have a strange animistic power or charm. Form is as mysterious as life itself. The artist is a man who reveals the mystery of form.

Even the child as it scribbles can do this. An American teacher, Rhoda Kellogg of the Golden Gate Nursery School in San Francisco, has classified children's scribbles and revealed their symbolic significance. A comparison of abstract art with children's scribbles does not make abstract art ridiculous; on the contrary, it connects it organically with the beginnings of all visual symbols.

As for the technique, much as this may baffle the critic of abstract art, I would say that the standard is the same as in representational art. It is a question of the artist's skill in using his tools and materials to their best advantage. There are badly painted abstract pictures just as there are badly painted representational pictures; and there are well-painted pictures of each kind. Even spontaneity, which is characteristic of abstract expressionist art, is also found in representational art — in Tiepolo or Magnasco, in the impressionists and the expressionists.

In abstract art and in representational art, the standards are the same. There is only good art and bad art.

Coherent composition, sensibility to colour harmonies, rhythmic movement, and significant imagery — abstract art possesses all the essentially aesthetic qualities that have been present in the art of the past. David Jones, an English painter who is not abstract, has made this point in *Epoch and Artist*: 'Those of us whose work no one, I imagine, would call "abstract" know, nevertheless, that it is an abstract quality, however hidden or devious, which determines the real worth of any work.'

A third criticism often made of abstract art is that it represents novelty for novelty's sake. There is a primary concern with being 'different' that leads to mere sensationalism. What began as a genuine experiment has become a fashionable cult.

It is true that modern art of all kinds, including poetry and music, has been deliberately concerned to 'make it new'. At the most general and perhaps profoundest level, this is a reflection of our historical situation. We live in a revolutionary period, and the changes in art are but reflections of the changes in society.

More direct causes for the novelty of modern art are to be found in the scientific and technical discoveries of our time. The invention of photography and the moving picture had a profound effect on the art of painting. So did technical advances in speed, the new dimensions of space given by the airplane, the new world of form revealed by the microscope. Form itself was established as a guiding principle in nature, in the universe, and form inevitably (and perhaps unconsciously) became the preoccupation of the artist. It would be absurd to complain of novelty for novelty's sake in science; it is equally absurd to complain of it in art. Art has merely kept in step with a changing world, and the more art has changed the more it has remained the same thing — the symbolic representation of reality.

The suggestion that such an activity constitutes a 'cult' is far from the truth. There have been cults in the past — the Pre-Raphaelite Brotherhood was one. Abstract art, by contrast, is one of the most nearly universal movements in the history of art. It can accommodate all varieties of human temperament and expression, from severe classicism to wild romanticism.

A more serious charge against abstract art asserts that an abstract painting is mere decoration, no more profound than a pattern for wall-paper or draperies. It is suggested that the abstract artist works first toward the effect of his work on a museum wall, rather than toward the intensification of experience, which is regarded as the proper purpose of art.

The Nature of Abstract Art

Ruskin once said that all great art was essentially decorative. The great compositions of Titian, Michelangelo, and Rubens are 'decorative'. If the abstract artist works towards the effect of his work on a museum wall, he is doing exactly what Titian, Michelangelo, and Rubens did.

It is true that some abstract pictures are empty, but that is because they are poor compositions, not because they are abstract. 'Intensification of experience' is not a question of size, but of the effectiveness of the symbols used.

Finally it is often said that abstract art is devoid of human emotion — that it has no philosophical foundation, no concern with basic and permanent values, as great art always had.

No art could have deeper philosophical foundations than abstract art. The many books on the subject constitute a wealth of speculation on the principles of art without rival in history. All these writings are concerned with 'basic and permanent values', and such values are human values.

Nevertheless, the charge that abstract art is 'devoid of human emotion' has some force if by human emotion is meant the day-to-day feelings of joy and sorrow, hope and despair, which are our normal experiences. If the purpose of art were to 'express' such feelings, to embody them in realistic pictures, in music or in drama, then art would be identical with life: a transcript, a report, a reflection.

The purpose of the artist is not to represent emotion, but to transcend it. There are two aphorisms of Georges Braque's which describe the true function of emotion in art: 'Emotion is neither added nor imitated: it is the seed, and art is the blossom' and 'I love the rule that corrects emotion; I love the emotion that corrects the rule'.

Art is a dialectical process — the resolution of contradictions and ambiguities. A work of art is removed from mundane strife; it is an object of disinterested contemplation.

Art is a dialectical process — the resolution of contradictions and ambiguities that are present in our mode of life, in our social constraints and frustrations. For the final and most important justification of abstract art we must therefore turn to our historical situation, and ask whether there are any world-wide material conditions that might account for a universal will to abstraction.

The first that might occur to us is the almost universal mech-

294

anization of the processes of production, and this phenomenon does indeed merit our careful consideration. Mechanization, and the division of labour that goes with it, is an affront to our humanity, which is nurtured and reproduced by organic processes. How often, through our greatest spiritual leaders, we have protested against mechanization and the alienation of man. Ruskin and Marx, Nietzsche and Bergson, Tolstoy and Lawrence, Jaspers and Schweizer, Gandhi and Vinoba, all speak with one voice, prophetic of doom. It would be inconceivable that such a fundamental revolution in the life of mankind should not have had a profound effect on man's artistic volition. Is this the single and adequate explanation of the artistic phenomenon that confronts us in all its magnitude and mystery?

It is surely a great part of the explanation, especially if we trace the reaction, not on the superficial level of mechanized living (potent as this might be as a superficial influence on the forms of art), but on the deeper levels known since Marx first used the word as *alienation*. Alienation is, indeed, the word also used by Worringer to describe Northern man's reaction to an unfriendly or inclement environment of a natural kind; how much more appropriate, therefore, as a word to describe universal man's reaction to an environment that is not merely organically inclement, but positively unnatural? But alienation itself is not a superficial or merely sensational reaction: it is a process involving the mind and spirit of man in their most intimate recesses. It is a social psychosis, a metaphysical disease. Its social effects have often been described by sociologists, by pioneers like Adam Smith and Karl Marx, by contemporary sociologists like Hannah Arendt and David Riesman; its spiritual effects never more eloquently than by Ruskin, significantly when discussing the 'savageness' of Gothic art. 'Men', he wrote, 'were not intended to work with the accuracy of tools, to be precise and perfect in all their actions. If you will have that precision out of them, and make their fingers measure degrees like cog-wheels, and their arms strike curves like compasses, you must unhumanize them. All the energy of their spirits must be given to make cogs and compasses of themselves. All their attention and strength must go to the accomplishment of the mean act. The eye of the soul must be bent upon the finger-point, and the soul's force must fill all the invisible nerves that guide it, ten hours a day, that it may not err from its steely precision, and so soul and sight be worn away, and the whole human being be lost at last — a heap of sawdust, so far as its intellectual work in this world is concerned: saved only by its Heart, which cannot go into the form of cogs and compasses, but expands, after the ten hours are over, into fireside humanity.'[1] When work is 'a perpetual and exquisitely timed palsy', then art, which is the only freedom left to mankind, must expand into savage liberty.

There are two possible objections to such a theory of action and reaction. Is it not true, in the first place, that modern art has to a considerable extent been inspired by the 'engineering rationality' of our time? If the idealization of the machine by the Futurists is in the objector's mind, then I would say that their work ought to be interpreted as a protest against academic realism rather than as 'machine art'; at any rate, it was soon to turn, in the significant work of Marcel Duchamp, into machine mockery. Nevertheless, the movement had its serious, even its metaphysical elements, and these were to inspire Tatlin and other precursors of the Constructivist movement in Russia. It is true that as it developed, this later movement, in the work of Gabo and Pevsner, left the machine and all utilitarian tectonics far behind it, to concentrate on the invention of new images of reality — an intuitive spiritual enterprise far removed from engineering rationality. But it can be said with truth that engineering and machinery generally had made the artist more fully aware of certain kinetic elements — movement and rhythm, for example — and modern art, which can be characterized in a certain general sense as dynamic (as opposed to the static character of Greek art) may have been influenced in this sense by its mechanistic environment. But the opposite thesis would be tenable: namely, that the sense of movement that characterized the art of the Baroque period — the steam engine, we should remember, was an invention of this period — inspired, however subconsciously, the first machines.

The other possible objection is that the reaction in art is far too partial to correspond to a phenomenon so widespread as mechanization: the machine is so universal and so penetrates every recess of life, that the reaction should be universal too, and not confined to an artistic coterie. But the reaction is by no means confined to the arts or to a coterie of artists: it shows up equally in the desperate search for leisure and amusement, in the unprecedented development of tourism, motoring, camping, and sport — all forms of escape from a perpetual and exquisitely

[1] *Stones of Venice,* II, vi, 12.

timed palsy. Grosser aesthetic reactions are to be found in so-called 'pop-art', which in an industrial civilization is a substitute for folk art: strip cartoons, 'westerns', the Hollywood film — these are in no sense an empathetic reaction to a congenial environment; on the contrary, they represent an impulse to self-alienation as powerful and as apprehensive as the urge to abstraction. The need for empathy, for objectified self-enjoyment, is satisfied in idealized archetypes (the dumb blonde, the epicene crooner, the heroic gangster) as remote from daily life on the assembly line as is a painting by Mondrian from a tree in the park.

To characterize abstract art as a reaction to the mechanization of life is not to remove art from the realm of reality, for reality is what we discover by our senses and shape by our intelligence. Its frontiers are continually under revision, and each step into unknown territory is established by some new intuition, some fresh image, some dimension first realized in the plastic forms of art. Art is a dialectical process, a process, in the words of Marx, 'in which man of his own accord starts, regulates, and controls the material reactions between himself and nature.' Art is a sensuous human activity that gives man a reasoned relation to the surrounding world, and I see nothing in the origins, scope and development of abstract art in our time that does not correspond to this dialectical conception of the process. Mechanization has taken command of our economic activities, but for that very reason the artistic will of man manifests a greater freedom than it has ever known.

Henry Moore[1]

Within a comparatively short time the fame of the English sculptor, Henry Moore, has become world-wide. In Great Britain his importance had been fully recognized as long ago as 1928, when at the age of thirty, he was commissioned to carve one of the four bas-reliefs that decorate the St. James's Underground Station in London. A series of one-man shows in the 1930's won increasing admiration for his work, but then came the war and a temporary check to his activities — it was no longer possible to obtain the stone for his carvings. But Moore's creative energy was not to be suppressed by such material limitations. As a sculptor he had used the medium of drawing for his preliminary studies of a subject, so he began to make many drawings in colour, partly as a record of subjects for future use, but partly also because the medium interested him for its own expressive virtues. Invited to make drawings of war-time subjects, he chose the Dantesque imagery of the underground shelters. In a long series of sketches he gave moving expression to the tragic reality of war as experienced by the ordinary citizen, and this achievement, though a divagation from his main purpose, enormously extended his public.

At the end of the war Moore was invited to hold a retrospective exhibition of his work at the Museum of Modern Art, New York. The exhibition was subsequently shown at Chicago and San Francisco, and everywhere it was admitted that a sculptor of international importance had emerged. The final triumph came in 1948 when the sculptor was invited to show his work at the Biennale in Venice. Moore was awarded the International Prize for Sculpture. After that, even Paris had to admit the existence of an English sculptor. An exhibition of his work was held at the Musée d'Art Moderne in 1949, and was more successful than any

[1] An address (delivered *in absentia*) at the opening of an exhibition in Berlin in July, 1961, with additions from earlier writings on this artist.

comparable exhibitions held there in recent times. This exhibition was afterwards shown in Brussels, Amsterdam, Hamburg, Düsseldorf and Berne and from 1950 onwards retrospective exhibitions of Moore's work have circulated throughout the world.

When Henry Moore received the first prize for sculpture at the Venice Biennale there was a general agreement among the world's leading art critics, not only that this artist had become the greatest sculptor of our time, but also that he was an artist whose images were in some manner peculiarly apt to express a consciousness specifically modern in its range and depth. Moore's work must finally be justified on grounds that are primarily technical and aesthetic, but that would not be a difficult task: all he has done exhibits the same perfect mastery of the plastic values of sculpture — its coherence as mass or volume, its balance and rhythm, the harmonic relationship of part to part, and of each part to the whole. Nevertheless — and this, we may suspect, explains the immediate appeal of his work — these formal elements are always used for an expressive purpose. There is throughout his work a discursive power, an implicit potency, that comes from some deep level of consciousness. His images are archetypal, and are, indeed, confined to a very few archetypes. But this very limitation of Moore's subject-matter indicates a concentration of power reaching deep down into the unconscious, rather than an attention dispersed among superficial phenomena. This strength-by-limitation (characteristic of so many great artists) does not come by conscious choice: it is an imperious and almost impersonal impulse that uses the artist as its medium.

It is not easy to give a brief and simple explanation of the qualities in Moore's work which have ensured the universal recognition of his genius. It is partly a question of his integrity. Endowed with a certain feeling for formal relations, he has striven all his life to give expression to this plastic vision. He has taken the most difficult path, working directly in wood, stone or metal, taking care that the forms which he 'discovered' were always forms natural to the chosen material. This led to a characteristic distortion of natural forms, for if flesh is represented in stone it should take on the material and structural nature of stone — it should not be disguised to look like flesh. Sculptors in other ages had established this same 'law', and in this respect Moore is following the tradition of ancient Egyptian, Chinese and Mexican sculptors, as well as the sculpture of the Saxon churches in England itself. But to follow a tradition is not enough. The great artist has in addition a personal 'vision', which is a quality that must be appreciated in front of the work of art itself; it cannot be adequately described in words. It is a question of creating, by abstract means, an impression of vitality. Vitality is, in organic objects, an effect of movement, of growth. The sculptor's problem is to give this dynamic quality to objects that do not move or grow. It is done by creating certain relations between a solid mass and its surrounding space, and by dividing the mass into contrasted areas — convexities and concavities which are rhythmically related and *seem* to move into one another. To create such vitality in an inanimate mass is an infinitely difficult task, and only the greatest sculptors have been capable of it. It demands not only a particular kind of plastic sensibility, but in addition the capacity to translate this sensibility into objective material form.

In modern Europe a sculptor cannot avoid certain humanistic preoccupations. We live in cities, and our whole outlook is anthropocentric. The modern sculptor, therefore, seeks by preference to interpret the human form; at least, this has been the normal tendency of sculpture for many centuries, and in this respect Henry Moore is normal. In his case the tendency has been modified by a desire to relate the human form to certain universal forms found in nature; this aspect of his work I will deal with presently. But first I wish to emphasize the fact that Henry Moore's sculpture is based primarily on the close observation and study of the human form. As a student he drew and modelled from life for many years, and he still periodically returns to life drawing. It is so important to stress this fact, that I would like to quote his own words to me:

'Every few months I stop carving for two or three weeks and draw from life. At one time I used to mix the two, perhaps carving during the day and drawing from a model during the evening. But I found this unsatisfactory — the two activities interfered with each other, for the mental approach to each is different, one being objective and the other subjective. Stone is so different from flesh and blood that one cannot carve directly from life without almost the certainty of ill-treating the material. Drawing and carving are so different that a shape or size or conception which is satisfying as a drawing might be totally wrong realized in stone. Nevertheless, there is a connection between my drawings and my sculpture.

Drawing from life keeps one visually fit — perhaps acts like water to a plant — and it lessens the danger of repeating oneself and getting into a formula. It enlarges one's form repertoire, one's form experience. But in my sculpture I do not use my memory or observations of a particular object, but rather whatever comes up from my general fund of knowledge of natural forms.'

That is to say, the artist makes himself so familiar with the ways of nature — particularly the ways of growth — that he can out of the depth and sureness of that knowledge create ideal forms which have all the vital rhythm and structure of natural forms. He can escape from what is incidental in nature, and create what is spiritually necessary and eternal.

But there is just this difficulty: most of the forms of natural growth are evolved in labile materials — flesh and blood, tender wood and sap — and these cannot be translated directly into hard and brittle materials like stone and metal. Henry Moore has therefore sought among the forms of nature for harder and slower types of growth, realizing, that in these he would find the forms natural to his carving materials. He has gone beneath the flesh to the hard structure of bone; he has studied pebbles and rock formations. Pebbles and rocks show nature's way of treating stone — smooth sea-worn pebbles reveal the contours inherent in stones, contours determined by variations in the structural cohesion of stone. Stone is not an even mass, and symmetry is foreign to its nature; worn pebbles show the principles of its asymmetrical structure. Rocks show stone torn and hacked by cataclysmic forces, or eroded and polished by wind and rain. They show the jagged rhythms into which a laminated structure breaks; the outlines of hills and mountains are the nervous calligraphy of nature. More significant still are the forms built up out of hard materials, the actual growth in nature of crystals, shells, and bones. Crystals are a key to geometrical proportions assumed naturally by minerals, whilst shells are nature's way of evolving hard hollow forms, and are exact epitomes of harmony and proportion. Bones combine great structural strength with extreme lightness; the result is a natural tenseness of form. In their joints they exhibit the perfect transition of rigid structures from one direction to another. They show the ideal torsions which a rigid structure undergoes in such transitional movements.

Having made these studies of natural form (and always continuing to make them), the sculptor's problem is then to apply them in the interpretation of his mental conceptions. He wishes to express in stone his emotional apprehension of, say, the human figure. To reproduce such a figure directly in stone seems to him a monstrous perversion of stone, and in any case a misrepresentation of the qualities of flesh and blood. Representational figure sculpture can never be anything but a travesty of one material in another — and actually, in most periods, sculptors have tried to disguise the stony nature of their representations by painting or otherwise colouring their statues. It is only in decadent periods that the aim has persisted of trying to represent flesh in naked stone. The aim of a sculptor like Henry Moore is to represent his conceptions in the forms natural to the material he is working in. I have explained how by intensive research he discovers the forms appropriate to his materials. His whole art consists in effecting a credible compromise between these forms and the concepts of his imagination. A similar aim has, I believe, characterized all the great periods of art; the only exception being those rare types of art in which all connection with nature is abandoned in favour of some abstract and disinterested ideal of beauty.

Moore's integrity is not merely artistic: it is also personal. Of simple origins (his father was a miner), he has retained throughout his life a simplicity of manner and a freshness of vision which only those who know him personally can properly experience. But I believe that this quality in the man is transferred to his work. Much modern art can be justly accused of sophistication — sophisticated art being the product of knowledge and imitation rather than of feeling and intuition. I have already admitted that Moore owes his debts to the great masters of the past — no genuine artist would dare to ignore such a treasury of experience. But there is all the difference in the world between the artist who steals from that treasury and the one who adds to it. Moore's sculpture is one of the richest gifts made in modern times to our common stock of enduring art.

Though his work is among the most inventive and experimental of our time, Moore is not a sophisticated artist. Nor is he a conceited artist — he fully admits his debt to his immediate predecessors and his profound admiration for the great sculptors and painters of the past. The word that most naturally occurs to one in writing about him — and it is a word I have already used — is *integrity*: integrity of spirit and of vision. It is this quality which,

transcending the ebb and flow of inspiration, gives to his work its
continuing influence and power.

For more than thirty years it has been my good fortune to
follow with intimate sympathy the unfolding of the genius of
Henry Moore. This man was not born with any special privileges.
His social origins were lowly and only a strong will and a compelling sense of his own destiny could have carried him through
the obstacles that beset an artist in an age committed to the pursuit of material values. Great art has always been the reward for
an overcoming of great difficulties, and we may consider lucky a
man who is challenged by his fate. Just as the best statues are
hewn out of the hardest stone, so the spirit of a great artist is
tempered in adversity. Moore came to maturity in the midst of the
First World War, but out of this experience (he served at the
Front and was wounded) he snatched an opportunity to pursue
his studies at a school of art. Once committed to the art of sculpture, he willingly submitted to its discipline. He served long years
of apprenticeship with hammer and chisel and stone, and thus
acquired a sense of mass and volume, of truth to material and of
three-dimensional integrity, which have remained the criteria of
all his subsequent work.

Perhaps I give the impression of a ruthless and self-centred
egotist, impatient, intolerant and proud; but those are not the
characteristics of a great artist, whose strength is always allied
to gentleness, whose self-regard is always modest, whose deepest
feeling is always humane. As the years have passed we have seen
this artist's work increase by some natural process of procreation,
until it now populates a whole world with its forms. How shall we
characterize these creatures of his imagination? First, by their
organic vitality. They are not intellectual abstractions of any
kind; they are nervously articulated, and seem to breathe with
the spontaneous rhythm of a hidden heart. This is not indeed the
only kind of sculpture to which we can give our allegiance — there
is another kind that depends on mathematical law, on the intuitive perception of geometric proportion, and Moore has occasionally shown that he can be master also of this kind. But in
general he has preferred, in the words of Ruskin, to unite the
'implacable severities of mathematics' with 'the softest mysteries
of emotion'. As Ruskin observed, only the greatest sculptors
have been capable of achieving such a perfect and errorless
balance.

Although Henry Moore has always been an experimental artist, capable of great daring in his formal inventions, yet all his adventures have been guided by a scientific knowledge. He innovates on a foundation of fact. He is familiar with the laws of growth and form, and any strangeness in his proportions is due to his discovery of the secrets of nature. He may assimilate one form to another, see a mountain in a bone, or a deep cave in a human breast; but every feature is organic, and can be referred back to prototypes in the realm of Nature. But he does not, like so many contemporary artists, have recourse to the microscopic world of forms revealed by scientific instruments; he remains faithful to human vision, and for this reason his work retains a sensuousness which is denied to unfamiliar shapes. All Moore's shapes are animistic, haunted by a vital spirit. The spirit may sometimes be imprisoned and tormented, but always it cries out in accents that are human.

To repeat another phrase of Ruskin's, Moore is 'as much master of all the laws of balance and weight in the human body as Michael Angelo himself'. But, as Ruskin said of the sculptor he was discussing, Jacopo della Quercia, the sculptor does not wish that you should think of such laws. Perfect knowledge ensures effortless equilibrium. Observe one of Moore's reclining figures. To recline gracefully is in life itself a difficult art for human beings, but in Moore's pieces of sculpture the disposition of the four limbs, the inclination of the torso, the swelling breasts and rounded head, all cohere to form a rhythmical revolution round some imaginary but true centre of gravity. Bosses and hollows, ridges and slopes, move rhythmically in relation to each other — cohere in a linked sequence of modulations. There is nothing violent or abrupt in this world of forms, but there is sometimes an element of terror, of *terribilitá*.

This brings me to the most difficult aspect of Moore's work. The modern movement in general has rejected the classical tradition in art. Henry Moore himself has declared, in a well-known statement, that 'beauty in the later Greek or Renaissance sense', is not the aim of his sculpture. But the rejection of beauty does not mean a total rejection of the ideals of art as they have been conceived in the past. Distinct from beauty there was always an ideal of sublimity, and first the author known to us as Longinus, who wrote in the second century, and then in the seventeenth and eighteenth centuries philosophers such as Boileau and Burke,

Schiller and Kant, made it clear that there are elements in art, and these of the highest, which have in their nature more of strangeness and terror than of measure and calm. It was Longinus who first suggested that emotional intensity is the mark of the sublime, and this was to be the principle upon which, from the middle of the eighteenth century, and largely on the basis of Burke's interpretation of Longinus, the whole Romantic Movement was to be founded. We are still romantics, however much we may dislike the fact and disown the label, and that 'delightful horror', which for Burke was the true test of the sublime, has never been so evident as in the art of our time, a time in which, as Rilke said:

> *das schöne ist nichts*
> *Als des schrecklichen anfang....*

The present is not the appropriate occasion to discuss such an aesthetic of terror, but Henry Moore has been its greatest representative in our time, and all I wish to emphasize is that in this respect his art should be considered under the rubric of sublimity, not of beauty.

There is perhaps just one other aspect of Moore's work which I should mention, though it is not one of which the artist himself is conscious — I mean its unconscious power. This is but another aspect of its sublimity. By virtue of its intensity and vitality, art of this kind has an ability, which Burke in his *Enquiry* had already observed, 'to pierce into the inmost, and what might appear inaccessible parts of our nature.' Much has been written of the archetypal significance of the images created by Moore, their relationship to the ancient images of the earth goddess, nature goddess or life goddess. There is certainly no deliberate intention on the artist's part to refer us to such archaic symbolism, but Moore's work has always returned to two or three feminine themes, the mother and child and the reclining figure, and there can be little doubt that this obsession has a spiritual significance, and proceeds from the inaccessible parts of Moore's own nature, those parts which merge with the terrors and mysteries of the whole human race.

I have known this artist well, and feel an intimate sympathy for his personality based on our common origins and common aspirations, above all on our sharing of the difficulties of the days before his genius was recognized, when there was much work to be done for little return, and when misunderstanding, bitter opposition and sometimes violent denunciation was our lot. Twenty-seven years ago, when my first appreciation of his work was published,[1] I already wrote that Moore, like all great artists, was consumed by an endless curiosity — curiosity concerning the possibilities of his materials, curiosity concerning the nature of life; and I already noted, as a matter for wonder in the case of this artist, then only thirty-five years old, 'the consistency of his course, the gathering power, the increasing clearness of his intention.' The life of an original artist, I concluded, be he painter, sculptor, poet or musician, is hard; 'only an unfailing integrity of purpose can carry him through those years of financial failure, of public neglect and derision which are his inevitable lot. All but a few are compelled to compromise.' But I said then, and can repeat now, that there has been no compromise in the life of Henry Moore; and now, as then, in the fullness of his powers, he offers us the perfected product of his genius.

[1] *Henry Moore* (London, Zwemmer, 1934).

V. Social Criticism

The Philosophy of Anarchism[1]

The characteristic political attitude of today is not one of positive belief, but of despair.

Nobody seriously believes in the social philosophies of the immediate past. There are a few people, but a diminishing number, who still believe that Marxism, as an economic system, offers a coherent alternative to capitalism, and socialism has, indeed, triumphed in one country. But it has not changed the servile nature of human bondage. Man is everywhere still in chains. The motive of his activity remains economic, and this economic motive inevitably leads to the social inequalities from which he had hoped to escape. In face of this double failure, of capitalism and of socialism, the desperation of the masses has taken shape as fascism — a revolutionary movement which aims at establishing a pragmatic organization of power within the general chaos. In this political wilderness most people are lost, and if they do not give way to despair, they resort to a private world of prayer. But others persist in believing that a new world could be built if only we would abandon the economic concepts upon which both socialism and capitalism are based. To realize that new world we must prefer the values of freedom and equality above all other values — above personal wealth, technical power, and nationalism. In the past this view has been held by the world's greatest seers, but their followers have been a numerically insignificant minority, especially in the political sphere, where their doctrine has been called *anarchism*. It may be a tactical mistake to try and restate the eternal truth under a name which is ambiguous — for what is 'without ruler', the literal meaning of the root of the word, is not necessarily 'without order', the meaning often loosely ascribed to it. The sense of historical continuity, and a feeling for philosophical rectitude cannot, however, be compromised. Any vague or romantic associations which the word

[1] London (Freedom Press), 1940.

309

has acquired are incidental. The doctrine itself remains absolute, and pure. There are thousands if not millions of people who instinctively hold these ideas, and who would accept the doctrine if it were made clear to them. A doctrine must be recognized by a common name. I know of no better name than Anarchism. In this essay I shall attempt to restate the fundamental principles of the political philosophy denoted by this name.

(i)

Let us begin by asking a very simple question: What is the measure of human progess? There is no need to discuss whether such progress exists or not, for even to come to a negative conclusion we must have a measure.

In the evolution of mankind there has always been a certain degree of social coherence. The earliest records of our species point to group organizations — the primitive horde, nomadic tribes, settlements, communities, cities, nations. As these groups progressed in numbers, wealth and intelligence, they subdivided into specialized groups — social classes, religious sects, learned societies, and professional or craft unions. Is this complication or articulation of society in itself a symptom of progress? I do not think it can be described as such in so far as it is merely a quantitative change. But if it implies a division of men according to their innate abilities, so that the strong man does work requiring great strength and the subtle man does work requiring skill or sensibility, then obviously the community as a whole is in a better position to carry on the struggle for a qualitatively better life.

These groups within a society can be distinguished according to whether, like an army or an orchestra, they function as a single body; or whether they are united merely to defend their common interests and otherwise function as separate individuals. In one case an aggregation of impersonal units to form a body with a single purpose; in the other case a suspension of individual activities for the purpose of rendering mutual aid.

The former type of group — the army, for example — is historically the most primitive. It is true that secret societies of medicinemen appear quite early on the scene, but such groups are really of the first type — they act as a group rather than as separate individuals. The second type of group — the organization of individuals for the active promotion of their common interests —

comes relatively late in social development. The point I am making is that in the more primitive forms of society the individual is merely a unit; in more developed forms of society he is an independent personality.

This brings me to my measure of progress. Progress is measured by the degree of differentiation within a society. If the individual is a unit in a corporate mass, his life will be limited, dull, and mechanical. If the individual is a unit on his own, with space and potentiality for separate action, then he may be more subject to accident or chance, but at least he can expand and express himself. He can develop — develop in the only real meaning of the word — develop in consciousness of strength, vitality, and joy.

All this may seem very elementary, but it is a fundamental distinction which still divides people into two camps. You might think that it would be the natural desire of every man to develop as an independent personality, but this does not seem to be true. Because they are either economically or psychologically predisposed, there are many people who find safety in numbers, happiness in anonymity, and dignity in routine. They ask for nothing better than to be sheep under a shepherd, soldiers under a captain, slaves under an overseer. The few that must expand become the shepherds, the captains, and leaders of these willing followers.

Such servile people exist by the million, but again I ask: What is our measure of progress? And again I answer that it is only in the degree that the slave is emancipated and the personality differentiated that we can speak of progress. The slave may be happy, but happiness is not enough. A dog or a cat can be happy, but we do not therefore conclude that such animals are superior to human beings — though Walt Whitman, in a well-known poem, holds them up for our emulation. Progress is measured by richness and intensity of experience — by a wider and deeper apprehension of the significance and scope of human existence.

Such is, indeed, the conscious or unconscious criterion of all historians and philosophers. The worth of a civilization or a culture is not valued in the terms of its material wealth or military power, but by the quality and achievements of its representative individuals — its philosophers, its poets, and its artists.

We might therefore express our definition of progress in a slightly more precise form. Progress, we might say, is the gradual establishment of a qualitative differentiation of the individuals within a society.[1] In the long history of mankind, the group is to be regarded as an expedient — an evolutionary aid. It is a means to security and economic well-being: it is essential to the establishment of a civilization. But the further step, by means of which a civilization is given its quality or culture, is only attained by a process of cellular division, in the course of which the individual is differentiated, made distinct from and independent of the parent group. The farther a society progresses, the more clearly the individual becomes the antithesis of the group.

At certain periods in the history of the world a society has become conscious of its personalities: it would perhaps be truer to say that it has established social and economic conditions which permit the free development of the personality. The great age of Greek civilization is the age of the great personalities of Greek poetry, Greek art, and Greek oratory: and in spite of the institution of slavery, it can be described, relatively to the ages which preceded it, as an age of political liberation. But nearer our time we have the so-called Renaissance, inspired by this earlier Hellenic civilization, and even more conscious of the value of free individual development. The European Renaissance is an age of political confusion; but in spite of tyrannies and oppression, there is no doubt that compared with the previous period,[2] it also was an age of liberation. The individual once more comes into his own, and the arts are cultivated and appreciated as never before. But still more significantly, there arises a consciousness of the very fact that the value of a civilization is dependent on the freedom and variety of the individuals composing it. For the first time the personality is deliberately cultivated as such; and from that time until today it has not been possible to separate the achievements of a civilization from the achievements of the individuals composing it. Even in the sciences we now tend to think of the growth of knowledge in particular and personal terms — of physics, for

[1] It is worth observing that this is Plato's measure of progress in the *Republic*, II, 369 ff.

[2] Stylistically it is no longer possible to regard the Renaissance as an epoch which begins arbitrarily about 1400. Giotto and Masaccio can fairly be regarded as the culmination of Gothic art no less than as the forerunners of Renaissance art. There was actually a continuous process of growth, which began imperceptibly as the new force of Christianity penetrated the dead forms of late Roman art, which reached maturity in the Gothic style of the twelfth and thirteenth centuries, and which then grew in richness and complexity as it became more personal and individual during the fourteenth and succeeding two centuries. From an aesthetic point of view the earlier and later phases of this process (Gothic and Renaissance) cannot be judged absolutely: what the one gains from co-operative unity it loses in variety, and vice versa.

example, as a line of individuals stretching between Galileo and
Einstein.

(ii)

I have not the slightest doubt that this form of individuation
represents a higher stage in the evolution of mankind. It may be
that we are only at the beginning of such a phase — a few centuries are a short time in the history of a biological process.
Creeds and castes, and all forms of intellectual and emotional
grouping, belong to the past. The future unit is the individual, a
world in himself, self-contained and self-creative, freely giving
and freely receiving, but essentially a free spirit.

It was Nietzsche who first made us conscious of the significance
of the individual as a term in the evolutionary process — in that
part of the evolutionary process which has still to take place.
Nevertheless, there exists in Nietzsche's writings a confusion
which must be avoided. That it can be avoided is due mainly to
scientific discoveries made since Nietzsche's day, so Nietzsche
must to some extent be excused. I refer to the discoveries of psycho-
analysis. Freud has shown one thing very clearly: that we only
forget our infancy by burying it in the unconscious; and that the
problems of this difficult period find their solution under a disguised form in adult life. I do not wish to import the technical
language of psycho-analysis into this discussion, but it has been
shown that the irrational devotion which a group will show to its
leader is simply a transference of an emotional relationship which
has been dissolved or repressed within the family circle. When we
describe a king as 'the Father of his People', the metaphor is an
exact description of an unconscious symbolism. Moreover, we
transfer to this figure-head all sorts of imaginary virtues which we
ourselves would like to possess — it is the reverse process of the
scapegoat, who is the recipient of our secret guilt.

Nietzsche, like the admirers of our contemporary dictators,
did not sufficiently realize this distinction, and he is apt to praise
as a superman a figure who is merely inflated with the unconscious desires of the group. The true superman is the man who
holds himself aloof from the group — a fact which Nietzsche
acknowledged on other occasions. When an individual has become conscious, not merely of his 'Eigentum', of his own closed
circuit of desires and potentialities (at which stage he is an egoist)
but also of the laws which govern his reactions to the group of

which he is a member, then he is on the way to become that new type of human being which Nietzsche called the Superman.

The individual and the group — this is the relationship out of which spring all the complexities of our existence and the need for unravelling and simplifying them. Conscience itself is born of this relationship, and all those instincts of mutuality and sympathy which become codified in morals. Morality, as has often been pointed out, is antecedent to religion — it even exists in a rudimentary form among animals. Religion and politics follow, as attempts to define the instinctive conduct natural to the group, and finally you get the historical process only too well known to us, in which the institutions of religion and politics are captured by an individual or a class and turned against the group which they were designed to benefit. Man finds his instincts, already deformed by being defined, now altogether inhibited. The organic life of the group, a self-regulative life like the life of all organic entities, is stretched on the rigid frame of a code. It ceases to be life in any real sense, and only functions as convention, conformity, and discipline.

There is a distinction to be made here between a discipline imposed on life, and the law which is inherent in life. My own early experiences in war led me to suspect the value of discipline, even in that sphere where it is so often regarded as the first essential for success. It was not discipline, but two qualities which I would call initiative and free association, that proved essential in the stress of action. These qualities are developed individually, and tend to be destroyed by the mechanical routine of the barrack square. As for the unconscious obedience which discipline and drill are supposed to inculcate, it breaks as easily as eggshell in the face of machine-guns and high explosives.

The law which is inherent in life is of an altogether different kind. We must admit 'the singular fact', as Nietzsche called it, 'that everything of the nature of freedom, elegance, boldness, dance, and masterly certainty, which exists or has existed, whether it be in thought itself, or in administration, or in speaking and persuading, in art just as in conduct, has only developed by the means of the tyranny of such arbitrary law; and in all seriousness, it is not at all improbable that precisely this is "nature" and "natural".' (*Beyond Good and Evil*, §188.) That 'nature' is penetrated throughout by 'law' is a fact which becomes clearer with every advance of science; and we need only criticize Nietzsche for calling such law 'arbitrary'. What is arbitrary is not the law of nature, in whatever sphere it exists, but man's interpretation of it. The only necessity is to discover the true laws of nature and conduct our lives in accordance with them.

The most general law in nature is *equity* — the principle of balance and symmetry which guides the growth of forms along the lines of the greatest structural efficiency. It is the law which gives the leaf as well as the tree, the human body and the universe itself, an harmonious and functional shape, which is at the same time objective beauty. But when we use the expression: *the law of equity*, a curious paradox results. If we look up the dictionary definition of equity we find: 'recourse to principles of justice to correct or supplement law.' As so often, the words we use betray us: we have to confess, by using the word equity, that common and statute law which is the law imposed by the State is not necessarily the natural or just law; that there exist principles of justice which are superior to these man-made laws — principles of equality and fairness inherent in the natural order of the universe.

The principle of equity first came into evidence in Roman jurisprudence and was derived by analogy from the physical meaning of the word. In a classical discussion of the subject in his book on *Ancient Law*, Sir Henry Maine points out that the Aequitas of the Romans does in fact imply the principle of equal or proportionate distribution. 'The equal division of numbers or physical magnitudes is doubtless closely entwined with our perceptions of justice; there are few associations which keep their ground in the mind so stubbornly or are dismissed from it with such difficulty by the deepest thinkers.' 'The feature of the Jus Gentium which was presented to the apprehension of a Roman by the word Equity, was exactly the first and most vividly realized characteristic of the hypothetical state of nature. Nature implied symmetrical order, first in the physical world, and next in the moral, and the earliest notion of order doubtless involved straight lines, even surfaces, and measured distances.' I emphasize this origin of the word because it is very necessary to distinguish between the laws of nature (which, to avoid confusion, we ought rather to call the laws of the physical universe) and that theory of a pristine state of nature which was made the basis of Rousseau's sentimental egalitarianism. It was this latter concept which, as Maine dryly remarked, 'helped most powerfully to bring about the grosser disappointments of which the first French Revolution was fertile.' The theory is still that of the Roman lawyers, but the theory is, as it were, turned upside down. 'The Roman had conceived that by careful observation of existing institutions parts of them could be singled out which either exhibited already, or could by judicious purification be made to exhibit, the vestiges of that reign of nature whose reality he faintly affirmed. Rousseau's belief was that a perfect social order could be evolved from the unassisted consideration of the natural state, a social order wholly irrespective of the actual condition of the world and wholly unlike it. The great difference between the views is that one bitterly and broadly condemns the present for its unlikeness to the ideal past; while the other, assuming the present to be as necessary as the past, does not affect to disregard or censure it.'

I am not going to claim that modern anarchism has any direct relation to Roman jurisprudence; but I do claim that it has its basis in the *law* of nature rather than in the *state* of nature. It is based on analogies derived from the simplicity and harmony of universal physical laws, rather than on any assumptions of the natural goodness of human nature — and this is precisely where it begins to diverge fundamentally from democratic socialism, which goes back to Rousseau, the true founder of state socialism.[1] Though state socialism may aim at giving to each according to his needs, or, as nowadays in Russia, according to his deserts, the abstract notion of equity is really quite foreign to its thought. *The tendency of modern socialism is to establish a vast system of statutory law against which there no longer exists a plea in equity. The object of anarchism, on the other hand, is to extend the principle of equity until it altogether supersedes statutory law.*

This distinction was already clear to Bakunin, as the following quotation will show:

'When we speak of justice, we do not mean what is laid down in codes and in the edicts of Roman jurisprudence, founded for the most part on acts of violence, consecrated by time and the benediction of some church, whether pagan or christian, and as such accepted as absolute principles from which the rest can be deduced logically enough; we mean rather that justice which is

[1] This is clearly demonstrated by Rudolf Rocker in *Nationalism and Culture* (New York, 1937).

based solely on the conscience of mankind, which is present in the conscience of each of us, even in the minds of children, and which is simply translated as *equalness* (équation).

'This justice which is universal but which, thanks to the abuse of force and to religious influences, has never yet prevailed, neither in the political nor in the juridical, nor in the economic world — this universal sense of justice must be made the basis of the new world. Without it no liberty, no republic, no prosperity, no peace!' (*Œuvres*, I (1912), pp. 54–5.)

(iii)

Admittedly a system of equity, no less than a system of law, implies a machinery for determining and administering its principles. I can imagine no society which does not embody some method of arbitration. But just as the judge in equity is supposed to appeal to universal principles of reason, and to ignore statutory law when it comes into conflict with these principles, so the arbiter in an anarchist community will appeal to these same principles, as determined by philosophy or common sense; and will do so unimpeded by all those legal and economic prejudices which the present organization of society entails.

It will be said that I am appealing to mystical entities, to idealistic notions which all good materialists reject. I do not deny it. What I do deny is that you can build any enduring society without some such mystical ethos. Such a statement will shock the Marxian socialist, who, in spite of Marx's warnings, is usually a naïve materialist. Marx's theory — as I think he himself would have been the first to admit — was not a universal theory. It did not deal with all the facts of life — or dealt with some of them only in a very superficial way. Marx rightly rejected the unhistorical methods of the German metaphysicians, who tried to make the facts fit a pre-conceived theory. He also, just as firmly, rejected the mechanical materialism of the eighteenth century — rejected it on the grounds that though it could explain the existing nature of things, it ignored the whole process of historical development — the universe as organic growth. Most Marxians forget the first thesis on Feuerbach, which reads: 'The chief defect of all hitherto existing materialism — that of Feuerbach included — is that the object, reality, sensuousness, is conceived only in the form of the *object* but not as *human sensuous activity*, *practice*, not subjectively.' Naturally, when it came to interpreting the history of religion, Marx would have treated it as a social product; but that is far from treating it as an illusion. Indeed, the historical evidence must tend altogether in the opposite direction, and compel us to recognize in religion a social necessity. There has never been a civilization without its corresponding religion, and the appearance of rationalism and scepticism is always a symptom of decadence.

Admittedly there is a general fund of reason to which all civilizations contribute their share and which includes an attitude of comparative detachment from the particular religion of one's epoch. But to recognize the historical evolution of a phenomenon like religion does not explain it away. It is far more likely to give it a scientific justification, to reveal it as a necessary 'human sensuous activity', and therefore to throw suspicion on any social philosophy which arbitrarily excludes religion from the organization it proposes for society.

It is already clear, after many years of socialism in Russia, that if you do not provide your society with a new religion, it will gradually revert to the old one. Communism has, of course, its religious aspects, and apart from the gradual readmission of the Orthodox Church,[1] the deification of Lenin (sacred tomb, effigies, creation of a legend — all the elements are there) is a deliberate attempt to create an outlet for religious emotions. Still more deliberate attempts to create the paraphernalia of a new creed were made by the Nazis in Germany, where the necessity for a religion of some kind was never officially denied. In Italy Mussolini was far too wily to do anything but come to terms with the Catholic Church, and a deep and frustrating ambiguity exists in the minds of many Italian communists. Far from scoffing at these irrational aspects of communism and fascism, we should rather criticize these political creeds for the lack of any real sensuous and aesthetic content, for the poverty of their ritual, and above all for a misunderstanding of the function of poetry and imagination in the life of the community.

It is possible that out of the ruins of our capitalist civilization a new religion will emerge, just as Christianity emerged from the ruins of the Roman civilization. Civilizations monotonously repeat

[1] For an account of the relations between the Soviet Government and the Church, see A. Ciliga, *The Russian Enigma* (London, Routledge, 1940), pp. 160–5.

certain patterns of belief in the course of their history, elaborate parallel myths. Socialism, as conceived by its pseudo-historical materialists, is not such a religion, and never will be. And though, from this point of view, it must be conceded that fascism has shown more imagination, it is in itself such a phenomenon of decadence — the first defensive awareness of the fate awaiting the existing social order — that its ideological superstructure is not of much permanent interest. For a religion is never a synthetic creation — you cannot select your legends and saints from the mythical past and combine them with some kind of political or racial policy to make a nice convenient creed. A prophet, like a poet, is born. But even granted a prophet, we are still far from the establishment of a religion. It needed five centuries to build the religion of Christianity on the message of Christ. That message had to be moulded, enlarged, and to a considerable extent distorted until it conformed with what Jung has called the archetypes of the collective unconscious — those complex psychological factors which give cohesion to a society. Religion, in its later stages, may well become the opium of the people; but whilst it is vital it is the only force that can hold a people together — that can supply them with a natural authority to appeal to when their personal interests clash.

I call religion a natural authority, but it has usually been conceived as a supernatural authority. It is natural in relation to the morphology of society; supernatural in relation to the morphology of the physical universe. But in either aspect it is in opposition to the artificial authority of the State. The State only acquires its supreme authority when religion begins to decline, and the great struggle between Church and State, when, as in modern Europe, it ends so decisively in favour of the State, is from the point of view of the organic life of a society, eventually fatal. It is because modern socialism has been unable to perceive this truth and has instead linked itself to the dead hand of the State, that everywhere socialism is meeting its defeat. The natural ally of socialism was the Church, though admittedly in the actual historical circumstances of the nineteenth century it was difficult to see this. The Church was so corrupted, so much a dependency of the ruling classes, that only a few rare spirits could see through appearances to the realities, and conceive socialism in the terms of a new religion, or more simply as a new reformation of Christianity.

Whether, in the actual circumstances of today, it is still possible to find a path from the old religion to a new religion is doubtful. A new religion can arise only on the basis of a new society, and step by step with such a society — perhaps in Russia, perhaps in Spain, perhaps in the United States: it is impossible to say where, because even the germ of such a new society is nowhere evident and its full formation lies deeply buried in the future.

I am not a revivalist — I have no religion to recommend and none to believe in. I merely affirm, on the evidence of the history of civilizations, that a religion is a necessary element in any organic society.[1] And I am so conscious of the slow process of spiritual development that I am in no mood to look for a new religion, and have no hope of finding one. I would only venture one observation. Both in its origins and development, up to its zenith, religion is closely associated with art. Religion and art are, indeed, if not alternative modes of expression, modes intimately associated. Apart from the essentially aesthetic nature of religious ritual; apart, too, from the dependence of religion on art for the visualization of its subjective concepts; there is, besides, an identity of the highest forms of poetic and mystic expression. Poetry, in its intensest and most creative moments, penetrates to the same level of the unconscious as mysticism. Certain writers — and they are among the greatest — Saint Francis, Dante, Saint Teresa, Saint John of the Cross, Blake — rank equally as poets and as mystics. For this reason it may well happen that the origins of a new religion will be found if not in mysticism, then in art rather than in any form of moralistic revivalism.[2]

What has all this to do with anarchism? Merely this: socialism of the Marxist tradition, that is to say, state socialism, has so completely cut itself off from religious sanctions and has been driven to such pitiful subterfuges in its search for substitutes for religion, that by contrast anarchism, which is not without its mystic strain, is a religion itself. It is possible, that is to say, to

[1] For a sociological explanation of this fact see Pierre Mabile, *Egrégores* (Paris, Jean Flory, 1938).

[2] It may not be without significance that the most authentic types of modern art — the paintings of Picasso or the sculpture of Henry Moore — succeed in creating symbols whose nearest parallels are to be found in the magical accessories of primitive religions. Cf. my chapter 'The Created Form' in *The Forms of Things Unknown* (London and New York, 1960); and *Le Mythe de l'éternel retour*, by Mircea Eliade (Paris, Gallimard, 1949).

conceive a new religion developing out of anarchism. During the Spanish Civil War many observers were struck by the religious intensity of the anarchists. In that country of potential renaissance anarchism has inspired, not only heroes but even saints — a new race of men whose lives are devoted, in sensuous imagination *and in practice*, to the creation of a new type of human society.

(iv)

These are the resounding phrases of a visionary, it will be said, and not the practical accents of 'constructive' socialism. But the scepticism of the so-called practical man is destructive of the only force that can bring a socialist community into existence. It was always prophesied, in the pre-war years, that State socialism was a visionary ideal, impossible of realization. Apart from the fact that every industrial country in the world has been moving rapidly towards State socialism during the twentieth century, there is the example of Russia to prove how very possible a central organization of production and distribution is, provided you have visionaries ruthless enough, and in this case inhuman enough, to carry an ideal into practice. I do not believe that this particular kind of social organization can endure for long, simply because, as I have already suggested, it is not organic. But if such an arbitrary (or, if you prefer the word, logical) form of society can be established even for a few years, how much more likely it is that a society which does not contradict the laws of organic growth can be established and will endure. A beginning was being made in Spain, in spite of the Civil War and all the restrictions that a condition of emergency implied. The textile industry of Alcoy, the wood industry of Cuenca, the transport system in Barcelona — these are a few examples of the many anarchist collectives which were functioning efficiently for more than two years.[1] It has been demonstrated beyond any possibility of denial that whatever may be the merits or demerits of the anarcho-syndicalist system, it can and does work. Once it prevails over the whole economic life of the country, it should function better still and provide a standard of living far higher than that realized under any previous form of social organization.

I do not intend to repeat in any detail the syndicalist proposals

[1] See Gaston Leval, *Social Reconstruction in Spain.* Also D. A. de Santillan, *After the Revolution.*

for the organization of production and distribution. The general principle is clear: each industry forms itself into a federation of self-governing collectives; the control of each industry is wholly in the hands of the workers in that industry, and these collectives administer the whole economic life of the country. That there will be something in the nature of a parliament of industry to adjust mutual relations between the various collectives and to decide on general questions of policy goes without saying, but this parliament will be in no sense an administrative or executive body. It will form a kind of industrial diplomatic service, adjusting relations and preserving peace, but possessing no legislative powers and no privileged status. By such means the antagonism of producer and consumer, so characteristic of capitalistic economy, will disappear, and the cadres of a competitive economy will be rendered obsolete by an interflow of mutual aid.

Admittedly there will be all sorts of practical difficulties to overcome, but the system is simplicity itself compared with the monster of centralized State control, which sets such an inhuman distance between the worker and the administrator that there is room for a thousand difficulties to intervene. On the other hand, if the motive for association and mutual aid is the wellbeing of the community, then that end is most effectively assured by an economy decentralized on a regional or local basis. There will be complexities (such as those involved in the exchange of surpluses) but they will be resolved by methods which secure the maximum benefit for the community as a whole. No other method will exist, but this motive will create the necessary enterprise.

The only other practical problem to consider at this stage is what I will call the interpretation of equity rather than the administration of justice. Obviously the great mass of civil and criminal proceedings will simply disappear with the disappearance of the profit motive; such as remain — unnatural acts of acquisitiveness, of anger, and self-indulgence — will to a great extent be dealt with by the collectives, just as the old manor courts dealt with all offences against the peace of the parish. If it is true that certain dangerous tendencies will persist, these must be kept in check. 'Kept in check' is the cliché that first springs to the mind, but it indicates the repressive methods of the old morality. The more fashionable word would be 'sublimated', and by this we mean the devising of harmless outlets for emotional energies which, when repressed, become evil and anti-social. The aggressive instincts, for example, are expended in competitive games of various kinds — the most playful nation is even now the least aggressive.

The whole case for anarchism rests on a general assumption which makes detailed speculations of this kind quite unnecessary. The assumption is that the right kind of society is an organic being — not merely analogous to an organic being, but actually a living structure with appetites and digestions, instincts and passions, intelligence and reason. Just as an individual by a proper balance of these faculties can maintain himself in health, so a community can live naturally and freely, without the disease of crime. Crime is a symptom of social illness — of poverty, inequality, and restriction.[1] Rid the social body of these illnesses and you rid society of crime. Unless you can believe this, not as an ideal or fancy, but as a biological truth, you cannot be an anarchist. But if you do believe it, you must logically come to anarchism. Your only alternative is to be a nihilist and authoritarian — a person who has so little faith in the natural order that he will attempt to make the world conform to some artificial system of his own devising.

(v)

I have said little about the actual organization of an anarchist community, partly because I have nothing to add to what has been said by Kropotkin and by contemporary syndicalists like Dubreuil;[2] partly because it is always a mistake to build *a priori* constitutions. The main thing is to establish your principles — the principles of equity, of individual freedom, of workers' control. The community then aims at the establishment of these principles from the starting-point of local needs and local conditions. That they must be established by revolutionary methods is perhaps inevitable. But in this connection I would like to revive the distinction made by Max Stirner between *revolution* and

---

[1] By this last word I mean the general restriction of emotional maturity due to social conventions and the petty tyrannies of the family. For a scientific demonstration of the social origins of crime, see G. W. Pailthorpe, M.D., *What We Put in Prison* (London, 1932), and the same author's official report on *The Psychology of Delinquency* (H.M. Stationery Office). An earlier treatment of the subject from the anarchist point of view is Edward Carpenter's *Prisons, Police and Punishment*. Cf. also Alex Comfort, *Authority and Delinquency in the Modern State* (London, Routledge & Kegan Paul, 1950).

[2] See Hyacinthe Dubreuil, *A chacun sa chance* (Paris, Grassel, 1935).

insurrection. Revolution 'consists in an overturning of conditions, of the established condition or *status*, the State or society, and is accordingly a *political* or *social* act'. Insurrection 'has for its unavoidable consequence a transformation of circumstances, yet does not start from it but from men's discontent with themselves, is not an armed rising, but a rising of individuals, a getting up, without regard to the arrangements that spring from it'.[1] Stirner carried the distinction farther, but the point I wish to make is that there is all the difference in the world between a movement that aims at an exchange of political institutions, which is the bourgeois socialist (Fabian) notion of a revolution; and a movement that aims at getting rid of these political institutions altogether. An insurrection, therefore, is directed against the State as such, and this aim will determine our tactics. It would obviously be a mistake to create the kind of machinery which, at the successful end of a revolution, would merely be taken over by the leaders of the revolution, who then assume the functions of a government. That is out of the frying-pan into the fire. It is for this reason that the defeat of the Spanish Government, regrettable in that it leaves the power of the State in still more ruthless hands, is to be looked upon with a certain indifference; for in the process of defending its existence the Spanish Government had created, in the form of a standing army and a secret police, all the instruments of oppression, and there was little prospect that these instruments would have been discarded by the particular group of men who would have been in control if the war had ended in a Government victory.

The natural weapon of the working classes is the strike, and if I am told that the strike has been tried and has failed, I must reply that the strike as a strategic force is in its infancy. This supreme power which is in the hands of the working classes has never yet been used with intelligence and with courage. It has been conceived in the narrow terms of class warfare, a war of trade unions against bosses. As the General Strike of 1926 showed with a logic that the strikers themselves had to accept, a third party is involved — the community. It is merely stupid for a group of workers — even for the workers organized as a national group — to invite the making of a distinction between themselves and the community. The real protagonists in this struggle are the com-

---

[1] Cf. Albert Camus, *L'homme révolté* (Paris, 1952); English trans. *The Rebel* (London, Hamish Hamilton, 1953).

munity and the State — the community as an organic and n-clusive body and the State as the representative of a tyrannical minority. The strike, as a weapon, should always be directed against the State — a strategy that has been made easier by the State taking over, in several industries, the functions and practices of the capitalist. The General Strike of the future must be organized as a strike of the community against the State. The result of that strike will not be in doubt. The State is just as vulnerable as a human being, and can be killed by the cutting of a single artery. But the event must be catastrophic. Tyranny, whether of a person or a class, can never be destroyed in any other way. It was the Great Insurgent himself who said: 'Be ye wise as serpents.'

An insurrection is necessary for the simple reason that when it comes to the point, even your man of good will, if he exercises power, will not sacrifice his personal advantages to the general good. In the rapacious type of capitalism existing in Europe and America, such personal advantages are the result of an exercise of low cunning hardly compatible with a sense of justice; or they are based on a callous speculation in finance which neither knows nor cares what human elements are involved in the abstract movement of market prices. For the last fifty years it has been obvious to anyone with an inquiring mind that the capitalist system has reached a stage in its development at which it can only continue under cover of imperial aggression — at which it can only extend its markets behind a barrage of high explosives. But even that realization — the realization that capitalism involves a human sacrifice beyond the lusts of Moloch — even that realization has not persuaded our rulers to humanize the social economy of nations. Nowhere — not even in Russia — have they abandoned the economic values upon which every society since the Middle Ages has vainly tried to base itself. It has only been proved, again and again, that on the question of spiritual values there can be no compromise. Half-measures have failed and now the inevitable catastrophe has overwhelmed us. Whether that catastrophe is the final paroxysm of a doomed system, leaving the world darker and more despairing than ever; or whether it is the prelude to a spontaneous and universal insurrection, will depend on a swift apprehension of the destiny that is upon us. Faith in the fundamental goodness of man; humility in the presence of natural law; reason and mutual aid — these are the qualities that can save us. But they must be unified and vitalized by an insurrectionary passion, a flame in which all virtues are tempered and clarified, and brought to their most effective strength.

The Politics of the Unpolitical[1]

If certain writers feel emancipated enough from all that is human — they would say *intellectual* enough — to continue to fulfil, under any circumstances whatever, the strange functions of purely abstract thought, good luck to them. But those who can only conceive their role as writers to be a means of experiencing more deeply and of establishing more fully a mode of existence which they want to be human, those who only *write* in order to feel themselves *living* integrally — such people no longer have the right to be disinterested. The trend of events, and the evolution of ideas, if they run out their course, will lead straight to an unparalleled deformation of the individual human being. Whoever gazes into the future which is being forged for us, and can there perceive the monstrous and denatured brother whom one will necessarily resemble, cannot react except by a revolt into extreme egoism. It is this egoism which must now be rehabilitated. Today the problem of the person effaces all others. The intelligence is placed in such circumstances that for it disinterestedness and resignation come to the same thing.

THEIRRY MAULNIER, *La Crise est dans l'homme* (Paris, 1932)

The politics of the unpolitical — these are the politics of those who desire to be pure in heart: the politics of men without personal ambition; of those who have not desired wealth or an unequal share of worldly possessions; of those who have always striven, whatever their race or condition, for human values and not for national or sectional interests.

For our Western world, Christ is the supreme example of this unselfish devotion to the good of humanity, and the Sermon on the Mount is the source of all the politics of the unpolitical. But others who came before Christ and who may have influenced him elaborated their political ideals in pureness of heart — Lao-Tzu and Zeno, for example; and among Christ's direct disciples we must include several philosophers and prophets nearer to our time, whose message is still insistent and directly applicable to our present condition — Ruskin and Kropotkin, Morris and Tolstoy, Gandhi and Eric Gill. These modern representatives of what we might well call an ancient tradition form a closely inter-related body of thought: Gandhi, for example, declared his debt to Ruskin and Tolstoy; Gill was a disciple of Morris, who was himself a disciple of Ruskin; Kropotkin was closely associated

[1] *Transformation*. Personalist anthology edited by Stefan Schimanski and Henry Treece, (London, 1943).

with Morris. Ruskin, in this succession, has a certain pre-eminence and originality: the vitality and transforming power[1] of his writings seem to come straight from his deep study of the Bible and from his prolonged meditation on the words of Christ; though he had in himself that rare power which Gandhi recognized as the specifically poetic power — his power 'to call forth the good latent in the human breast'. We are still far from estimating the full extent of this great man's influence, but we can describe it as ethical and aesthetic rather than as religious or political. Ruskin's eloquence did not bring into being either a new sect or a new party; his power is emotive and not calculative, and in this as in other respects he is nearly related to Rousseau, having for our own revolutionary period almost exactly the same significance as Rousseau had for the French Revolutionary period. We may still come to regard *Unto this Last* as the *Contrat Social* of a new society — as the Manifesto of those communists who renounce political action in their efforts to establish a new society.

Of the six names mentioned, Morris was the only one who compromised on this political issue, but he never, to the end of his life, reconciled himself to the political methods advocated by his friends. His lecture on 'The Policy of Abstention' (1887) is the best statement of the case against parliamentary action ever made in English, and it is a pity that it is so entirely forgotten by socialists today, and that it is only available in a limited and expensive publication.[2] Towards the end of his life Gandhi also, it might be said, made a tactical compromise of some kind with the politically minded leaders of the Congress Party. He worked in close association with them, but always in a relationship which he himself has described as 'experimental'. For the whole of Gandhi's life and teaching were directed against parliamentary action: the doctrine of *ahimsa*, or non-violence, rejected the violence of majority government no less decisively than the violence of military oppression. In the end his methods met with complete success.

It is characteristic of these six teachers that although they would be included among the most revolutionary figures of the past hundred years, we do not spontaneously associate the word

---

[1] 'The one book that brought about an instantaneous and practical transformation in my life was *Unto this Last*.' (*Mahatma Gandhi: His Own Story* (London, 1930), p. 163.)

[2] May Morris, *William Morris: Artist, Writer, Socialist* (2 vols., Oxford, Basil Blackwell, 1936), vol. ii, pp. 434–53.

'democracy' with any of them. Democracy is a very ambiguous word, and its meanings vary from a sentimental sympathy for the poor and oppressed such as we get in Christian Socialism, to a ruthless dogma of proletarian dictatorship such as we have seen established in Russia. Our Six were all democrats in the former sense; none of them was a democrat in the latter sense. But it is an important distinction, and if in the name of democracy we are more and more inevitably compelled to commit ourselves to the political machinery of the state — to the nationalization of industry, to the bureaucratic control of all spheres of life and to the doctrine of the infallibility of the People (divinely invested in a unique Party) — then it is time to renounce the democratic label and seek a less equivocal name. My use of the word 'democracy' is always subject to this consideration.

A complete renunciation of the word is not easy: indeed, it has been deliberately made difficult for us, not only by the common usage of many ardent seekers after the truth, but also by the deliberate propaganda of the enemies of liberty. A common form of this Machiavellian sophistry consists in presenting your opponent with an apparently inescapable alternative — an 'either/or' which you accept as covering all the known facts. In our own time, in the sphere of world politics, this either/or is *either* democracy *or* fascism. Such an alternative seems to leave communism out of account, but not in reality. If you question people about the relation of communism to democracy, the communists among them will tell you that communism is the extreme form of democracy, and the anti-communists will say that communism as it exists in Russia is merely another form of totalitarianism.

Both these views are right. Communism is an extreme form of democracy, and it is totalitarian: but equally the totalitarian state in the form of fascism is an extreme form of democracy. All forms of socialism, whether state socialism of the Russian kind, or national socialism of the German kind, or democratic socialism of the British kind, are professedly democratic: that is to say, they all obtain popular assent by the manipulation of mass psychology. All are actually majority governments.

The weaknesses of democracy have been exposed by every political philosopher since Plato and Aristotle. Even Rousseau, the so-called Father of Democracy, rejected it as a system practicable for any society larger than a city state. The philosophers, being men of intelligence, have never been able to suggest anything better than a dictatorship of the intelligentsia; but knowing how unlikely it is that such a dictatorship would be long tolerated by the ignorant masses, they have tried to disguise the inevitability of some alternative form of dictatorship under a picturesque formula. Historically the most effective of these is constitutional monarchy. It has always been recognized that a king might easily degenerate into a tyrant, but his natural life is limited and can at a pinch be artificially shortened; whereas the reign of an aristocracy, which is the next best possibility, has no mensurable limit: it can only be brought to an end by a civil war with all its miseries.

The plain fact about democracy is that it is a physical impossibility. In an aggregation of millions of individuals such as we always have in modern society, we may get government *of* the people and even government *for* the people, but never for a moment government *by* the people. But that is the essential test, for if a people does not govern itself, it is governed by somebody else; *ipso facto* it is no longer a democracy. This is not merely a logical quibble: democracy never has in fact existed in modern times. In our own country, for example, the monarchical system was overthrown by an oligarchy, and since the 'Great' Revolution of 1688 we have been governed by a succession of oligarchies, which might be Whig or might be Tory, might represent the landed interests or the moneyed interests, but never for a moment represented the people as a whole. In our own time a new oligarchy, the oligarchy of the trade unions, as exclusive a caste as ever aspired to power, has competed, luckily in vain, for the control of the state. It is now openly merging itself with the ascendant oligarchy of monopoly capitalism, to form what James Burnham has called 'the managerial class'.

All this is such an obvious interpretation of the historical facts that no one but a fool can deceive himself in the belief that democracy has ever been, or is ever likely to be, a reality in a modern industrial community. A constitutional monarchy as a cloak for competing sectional interests, as a symbol of unity in a society which would otherwise distintegrate from ruthless class warfare — that is the definition of the British constitution. The French Republic, the United States of America, the German and Italian Republics are all constitutions of the same character: they only differ in nomenclature and the trimming on their uniforms.

Nevertheless this must be said (if only in justification of the lip service which so many of us have paid to democracy at various times): the political doctrine known as democracy has implied an important principle which, if it were not systematically misinterpreted and misunderstood, would still justify us in using the word. This is the *principle of equality* — an ethical doctrine, even a religious dogma. The equality of man implies many things, but never its literal meaning. No one believes that all men are equal in capacity or talent: they are in fact outrageously diverse. But nevertheless, in Christian phraseology, they are all equal in the sight of God; and to affirm our common humanity is the first article of freedom. Whatever government we establish, whatever way of life we follow, all our faith is built on error unless we respect the rights of the person — that is to say, his right to be a person, a unique entity, 'human left, from human free'.

This is the fundamental doctrine of a Christian community and of all other types of essential communism. It is even fundamental to the communism of Marx and Engels. But the equality acknowledged by democracy has in practice been something very different. God has been eliminated from the formula and we are left with a mere equalization or levelling of man with man. The spiritual measure has been discarded, and man is left to dangle in material scales; and for centuries the counter-weight has been a piece of silver. The only way in which democracy has been able to assess equality is in terms of money, and it is the inability of the trade union movement, especially in Great Britain and Germany, to break away from this cash valuation of humanity which has, more than any other single factor, made the democratic working-class movement a futile diversion of revolutionary effort.[1]

By what values a man shall be judged absolutely we will not discuss here, but socially, as a man among his fellow-men, he should be judged by his creative ability, by his power to add to the common stock of goods. The value of a man is the value of the art he practises — whether it is the art of healing or the art of making music, the art of road-mending or the art of cooking.

---

[1] Chiefly because it has prevented the workers from concentrating on the enhancement of their human dignity by the acquisition of responsibility for the direction and control of industry. But also because, as Franz Borkenau has shown so effectively, it has prevented the development of international solidarity among the workers, for the wage-rate is directly dependent on the international market, not only of labour, but of commodities. For this reason the workers have been forced to realize that their interests are bound up, not only with the interests of their employers, but also with the competitive expansion of the national economy. Cf. F. Borkenau, *Socialism, National or International* (Routledge, 1942).

We might place first of all the art of making children, because on that the continuance of the human race depends. Procreation is perhaps the only art which is literally creative: the rest of the arts are merely inventive.

For this and for reasons more strictly sociological, our social philosophy must begin with the family. From whatever realistic angle we approach the problems of human life, the family is seen as the integral unit, without which there is no social organization, no social progress, no social order or human happiness. But we must insist that this is a sociological problem, and we must dissociate ourselves from those who think it can be solved by moral persuasion. Families are encouraged and sustained by security of life and property, decent housing, and an environment in which nurture and education can be natural and serene. Morality and religion may give their sanction to the social unit thus established: it is the fascist way of thinking to imagine that such sanctions are a substitute for economic action.

The next essential group is the guild — the association of men and women according to their calling or practical function. (I obstinately retain the word 'guild', in spite of its medieval and sentimental associations, because it is more human, and euphonious, than such expressions as 'collective', 'co-operative', 'soviet', etc.) The guild is a vertical and not a horizontal organization: it includes all persons associated together in the production of a particular commodity. The agricultural guild, for example, would include the drivers and mechanics who run the tractors: the engineers' guild would include the men who make the tractors. But the vertical organization will be divided into regional and district units, and the main business of the guilds will always take place in the district units; decisions will arise out of personal contacts and not from the abstract and legalistic conclaves of a central bureau.

Decentralization is thus also of the essence of this alternative to democracy. 'Real politics are local politics', and power and authority should be devolved and segmented to the utmost limit of practicability. Only in such a way can the person — every person in society — be assured of an adequate sense of responsibility and human dignity. These qualities for the average person only emerge in his actual sphere of work and in his regional environment.

The trend to centralization is a disease of democracy, and not, as is so often assumed, of the machine. It arises inevitably from the concentration of power in parliament, from the separation made between responsibility and creative activity, from the massing of production for greater profits and higher wages. The evolution of democracy is parallel to the growth of centralization, and centralization is in no sense an inevitable process. Modern warfare has revealed its extraordinary inefficiency. The guerillas of Jugoslavia showed more initiative than the bureaucrats of London or Berlin. The centralization of control in a democratic state is clumsy, inhuman and inert. Incapable of thought, originality or enterprise, it can only act under the dictatorship of a Hitler or a Churchill — even the shrill voices of an exasperated Press have no effect on it.

The health and happiness of society depend on the labour and science of its members; but neither health nor happiness is possible unless that work and science are directed and controlled by the workers themselves. A guild is by definition autonomous and self-governing. Every man who is a master of his craft acquires thereby the right to a voice in the direction of his workshop. He also acquires security of tenure and of income. Indeed, his income and his tenure should depend on his qualifications rather than on the tally of his labours. He should begin to receive an income from the moment he has chosen a calling and been admitted as an apprentice of a trade or profession — which will be long before he has left school. His income will rise with his qualifications, and will depend entirely on his qualifications. Any rational society will naturally make use of the services of a qualified worker, because it thereby increases the general well-being. If it fails to do so, that society is restricting production; and if such restriction is in the general interest, then society should pay the worker for his qualifications until they can be used, or otherwise pay the worker to train and acquire more immediately useful qualifications. The talents and acquired skill of a person are his property: his contribution to the common wealth. Society should be organized to secure the maximum utilization of its inherent wealth, and the productive organizations themselves will then decide how this common wealth is best increased — by machinery or handicraft, by large factories or small workshops, in towns or villages. The human values involved, and not an abstract and numerical profit, will be the criterion.

Education, in such a society, is initiation. It is the revelation of innate capacities, the training of these capacities in socially useful activities, the disciplining of these activities to aesthetic and moral ends.

Such a natural organization of society leaves little activity to the state as such. The state remains merely as the arbiter, to decide in the interests of the whole the conflicts which emerge in the parts. Such a function is already exercised by an independent judiciary, which might well extend its functions to cover the rights of the citizen as consumer. An Economic Council, constituted by much the same means as the Bench, would be necessary to safeguard society as a whole against a policy of restrictionism in any particular guild, to direct the general volume of production and to maintain a balanced output among its tributary guilds. It is difficult to see the necessity for any other central authority.

All this may seem to amount to a programme far more definite and dogmatic than the title of my essay promised, but to be unpolitical does not mean to be without politics: every attitude that is more than egoistic is to that extent social, and a social attitude is a political attitude. But it is one thing to have politics, and another thing to pursue them. It is one thing to have a faith, and another thing to trade on the credulity of the faithful. It is not the substance of politics we should object to, but the methods of the politician. We should refuse to invest our private interests in a public policy, for we know that what cannot be won by a change of heart, which is also a revolution of reason, is only won by cheats and impostors.

Let me summarize the essential features of a natural society:

    I. The liberty of the person.
    II. The integrity of the family.
    III. The reward of qualifications.
    IV. The self-government of the guilds.
    V. The abolition of parliament and centralized government.
    VI. The institution of arbitrament.
    VII. The delegation of authority.
    VIII. The humanization of industry.

The social order thus envisaged is international because it is essentially pacific: it is pacific because it is essentially international. It aims at the production of world-wide plenty, at the humanization of work, and at the eradication of all economic conflicts. It may be, as some philosophers hold, that an aggressive instinct is innate in man, and that no organization of society can guard against its expression. In that case the world can only be made tolerable in the degree that this instinct can be controlled by reason. Reason has no chance if men are starving, or even if they have undue cause for envy. But granted an economy that is no longer competitive, in which the highest yield of production is wisely and evenly distributed among all mankind, then reason will have a chance. Instincts are not immutable: they can be transformed, sublimated, diverted into creative channels. Energy itself is not evil: it only becomes evil by being applied to evil ends.

Towards a Duplex Civilization[1]

On several occasions when I have been concerned with the problem of education, I have suggested that unless you have some system of education, or mode of upbringing, which quite naturally and inevitably instils into the general body of the people *skill* in the making of things and *taste* in the consumption of things, all other efforts to give *style* to the products of the machine will be in vain. On the present occasion I would like to be a little more specific — to discuss these problems in relation to the existing structure of our industrial society and to speculate on what changes in that structure must take place before our ideals can be realized.

I have ridiculed the notion that you can take a pupil who has had a miscellaneous education up to the age of fourteen or sixteen, and then begin to turn him into an artist, or, more specifically, an architect or industrial designer, by means of a more or less extensive course of vocational training. The miscellaneous — multilateral is the more obscure word used by our educationists — the miscellaneous education to which that pupil has been subjected before he reaches the age of twelve or fourteen most likely will have destroyed that basic sensibility without which a vocational training in design is a mere waste of time. The education of an artist begins at birth: it is the education, or rather *preservation*, of virgin sensibilities, and these sensibilities are so important in all walks of life (not least in the moral walks) that a few exceptionally perceptive philosophers such as Plato, Schiller and Bernard Shaw have maintained that aesthetic education is the only kind of education that really matters. As Shaw puts it with his usual force: 'The education that sticks after school is aesthetic education. Such terms as scientific education and secular education are thoughtless nonsense: science transcends all pigeon-holes; and

---

[1] Originally delivered as a lecture at Yale University, 1946. From *The Grass Roots of Art* (New York, 1946; London, 1947).

secular education means teaching with a cane instead of a creed. The classification proper for statesmen is into aesthetic and technical education.'[1]

Granted a basic aesthetic education, a pupil can be made anything of, a good engineer or a good accountant, as well as a good designer. If the stock is good, any variety of vocation can be grafted on to it, by an operation that is painless and unobserved. A sensible system of education would not impose vocational training at any arbitrary age: vocation would grow out of natural aptitude, and our object should be to devise a system which allows such aptitude to emerge as naturally as a stem from the growing plant.

Existing educational systems are not aesthetic, and only a minority who have managed by luck or illness to escape their deadening influences show any natural desire to become artists or designers. This minority can at present pursue vocational courses, but few of these have any relevance to the immediate needs of industry. They can, it is true, become architects, and architects have their place in industry. In the existing situation industrial designers have been drawn largely from the ranks of trained architects, but no one would maintain that an architect's training is wholly adequate for the industrial designer. Apart from architecture, the potential industrial designer can only be trained as an artist — which, if the word conveyed its right meaning, would be perfect. But in fact this means that a pupil can attend a school or college of art which trains him to become a painter or sculptor, or, alternatively, a 'commercial' artist, which term might include poster-artist, fashion-designer, book-illustrator or artist-potter. Never, so far as my experience goes, could the product of these schools immediately take his place in industry as the designer of a motor-car, a machine-tool, or even a domestic utensil.

There are, of course, the technical colleges and institutes, and some of these run, like a trailer, a course in art. The degree to which this course is integrated with technical education may vary a little from one institution to another, but the link is never vital. Art is an 'extra', and it often implies no more than a superficial acquaintance with the historical conventions of 'ornament' and 'decoration'.

Aesthetic education, design centres, colleges of art, post-graduate courses in industrial design — these no doubt represent efforts

[1] *Everybody's Political What's What* (London, 1944).

which might eventually seal off oases of order in the productive chaos, but I do not see any certain hope of salvation unless all these measures to promote good design are spontaneous expressions of a social conscience. That is a somewhat metaphysical way of stating the evident truth that a style, in the historical sense, can only arise out of, and be a reflection of, a specific social and industrial structure. Or more simply still, a society gets the style it deserves. The predatory capitalism of the nineteenth century got the style it deserved — the worst in the history of taste. There is no escape from this interdependence of art and society, of style and custom. You can have great artists, exceptional individuals, who rise superior to their circumstances; but the daily bread of things made and used is sweet if the daily life is sweet, sour if it is sour, and just stinking rotten if the basis of society is injustice and misery.

I do not pretend to know what kind of industrial structure will eventually emerge from the evident breakdown of laissez-faire capitalism, but it would seem that the only immediate choice is between some form of monopoly capitalism and some form of state socialism: most of the economists one reads or talks to seem to expect a combination of both systems, the essential feature being an 'economics of control'. Such economists do not ask for the direct supervision of industry; they would be content to operate through the central instruments of credit issue, taxation, export licences, etc.

These alternative systems of industrial organization are nowhere fully established: we are dealing with tendencies. This is true even in a country like the U.S.S.R., where the economic and industrial structure of society has undergone vast changes since the Revolution of 1917, and is still changing.

We should first note that these tendencies, in all advanced industrial countries, are both economic and technical. I shall deal with these distinct aspects separately, and first with the economic tendencies.

The general economic character of the industrial system of the past 150 years may be described as competitive, and is openly defended as such by economists like Robbins, Hayek and Röpke. Its structure was determined by the profit motive, and all the subsidiary activities of distribution and sale depended on whether articles manufactured could be 'made to pay'. We may have various opinions about the fairness and efficiency of such a system, but no one is likely to question this general description of its mode of operation.

Towards a Duplex Civilization

About the general economic character of the industrial system towards which we are now moving, there may be some legitimate difference of opinion, but I think we can agree that all the various alternatives rely on some form of centralized control. This is probably an inherent tendency of the democratic system itself, in so far as democracy is identified with majority rule. But the control may be either industrial or governmental. If it is to be industrial, the whole field of production will gradually crystallize into a few powerful cartels or combinations, international in scope, and to some degree competitive with one another — the heavy metals compete with the light alloys, synthetic rubber with plantation rubber and the shipping combines, shipping with airways, coffee with tea, and so on. If the centralized control is governmental, it tends to be nationalistic and totalitarian — it comes into direct conflict with the internationally organized cartels and in time of war takes action against them. This totalitarian control of industry is, from the economic point of view, essentially practical — it may be combined with either a fascist or a socialist ideology. The monopolist control is also essentially practical and does not aspire to an ideology. It knows that an ideology can easily be created once its power is secure.

We may not like either of these systems — we may long to be back to the good old days of private enterprise and laissez-faire competition; or we may think, as I do, that there is still another system to be evolved, based on co-operation and mutual aid. But both these attitudes are idealistic, and I think that we are forced to admit that the only practical choice, in the immediate future, is between the totalitarian and the monopolistic organization of industry.

This may seem a gloomy prognostication to those who believe in democratic control, but how precisely can such control operate if it is to operate from a centre? We may enact anti-trust laws, as has been done in the United States, but such laws are operative within a sovereignty that is limited in territorial extent. The trusts will register their offices in Luxembourg or Timbuctoo, and operate through anonymous holding companies. We cannot control an international organization by piecemeal national legislation. But even if we suppose that we can — if we suppose that by sanctions and other forceful measures we can compel all nations to take action against the cartels — what do we put in their places? The most rigid state control. And what does this control amount to in terms of personnel? An exclusive civil service, trained in new technical colleges and universities. Our wartime experience has shown the impracticability of that solution. We are compelled sooner or later to import into our civil service that same managerial class, expert in the administration of big business, which would otherwise run the cartels.

The more we concentrate, the more completely we deliver ourselves into the hands of the managers, or, as we now tend to call them, the controllers. This group, whether working for a cartel or for the State, will give us the goods: they will promise, and will achieve, a higher standard of living for the worker. In return all they will ask of the worker is that he should surrender his freedom — his freedom of movement, so that industries can be scientifically located; his freedom of association, so that labour can be docile and flexible; his freedom of opinion, so that the worker can concentrate on the job in hand. And I do not doubt that many workers will be glad to surrender these privileges which never filled their bellies, for a future of high wages, short hours, cheap amusements and every man a car.

Let us now glance at the technical tendencies of our time. There is little doubt about their dominant nature. The Industrial Revolution, such as we have known it in the past, was essentially mechanical. From the invention of the steam-engine to the electric dynamo and the internal combustion engine, it was a revolution exploiting power, and took the form of a progressive development of more and better machines. For that reason we call this period of development the Machine Age. Combined with the economics (and the ethics) of competitive enterprise, the machine had little thought for its material. Exploitation was its motive, and the natural resources of the earth — coal, metal, stone, wood, organic fibres, etc. — seemed sufficient unto the day.

But all the time, parallel to this physical revolution, a chemical revolution was taking place; and, though it had many important applications to industry, it was not until comparatively recent times that chemistry began to take a lead and even to threaten the whole structure of the mechanical industries. Power is, of course, still an essential, but the direction in which this power is to be applied may be completely switched over — switched from the exploitation of natural resources to the elaboration of synthetic materials. Not all these new materials are, strictly speaking, synthetic, but all are, on almost every score, infinitely preferable to the old materials. Plastics can replace wood, glass, rubber, and leather; aluminium and magnesium alloys can replace iron, steel, tin, zinc, etc.; rayon, nylon, and such synthetic fibres can replace cotton, jute, wool, etc., and even eliminate the process of weaving. Hundreds of existing crafts are threatened with extinction. The chemical phase of the industrial revolution is going to be more violent and far-reaching than the mechanical phase.

We may have all sorts of political and moral objections to these economic and technical tendencies, but I want to confine our attention to their likely effect on design. It is an effect which is already partly apparent, but the final outcome is anything but obvious.

As far as the economic tendencies are concerned, we may be fairly certain that design will not fare worse than it has done under laissez-faire capitalism. The effect of the profit motive was always detrimental to design. Art was the first luxury to be eliminated in cut-throat competition, and the number of people who were willing to pay more for a well-designed article was always, from the market point of view, inconsiderable. It is not a point that need be argued — we have only to look at the dreary products of the system. All attempts to improve it — the Prince Consort with his museums and exhibitions, William Morris with his craftsmen and workshops — were movements against the predominant economic motive and were doomed to failure.

There have been, perhaps, some stirrings of remorse in recent years. Some manufacturers did begin to realize that, other things being equal, design would pay. The efforts of a century of propaganda were beginning to have some effects on the buying public, which was becoming design-conscious. But the lead really came, not from the typical capitalists of the past, but from the managers of the first public corporations and industrial combinations. When competition is cut out, when profit is no longer the dominant motive in an industrial organization, when, in short, public service is the guiding motive, then good design becomes a decisive factor — simply because it brings prestige to the managerial class.

Logically, the same considerations ought to apply to the totalitarian control exercised by the State, but the evidence so far is not unequivocal. In the State where totalitarian control has been most absolute for the longest period — in Russia — there is little sign of grace. Aesthetic factors were left out of the Five Year Plans. It would not have cost anything to put them in — but they were left out.

The evidence from pre-war Germany and Italy was more favourable to the totalitarian system. Both regimes were design-conscious, but both illustrated the ambiguity of such a situation. The design did not arise out of the industrial system, but was imposed on it and, if not political, was merely academic. In Germany, after 1933, there was a deliberate return to the heavy, solid style of the Bismarck era, tempered with some influence of that Graeco-Roman classicism which dictators usually favour. In Italy there was more originality and, indeed, some attempt to form a modern style. It was mostly confined to public works, monumental art of various sorts, and did not penetrate very deeply into the industrial system. In both Germany and Italy the change, such as it was, was forced — it never became a natural function of industry.

We come then to that other form of central control which is exercised by industrial cartels, usually of international scope. Here the evidence is more difficult to collect. As a matter of fact, these international combines have so far in the main been confined to the manufacture of primary materials — metals and chemicals — and they have not attempted to control the making-up of these materials into articles for the retail market. There is perhaps some exception in the electrical industry. Generally, however, a cartel like the Imperial Chemical Industries, or Du Pont and its subsidiaries, has been content to supply the raw material of, say, plastics and leave it to small manufacturers to make what use they liked of such raw material. The vulgarity of most plastic articles is explained by this fact. No research has gone into the design of plastic objects — certainly no research comparable to the chemical research which produced the actual substances.

There are signs, however, that this position is changing. The wartime concentration of industry was one aspect of the change. The desire of industrial combinations to extend their tentacles vertically as well as horizontally is another explanation. When the utilization of their raw materials becomes the concern of the cartels, I believe that there is every likelihood that we shall see an immense improvement in design. Design will become one of the functions of management, and it will be governed by the same ideals of efficiency which prevail in the scientific and administrative departments of the cartels.

Towards a Duplex Civilization

In political economy we associate cartels and trade combinations of all kinds with a policy of restrictionism, and it may be that this tendency will have to be brought under State control, thus destroying whatever virtues the system possesses. But cartels are not the only restrictionist organizations in our industrial system. Trade unions, with their policies directed against the dilution of labour, are potentially and even actually a far greater obstacle to the improvement of design. One has only to read of the opposition which a great and original architect like Frank Lloyd Wright received from the labour unions in America to realize the practical veto which they exercise on new materials and processes. Anything that disturbs the traditional hierarchy of the labour market has been and will be bitterly opposed by the trade unions. There will be a big fight on the issue of pre-fabrication, and every new process which brings to an end an old craft, every new material which makes an old industry obsolete, will be opposed as bitterly and as unavailingly as the workers of 150 years ago opposed the first machines.

I do not pretend to trace a clear line through the obscure jungle of industrial change which lies ahead. I see no future which I can anticipate with any personal pleasure — the managerial revolution, whether in its monopolist or totalitarian form, seems to me to offer but different names for an essential serfdom, in which there will be little liberty, no equality, and only the fraternity of the barrack-room. But I feel fairly sure that that barrack-room will have more amenities under monopoly capitalism than in the totalitarian State. Monopoly capitalism still preserves a competitive spirit, if it is only the competitive spirit of rival industries. The fight between gas and electricity, between aluminium and steel, between plastics and a hundred materials, is a fight in which cost will be reduced to an absolute minimum and quality will tell as it never has told in the fight between private enterprises and national interests. The fight between industries is more promising for the consumer than the fight *within industries*. The very totalitarianism of the collective State, on the other hand, abolishes all competitive spirit — it even tends, by pursuing a policy of autarky, to eliminate international struggles. The English automobile, for example, so long as it had to fear the competition of the American car, was spurred on to some progressive sense of design. Abolish this competition, unify production under State management, and what motive remains for progress?

The State car would be a utility car, economical to run, possibly cheap to buy, but as dull as a blue book or a postage stamp, or any other typical product of existing State industries.

When I say that a society gets the style it deserves, the implication is that we lack a great style in the arts today because we have not yet evolved a form of society from which a style can spontaneously emerge. This is another way of saying that as a people we lack *taste*, and once we have stated the truth in that brutal way, we have put the blame where it properly belongs — on ourselves, on our present social structure.

In discussing the problems of industrial art, and indeed the problems of art in general, we have tended in recent years to adopt an attitude which is too objective. We have thought in terms of the *thing*, the work of art or piece of craftsmanship, and too little in terms of the *person*. It is true that we have said quite enough about the person of the artist, even enough about the psychology of the creative process which determines the nature of the work of art. But art is meant for communication, for consumption; and what we have neglected is the psychology of the consumer, the person for whose enjoyment or use the work of art is intended. What we have neglected, in short, is the whole phenomenon of *taste*, and we have even become a little shy of using the very word.

An inquiry into the etymology of the word itself would carry us into some interesting by-ways of history, but it is only essential for our present purposes to note that originally taste meant something very definitely physical or sensational: the actual process of testing by touch (the word *tact* is related to it), and, in the sense still normal, the act of testing the flavour of food by means of the tongue. It was with that physical analogy in mind that the use of the word was gradually extended to describe the reception and appreciation of works of art.

When in the eighteenth century philosophers began to turn their attention to the sensory experience involved in the appreciation of works of art, they used this word taste. It plays a great part in the philosophy of Kant, for example, who defined it as 'the faculty of judging (or estimating) an object or the representation of an object by an entirely disinterested satisfaction or dissatisfaction'. Such a definition does not carry us very far, but it was the disinterestedness of aesthetic judgements which attracted the attention of these philosophers. Back in the seventeenth century Leibniz had pointed out that whilst intellectual ideas were judged by their clarity, and knowledge depended on the distinctness to which ideas were reduced by philosophy, another class of ideas did nevertheless exist which could not be reduced to clarity, which were essentially confused and only accessible to the senses, and only to be estimated by that faculty which we agree to call intuition. An artist, Leibniz pointed out, could not always give a reason for what is right and what is wrong in a work of art: if pressed, he replies that the work he dislikes lacks a *je ne sais quoi*.

I do not think that the innate nature of taste has ever been challenged except by the behaviourist school of psychology, which challenges everything that cannot be reduced to ounces or grammes. In general, taste has always been and still is recognized as personal and fundamentally irrational. What an individual *likes* or *prefers* is that individual's taste: what the aggregate, or perhaps the average of individuals in any age or civilization likes or prefers, is the taste of that age or civilization.

The irrational basis of taste is recognized in the old adage: *de gustibus non est disputandum*. It has been universally recognized that taste relates to the sensuous and physical constitution of the individual, and that therefore it is not possible to argue with him about it — you accept it as part of his disposition, as something that can no more be altered than the colour of his eyes or the shape of his head. In other words, it is assumed that taste is an innate and not an acquired characteristic.

This is, of course, a popular fallacy. It is true that we are born with innate physical peculiarities, and these determine the basic nature of the organs through which we receive sensuous experience. It may be true that the sensuous reactions of the newborn infant have an instinctive rightness about them and remain instinctively right so long as the child is adapting itself in a purely physical sense to its environment: the child, that is to say, has the same kind of instinctive grace as the kitten or the foal. But from the moment of birth and during the whole course of its upbringing, the human child is subjected to innumerable influences which distort its natural development — the influences of a man-made and artificial environment, and the more profound influences of the complex emotional relationships evolved by civilization. To take an elementary example: an individual's colour preferences are not always, or even generally, based on direct sensational reactions. Certain colours have acquired associational values, and one individual may like blue because it is the colour of his mother's eyes, and another may hate it because it was the colour his baby brother used to be dressed in, or because he unconsciously associates it with the sea and seasickness.

These associational factors have been studied in great detail by psychologists like Bullough and Myers, and more recently by the psychoanalysts. We need not pursue this aspect of the matter here, though we should remember that what some people mean by taste is precisely such an accumulation of whimsies or predilections. 'In decoration as in clothes,' we are told in an issue of the magazine *Vogue* (September 1945), 'taste is opinion, never standard, but a conscious development that gives one the courage of one's convictions'; and to illustrate what is meant by this vague but dogmatic statement, we are told that 'Princess Gourielli's flat in New York is rather like a collector's heaven. Everywhere "irreconcilables" of Period meet in fabulous amity. . . . Princess Gourielli (who is Madame Helena Rubenstein) is a great and catholic collector with a splendid barbaric sense of colour. She has filled her London and Paris houses and New York apartment with objects that amuse or interest her, resulting in a fine *tour-de-force* mixture of modern colour and period pieces.' The illustrations opposite this statement show what is described as an 'eclectic mélange' of 'Victorian chairs; chartreuse rug; on the pickled-oak walls a Rouault in needlepoint, three African sculptured pieces and two Picassos . . . the Spanish Colonial bookcase was a find in Mexico; afterwards lined with mirror to reflect a Bristol glass collection'.

This might be described as an extreme case of eclecticism, but the more timid and less barbaric taste which indulges in Queen Anne silver and Chippendale or Shaker furniture is not essentially different: it merely substitutes, for the 'irreconcilables' which it needs a certain courage to display, the 'perfect match' which is dictated by historical knowledge or a dealer's certificate. I have no wish to decry such acquired taste: it has created some very pleasant oases in the desert of our ugliness. But it can never transform that desert. It is a dilettante and individualistic affair, and has no particular relevance to our present inquiry. What we have been considering is *generalized* taste, taste which is characteristic of a people or a period, of a class or a civilization. This is an aesthetic and sociological problem of some importance.

Towards a Duplex Civilization

There are at least three ways in which taste becomes generalized:

(1) by social pressures,
(2) by economic processes,
(3) by material or technical discoveries.

We need not pay much attention to the third way. Obviously if a new material, such as plastic, is invented, or a new method of construction, such as ferro-concrete, is evolved, or a new method of production, such as machine production, is introduced, then the material limits are expanded: taste has more (or perhaps less) freedom of choice, more or less scope for indulgence. But it is doubtful if these material factors affect the quality of taste: they merely feed the taste which has already been formed by social and economic factors.

An orthodox Marxian would no doubt argue that the social pressures which influence taste are merely a reflection of the underlying economic processes. In an obvious sense this is true enough; but once the economic differentiations have been set up, then the way in which taste develops within each economic group is determined by factors that are not essentially economic.

An obvious distinction exists between the taste of the rich and the taste of the poor, but it is not a distinction that follows predictable or consistent lines. Simplicity, for example, which may be an economic necessity for the poor, may become the last stage of sophistication for the rich; and the poor, by a natural process of compensation, will have a love of ostentation, a taste which is the meretricious imitation of the rich man's taste. But nevertheless, certain distinct class standards do develop within a class society.

But then another complicating factor comes into play, one which shows the superficiality of any too simple economic parallelism. This is the force of *tradition*. If the rich man could acquire his taste as simply as he acquires his riches, there would be no difference between, say, the taste of a successful manufacturer of pills and that of an aristocratic landowner. But the successful *parvenu* (admittedly there are a few exceptions) is probably a man who could only have gained his riches by virtue of his aesthetic insensibility. He is rich, but vulgar; and the one thing he cannot buy with his money is an instinctive feeling for beauty.

In his dilemma he is helped to some extent by *fashion*. He finds that 'the best people' furnish their houses with Chippendale furni-

347

ture, seventeenth-century Dutch pictures, Persian rugs; he may even perceive that a minority among the best people collect less obvious things, 'Empire' furniture, impressionist paintings, or Chinese porcelain. He can be selective in his imitation; moreover, he can even employ an 'expert' to buy these things for him, and that is perhaps his safest course. But within his heart he must from time to time realize that these things are not *his* taste, but only, as it were, a passport to social prestige. He may be honest enough to preserve in some corner of his mansion a 'den' or billiard-room where he is not embarrassed by *objets d'art* and can 'feel comfortable' — or perhaps 'cosy' is the word.

The traditional taste which some people possess by inheritance and others acquire during the course of their upbringing, is a complex cultural product, maintained by the inherent social stability of a class, and perpetuated by the educational system instituted by that class. The only coherent tradition today, which still survives in spite of the violent social upheavals of our time, is that standard of taste which was introduced into European society at the time of the Renaissance. The new middle-class or bourgeoisie which came into existence during this period found in the accumulation of works of art, and in the support of artists, a means of expressing their class consciousness, the power of their wealth. Taste became a visible sign of success, and once this link between wealth and art had been established, there was a tendency to stabilize the existing values. If, that is to say, a merchant of the sixteenth century had converted his wealth into the tangible form of sculpture of the Hellenic period, or paintings of the Florentine school, the 'taste' thus expressed became a vested interest and as such was passed down from father to son. Moreover, the whole system of education was influenced in the same direction, so that the sons in question, and the younger generations as a whole, in so far as they were educated, were taught to appreciate the 'values' of such accumulated possessions. Academies were formed to perpetuate these same values in the practice of future artists, and the eventual result was an academic tradition strictly graded to the prevailing economic order, imitative and not originative in its ideals. Taste in this way became an intellectual category, a subject to be taught in schools; and the innate sensibility of the individual was trained to conform to this traditional standard. Sensibility as a spontaneous function only survived in folk art and in savage art — in the art, that is to say, outside the bourgeois pale. For a time, perhaps, we can trace the survival of the aristocratic or religious standards of the previous epoch, but by the seventeenth century it is already difficult to distinguish them. When an artist does by chance emerge outside the bourgeois pale (William Blake is the example that comes to mind) he is considered an eccentric and completely neglected during his lifetime. Later his eccentricity may be turned to good account by the bourgeoisie, for his works acquire the adventitious values of scarcity and antiquity.

As bourgeois society matures, it becomes more complex and divides into distinct groups or sub-divisions, and each of these may develop a minor variation of the established canon. Such sub-divisions usually have either a vocational (professional) basis, or a regional one. The taste of the clergy, for example, is more ascetic than the taste of the landowners, and bankers may be more cultured than brokers (even when their personal incomes are comparable). Lower in the social scale, the possession of a television apparatus becomes a hall-mark of respectability.[1] There is a subtle distinction between lace curtains and gingham, between plush and rexine, between oak and mahogany. More interesting, however, are the regional variations. These sometimes express a local tradition, originally derived from folk art (e.g., the tartans of Scotland), but in great cities like London or Paris they express the segregation which naturally takes place in large communities. Bloomsbury and Mayfair are typical examples of what I mean. The reason why intellectuals of a certain type formerly tended to congregate in that district of London known as Bloomsbury may be found in various factors — the proximity of the British Museum and the Slade School of Art, the existence of tasteful houses of the right rentals, the desire of like-minded people to live within easy distance of one another. This last factor is probably the only reason which brings together the fashionable set of Mayfair. But in both these districts, and in other similar segregations, we find the emergence of that intangible factor which we call *snobism*.

The snob is a social phenomenon of some pathological interest, but it is doubtful whether he has any real taste. His values are predominantly social and not artistic. But undoubtedly there exists a sub-variety which we call the artistic snob, and again he is a com-

---

[1] Almost the contrary is now true—*not* to possess a television 'set' is sometimes considered to be a sign of cultural superiority. (1963).

plex growth, typical of an ingrown and sophisticated civilization. He is a great hindrance to the true appreciation of art, not so much because he extols false values but rather because he is apt to fix on real values for the wrong reasons. Like the dilettante, he may have real sensibility, but he can only exercise it within a socially-approved range. He is fairly safe in relation to the past, for there he has the aid of the educational conventions already mentioned. But in relation to his contemporaries he must play an agile game, for artists are usually approved or disapproved for reasons which have little to do with the quality of their work. A good artist may be a bad 'mixer', a social boor, or merely a dull conversationalist, or he may have an inconvenient wife. Whatever the interest of his work, the fashion will turn against him and he will remain poor and undistinguished until a future age, to which his personality is a matter of indifference, re-discovers him. Contrariwise, many an inferior artist is exalted far above his merits during his lifetime simply because he is socially charming, or has made a good marriage.

All these considerations may be commonplace, but they show the difficulties that beset anyone who would exercise a natural taste. If such a person is an average member of our present society, he will have to contend against the following forces:

(*a*) acquired prejudices, chiefly those absorbed at school, through literature, the Press, and the film;

(*b*) inherited possessions. All but the very poor inherit bad furniture, bad pictures, tasteless or positively ugly objects of all kinds. To sacrifice such things may be economically impossible, or sentimentally undesirable. Many possessions which we value for their associations may be aesthetically disgusting. To be surrounded by such things may eventually corrupt our taste, making us indifferent to everything we possess;

(*c*) our environment. Our civilization has gone from bad to worse, until a point has been reached where the greater part of humanity live in surroundings which deaden their sensibility and reduce them to an apathetic acceptance of whatever is offered to them by the prevailing commercial system.

Generally speaking, we exist, as a civilization, in a state of frustrated sensibility. We simply have no taste, except bad taste. To get out of this state, some very drastic measures of reform will obviously be necessary.

Towards a Duplex Civilization

I have tried to give a realistic picture of the problems of style, taste, and design as they emerge from the prevailing tendencies of the industrial system, and it may not be found a very cheerful picture. But I am now going to ask you to assume that any defects in the prevailing economic system have been removed, and that there are no further obstacles to the full and free application of design to the products of the industry. Production is for use rather than profit, everything is made fit for the purpose it is to serve, and everyone has the necessary means to acquire the essentials of a decent life at the highest level of cultivated taste. Of course, there will still be plenty of problems left — those problems of individual taste and periodic fashion which I have already discussed. But virtually we shall have, not only a machine age, but also, what we have so far lacked, a machine art. It is, let me emphasize, a very possible Utopia. The necessary steps can be clearly defined and the only obstacles could be easily removed. The main requisite is a more flexible economic system, that will allow the industrial system to function freely without those restrictions on ouput and quality which are at present dictated by the profit motive. And there are many signs that the economic system is changing and will continue to change in this direction; indeed, it must change in accordance with the process of economic stabilization which is everywhere taking place and to which we must adapt ourselves if we are to avoid an unending series of world wars and the ultimate extinction of our civilization. All forward-looking economists and sociologists are agreed on this: a balanced economy is the 'essential foundation for the next step in human development'. I take that phrase from a pamphlet by Lewis Mumford, who continues: 'The conditions which favoured expansion during the last three centuries are all definitely over; expansion on past terms is possible only for the purpose of waging war. If stablization should continue in purely pecuniary terms of monopoly, insurance, class privilege, the result will be self-defeating; whereas, if it is resisted, it must lead to a complete breakdown of our whole economy. . . .'[1] Just as surely as we can forecast the inevitability of this process of stabilization, so surely can we predict that stabilization when it comes will be expressed in a general tendency to substitute qualitative for quantitative standards. If there are any laws of history (which I doubt), this is one: that a stable civilization is biased towards quality of

[1] *The Social Foundations of Post-war Building* (London, 1943), p. 20.

achievement, a bias which has hitherto eventually led to over-refinement and sophistication. But that is the danger I am leading up to.

I have asked you to imagine that a stable civilization has been achieved, and that the industrial system is then devoted to the mass production of articles which satisfy the aesthetic standards that we have established for machine art:[1] economy, precision, fitness for purpose — the classical attributes of beauty. What then? We shall have factories full of clean automatic machines moulding and stamping, punching and polishing, innumerable objects that are compact in form, harmonious in shape, delectable in colour. Gone are the jointed and fragile objects which today we ingeniously construct from wood and metal: almost everything will be made from one basic plastic material, and beds and bathtubs, plates and dishes, radio cabinets and motor-cars, will spill out of the factories like an unending stream of glossy jujubes. I am perhaps exaggerating: if we get tired of glossiness, we can have our surfaces matt. Nothing will be impossible. The technologist and the designer between them will be able to satisfy every whim and fancy. From a technical point of view, it will all be fearfully easy, and we may well ask ourselves: where is the restraint to come from? What is to prevent this search for quality and variety from degenerating into an avalanche of vulgarity?

Prophets have a pre-emptive right to be gloomy, and in that role I would warn you that nothing whatever can save us from that avalanche unless we take preventive measures now. The children who are being educated in our schools today are the people who will inherit the Plastic Age we are preparing, and what powers of resistance will they have when they enter into the glossy land of promise? They will have less than we have, much less than our ancestors had. For what is 'good taste' as opposed to vulgarity? Is it something which can be taught at school, like Latin or arithmetic? Something you pick up at Oxford like an accent? Is it something innate, like an ear for music or a passion for oysters? Before answering such rhetorical questions — they are not meant to be answered — let us glance once again at the historical evidence.

The most striking fact about the great epochs of art, as I have emphasized again and again, is their homogeneity. If we could transport ourselves into the sixth century B.C. in Greece, to the eleventh century in China, into the twelfth century in Northern

[1] Cf. my *Art and Industry* (fourth edition, London, 1956).

France, the thirteenth century in Italy, the eighteenth century in
England, we should find not only great monuments of art in the
cities and public places: diffused everywhere throughout those
lands, in houses and clothes, in ordinary objects of utility and
ornament, we should find the ubiquitous stamp of a civilization. It
would not all be refined: it might be rough in texture, even crude
in conception. But it would never be vulgar. The shape would
be good, the ornament appropriate, the colour harmonious.

Now, the usual assumption is that somehow or other the high
cultural achievements of an élite at the top of such a society trickle
downwards until they reach the lowest cottage in the land. But
such a theory is not borne out by the facts. Apart from the absence of any means of diffusion, such as we possess nowadays in
the Press and the radio, in mass production and mechanical distribution, the chronological evidence is all against it. The peasant
art comes first — we can prove it in the evolution of an art such as
Greek pottery. But more than this: I believe that the peasant art
is there all the time until it is corrupted by influences coming from
a more artificial class. What I want to assert, in relation to our
own particular problems, is that good taste is always built up from
a broad basis; it is a slow elaboration and refinement of instinctive
activities natural to man, and this slow process is what we call a
tradition in art. It is only in so far as the constructive instincts of
man are progressively refined by application to specific problems
of form and function that anything in the nature of an artistic
tradition can develop. That is a difficult sentence to grasp, perhaps, but let me be quite clear. I mean that the fingers must feel
the clay, the crisp substance of the wood, the tension of the
molten metal; there must be sensuous contact of hand and eye
with the grain and grit. Otherwise we have made a divorce between
man's senses and man's artifices which has never existed before in
history and from which consequences will flow of a quite unpredictable nature.

Such consequences are unpredictable only in their sympto-
matic detail: broadly we may say that the atrophy of sensibility
which is involved in such a cessation of handwork involves the
decay of our civilization — some of us would say that the evidence
is already plain to see, that the decomposition has begun. Now,
I think it would be possible to elaborate an up-to-date psychological theory to explain why this should happen: it is summed up
in one of the most ancient of psychological maxims: *nihil est in*

intellectu quod non fuerit prius in sensu, which means that the basis of intelligence is a lively sensibility. But there is another and even more familiar maxim which gives the common-sense view of the process: Satan finds some mischief still for idle hands to do. If by advances in technology, in machine-tool design, by factory organization, and so on, the human element is largely eliminated from production, then, apart from the problem of the adequate distribution and consumption of these mechanically produced goods — a problem which, as I have already said, could conceivably be solved by some scheme of social credit — there remains not only what the sociologists with unconscious irony call the problem of leisure, but this much more serious aspect of the problem which I have called 'the atrophy of sensation'. You might conceivably solve the problem of leisure, not only by employing a greater number of people in distributive trades and social services, but also by various forms of cultural entertainment. It is an only too credible possibility — a vast conglomeration of shop-walkers and civil servants, ticket-punchers and typists, their hands getting more and more refined, their minds more and more cultured. Even the peasant's fingers will have forgotten the knack of milking a cow, and the spade and fork will have joined the rest of the tools of the Iron Age in our museums.

It might be said that I have forgotten the designer, and the pattern maker and the machine-tool maker. But these people who may still be required to use their hands in creative contact with a material will always be an insignificant minority in any individual community, and quite unable to retard a general atrophy of sensibility in a civilization. No: if we are to go forward to the logical conclusion of the machine age — and I am not suggesting that we should attempt to arrest an historical process of such acquired momentum — then we must create a movement in a *parallel* direction, and not in opposition.

We must, in other words, establish a double-decker civilization. That is not so fantastic as at first sight it might seem. Such a phenomenon has, indeed, appeared many times in the course of history, chiefly in primitive communities where a secret art was practised by the priesthood in complete independence of the utilitarian or decorative arts of the common people. But the most striking example of a binary or duplex civilization is that of Ancient Egypt, and it is one which offers some striking parallels to our own. In the valley of the Nile there existed for many centuries side by side two types of art of entirely distinct character. One, consisting mainly of public buildings and sculptured monuments, was religious; the other, consisting mainly of paintings, small carvings and decorated vessels of various kinds, was domestic. The religious art was geometric, rational, objective, abstract; the other was naturalistic, lyrical, even sentimental. These two arts did not represent the highbrow and lowbrow extremes of expression within a social unity: they were completely divorced styles, uninfluenced by each other, almost unaware of each other.

A similar stylistic division has already become evident in our own time, though few people are yet conscious of it, and fewer still are aware of its significance or willing to draw conclusions from it. But surely between the constructive art of Gabo or Nicholson, the functional architecture of Le Corbusier or Niemeyer on the one hand, and what generally passes for art and architecture on the other hand, there is not merely a separation, but a decree absolute. The second group includes much that is merely bad and imitative, and I would not in any case wish to force it all into one category. But among it we shall find the naturalistic, the lyrical and sentimental modes of expression which correspond strictly in character to the domestic arts of Ancient Egypt.

So therefore we are already a double-decker civilization, though there seems to be some confusion on the lower deck. But now let us carry the comparison a little further. I have already, in my book on *Art and Industry* and elsewhere, formulated the abstract principles which should govern machine art. The art of the machine can never be naturalistic or humanistic: it is an art of geometrical proportions, of purely formal harmonies. Though my last wish is to exclude those intuitive faculties which only the artist can bring to bear on industrial design, its general character can best be described as 'objective rationality', which is a translation of the very phrase which a German historian of art has used to describe Egyptian architecture. 'The characteristic which speaks out most clearly in it as a phenomenon in general is that naked, abstract absoluteness of the constructive spirit in its cold grandeur, its terse decidedness, its renunciation of every superfluous articulation.'[1] That is Professor Worringer's description of Egyptian architecture, but it might equally well be a description

[1] Wilhelm Worringer, *Egyptian Art*, trans. by B. Rackham (London, 1928), p. 24.

of contemporary functional architecture. The spirit underlying
Egyptian architecture and the spirit underlying modern architecture is the same spirit, and it is something quite distinct from the
naturalistic or humanistic art which led a separate existence in
Egypt, but which is being slowly eliminated from our own civilization by the machine.

We cannot, at this stage of development, oppose the machine:
we must let it rip, and with confidence. Egyptian art proves that a
spirit of objective rationality is capable of the most magnificent
and awe-inspiring achievements. We can already see its potentialities around us, in the functional buildings which have already been
erected, and in some of the products of the machine industry.
But do not let us make the mistake of assuming that a civilization
can be based on rationality or functionalism alone. The foundations of a civilization rest not in the mind but in the senses, and
unless we can use the senses, educate the senses, we shall never
have the biological conditions for human survival, let alone human
progress.

We must look forward, therefore, to some division of our human
and social activities which will insure a due proportion of time
devoted to manual craftsmanship. It would be quite impracticable
to achieve this by any artificial interference with industrial development. We cannot select several industries — say furniture
and pottery — and reserve these for handicraft. Such vertical
rifts in the industrial system would lead to economic anomalies
and social inequalities. They would divide the industrial world
into a technological priesthood and a lower order of handicrafts-
men. That solution might be possible under some system of centralized planning, but I think we can dismiss it as undesirable
and as only partial in its effects.

But there is another possiblity, and this is to make the division
horizontal, affecting every industry and every individual, but only
up to a certain point. In other words, let every individual serve an
apprenticeship in handicrafts. In the next part of this volume I
make a plea for the aesthetic basis of education; what I am here
advocating is an extension of that method beyond the school age,
into the period of apprenticeship, into the hours of adult leisure.
If, between the ages of five and fifteen, we could give all our children a training of the senses through the constructive shaping of
materials — if we could accustom their hands and eyes, indeed all
their instruments of sensation, to a creative communion with

sounds and colours, textures and consistencies, a communion with nature in all its substantial variety, then we need not fear the fate of those children in a wholly mechanized world. They would carry within their minds, within their bodies, the natural antidote to objective rationality, a spontaneous overflow of creative energies into their hours of leisure.

The result would be a private art standing over against the public art of the factories. But that — in our painting and sculpture, our poetry and dancing, our artist-potters and artist-weavers — we already have. That is to say, we have a tiny minority of people calling themselves artists. I am recommending that everyone should be an artist. I am not recommending it in a spirit of dilettantism, but as the only preventive of a vast neurosis which will overcome a wholly mechanized and rationalized civilization.

I make a further claim. The art of that completely mechanized civilization can never, if it is to be an art, arise from the purely rational solution of functional problems. The function, after all, always relates to human needs. Human needs, in their turn, are always related to a natural environment. There can be no artificial separation of art from nature, of the machine from its environment. The great air liners of the future will soar above the clouds, but their very shape and size will be determined by the element which sustains them. We can fly because we understand the natural properties of air; and in every sense, in every direction, we shall only advance on an understanding of nature. Let our children therefore first learn about the potentialities of nature, and about the potentialities of those senses by means of which they can give a pleasing shape to the products of nature. In this way the community at large will gradually acquire a spontaneous desire to give expression to creative impulses, and hands will never again lose their cunning, nor eyes their delight in colour and form.

Only a people serving an apprenticeship to nature can be trusted with machines. Only such a people will so contrive and control those machines that their products are an enhancement of biological needs, and not a denial of them. Only such a people will be secure from the debilitating effects of mass production and mass unemployment (miscalled 'leisure'). Only such a people, with sensations still vivid and intelligence ever active, can hope to form a stable and integrated society in the industrial world of the future.

VI. Education

Education through Art

The history of modern education reveals a series of successive readjustments not only to the changing needs of our practical life, but also to our deepening understanding of human psychology. We have introduced into the curriculum new subjects of a technological nature; we have established close links between schools and industry, we have developed physical training and organized recreation — all to the end of creating a useful and efficient citizen. The more spiritual aspects of life have not fared so well, but they have not been altogether neglected. Literature has been firmly established as a school subject, drama has been introduced as a group activity, music is no longer merely an accompaniment to gymnastics. Even the particular activities I am about to discuss — the plastic arts of painting and sculpture — now have a recognized place in the curriculum, and are taught by methods that are comparatively enlightened. Great reforms have taken place in the past thirty years, and are still in progress. We must ask, however, not merely whether these reforms are yet adequate, but also whether they have any guiding principle, and, in particular, whether they succeed in preserving the right balance between the various mental faculties which make the whole man, by which I mean a man alive, alert and creative.

Ever since the Middle Ages our ideal of education has been dominated by what might be called the intellectual prejudice. Knowledge has been the overriding purpose: observation and memory the means. 'The mind is the man, and the knowledge of the mind. A man is but what he knoweth.' That was Francis Bacon's ideal at the very beginning of systematic education in the modern world. It will at once be seen that it allows no place for feeling or sensibility — no place for intuition as a mode of knowledge nor for appreciation as a mode of experience. Contrast Pascal's perception: 'The heart has its own reasons which Reason does not know; a thousand things declare it — ' and among these thousand things are not only the religious instincts with which Pascal was concerned, but also the creative instincts with which we are concerned. The true end of education, we would say, is not the quantity of known facts, nor even the use of such knowledge in practical affairs, but rather the possession and instinctive use of a sense of values. By a sense of values we do not mean utilitarian values, nor even ethical values, for these again are secondary aspects of knowledge; we mean, if the distinction is to be kept sharp and final, the sensuous apprehension of the facts themselves — the sensuous cognition, we might say, of reality itself.

We must always distinguish two faculties in the life of man: intellect and sensibility. Intellect begins with the observation of nature, proceeds to memorize and classify the facts thus observed, and by logical deduction builds up that edifice of knowledge properly called science. Sensibility, on the other hand, is a direct and particular reaction to the separate and individual nature of things. It begins and ends with the sensuous apprehension of colour, texture and formal relations; and if we strive to organize these elements, it is not with the idea of increasing the knowledge of the mind, but rather in order to intensify the pleasure of the senses. But admittedly we also know by feeling, and we can combine the two faculties, and present knowledge in the guise of art, which is precisely the secret of teaching. But to neglect the senses, either through ignorance of their epistemological significance, or from mere puritanical prejudice, is to neglect one half of our being. Neither in teaching nor in learning, neither in making things nor in our dealings with one another, can we afford to ignore the sensuous reactions that record the quality of experience.

It follows that in any ideal system of education we should educate the senses, and to this end each of the arts should have its appropriate place in the curriculum. If, on the present occasion, I seem to neglect the arts of music, drama and dance, it is only for the sake of simplifying the issue. The conclusions we reach in respect of the visual or plastic arts should be of general application. A 'psychogenetic education', which is a comprehensive description of our aim, cannot neglect any mode of sensuous expression and communication.

Up to very recent times, the art education which was given in our schools was designed to aid rather than supplement the normal curriculum. Confined for the most part to drawing lessons, it attempted to train the child in the close observation of nature and in the accurate recording of the observed facts. Art was a visual aid to memory, and skill was the only requisite for success. But in some schools it was recognized that art is a profession, and that if talent could be discovered, it should be directed into this remunerative channel. Art schools were established to take over these promising pupils, and to train them in the same sense that other pupils would be trained as engineers or doctors. Art education in this professional sense should be excluded from the present discussion; it only confuses the issue, which is not the education of the artist, but the place of art in the education of every child. From our present point of view, the whole question of talent is immaterial; we begin with the assumption that every individual has certain sensations, emotions, intuitions, and certain impulses to express these states of mind; and that it is desirable to encourage these tendencies. We believe that human life includes an aesthetic activity as well as a practical activity, and that an education that ignores the aesthetic activity is only a half-education, or no education at all.

How, then, shall we proceed? Various teachers have experimented in recent years and have discovered that with rare (and probably pathological) exceptions, every child lives in a world of imagery which is far more real than the world of appearances, and that given the means (colour and paper, clay, etc.,) the child will express these images naturally and with great effectiveness. Certain methods have been devised for encouraging this impulse to expression, but the greatest necessity is a negative one: the avoidance of the imposition of any preconceived standard of skill or verisimilitude. The child is not observing nature, and its activity has nothing to do with objective reality; the child is giving a symbolic representation of its inner or mental life. The child, that is to say, is wholly concerned with a reality that is subjective and personal.

It may be that some educationist can make out a case against this symbolic activity; it may be that the life of the intellect and the stability of society demand the repression of fantasy in the child. I do not believe this myself; the evidence of anthropology and of history points rather to the conclusion that the happiest communities are precisely those which have a rich life of fantasy, and that the repression or neglect of this life of the imagination leads to social apathy and cultural decadence. The expression of imagination is a natural and not an unusual activity in human societies, and by expression we mean the creation and communication of non-discursive symbols to represent states of feeling and intuition that are outside the range of conceptual thought. Pascal's reasons that Reason does not know. In giving expression to the images which crowd its innocent mind, and which alone correspond to its mental requirements at a particular stage of development, the child will use colour, make gestures, arrange objects in relation to each other and to the available space — in short, exercise its aesthetic faculty. In however humble a way, each child becomes an artist.

But that is only half the story. The child must next be encouraged, not merely to project its own images in plastic form — that is to say, to create symbols that correspond to its own state of mind — the child must also learn to appreciate this mode of expression in others. The meaning of art in contemporary life and the significance of the art of the past can only become fully available to the child if we succeed in developing a receptive attitude towards works of art as such, and in educating those faculties by means of which we appreciate the qualities of such works. This seems to me to be by far the most difficult aspect of art education. We have to take care that we do not revert to our intellectual concepts and turn the appreciation of art into an accumulation of facts about art. As the child grows up it will be necessary to relate the great works of the past to their social background, to see them in their chronological sequence and their psychological significance — if only because such knowledge can deepen the enjoyment of our own aesthetic activities. But aesthetic enjoyment proceeds from a source as natural and spontaneous as any of the pleasure-giving instincts of life, such as the satisfaction of hunger and of love. It must be developed from the young child's direct delight in the colour and quality of material things, and not from books or lectures or museums. These will play their part, but passively. I personally would not exclude paintings and reproductions of paintings from the school; and, what is even more important, I would like to see every school itself a work of art and all its furniture and fittings works of art. But these should work on the child unconsciously — should be an ambience as wide and as accepted as nature itself.

These are practical ideals, already partly realized, as I have said, in a number of schools in various parts of the world. But much more is necessary, and in particular there is the problem of the teacher, for it may be said that only rarely, and then by accident, does the present system of training teachers produce one capable of teaching art in the sense here indicated. Some people believe that only an artist, and an artist in the process of development, can teach art to children. With certain reservations I believe this to be true. Art is not 'taught' by any formal, instructional method: it is communicated by example. But just at this point lies a subtle danger, for what should be communicated is not a style, nor even a technique, but confidence in the child's own uninhibited activity. Because of the danger that always exists of a child imitating the mannerisms of an adult artist, the artist-teacher should be careful not to impose his personality on the children under his tuition. He should be capable of identifying himself for the time being with the distinct personality of each child — a tough requirement for the average artist! That is why I make my reservation, for I have observed that it is by no means the best artist that makes the best teacher. The main qualification in the teacher is sympathy — what Sylvia Ashton-Warner has called the ability to draw out and preserve the child's own line of thought.[1] If this attitude takes the form of a practical activity that gives the child the assurance that its own activity is not merely childish, then we have the perfect teacher of art.

It should by now be obvious that what is involved is not merely reform in one branch of education: it is education itself, as it has so far existed, that is challenged by the ideas I am outlining.

In *Education Through Art* I suggested that aesthetic education had five separate aims. These are all means of self-realization, but I now feel that this phrase is a little deceptive, for in general it will be discovered that group activities are involved—that the self can only be realized in a relationship of mutuality. I propose here to give a separate description of these aims, and of the methods by which they are to be achieved, and in this way what is meant by 'education through art' will become clearer.

The first aim is *to preserve the natural intensity of all modes of perception and sensation.*

That the child sees and feels with a certain virgin freshness is a commonplace observation, and in a sentimental way all ages have paid tribute to the innocent eye. What has been more rarely perceived and is perhaps difficult to admit is the possible connection

---

[1] *Teacher* (New York, 1963).

between this original sensibility and what we call inspiration in art and science. Inspiration is, of course, a dangerous word to introduce into a serious discussion. However, I am not dealing in superhuman faculties, but referring to a mental process that might occur in anyone. We have all experienced the mental restraint or mere blankness which comes from our inability to solve a particular problem, or even to remember a particular name. Then, in a flash, comes the 'inspiration' — the release of mental tension which accompanies the solution of the problem. At a higher or 'creative' level, the inspiration of the artist or the scientist is of the same kind, and is distinguished only by a wider range of connections, which gives the effect of originality.

There is a distinction to be made which is of some importance between creation and invention, but it does not affect the point under discussion. Whether we call the mental process creation or invention, it depends for its occurrence on acuteness of perception and sensation — on the range and vividness of the imagery present at any particular moment in the mind. Vividness of sensation is a birthright — I do not doubt that it varies from child to child, and there is perhaps little we can do to develop or intensify it. But we can make the child aware of its sensations — of the range and subtle variations of any given sensation. Take, for example, the sense of touch — tactile sensation. This can be developed by elementary 'tactile exercises'. At the Bauhaus, the famous school established by Walter Gropius in Germany in 1919, tables were constructed on which different materials were arranged in rows — for example, fabrics, metals, bits of bread, leather, paper, porcelain, sponge, etc., and the student learned by experience to distinguish by sight and touch the various sensations aroused by these materials, or by these materials under pressure or in vibration. Education of this kind may seem so elementary as to be futile, but the disciplining of sensation is only to be attained by its persistent exercise. We are all familiar with the training of the voice for singing; but not only the vocal organs, but all the organs of sensation and expression should be trained by similar methods, the aim being to develop the range and flexibility of all modes of perception and sensation at the elemental, somatic level. Such is the first stage in aesthetic education, and it is one that is completely neglected in our normal methods of education.

The second aim of aesthetic education is *to co-ordinate the various*

modes of perception and sensation with one another and in relation
to the environment.

We should try, in the first phase of education, to develop to their fullest potentiality the separate senses of sight, touch, hearing, muscular rhythms, voice pitch and pronunciation. But such modes of perception or sensation must then be combined and correlated. An obvious example is the matching of voice to music, but there should be an infinite extension of this marriage of true sensations. When we *see* something we should at the same time experience by association the tactile values of the surface of that object. Images should spontaneously accompany sounds, and the whole range of perception and sensation should be like an orchestral symphony, in which each clearly distinguished instrument contributes to an harmonious whole. This coordination of the senses leads naturally to the third aim of aesthetic education, which is *to express feeling in communicable form.*

I think most of us are aware of our shortcomings in this respect. It may be that we can express spontaneously enough the more elementary emotions of joy or sorrow, but life involves us in complex states of feeling which demand, for their communication to others, not only infinite subtleties of verbal expression, but also various forms of symbolic expression.

The modern world has largely forgotten, and our educational systems ignore, the primary importance, in the evolution of man, of various types of symbolic communication — the communication embodied in gesture, ritual, dance, music, myth, and poetic metaphor. All these modes of expression constitute a language of feeling, a non-discursive form of thought, absolutely essential to our individual development and to the unity of social life. Adult civilized societies have developed language and discursive logic to such a pitch of refinement that they tend to ignore what may be called the primary non-discursive language of symbols. We may question the adequacy of a logical syntax for communication even in a developed civilization. I will return to that general problem later, but there is no doubt whatever that intellectual modes of communication do not meet the needs of a child. The child is utterly dependent on symbolic modes of communication, and that is the crux of the whole problem. It is precisely because the child, as it matures and develops complexities of feeling, cannot at the same time express these complexities of feeling in verbal and logical form, that frustration results with all its melancholy neurotic aftermath. The ability to represent inner feeling in outward forms is the essential instrument of self-realization, and this ability is a technique that can be taught. We can only 'realize' ourselves adequately if we know how to express ourselves significantly; and we only know how to express ourselves significantly if we have preserved the natural intensity of our modes of perception and feeling and are able to coordinate these modes into significant patterns — into forms which effectively communicate the quality of our sentience to other people.

All that is difficult enough, and it is perhaps as far as elementary or primary education can go in the time at its disposal. But there are two further aims of any adequate method of education. Modern psychology has taught us that there is more in the mind than is put there by perception and sensation. I do not want to be dogmatic about this point, and if you cannot admit the hypothesis of the unconscious, and more particularly the concept of the collective unconscious, no harm is done to my general argument. But I do admit the possibility of these submerged depths of the personality, and I think that education should develop modes for their expression in communicable form. Here again, the symbol is the unit of expression, and the work of art, whether in plastic or verbal or musical form, or elaborated in ritual and myth, is the mode of communication. I do not think the projection of images from the unconscious is necessarily more important than the expression of more conscious states of sensibility, but we should allow for the perfecting of all modes of communication. I must be a little vague at this point, because I am indicating modes of education that have never been conceived, much less reduced to practical formulas. Education through mythology — I mean the creation of new myths — sounds like a contradiction in terms. Let us call it education through constructive fictions — that sounds more scientific. To the degree that we preserve spontaneity, we liberate constructive forces in the imagination.

Finally, and with most difficulty, we must teach children *how to express thought in required form* — by which I mean education in constructive crafts, a practical craft like engineering, a conceptual craft like logic. And here it might seem to some of my readers that at last I am beginning to talk sense. But constructive education only makes sense if it is firmly based on the other forms of education I have mentioned — visual, plastic, musical, kinetic, verbal and symbolic education. That is to say, there is a necessary connection between the validity of thought and the form in which that thought is expressed. I am not, I hope, confusing validity and perdurability, truth and history; but *is* it an accident that the philosophy of Plato, for example, is expressed in prose works of aesthetic perfection? Is it an accident that the greatest scientists, as a general rule, command the clearest style? There is some quality in the very substance of thought that demands vitality in expression and significance in form.

Such are the aims of education *through* art, and I again emphasize the preposition because it is not the education *in* art that I have been describing, but education *by means of* art. The claim I make is that the experience involved in the process of artistic *creation* is in itself an educative one, and that art is therefore an essential instrument in any complete method of education. But to speak of art as 'an instrument of education' is unconsciously to accept an authoritarian conception of education foreign to the artistic process. Art is not an arbitrary discipline to which the child has to be subjected; it is a discipline inherent in our reactions to the natural order; and in conforming to this discipline the child finds perfect freedom. Art is also — and its educative influence derives largely from this fact — a social process, for not only is it communicative — in that it is directed to an audience, but also communal, in that it can be a means to common ends. 'Man is, above all, he who creates. And theirs alone is brotherhood who work together.' That is a quotation from *Citadelle* by Antoine de Saint-Exupéry (translated as *The Wisdom of the Sands*[1]), and when the speaker is asked to explain what he means by 'creation', he does so in words which I find illuminating.

'To create may be to miss a step in the dance; or to deal a chisel stroke awry when you are carving stone. Little matters it what the gesture brings forth. To you in your blindness such an effort may seem fruitless, for you may bring your eyes too close. Only stand back and observe from a distance the activity in this quarter of the city. You shall see there a vast ardor and a golden cloud of dust billowing above the work. No longer will you notice gestures that go astray. Intent on their task, all these men are building, whether they will or no, palaces, cisterns, hanging gardens. Their hands are spellbound and these things are born of their enchantment. And, mark my words, these noble works are shaped no less by those who botch their gestures than by those who make

---

[1] By Stuart Gilbert (London, 1952).

them deftly; for you cannot divide men up, and if you will have none but great sculptors, you will soon have none at all. . . . The great sculptor springs from the soil of poor sculptors: they are steps whereon he climbs towards the heights.' (Pages 43–4.)

'The one thing that matters is the effort.' (Page 141.)

Such statements are firmly based in human psychology. The human psyche, as we realize more clearly with every advance of mental science, is a delicate adjustment of sensation, feeling, intuition and thought, and although we call man the rational animal, because he alone among living beings possesses the capacity to form concepts and to relate new experiences to universal abstractions, nevertheless his real needs are for creative activites. Education has generally been conceived as a process for training and strengthening the faculty of reasoning, on the supposition that rational or discursive thinking gives a man the best control of himself and of his environment. It has for long been obvious that such a rational bias in education involves a suppression of the instinctual and emotional components of the human personality, and although this has been accepted as a necessary social safeguard, even by such a champion of the unconscious as Freud, it is now realized that no progress is made, even in the moral sphere, by a bird with one wing.

The notion that men's impulses can be controlled by his reason is the Faustian illusion, and has again and again in the history of the world involved mankind in the bitterest disillusion. We are now forced to the realization that the human psyche cannot be unified, either in its individual or collective aspect, by any coercion proceeding from the intellect, but that there must be an open reconciliation of those two sides of our nature which we may represent variously as intuition and intellect, imagination and abstraction. I am conscious of the fact that in using words like 'intuition' and 'imagination' I am ignoring the existence of instincts and impulses that deserve an uglier name, but this is not really the case. It is an overvaluation of the powers of reason, and an undervaluation of the powers of the imagination, that permits the easy triumph of evil. 'Barbarism', as Jung has said, 'is one-sidedness, lack of moderation — bad proportion generally.'

The reconciliation of intuition and intellect, of imagination and abstraction, can only take place objectively, or, as I would rather say, creatively. It is only by projecting the two sides of our nature into a concrete construction that we can realize and

370

contemplate the process of reconciliation. That is precisely the function of the work of art, and that has been its function all down the ages. It is the symbol of reconciliation, the physical artefact in which our impulses submit to the aesthetic discipline of rhythm and proportion, in which reason informs itself with the vital energies of the animal.

That, at any rate, is the philosophical faith on which we must base a plea for education through art. I call it a faith, but already in Plato it was a philosophy based on empirical observation, and in Schiller's Letters *On the Aesthetic Education of Man* it received a formulation that is already complete. The conspicuous neglect of Schiller's treatise — incomparably the profoundest treatise on education ever written — can only be explained by its appearance at an unfortunate moment in history (1795), that moment when Europe was entering into an epoch of industrial expansion and mechanical invention which required in its leaders, its managers and executives, a form of education that was precisely the opposite to the one recommended by Schiller. The very concept of 'living form', which is central to Schiller's philosophy, is contrary to the dead forms of machine production and industrial organization; and how could one seriously recommend to the apostles of profit, to whom human labour is but one of the economic factors in production, a development of *the play instinct*. Even to the enlightened manufacturers of the nineteenth century, even to the educational reformers themselves, a philosopher who, in an educational treatise, asked them to admit, *once and for all*, that 'man only plays when he is a man in the fullest meaning of the word, and is only completely man when he is playing', must have seemed like a madman.

I have already referred to the function of the symbol in the mental and social life of man, a function which has been largely ignored by modern education, with impoverishing results for our culture. Schiller's emphasis on the play-instinct was not arbitrary. He realized that this instinct is the energetic aspect of all phantasy, and therefore of all symbolic and metaphorical activity. By virtue of this instinct it is possible to mediate between the world of sensuous experience and the world of form, and thus to provide the basis for all symbolic discourse whatsoever — not only for art, but also for language and myth, philosophy and science. This evolution has been traced by the German philosopher Ernst Cassirer, to whom we also owe a warning of the price that must be paid for the transformation of language into a vehicle of thought, into an instrument for the expression of concepts and judgements. That price is the sensuous and spiritual impoverishment of language, and Cassirer was of the opinion that language must be constantly regenerated by its use as a medium of artistic expression — as poetry. Only in so far as the mind uses the sensuous forms of word and image to express the realm of pure feeling can it maintain a complete hold on reality. One might say, in short, that there exists a whole language of feeling distinct from the language of thought. This language, even when it consists of visual images or of tonal movements in music, is just as capable of articulation as the language of words, but it is not discursive. Susanne Langer, in a book that extends Cassirer's philosophy of symbolism to the world of art, has shown the enormous significance which these non-verbal, non-discursive forms of thought have for the development of human intelligence. To neglect them in favour of purely conceptual and discursive modes of thought is to leave the world of feeling unarticulated, unexpressed, with consequences that are individually neurotic and socially disastrous.

Once it is realized that the forms abstracted in art as symbols are radically different from the forms of rational discourse, and that they serve the all-important purpose of 'symbolizing the dynamics of subjective experience, the pattern of vitality, sentience, feeling and emotion' (to use Mrs. Langer's words), the necessity for encouraging the use of such forms in the educative process becomes immediately apparent. Education, as we have seen, has a twofold purpose: to develop sensuous expression and communication in the individual, and to effect an understanding 'between man and man'. It is doubtful if the personality itself can be fully developed unless it can project subjective experience into concrete forms, and do this with increasing skill and exactitude; but obviously the second and equally important aim of education remains frustrated unless the individual can communicate subjective experience, and such experience can *only* be communicated by specific symbols. Such symbols are effective as media of communication to the degree that they are expressive as works of art. If we do not encourage our children to express themselves in symbolic forms, we fail to develop the most efficient modes of communicating experience. We leave the world dependent on a language of thought and a mode of reasoning that can give expression only to the abstract realm of concepts and judgements.

However narrow and exclusive it may be, discursive reasoning of this kind is admittedly of the utmost importance for the development of humanity. But the vitality of thought is dependent on feeling — it is impossible for us to *think* of any thing, as David Hume said, which we have not antecedently *felt*, either by our external or internal senses. Again and again scientists and philosophers have confessed that their moments of inspiration and invention have been metaphorical. That is to say, at the critical moment in the rational argument they have had to desert their abstract concepts and 'think in images'. The metaphorical faculty, as we may call it, is of the highest importance in thought itself, and the greatest works of philosophy and science are precisely those in which the metaphorical faculty is seen in action. One of the principal aims of education should therefore be to preserve what every child is born with — a physical intensity of perception and sensation. These will inevitably be dulled by the growth of conceptual thought; but these conceptual modes of thought have greater effectiveness to the extent that they retain acuteness of perception and a ready faculty for the recognition of similitudes.

Finally I must mention the argument for aesthetic education which Plato regarded as the most important of all — the moral argument. The same idea is implicit in Schiller, in Herbart, in Nietzsche, and even in Rousseau and Pestalozzi — even in Pavlov! — the idea that a causal connection exists between action and character, between physical form and ethical form, between environment and virtue. All these educators were disciplinarians, but they recognized that discipline is not an abstraction (or if regarded as such, is always ineffective), and so they put forward the idea that discipline is a physically conditioned disposition to harmony. Children are not born with such a disposition; it has to be induced. We must take care, however, that the harmony we take as a pattern is a natural one — or, as Herbart said, a *necessary* one; and all these philosophers agree that the only natural or necessary harmony is aesthetic harmony. Bring up your children, therefore, in automatic obedience to the laws of aesthetic harmony, and you will naturally, inevitably, create in them an harmonious state of mind and feeling.

The distinctions commonly made between mind and feeling,

between intellect and sensibility, between knowledge and taste, do not imply a separation of the mind and the senses. On the contrary, a healthy intellect or reason is every bit as dependent on the exercise of the senses as is a healthy taste. And this is true at every stage of education. Whitehead, that great philosopher who was not least a great philosopher of education, towards the end of his book *Science and the Modern World* considers the very problem of the balance of general and specialist education and comes to the conclusion that the make-weight which balances the thoroughness of specialist intellectual training should be of a kind radically different from purely intellectual analytical knowledge. He can see no solution of the problem in a combination of the gross specialized values of the mere practical man and the thin specialized values of the mere scholar. 'Both types have missed something; and if you add together the two sets of values, you do not obtain the missing elements.' What Whitehead asks for is a faculty for the direct perception of the concrete achievement of a thing in its actuality, and he finds this faculty in aesthetic apprehension; but merely passive apprehension is not enough. We must foster creative initiative. Impulse as well as sensitiveness is essential, for 'sensitiveness without impulse spells decadence, and impulse without sensitiveness spells brutality'. And the *habit* of art he defines as the habit of enjoying vivid values.

I quoted those words in an inaugural address I gave many years ago when I took up a professorship of Fine Art in Edinburgh University. They seem to me truer than ever today, and so does something else I said on that occasion:

'Art, just because it demands an intuitional apprehension, cannot be dismissed as history. It is a present activity, and I should regard my duties as but half done if, in teaching the enjoyment of art of the past, I did not also lead my students to enjoy the art of the present day. Art today is a testimony to our culture, a witness to its positive qualities and to its limitations, just as the arts of the past are to the cultures of the past. We cannot fully participate in modern consciousness unless we can learn to appreciate the significant art of our own day. Just because people have not learned in their youth the habit of enjoyment, they tend to approach contemporary art with closed minds. They submit it to intellectual analysis when what it demands is intuitive sympathy. They have no pureness of heart and therefore they cannot share the artist's vision. That is a sad state, and it seems to me that it is one of the primary functions of a university, which sends out its thousands of young men and women to be teachers and preceptors of their fellow-men, to send them out with open eyes and active sensibilities, so that what they see they may enjoy. For what they *seeing* enjoy (*id quod visum placet*), that is art. It is one of the qualities of enjoyment that it is infectious, and everywhere we should try to diffuse an awareness of the vividness of this habit of enjoyment which is art. It will then be possible to lift our heads above the ugliness which, like the rising flood after a storm, has followed in the wake of the Industrial Revolution. These islands were once beautiful and full of pleasures; the ugliness that then descended on them was a disease of the spirit. It was due, more than to anything else, to the divorce which philosophy and even religion made between spirit and matter. Art, even more than any other faculty, is stultified by such a divorce, for art is literally, as I have already insisted, spirit informing matter.'

Such a philosophy of education assumes modes of aesthetic perfection which may not be obvious in art as we know it today, and only fitfully apparent in the art of the past. But we must seek the best, and in any case must realize, as I have elsewhere said, that 'the perfection of art must arise from its practice — from the discipline of tools and materials, of form and function'. It is a mistake to define a world of art and set it apart from life. For that reason it is a mistake to confine the teaching of art to appreciation, for the implied attitude is too detached. Art must be practised to be appreciated, and it must be taught in intimate apprenticeship. The teacher must be no less active than the pupil. For art cannot be learned by precept, by any verbal instruction. It is, properly speaking, a contagion, and passes like fire from spirit to spirit.

Art and Life[1]

There is an early story of Tolstoy's, which has always seemed to me to have a fundamental bearing on the relation of the creative activities we call 'art' to the destructive forces we call 'crime'. Tolstoy describes a walk he took with three boys from the school on his estate at Vásnaya Polyana. In class they had been excited by the reading of a violent story by Gogol. It was a moonless winter night with snow on the ground and clouds in the sky. In a spirit of daring the boys wanted to go into the woods where wolves prowled but, being too afraid, they skirted round them, and began to talk about Caucasian robbers. Tolstoy told them tales about the Cossack braves he had known when he was a soldier, of one who, surrounded by his enemies, broke out into song and threw himself on his dagger. The children were struck by the strange fact that a man should sing when he was about to die. But their appetite for horrors was not satisfied, so Tolstoy went on to recount the gruesome murder of his aunt, whose throat had been cut by robbers. They stopped in a thicket at the end of the village, and Tolstoy, with his acute eye for significant detail, describes how one of the children picked up a dry stick from the snow and began striking it against the frosty trunk of a lime tree. Hoar frost fell from the branches on to their caps and the noise of the blows resounded in the stillness of the wood. Then another of the children, Fédka, a boy of ten 'with a tender, receptive, poetic yet daring nature', suddenly asked: 'Why does one learn singing? I often think, why, really, does one?' Tolstoy comments:

'What made him jump from the terror of the murder to this question, heaven only knows; yet by the tone of his voice, the seriousness with which he demanded an answer, and the attentive silence of the other two, one felt there was some vital and legitimate connection between this question and our preceding talk.

[1] *The Saturday Evening Post* (Philadelphia), September 26, 1959.

Art and Life

Whether the connection lay in some response to my suggestion that crime might be explained by lack of education (I had spoken of that), or whether he was testing himself — transferring himself into the mind of the murderer and remembering his own favourite occupation (he has a wonderful voice and immense musical talent), or whether the connection lay in the fact that he felt that now was the time for sincere conversation, and all the problems demanding solution rose in his mind at — any rate his question surprised none of us.'

'And what is drawing for? And why write well?' Tolstoy asked, not knowing how to answer the child's question. 'What is drawing for?' repeated Fédka, and Tolstoy adds: 'He was really asking, What is Art for? And I could not explain.'

Tolstoy thought about this question all his life, and it was not until thirty-seven years later, in *What is Art?* that he tried to explain the mysterious relationship that exists between beauty and truth, between art and life.

Tolstoy knew that the relationship was very profound, and even these children knew instinctively that there is some intimate connection between beauty and violence, between love and death. Such a connection is made by the great poets, by Homer and the Greek tragedians, by Shakespeare and by Tolstoy himself in *War and Peace*, but now we have lost it. Our technological civilization ignores all such values in its blind drive towards power and affluence, and pays the toll in a mass neurosis whose symptoms are fearful despair, apathy and violence.

In recent years violence has increased, especially among young people. Sometimes it seems to be motivated by race prejudice, not only in countries like the United States and South Africa where there is an indigenous and long-persisting racial problem, but even in Great Britain — we may recall the riots in London and Nottingham a few years ago when coloured immigrants from the West Indies were beaten up and their homes smashed. This particular outbreak seems to have had little to do with racial prejudice. Colour was only an excuse to exercise an impulse which would, if necessary, have found other outlets. The teen-age delinquent and, at a more literate level, the Angry Young Man are giving vent to suppressed feelings of frustration. Something in their nature has no disciplined outlet, and in their boredom and restless urge to action, these frustrated youths seek to hurt, to destroy; for destruction, as Bakunin said, is also creation. More exactly, it is a substitute for creation.

Such violence of action is no doubt related to the violence of expression that has increasingly become a feature, not only of novels, newspapers, films and television, but also of literature universally acclaimed as of great cultural value. America is not unique in this respect; the cynical brutality in William Faulkner's novels, for example, is but an outstanding example of a phenomenon characteristic of our civilization everywhere.

Violence, of course is not new to literature. There is violence in the *Iliad*, and the epic generally is a celebration of mutal slaughter among men. There is violence in Shakespeare and Cervantes, but the violence is never condoned by these writers. They view it as just retribution for sins against the divine order, or as a sacrifice sanctioned by heroism or martyrdom. What is peculiar to the modern literature is violence for the sake of violence, gratuitous violence. Perhaps our reverence for life has been dulled by mass slaughter, though mass slaughter has not been exceptional in the history of mankind. What is exceptional is the boredom that now alternates with war. The basic emotion in peace-time has become a *horror vacui*: a fear of being alone, of having nothing to do, a neurosis whose symptoms are restlessness, an unmotivated and undirected rage, sinking at times into vapid listlessness. This neurotic fear in the individual is intensified by the prevailing sense of insecurity. We do not consciously think about the threat of atomic war, but it has corrupted our faith in life itself, and given poignancy to our moods of boredom.

This universal neurosis has developed step by step with the technological development of our civilization. It is the neurosis of men whose sole expenditure of energy is to pull a lever, or push a button, of men who have ceased to make things with their hands, even to transport themselves with their legs. Such inactivity is a cessation not only of the muscular exercises and nervous combinations that constituted the normal life of man before the technological revolution; it is also a cessation of those formative or creative mental processes that even at the level of simple craft operations or manual tasks, engaged the will in a positive and productive action. If one could contrast visually, in the manner of the time-and-motion studies of the sociologists, the daily actions of an eighteenth-century chairmaker and those of a twentieth-century machinist, the latter would appear as a confined, repetitive clot, the former as a free and fantastic arabesque. But the most significant contrast could not be visualized, for it is mental: the contrast between a mind suspended aimlessly above an autonomous movement, and a mind consciously bent on the shaping of a material substance according to the persistent evidence of the senses.

Routine activities existed in other ages, but generally speaking human beings were in direct contact with nature and dependent on *things*. It was a realization of this fact which caused Jean-Jacques Rousseau, long before the Industrial Revolution, to lay down as one of the first principles of education: *Keep the child dependent on things only*. Rousseau believed that the child learns by trial and error better than by formula. This kind of pragmatic learning is essentially physical; skill develops in coping with material objects. It is true that skill of this kind is still involved in many industrial processes; we still divide labour into skilled and unskilled categories. But too often today skill means the understanding and control of a mechanical process, rather than the manual shaping of a physical substance. It is an activity more cerebral than sensual. This is true even of agricultural operations; the peasant who formerly used the spade and the scythe has been replaced by a mechanic driving a tractor. Sport also still implies skill in the physical sense, but the increasing professionalism of games confines the physical effects of such activities to a very small number of people. Sport, too, has become a mental activity.

I know of no detailed study of the universal cerebralization of productive activities that has taken place in all advanced technological civilizations during the past century and a half, and that has increased in intensity during the past fifty years.

But such a change in the basic modes of human activity must have deeply affected mental life and moral behaviour. The most obvious expression of such a change might well be aimlessly aggressive. Satan always finds some mischief for idle hands to do. Unused energies, deprived of traditional or habitual outlets, explode in violence.

I have spoken of 'skill', a word of Norse derivation whose original meaning implied discrimination. It is a curious fact that the word has no precise equivalent in French or German.[1] We use 'skill' in association with 'craft', an old English word that originally meant power or strength. The association of craft with words like

---

[1] The nearest equivalent in French is *habilité*, which is not the same thing. The German *Geschichtlichkeit* means 'giftedness'; *Fertigkeit* means 'readiness'.

skill, art or occupation exists in English only: a skilled craftsman is a worker with the power of discrimination. 'Know-how' is a popular equivalent.

The Greeks, though the source of our philosophy of *art*, had no word for art. They used *techne* — the equivalent of our word 'skill'. The word 'art' is derived from the Latin *ars*, which also implies skill, and this word is derived from the root *ar*, meaning to fit or join. The Romans were probably responsible for the distinction that gradually developed between arts and crafts, for they personified the Arts and began to think of them as refined (i.e. fine) activities. Nevertheless, during the Middle Ages the primary meaning of art remained skill — skill in making things, whether a chair, a tapestry, a painting, a 'piece of music' or a poem. The liberal arts were taught in schools as objective skills — grammar, rhetoric, logic; arithmetic, geometry, music and astronomy. We no longer speak of the liberal arts, but of *science*, that is to say, various categories of *knowledge* expressed in verifiable language. The arts were a way of 'doing', involving skill; the sciences are a way of 'knowing', implying logical consistency.

The history of words is a key to the history of ideas. We have now effected a complete divorce between the originally identical concepts of *techne* and *ars*. Technique, scientific method, skilled craft — all these terms imply intellectual know-how, and are characteristic of our technological civilization. But though moribund art schools still teach art as a skill, it is regarded more as an instinctual activity, exercised by a minority of gifted people, essentially inspirational in origin and personal in manifestation and significance. Its relevance to a technological civilization is considered marginal: an optional grace which most economies cannot afford. The controlling ideal of a technological civilization is not grace or beauty, but productive efficiency.

The Greeks did not distinguish between grace and efficiency; they considered them identical. Plato in his *Politicus* argued that statesmanship was a skill, comparable to that of the weaver (or, as we should say, an art, not a science), an intuition of Form in all things — not a tyrannical application of law. The modern philosopher does not agree with Plato. Politics he considers a science. We deliver ourselves into the remote hands of technical experts, who attempt to control our natural tendencies by means of scientific organizations.

To make a distinction between the art of government and the

science of government may now seem an academic exercise, but it is part of the vital problem of distinguishing between an art and a science of life itself. I call it a *vital* problem with a precise intention, because I believe that the future welfare of mankind depends on a realization of the issues involved, and then upon a clear choice of alternatives. To say that we stand at a cross-road of human development may be a rhetorical cliché, but is nevertheless a formidable fact.

Let us now look more closely at this human faculty we call 'skill'. Dr. Loren C. Eiseley, the distinguished American anthropologist, has suggested that it is the faculty upon which man has depended for his survival in the struggle for existence. Man has not reached his present superior status in the evolution of species by force alone, or even by adjustment to changes in his environment. He has reached it by the development of consciousness, enabling him to discriminate the *quality* of things. To quote Dr. Eiseley's own words: 'Man has become . . . a value-creating animal. He sets his own goals and more and more exerts his own will upon recalcitrant matter and the natural forces of the universe. In this activity he has passed from the specialized evolution of the parts of the body to a projection of such 'part' evolution upon his machines and implements. In this respect man is a unique being. Having achieved high intellectual ability, he may remain comparatively unchanged in structure while all around him other animals are still subjected to the old laws of specialized selection.'[1]

The long historical process whereby man became able to impose his will on recalcitrant matter can be reconstructed only speculatively. But there is nothing speculative about the process through which the child achieves this capacity. It has been studied in all its intricacy by the great Swiss pedagogue Jean Piaget who has published a whole series of books based on his patient observations of infantile behaviour. In one of them (*The Origin of Intelligence in the Child*) he defines intelligence as a relationship between the human organism and things. It is not, he insists, a power of reflection independent of the organism's particular position in the universe; rather it is linked, from the very beginning, with the organism's reaction to its physical environment. But this is not a simple reflex action; simultaneously with the organism's assimilation of external things, there is a mental

---

[1] *Adventures of the Mind* (from *The Saturday Evening Post*, New York, Knopf, 1959), p. 10.

organization of the things assimilated. The infant 'gropes' among its first confused experiences, becomes aware of certain relationships between the acts to be performed and an end to be attained, and *profits from experience*. Habits are formed, reactions to environment are automatically repeated, and gradually the groping becomes more continuous and consistent until it constitutes an *intention*. Intention is the essential characteristic of intelligence. An act is intentional, according to Piaget's definition, when it is determined by representation, as distinct from the elementary associations of the organism and its environment in which an act is determined by an external stimulus.

Intelligence presupposes intention. Intention is connected with the power of evoking images, and eventually with the whole process of symbolization and speech. In a series of observations on sucking reflexes in infants, Piaget shows that intentional adaptation begins as soon as the child transcends the level of simple corporal activities, such as sucking, listening, looking, grasping and *acts upon things and uses the interrelationships of objects*. In other words, intelligence develops (as Rousseau perceived) in contact with things, and increases in its range and capacity in so far as the images derived from this basic sensuous experience are formed and reformed in imaginative activity. Piaget defines imagination as 'invention through mental combination'.

Intention implies intention *towards* something. It is motivated by what Freud called the pleasure-principle, which in terms of bodily reactions is simply a sense of balance or ease. It will be seen that an element of choice is involved — a choice between the various mental combinations that might make for mental comfort. Where there is choice there is value. Value, as Piaget says, is the expression of desirability at all levels of experience, and it is my contention that the desirable values are always aesthetic — that is to say, determined by their contribution to whatever structure of experience gives the greatest pleasure to the organism. Such an ideal of equilibrium represents the final goal of our actions, and whatever means are used to attain this goal are the 'values' involved not only in life's primary processes, but also in the work of art. There is a continuous link between the methods that determine the origins of intelligence in the child and the methods that determine the beauty of a work of art.

We are still left with the problem of defining the values that make for ease and stability. There is a school of psychologists, of German origin but now active in the United States, which has concentrated on this problem — the problem of why things look the way they do. They find the solution in perception itself. Perception is a process that gives a coherent order to the jumble of images received by the senses. We *learn* to see. We learn to give these images a good lay-out or *Gestalt* (the German word from which the school takes its name). According to Professor Koffka, the nervous system, under the impact of the stimulations that impinge on the retina of the eyes, 'produces processes of organization in such a way that the pattern produced is the best possible under the prevailing conditions . . . thus colour and brightness, shape and space, figure and background, location and motion, are all *interdependent* aspects of the organized pattern which ordinary visual stimulation will produce.' In other words, the way the nervous system develops its organized patterns is not very different from the way the artist paints his pictures. It is by this faculty of assimilating sensuous impressions from material things and then combining them in significant relationships, that the human race found its place in the world, and it is this faculty that contemporary man utilizes less and less. Mental faculties can develop only through use. Thus, the whole structure of human intelligence is now threatened at its foundations.

An infinite distance may seem to separate the sucking reflexes of an infant from the constructive intelligence needed to build a cathedral or compose a symphony, but the same laws of perception are involved. They are involved in any process of discrimination, which we have found to be the meaning of words like craft or skill. It follows that the same laws are also involved in the appreciation of a work of art, for the appreciation is based on a play of perceptual images that re-enacts the processes underlying artistic creation. An artist works towards a unity that emerges progressively from his perception and manipulation of material quantities, whereas we who appreciate the result begin with this unity and afterwards become aware of the isolated quantities which have cohered to produce it.

We enjoy works of art because they possess these values of required order and unity. But what we do not often realize is that the same formal values differentiate intelligence from sensorimotor reflexes at every stage of human mental development.

Such facts in relation to the tendencies of a technological civilization are now seen to be far-reaching and devastating. It is true that we cannot yet generalize about our whole contemporary social structure; it varies from country to country, and there are entire nations, particularly in Asia and Africa, who, though enjoying the imported products of technology, are not yet subject to its immediate impact. What I have to say, therefore, applies mainly to North America and Europe. Here, too few men have little sensuous contact with the soil, with animals, with the handling of wood, clay or metal. Progressive schools make some attempt to give the child sensuous experience. But technology is a ruthless tyranny, and its processes demand from the educational system a training directed exclusively towards conceptual modes of thought. 'Money, mechanization, algebra. The three monsters of contemporary civilization.' So wrote Simone Weil in her *Notebooks*, and in another remarkable book, *The Human Condition*, Hannah Arendt confirms this intuition. Earth alienation, she says, is the hallmark of modern science. 'Under the sign of earth alienation, every science, not only physical and natural science, so radically changed its innermost content that one may doubt whether prior to the modern age anything like science existed at all. This is perhaps clearest in the development of the new science's most important mental instrument, the devices of modern algebra, by which mathematics "succeeded in freeing itself from the shackles of spatiality", that is, from geometry, which, as the name indicates, depends on terrestrial measures and measurements. Modern mathematics freed man from the shackles of earth-bound experience and his power of cognition from the shackles of finitude.' Virtually all higher education in the modern world aspires to this mathematical ideal, in which direct sensuous experience is no longer admitted as evidence — in which everything is reduced to a cosmic language of abstract symbols.

But these, it will be said, are the methods by which science has won its greatest victories; to logic and mathematics, to introspection rather than observation, to hypothesis rather than classification, we owe the wonders (and the terrors) of our atomic age.

All this is true, and I shall not try to balance these achievements against the evils that have accompanied them. What is more significant is the anxiety, the all-prevailing sense of insecurity which undoubtedly motivate the crime and violence of our age.

Many earnest people call for moral sanctions. Man's ethical standards, they point out, have not kept pace with his scientific knowledge. He has lost his sense of sin, and has no fear of retribution. But our moral philosophers and religious leaders fail to indicate any practical methods for imbuing a technological civilization with ethical standards. Morality is not so much a question of beliefs as of habitual behaviour, of tradition. Moral habits are acquired in the home, in the school, in the social milieu. One might say they are conditioned reflexes, like those of a domesticated animal. No man is good simply because he believes in goodness, but because the way of life in which he was brought up is good. What incentives to goodness exist in the mechanized ways of a technological society? This is not a political question, a question of the relative moral values of socialism or capitalism: all contemporary political systems are technological. In this respect their aims and ideals are identical. Technical idealism dominates the world, and displaces all forms of moral idealism.

What we must finally recognize is the existence of two distinct modes of intelligence: one, the Cartesian, Descartes having been the first philosopher to base reasoning on the pure consciousness of self (I *think*, therefore I am); and one, the aesthetic, since it maintains contact with the sensuous world at every stage of its reasoning (I *feel*, therefore I am: reality is a creation of my senses). To the Cartesian intelligence we owe the great structures of rational or idealistic thought; to the aesthetic intelligence the discoveries of the physical sciences and the creation of works of art. In the modern world we have never kept a sensible balance between these two modes of intelligence, and so we have reached the abyss which now separates the man of feeling from the man of thought, the geometrician from the mathematician, the practical scientist from the scientific philosopher. Higher education in the modern world aspires to an ideal of theoretical or intellectual perfection in which direct sensuous experience is no longer admitted as evidence. The only truths are logical, and they are of no practical importance.

To cultivate the aesthetic intelligence would require a complete change in the direction and ideals of education. To keep the child dependent on things only, as recommended by Rousseau, would mean a considerable sacrifice of the efforts which are now made to emancipate the child from things and make it dependent on words only, that is to say, on abstract thought. While not denying the disciplinary virtues of subjects like logic and algebra, their ideals should not be confused with those of the physical or natural sciences. Scientists like Newton and Einstein have proclaimed their dependence on the vivid imagery that comes from sensuous experience, or like Darwin have lamented a life devoted to abstractions.

Whether we are scientists or artists, our aim is what Wordsworth called 'joy in widest commonalty spread': a society rid of its neuroses, a civilization rid of the threat of annihilating war. This aim will never be achieved by political legislation or by any form of totalitarian coercion. The change must come about organically, and must correspond to those vital laws which from the moment of birth determine the physical and psychological equilibrium of unfolding life.

These laws are known. It remains only to magnify them to the scale of our social problem and to animate them with that faith in life which is the final sanction of all human endeavour. Life, in its intimate recesses, is intelligence, is creative, is art. But how shall we penetrate to these recesses and ensure that life's creative forces are liberated?

Tolstoy had an answer to this question and I believe that it is the true answer. Tolstoy was not an impractical visionary. He was a man who had experienced to the full the passions and tragedies of life. He had been a soldier and a landowner, a father and a schoolmaster, a sinner and a saint; he had possessed great riches and given all that he had to the poor; he wrote the greatest prose epic of our time and he ranks with the few greatest figures of world literature. In *What is Art?* a mature work of his old age, he answered the question of the schoolboy Fédka — What is art for? He answered it in three clear sentences: the evolution of feeling proceeds by means of art; art is accessible to all men; art and only art can cause violence to be set aside. 'The task of art is enormous. Through the influence of real art, aided by science, guided by religion, that peaceful co-operation of man which is now maintained by external means — by our law-courts, police, charitable institutions, factory inspection, and so forth, — should be obtained by man's free and joyous activity.'

It is not necessary to agree with everything Tolstoy said about art — he sometimes allowed moral prejudices to cloud his aesthetic judgement. But he realized as no one since Plato had so clearly realized that art is not an ornamental addition to life, 'not a pleasure, a solace, or an amusement. . . . Art is an organ of human life transmitting man's reasonable perception into feeling.'

Not only is art a process or experience co-equally important with science for the life and progress of mankind, but it has the unique function of uniting men in love of each other and of life itself. Why does one learn singing? What is drawing for? Tolstoy could now answer these questions and we can now answer them. The cultivation of the arts is an education of the sensibilities, and if we are not given an education of this kind, if our hands remain empty and our perception of form is unexercised, then in idleness and vacancy we revert to violence and crime. When there is no will to creation the death instinct takes over and wills endless, gratuitous destruction.

An education of the sensibilities — what I have called an education through art — is not the present concern of our schools. Something is done at the primary stage — at kindergarten and infant schools; but the child is then quickly swallowed up in a system that ignores the evolution of feeling and provides no time for the free and joyous activity of art. To know becomes the exclusive aim of education: to create is the concern of a tiny minority that evades the social pattern of our technological civilization. The growing child gradually loses all contact with things, all capacity to manipulate materials or discriminate forms. Unless we can discover a method of basing education on these primary biological processes, not only shall we fail to create a society united in love: we shall continue to sink deeper into disunity, mass neuroses and war.

The Flower of Peace[1]

Peace is not the absence of war: it is a virtue born out of the strength of the heart.
SPINOZA, *Tr. politicus*, V, 4

Peace may be physical, a state of rest or harmony; or peace may be spiritual or psychic and is then better described as a state of silent growth. We must distinguish an arrest of movement, which in the human psyche would be death, and that harmony which is movement so perfect that it is imperceptible, like the movement of a spinning top. But even this harmonic movement does not represent the full meaning of peace, for the invisible movement of the human psyche is also an unfolding of form, a growth whose perfect analogy is the flower.

This was an image perfected in Hermetic philosophy, and beautifully expressed in a short poem by Henry Vaughan, the English metaphysical poet whose *Silex Scintillans, or Sacred Poems and Private Ejaculations*, was published in London in 1650. I would like to quote this poem, for all that I have to say on this theme of peace is by way of being a commentary on it:

> *My soul, there is a Countrie*
> *Far beyond the stars,*
> *Where stands a winged Centrie*
> *All skilfull in the wars,*
> *There above noise, and danger*
> *Sweet peace sits crown'd with smiles,*
> *And one born in a Manger*
> *Commands the beauteous files,*
> *He is thy gracious friend,*
> *And (O my soul awake!)*
> *Did in pure love descend*
> *To die here for thy sake.*

[1] *Eranos Jahrbuch*, Vol XXVII (Zurich, 1958). Reprinted, *The Forms of Things Unknown* (London, 1960).

The Flower of Peace

If thou canst get but thither,
There growes the flowre of peace,
The Rose that cannot wither,
Thy fortresse, and thy ease;
Leave then thy foolish ranges;
For none can thee secure,
But one, who never changes,
Thy God, thy Life, thy Cure.

Peace is here represented as an unwithering flower, growing in a far country, beyond the stars; its possession is security and ease, but it is only to be obtained by the intercession of the healing God, the God who in pure love had sacrificed his life so that man might possess this immortal flower.

Vaughan's master, both in piety and in poetry, was George Herbert, the gravest of our English metaphysical poets, and he also wrote a poem entitled 'Peace' which we might consider at the same time. It was composed at least twenty years earlier than Vaughan's poem, and is twice as long: it is at once simpler in diction and more elaborate in thought —

Sweet Peace, where dost thou dwell? I humbly crave,
Let me once know.
I sought thee in a secret cave,
And ask'd if Peace were there.
A hollow winde did seem to answer. No:
Go seek elsewhere.

I did; and going did a rainbow note:
Surely thought I,
This is the lace of Peace's coat:
I will search out the matter.
But while I lookt, the clouds immediately
Did break and scatter.

Then went I to a garden, and did spy
A gallant flower,
The Crown Imperiall: Sure, said I,
Peace at the root must dwell.
But when I digg'd, I saw a worm devoure
What show'd so well.

The Flower of Peace

At length I met a rev'rend good old man,
Whom when for Peace
I did demand, he thus began:
There was a Prince of old
At Salem dwelt, who liv'd with good increase
Of flock and fold.

He sweetly liv'd; yet sweetness did not save
His life from foes.
But after death out of his grave
There sprang twelve stalks of wheat:
Which many wondring at, got some of those
To plant and set.

It prosper'd strangely, and did soon disperse
Through all the earth:
For they that taste it do rehearse,
That vertue lies therein,
A secret vertue bringing peace and mirth
By flight of sinne.

Take of this grain, which in my garden grows,
And grows for you;
Make bread of it: and that repose
And peace, which ev'ry where
With so much earnestnesse you do pursue,
Is onely there.

Here again we have the discovery of a flower, the Crown Imperial, in a region beyond the clouds; but its 'crown' is deceptive, for as in Blake's poem, 'The Sick Rose',

The invisible worm
That flies in the night,
In the howling storm,
Has found out thy bed
Of crimson joy
And his dark secret love
Does thy life destroy.

Perhaps the worm in George Herbert's poem is not the same worm as Blake's, but we shall see. In Herbert's poem, the flower is apparently abandoned, and a familiar archetypal figure appears,

390

the Wise Old Man, and he directs the seeker for peace to the imaginary city of Salem, where, according to the Bible, Melchisidec, King of Peace, did dwell. But Melchisidec, who had lived at peace for many years, is overrun by foes and killed. From his grave, however, spring twelve stalks of wheat, which increase and multiply until they cover the whole earth. Bread which possesses a secret virtue is then made from this wheat, and those who then partake of it are granted that repose and peace which they have everywhere and so earnestly sought.

It may be that these poets, who were simple and pious men, were only inventing new allegories to illustrate the Christian legend. Melchisidec is the prototype of Christ, and the twelve stalks of wheat are the twelve apostles who spread the gospel of peace throughout the world. Christ as the Prince of Peace is one of his most familiar rôles. But both Herbert and Vaughan were adepts of Hermetic philosophy, and the images they used are archetypal. We have, in these two related poems, at least three such archetypal images: The unwithering flower, the Rose or Crown Imperial; The Wise Old Man and the transubstantiating bread, made from wheat which springs from the grave of the Prince of Peace. In what terms shall we interpret these symbols?

The unwithering flower is the *amaranth* (Gr. ἀμάραντος), sacred to Ephesian Artemis, the many-breasted goddess of fertility, who was served by eunuch priests. In Christian mythology also the amaranth (or amarant as it is more correctly spelt) has a symbolical significance; the crowns of the heavenly angels are inwoven of amarant and gold, and in *Paradise Lost* (III) Milton tells us why:

> *Immortal Amarant, a Flour which once*
> *In Paradise, fast by the Tree of Life,*
> *Began to bloom, but soon for man's offence*
> *To Heav'n remov'd, where first it grew, there grows.*
> *And flours aloft shading the Fount of Life,*
> *And where the River of Bliss through midst of Heav'n*
> *Rowls over Elisian Flours her Amber stream;*
> *With these that never fade the Spirits elect*
> *Bind their resplendent locks inwreath'd with beams,*
> *Now in loose Garlands thick thrown off, the bright*
> *Pavement that like a Sea of Jasper shone*
> *Impurpl'd with Celestial Roses smil'd.*

Here again the flower is associated with fertility, with the Tree of Life; it shades the Fount of Life, from which flows the River of Bliss, and with its immortal blossoms the multitude of Angels bind their resplendent locks.

Paradoxically the amarant is also associated with blood. Thus in Spenser's *Faerie Queene* we read (III, 45) of:

> *Sad* Amaranthus, *made a flowre but late,*
> *Sad Amaranthus, in whose purple gore,*
> *Me seemes I see Amintas wretched fate,*
> *To whom sweete Poets verse hath given endlesse date.*

The sweet poet is, of course, Torquato Tasso. I am not certain how the amarant would be represented, if represented it ever was, in Ancient or Renaissance painting; but when Herbert calls the flower of peace a 'Crown Imperial' he is suggesting something round and regular, something like the Golden Flower of the East, the symbol of balanced perfection. It serves well enough as a symbol of peace, as I intend to show.

We could spend a very pleasant hour tracing these archetypal images throughout classical and modern literature, but I am anxious to interpret these images in the terms of our practical need, which is to 'seek peace and ensue it'. This is a Biblical phrase, and it is significant that peace in ancient literature and in the English of the translators of the Bible was always referred to in this active or transitive sense. The people *held* their peace; or they *made* peace; peace was a positive condition that had to be created and maintained. It was not a state of inaction or passivity; rather a precarious balance to be achieved by conscious effort.

This necessity has always been present in the minds of political philosophers and statesmen, and they have therefore designed and even put into execution various systems of control or arbitration. These have usually been based on the rule of law, with sanctions either military or economic, for infringement of the law. Such systems of control have always broken down for the simple reason that force cannot be controlled by force. If the passions of mankind remain unruly, no rules will keep them in restraint. We are therefore driven to the logical conclusion that it is the passions themselves that must be subdued, and the only way of doing this is the way of love, or to use a more practical term, the way of education. The way of education, as we know from our knowledge of the human psyche, is the way of integration, and it remains to define this process in the terms of a political philosophy.

This problem was the subject of one of Plato's profoundest and nowadays most topical dialogues, the *Politicus*, which incorporates the myth of the Age of Kronos. The purpose of the *Politicus*, it must be remembered, is to define the Statesman, to prove that statesmanship is an art, not a science, and the myth is introduced to show that the Universe being what it is, the art of the statesman is necessary to save mankind from the bottomless abyss of non-being. The Universe was not always 'what it is'; in the Age of Kronos its affairs were directed by the Shepherd King, who ruled mankind through the agency of divine guardians. Life was supported without labour. There was no war and no politics. Men and beasts shared this paradise and were born, not from physical intercourse, but directly from the earth. They lived from maturity to infancy in the opposite course to us, and disappeared in utmost infancy into the earth to be the seed of future generations of the earth-born. All this was part of one great cycle of time, a God-directed cycle. But at a certain point of time there was a reversal: the Universe began to turn in the opposite direction, and mankind lost the guidance of the Divine Pilot. In this new cycle of time, the so-called Age of Zeus in which we live, the Divine Pilot abandons the helm, and chaos begins to reassert its sway. 'Bereft of the guardian care of the Daemon who had governed and reared us up, we had become weak and helpless, and we began to be ravaged by wild beasts — for the many evil-natured beasts had by now turned savage. Men lacked all tools and all crafts in the early years. The earth no longer supplied their food spontaneously and they did not yet know how to win it for themselves: in the absence of necessity they had never been made to learn this. For all these reasons they were in the direst straits. It was to meet this need that the gifts of the gods famous in ancient story were given, along with such teaching and instruction as was indispensable. Fire was the gift of Prometheus, the secrets of the crafts were made known by Hephaestus and his partner in craftmanship, and seeds and plants were made known by other gods. From these gifts everything has come which has furnished human life since the divine guardianship of men ceased . . . and men had to manage their lives and fend for themselves in the same way as the whole Universe was forced to do.'[1]

---

[1] I quote from Prof. J. B. Skemp's edition: *Plato's Statesman* (a translation of the *Politicus* of Plato with Introductory Essays and Footnotes, London, 1952).

Plato's point in relating this myth is to distinguish between the task of the Divine Shepherd, who is all-powerful and whose flock is docile to his wisdom, and the task of the Statesman, who is a man like other men, mortal, who has to discover methods of tending his human herd. 'Tendance of human herds by violent control is the tyrant's art; tendance freely accepted by herds of free bipeds we call statesmanship.' How does the Statesman persuade herds of free bipeds (there is a reason for this somewhat contemptuous description of humanity which has to do with parts of the argument that do not concern us now) — how does the Statesman persuade the common herd to follow in the path of wisdom?

Before we go on to consider Plato's answer to this question, let us note that all present proposals for making and preserving peace either assume that we still live in the Age of Kronos, and that mankind can be governed by a Divine Shepherd, whether the resurrected Christ or, a not less chiliastic proposition, Divine Guardians operating as a World Security Authority; or they assume that since we live in the Age of Zeus, tyranny is the only solution, and we must live forever under the threat of an International Police Force, or some such concentration of power. That was not Plato's conception of statesmanship, or of peace.

Plato suggested that statesmanship should work through what he called the method of Example, or Paradigm. He believed in the existence of certain concrete patterns or forms (the whole idea is an extension of his theory of Forms) which if imitated would establish order in the State. There exist types of activity which if practised stamp in a particular way the actions and experiences of men. 'They are specific forms of activity in imitation of which the human or animal soul may be said to be functioning at a given time. Most important among them are the group of Forms represented by the arts; for they represent the ordering and formative intelligence in a particular way to a particular end. To think of such Forms is to make it easier at once to think of all Forms whatsoever as imposing a Limit upon the Unlimited.'[1]

Behind the Paradigm is the concept of 'due measure', the central ideal of Platonic and indeed of all Greek wisdom. But before examining the methods by means of which this ideal is to be realized in the State, or in mankind generally, let us glance at the extraordinarily elaborate analogy which Plato draws, in *Politicus*,

[1] Skemp, op. cit., p. 77.

from the craft of Weaving. It has an application to our present problem which even Plato did not fully exploit.

Plato realized that in this Age of Zeus men would always react in one way or another according to the affinities of their own dispositions.[1] 'They favour some forms of action as being akin to their own character, and they recoil from acts arising from opposite tendencies as being foreign to themselves. Thus men come into violent conflict with one another on many issues.' The purpose of his long-drawn-out analogy is to suggest that true statesmanship consists in weaving together the woof and warp of these diverse temperaments to make an enduring fabric. But he assumes a previous stage of carding: the diverse strains of which the fabric is made are good according to their kind: one is gentle, the other brave, and the ideal of the statesman is to avoid the extremes of these qualities, dullness and incapacity for action on the one hand, sheer fury and madness on the other, and by miscegenation produce a citizen of balanced temperament.

But what of the discarded, one might ask; what of the weak and the vicious among the children of Zeus? Plato leaves us in no doubt, at any rate in the *Politicus*, about their fate: they will be 'liquidated', banished or put to death. As for those who are merely mentally or morally deficient, they will serve the community as slaves. They are 'slaves by nature'.

Such inhumanity shocks the modern conscience, but it must be seen against the wider background, not only of a civilization fundamentally different from our own, but of Plato's theory of education. After all, in our much more humane age (or those aspects of it to which we give our passionate allegiance) we, too, banish the mentally deficient to asylums, our criminals to prison, and we put the murderers among them to death. As for Greek slavery, that is an old bone of contention, but one may wonder how many Greek slaves would have exchanged their position for the dark coal-pits and monotonous production-lines of modern industry. 'Slavery' is one of those rogue words referred to by Ruskin, and best left out of the discussion unless carefully defined.

The whole point of the *Politicus* is to show that 'law can never issue an injunction on all which really embodies what is best for each; it cannot prescribe with perfect accuracy what is good and right for each member of the community at any one time. The differences of human personality, the variety of man's activities

[1] *Politicus*, 307d.

and the inevitable unsettlement attending all human experience
make it impossible for any art whatsoever to issue unqualified
rules holding good on all questions at all time.'[1] So much for the
rule of law, on which modern politicians rely for the maintenance
of peace. The only alternative is the rule of wisdom, which we also
call the rule of love.

Before passing on to Plato's definition of wisdom, which is also
his prescription for peace, I would ask the reader to observe how
perfectly his use of the craft of weaving as a metaphor for the art
of statesmanship could be used as a metaphor for the process of
individuation. Our contrary impulses, our introversive and extra-
versive tendencies, our rationalism and empiricism, idealism and
materialism, our tough-mindedness and our tender-mindedness —
all these as well as Love and Force are the woof and the warp that
have to be woven into the enduring fabric of the personality. And
what of our weak and vicious promptings, what of the shadowy
Strife that is continually threatening the web of psyche? Can we
discard this Shadow, banish aggressive thoughts, put Satan behind us? The modern psychologist bids us recognize the Shadow,
come to terms with it, but how? It has never seemed to me that
the psychologist is very precise in his prescription of a method of
accommodation. I am going to suggest that the effective method is
the one recommended by Plato for the Statesman, the method of
Paradigm. For an account of this method we must go beyond
Politicus, indeed, to Plato's last work, *The Laws*.

This method is sometimes called 'the Argument from the Arts',
but it is very necessary to be forewarned of a misunderstanding
that has bedevilled the whole history of Platonism, until quite
recent times. The Greeks had no word for 'art', and though they
drew a distinction between the fine and the applied arts, all arts
were conceived as *techne*, as a specialized skill exercised produc-
tively on a specific material, whether it was the stone of the
sculptor, the leather of the shoemaker or the wool of the weaver.
This productive action, once perfected as a skill, implied a certain
infallibility. Plato goes so far, through the voice of Thrasymachus
in the *Republic*, as to assert that no one who practises a craft
makes a mistake. 'A man is mistaken when his knowledge fails
him; and at that moment he is no craftsman.'[2] The implication is
that there is an inherent rightness in the exercise of a craft, a
truth to form, and again Form (with a capital F) is implied. It

[1] *Politicus*, 294b.   [2] *Republic*, I, 340.

follows that what is true of the craftsman is true of the Statesman;
he is never mistaken so long as he is being true to his craft. Wisdom is the distinguishing characteristic of craftsmanship as such; the
Statesman is wise not as a man, but as one who exercises statecraft.

Plato's theory of education — and it is always a theory of education for citizenship — relies on this mystique of craftsmanship.
Even primary education, as we may gather from the references to
the teaching of spelling in the *Politicus*, was taught visually as a
craft. In the *Republic* the primary education of the Guardians is
divided into three stages, Grammatic, Music, and Gymnastic,
but the intention is the same at every stage: to condition the
mind to measure, proportion and harmony. Education is a process
of conditioning the malleable sensibility and mind of the child to
rhythm and metre, to skilful movements which are always grace-
ful movements, to the visible embodiment of perfection in any and
every form. For, says Plato, 'excellence of form and content in
discourse and of musical expression and rhythm, and grace of form
and movement, all depend on goodness of nature . . . so, if our
young men are to do their proper work in life, they must follow
after these qualities wherever they may be found. And they are to
be found in every sort of craftsmanship, such as painting, weaving, embroidery, architecture, the making of furniture; and also
in the human frame and all the works of nature: in all these grace
and seemliness may be present or absent. And the absence of
grace, rhythm, harmony is nearly allied to baseness of thought
and expression and baseness of character; whereas their presence
goes with that moral excellence and self-mastery of which they are
the embodiment.' All this is clear and precise enough, but Plato
continues to emphasize 'the decisive importance of education in
poetry and music: rhythm and harmony sink deep into the recesses of the soul and take the strongest hold there, bringing that
grace of body and mind which is only to be found in one brought
up in the right way'.[1]

All this is repeated, elaborated and emphasized in the *Laws*,
and is there related specifically to the view that the State should
be permanently organized with a view to peace, not to war. This
topic, familiar to us from its treatment in the third book of the
Republic, is in the second book of the *Laws* handled, as Professor
A. E. Taylor has said,[2] 'with a psychological thoroughness for

[1] *Republic*, trans. F. M. Cornford (Oxford, 1941), III, 400–1.
[2] Introduction to his translation of *The Laws of Plato* (London, 1934), p. xxiv.

which the *Republic* affords no parallel ... we have to lay it down as the foundation of a sound pedagogy that a child's first experiences in life are its feelings of pleasure and pain, and that education itself may very properly be said, at this stage, to be simply "learning to feel pleasure and pain about the right things", a declaration which called forth the unqualified applause of Aristotle.[1] And Professor Taylor (whom it was my privilege to know and admire for a brief time when we were academic colleagues in Edinburgh) further comments:

'To Plato, as a true Greek, the "ugliness" of conduct which is morally out of place is the most immediate salient fact about it, and "the beauty of holiness", if the scriptural phrase may be permitted, is something much more than a metaphor. To judge by the tone of much of our literature, we are less sensitive on the point; we seem slow to perceive ugliness in wrong-doing as such, or even ready to concede the "artistry" of great wickedness. It may be a wholesome discipline to consider carefully whether this difference of feeling may not be due less to a confusion on Plato's part between the beautiful and the morally good than to a certain aesthetic imperceptiveness on ours.'[2]

The *Laws* go into every aspect of the ideal curriculum in great detail, and I must not disguise the fact that this curriculum includes instruction in the arts of war, and that such instruction applies in all respects to girls as much as to boys. But when we see what such instruction amounts to — horsemanship and the use of the bow and arrow — we suddenly realize what a gulf separates us from Plato's world. Indeed, the widest part of the gulf, so to speak, stretches from the present to the immediate past, and if it is now ludicrous to compare a war of atomic missiles with a war of gunpowder and foot-soldiers, how much more unreal Plato's world of bows and arrows! Nevertheless it is the technology of war that has changed and not the eternal forms on which Plato's conception of education is based; and this is visibly demonstrated by the survival through all this accelerated strife, and mutilated though they be, of the still unravished, silent but teasing forms of Greek art. It would not now be possible to reconstitute Greek warfare; but the education envisaged by Plato is still a possibility, if we can still believe in the possibility of peace and goodness.

But I feel that I have not yet sufficiently driven home Plato's

---

[1] E.N. 1104, b. 11.   [2] *The Laws of Plato*, p. xxvi.

main contention, which is that a peaceful world is in itself a work of art — that the peace within a state, and *a fortiori* the peace between states, is a condition of equilibrium attained by the skilful adjustment of human desires to absolute values, specifically to the values revealed to the senses as harmony. One might say universal values, for these harmonic values are visibly embodied in the order of the Cosmos, in so far as science can reveal that order. But Plato does not imply that order and harmony are limited to their embodiments in what already exists. That would be to suggest that man has no formative or creative power — that the mind has no imaginative or creative function. In a difficult passage in the *Politicus* he deals with this point. There is a paradox, he says, which most thinkers have failed to notice: 'Likenesses which the senses can grasp are available in Nature to those real existents which are in themselves easy to understand, so that when someone asks for an account of those existents one has no trouble at all — one can simply indicate the sensible likeness and dispense with any account in words. But to the highest and most important class of existents there are no corresponding visible resemblances, no work of nature clear for all to look upon. In these cases nothing visible can be pointed out to satisfy the inquiring mind: the instructor cannot cause the inquirer to perceive something with one or other of his senses and so make him really satisfied that he understands the thing under discussion. Therefore we must train ourselves to give and to understand a *rational* account of every existent thing. For the existents which have no visible embodiment, the existents which are of the highest value and chief importance, are demonstrable only by reason and are not to be apprehended by any other means.'

In other words, such existents are essences. Plato, like Whitehead, was all for preserving a principle of novelty in the universe. The experience of art tells us, as Santayana has said, that beauty is 'a positive presence to the spirit and not a vague title conventionally bestowed. In a form felt to be beautiful an obvious complexity composes an obvious unity: a marked intensity and individuality are seen to belong to a reality utterly immaterial and incapable of existing otherwise than speciously.[1] This divine beauty is evident, fugitive, impalpable, and homeless in the world of material fact; yet it is unmistakably individual and sufficient unto itself, and although perhaps soon eclipsed is never really

[1] Cf. the Latin *speciosus*, meaning good looking, beautiful.

extinguished: for it visits time but belongs to eternity.' I do not think Plato himself ran such a danger, but one must not conceive form in art as inflexible, or the practice of an art as a routine. 'The sense of beauty', to quote Santayana again, 'is not a feeling separable from some intuition of form; on the other hand, it is a feeling, not a verbal or an intellectual judgment.' Realized beauty 'cannot be preserved mummified in any external object; it can belong to things only by being attributed to them by some living soul'.[1]

In the *Symposium* the experience of beauty is seen as a living experience, *ein Erlebnis*, to use the more expressive German word. It is a process of initiation, which is the word we ought to use instead of education: a heavenly ladder of learning as Plato calls it, leading from bodily beauty, the beauty inculcated by music and dance, to the beauty of institutions; from institutions to the beauty of knowledge, philosophical beauty: and from the beauty of philosophy to the beauty of holiness, the love of beauty itself, essential beauty. The final vision is 'an everlasting loveliness which neither comes nor goes, which neither flowers nor fades. . . . Nor will this vision of the beautiful take the form of a face, or of anything that is of the flesh; it will be neither words, nor knowledge, nor a something that exists in something else, such as a living creature, or the earth, or the heavens, or anything that is, but subsisting of itself and by itself in an eternal oneness; which every lovely thing partakes of it in such sort that, however much the parts may wax and wane, it will be neither more nor less, but still the same inviolable whole.'[2]

Shelley, the reincarnation of Plato in English poetry, said in his *Defence of Poetry* that: 'The great secret of morals is love; or a giving out of our own nature, and an identification of ourselves with the beautiful which exists in thought, action, or person, not our own. A man to be greatly good, must imagine intensely and comprehensively; he must put himself in the place of another and of many others; the pleasures and pains of his species must become his own. The great instrument of moral good is the imagination; and poetry administers to the effect by acting upon the cause. . . . Poetry strengthens the faculty which is the organ of the moral nature of man, in the same manner as exercise strengthens a

---

[1] *The Realm of Essence* (London, 1928), pp. 152–4.
[2] *Symposium*, 211, trans. Michael Joyce (London, Everyman Library, 1938), pp. 64–5.

limb.'[1] It would not be difficult to describe this process in our ugly scientific terminology, but I do not propose to do so. I have given the beautiful and simple words of Plato and Kierkegaard, of Shelley and Tolstoy, and there is not any need to translate them into an obscure jargon. Force, violence, fear on the one side; love, imagination, beauty on the other side. 'Perfect Love', we are told by St. John, 'casteth out fear.'[2] We have heard this a thousand times, and heard many theological interpretations of this profound utterance. Plato, I have been suggesting, gives us a very concrete and practical interpretation; so does Shelley. The creative imagination, conceived actively, as *paideia*, is the only effective instrument of peace.

To return to Herbert's poem, with which I began this phase of my argument. Peace, he said, is not to be found in some secret cave; we cannot find it by searching for it in remote places. It is not an insubstantial mirage, that eludes us; nor is it the gift of idleness and inaction. It is a seed which must be planted and set, brought to flower and fruition, harvested and milled, and then we must make bread of it, and this bread will possess a secret virtue, bringing peace and mirth to all who partake of it. A simple allegory, it may be thought, but I have tried, with the aid of Plato, to give it an application to our present discussion of the problem of peace. It may be that Plato's conception of the Statesman as the Prince of Peace is far removed from our conception of Christ as the Prince of Peace, but Simone Weil has drawn attention to the 'intimations' of Christianity in Plato, and of course Platonism is one element, and an important one, in the development of Christian mysticism. But I have resorted to Plato, not for a mystical doctrine, but for a practical solution to the problem of peace; and we have found, not moral exhortations, but the outlines of a precise discipline: a discipline combining organic growth and harmonic form, a discipline that is a reconciliation of Strife and Love, of what Tolstoy called the mutually exclusive and separately incomprehensible conceptions of freedom and inevitability; and the image of such a reconciliation is this 'flower of peace, the Rose that cannot wither'.

[1] *A Defence of Poetry*, 1821.   [2] *John* iv. 18.

Select Bibliography

(Compiled with the assistance of Philip Ward and Dr. Salma M. Ghanem)

1. *Songs of Chaos.* (Elkin Mathews, London 1915)

2. *Naked Warriors.* ('Art and Letters', London 1919)

3. *Eclogues*: a Book of Poems. (Beaumont Press, London 1919)

4. *Auguries of Life and Death.* Written in memory of Charles Read, Lieutenant of The Yorkshire Regiment, born April 24th, 1897, killed in action at Beaurevoir in France, October 5th, 1918. (Privately printed 1919)

5. *Mutations of the Phoenix.* (Hogarth Press, Richmond 1923)

6. *English Pottery*: its development from early times to the end of the eighteenth century. By Bernard Rackham and Herbert Read. (Ernest Benn, London 1924)

7. *Speculations*: essays on humanism and the philosophy of art, by T. E. Hulme. Edited and Introduced by Herbert Read. (Kegan Paul, London; Harcourt Brace, New York 1924)

8. *In Retreat.* (Hogarth Press, London 1925)

9. *Reason and Romanticism*: essays in literary criticism. (Faber and Gwyer, London 1926)

10. *English Stained Glass.* (Putnam, London and New York 1926)

11. *Collected Poems 1913–1925.* (Faber and Gwyer, London 1926)

12. *English Prose Style.* (Bell, London 1928. Revised edition 1952. Beacon Press, New York)

13. *Phases of English Poetry.* (Hogarth Press, London 1928. Revised edition, Faber and Faber, London 1950. New Directions, New York)

14. *The Sense of Glory*: essays in criticism. (University Press, Cambridge 1929)

15. *Notes on Language and Style*, by T. E. Hulme. Edited by

Herbert Read. (University of Washington Bookstore, Seattle 1929)

16. *Staffordshire Pottery Figures.* (Duckworth, London 1929)

17. *Wordsworth.* The Clark Lectures 1929–1930. (Cape, London 1930. Revised edition Faber and Faber, London 1949. Hillary House, New York)

18. *Julien Benda and the New Humanism.* (University of Washington Bookstore, Seattle 1930)

19. *Ambush.* (Faber and Faber, London 1930)

20. *The Meaning of Art.* (Faber and Faber, London 1931. Revised editions 1936, 1951. Dodd, Mead, New York [as 'The Anatomy of Art'] 1932. Pitman, New York 1951)

21. *The London Book of English Prose,* selected and ordered by Herbert Read and Bonamy Dobrée. (Eyre and Spottiswoode, London 1931. Macmillan, New York [as 'Anthology of English Prose'] 1931. 2nd edition [as 'The London Book of English Prose'])

22. *The Place of Art in a University*: an Inaugural Lecture given at the University of Edinburgh. (Oliver and Boyd, Edinburgh 1931)

23. *Form in Modern Poetry.* (Sheed and Ward, London 1932. New edition, Vision Press, London 1948)

24. *Art Now*: an introduction to the theory of modern painting and sculpture. (Faber and Faber, London 1933. Revised editions 1936, 1948, 1960. Pitman, New York. 2nd edition 1961)

25. *The Innocent Eye.* (Faber and Faber, London 1933)

26. *The English Vision*: an anthology edited by Herbert Read (Eyre and Spottiswoode, London 1933)

27. *The End of a War.* (Faber and Faber, London 1933)

28. *Unit One: The Modern Movement in English Architecture, Painting and Sculpture.* Edited by Herbert Read. (Cassell, London 1934)

29. *Art and Industry*: The Principles of Industrial Design. (Faber and Faber, London 1934. 4th revised edition 1956. Horizon Press, New York 1954)

30. *Henry Moore, Sculptor*: an appreciation. (Zwemmer, London 1934)

31. *Poems 1914–1934.* (Faber and Faber, London 1935)

32. *Essential Communism.* (Freedom Press, London 1935)

33. *The Green Child*: A Romance. (Heinemann, London 1935. Eyre and Spottiswoode, London 1947. New Directions, New York)

34. *In Defence of Shelley*, and other essays. (Heinemann, London 1936)

35. *Surrealism*: edited with an introduction by Herbert Read. (Faber and Faber, London 1936)

36. *Art and Society.* (Heinemann, London 1937. Faber and Faber, London 1945. 3rd edition 1956)

37. *Poetry and Anarchism.* (Faber and Faber, London 1938)

38. *Collected Essays in Literary Criticism.* (Faber and Faber, London 1938. 2nd edition 1951. Horizon Press, New York [as 'The Nature of Literature'] 1956)

39. *The Knapsack*: a pocket-book of prose and verse edited by Herbert Read. (Routledge, London 1939)

40. *The Philosophy of Anarchism.* (Freedom Press, London 1940)

41. *Annals of Innocence and Experience.* (Faber and Faber, London 1940. New York [revised edition as 'The Innocent Eye'] 1947)

42. *Thirty-Five Poems.* (Faber and Faber, London 1940)

43. *To Hell with Culture.* (Kegan Paul, London 1941. New edition with additional essays, Routledge and Kegan Paul, London; Schocken Books, New York 1963)

44. *Kropotkin: Selections from his Writings*; edited with an introduction by Herbert Read. (Freedom Press, London 1942)

45. *The Politics of the Unpolitical.* (Routledge, London 1943)

46. *Education Through Art.* (Faber and Faber, London 1943. Pantheon Books, New York. Revised edition 1958)

47. *A World within a War.* (Hampden Press, London 1943 [title poem only]; Faber and Faber, London 1944)

48. *Henry Moore; Sculpture and Drawings.* Introduced by Herbert Read. (Lund Humphries, London 1944)

49. *The Education of Free Men.* (Freedom Press, London 1944)

50. *A Coat of Many Colours.* (Routledge, London 1945. Revised edition 1956. Horizon Press, New York 1956)

51. *Collected Poems*. (Faber and Faber, London 1946. New Directions, New York)

52. *The Grass Roots of Art*. (Wittenborn, New York 1946; Lindsay Drummond, London 1947. Revised edition, Faber and Faber and Wittenborn 1955)

53. *Aristotle's Mother* and *Thieves of Mercy*. Two radio scripts included in *Imaginary Conversations* edited and introduced by Rayner Heppenstall (Secker and Warburg, London 1948) [*Aristotle's Mother* republished separately by Philip Ward, North Harrow, Middlesex 1961]

54. *Ben Nicholson — Paintings, Drawings and Illustrations*. Introduced by Herbert Read. (Lund Humphries, London 1948)

55. *Coleridge as Critic*. (Faber and Faber, London 1949)

56. *The London Book of English Verse*, edited by Herbert Read and Bonamy Dobrée. (Eyre and Spottiswoode, London 1949. Macmillan, New York)

57. *Existentialism, Marxism and Anarchism*: Chains of Freedom. (Freedom Press, London 1950)

58. *Education for Peace*. (Scribners, New York 1949; Routledge, London 1950)

59. *Contemporary British Art*. (Penguin Books, Harmondsworth 1951. New edition 1963)

60. *Art and the Evolution of Man*. (Freedom Press, London 1951)

61. *Byron*. 'Writers and their work', No. 10. (Longmans, London 1951)

62. *The Philosophy of Modern Art*: Collected Essays. (Faber and Faber, London 1952. Horizon Press, New York 1953)

63. *The True Voice of Feeling*: Studies in English Romantic Poetry. (Faber and Faber, London; Pantheon Books, New York 1953)

64. *Anarchy and Order*: Essays in Politics. (Faber and Faber, London 1954)

65. *Icon and Idea*: The function of art in the development of human consciousness. (Harvard University Press, Cambridge, Mass.; Faber and Faber, London 1955)

66. *Moon's Farm*, and poems mostly elegiac. (Faber and Faber, London 1955; Horizon Press, New York 1956)

Select Bibliography

67. *The Art of Sculpture*. (Pantheon Books, Bollingen Series, New York; Faber and Faber, London 1956)

68. *The Psychopathology of Reaction in the Arts*. (Institute of Contemporary Arts, London 1956)

69. *The Tenth Muse*. (Routledge, London 1957; Horizon Press, New York 1958)

70. *A Concise History of Modern Painting*. (Thames and Hudson, London; Praeger, New York 1959)

71. *The Forms of Things Unknown*: essays towards an aesthetic philosophy. (Faber and Faber, London; Horizon Press, New York 1960)

72. *The Parliament of Women*: a drama in three acts. (Vine Press, Hemingford Grey 1960)

73. *Truth is More Sacred*: a critical exchange on modern literature between Edward Dahlberg and Herbert Read. (Routledge, London; Horizon Press, New York 1961)

74. *A Letter to a Young Painter*. (Thames and Hudson, London; Horizon Press, New York 1962)

75. *The Contrary Experience*: Autobiographies. (Faber and Faber, London; Horizon Press, New York 1963)

76. *Lord Byron at the Opera*: a play for broadcasting. (Philip Ward, North Harrow, Middlesex 1963)